Perl 6 Now: The Core Ideas Illustrated with Perl 5

SCOTT WALTERS

Apress®

Perl 6 Now: The Core Ideas Illustrated with Perl 5

Copyright © 2005 by Scott Walters

ISBN (pbk): 1-59059-395-2

Printed and bound in the United States of America 9 8 7 6 5 4 3 2 1

Lead Editor: Chris Mills
Technical Reviewers: Randal Schwartz and James Lee
Editorial Board: Steve Anglin, Dan Appleman, Ewan Buckingham, Gary Cornell, Tony Davis, Jason Gilmore, Chris Mills, Dominic Shakeshaft, Jim Sumser
Project Manager: Tracy Brown Collins
Copy Edit Manager: Nicole LeClerc
Copy Editor: Kim Wimpsett
Production Manager: Kari Brooks-Copony
Production Editor: Janet Vail
Compositor: Kinetic Publishing Services, LLC
Proofreader: Linda Seifert
Indexer: Kevin Broccoli
Artist: Kinetic Publishing Services, LLC
Cover Designer: Kurt Krames
Manufacturing Manager: Tom Debolski

Distributed to the book trade in the United States by Springer-Verlag New York, Inc., 233 Spring Street, 6th Floor, New York, NY 10013, and outside the United States by Springer-Verlag GmbH & Co. KG, Tiergartenstr. 17, 69112 Heidelberg, Germany.

In the United States: phone 1-800-SPRINGER, fax 201-348-4505, e-mail orders@springer-ny.com, or visit http://www.springer-ny.com. Outside the United States: fax +49 6221 345229, e-mail orders@springer.de, or visit http://www.springer.de.

For information on translations, please contact Apress directly at 2560 Ninth Street, Suite 219, Berkeley, CA 94710. Phone 510-549-5930, fax 510-549-5939, e-mail info@apress.com, or visit http://www.apress.com.

The source code for this book is available to readers at http://www.apress.com in the Downloads section.

Contents at a Glance

PART 4 ▪▪▪ Computer Science

Contents

PART 1 ■ ■ ■ Basics, Data Flow, and Program Flow

PART 2 ■■■ Variables, Arrays, and Control Structures

■CHAPTER 7   Multidimensional Arrays

■CHAPTER 8   Data Structures

PART 3 ▪▪▪ **Threads and Objects**

PART 4 ▪▪▪ Computer Science

About the Author

SCOTT **WALTERS** has been fixing things that weren't broken since he was five years old. After some brief dabbling with hardware, Scott quickly relegated himself to working on software. To this day, hardware hasn't forgiven Scott.

Scott Walters has been programming Perl since a lot of Perl 5 programmers still had their purple camels, which is to say years after Perl 5 came out, which isn't all that long ago. The period of time in that Scott managed to ignore Perl is much more impressive—he has been banging around the Internet since 1990, back when it wasn't lame. After hearing over and over that Perl is a messy language and that he should learn it (from two nonintersecting groups of people), Scott finally sat down and learned it—when someone offered him $1,000 to create a little dynamic Web site with it, that is.

For the past six or so years, he has worked (and hacked) primarily in Perl for various companies, working as technology lead in two startup companies and serving as lead programmer on a project to implement an intranet at a major healthcare provider, among other things. For the past four years, he has consulted full-time. Currently, most of his work is done for Pariyatti Book Services, which has tolerated his relative absence with relatively good humor.

Scott is involved in the Phoenix Perl Mongers, where he often speaks. He maintains http://projects.netbsd.org (and plans to do more as soon as he figures out how to get messages to go through on the NetBSD WWW mailing list) and, of course, works on numerous projects and modules related to Perl, including the budding http://perldesignpatterns.org free documentation project.

Scott has had love affairs with Forth, SNOBOL, and Scheme, and he has always liked C and bash. He picked up a smattering of Java back in the Java 1.0 beta days, and thinks it's OK. In fact, he likes most languages. He hails from Fountain Hills, Arizona, but considers himself a Minnesotan, even after baking in the desert heat for five years. He still has his long underwear and wool socks, just in case.

Thanks and Shouts

This book wouldn't be possible without the dedication and hard work of a whole cast of people who apparently love technology as much as I do (and a few who don't). Some of them pioneered Perl, some supported it, and others supported me in my efforts. Apologies to everyone I've forgotten. I'm reflecting on the road behind me as I write this, but the journey was long, and my memory is shoddy.

People I Don't Know

Larry Wall gave us Perl, which he really didn't have to do (and I didn't get Larry anything). Thanks to all of the Perl 5 Porters, who did, with almost no recognition, the hairiest of the work of building Perl as we know it.

Thanks go out to Randal Schwartz, Tom Christiansen, Nathan Torkington, and everyone else who shaped the community and wrote the documentation from which we all learned. They've given generously of themselves even after the books and software they've written. Thank you.

Damian Conway, I'm sorry I stole your guacamole. I'm deeply indebted to Damian. The ideas and implementations documented in this book came primarily from him. Damian wrote most of the modules I've documented in this book. After I started writing, he wrote more. In fact, I couldn't keep up with him.

People Who Worked on the Book with Me

Writing, I got to play newbie again, but thankfully the staff members I worked with at Apress were pros. I'd like to thank the people I got to work with directly.

Chris Mills, my editor, served the difficult role of speaking for my audience, who couldn't yet speak for themselves. Chris entertained all my crazy schemes with encouragement and enthusiasm, and that vote of confidence mattered a lot to me. He also set the standard for quality for this book.

Randal Schwartz, a man who needs no introduction, did technical review on many of the chapters, provided valuable insight into Larry's hopes and intentions, and defended the honor of Perl 5.

James Lee, author of *Beginning Perl* (Apress, 2004), did technical review on other chapters and offered a lot of great suggestions, many of which will unfortunately have to wait for the next edition.

Tracy Brown Collins managed the project, picking up where my organizational skills left off. Kim Wimpsett was a superbly knowledgeable copy editor. Janet Vail coordinated production and faithfully strived to integrate every last-minute correction.

I made a lot of extra and unusual demands on these folks, and they really came through for me. All errors are, of course, my own.

People Who Helped

Adam Turoff graciously allowed me to reprint part of his "The State of Perl" article. Juerd Waalboer wrote several of the tables contained in this book and contributed wording in several places. He looked at early manuscripts and gave valuable feedback that shaped the style and attitude of the book.

Marc Lehmann, the author of `Coro` and related modules, kindly commented my drafts of the two chapters covering his module. These comments were eye-opening, and the chapters are much better for it.

Craig DeForest, one of the Perl Data Language (PDL) Porters kindly commented on Chapter 7, which is about PDL. I've used examples of his in a few places, and he deserves credit. PDL is a truly wonderful creation, and Craig helped me understand some of the nuance of it. As Chapter 7 is meant primarily as a tutorial, I unfortunately wasn't able to include everything.

Thanks to Ernie Southrada and Dead Bunny Enterprises for hosting `straylight`, also known as `http://projects.netbsd.org`, `http://perldesignpatterns.com`, `http://perl6now.com`, and others. I've wanted a machine on the 'Net since I was a wee tyke, and after a gauntlet of dedicated SLIP connections, PPP connections, dorm coax connections, and cable modems, I've been able to depend on this critical facade of my existence.

Thanks to Doug Miles, the Phoenix Perl Mongers Pumpking, for his tireless dedication to the Phoenix Perl community, which he brought together. Writing Perl in the valley would be a lot lonelier without his hard work.

Tim Walters, Ian Patterson, Heather Macnaughtan, and a few people I lost track of each looked over other chapters and told me what they liked and didn't like.

Shouts to Friends and Family

Shouts to my family: Linda and James Walters who always taught me to work hard and work toward what I believe in; my brother, Tim, who shared my first passion, video games; my brother, Ryan, who made us proud but also makes us wonder.

Shouts to my friends Ernie Southrada, Blake Burgess, Robin McFarlane, Bill Lindley, Jan Lethen, Alicia Andrae, Michael and Tricia Schmidt, Phil Moseby, Mark Weaver, John Viega, and Michael Dorland. These are the people who teach, amuse, inspire, and entertain me. Shouts to my online friends of new and old: Lmg, Maddas, deyja, Bleys, the entire old crew of AfterHours LPMUD, and too many others to name.

Finally and most significantly, Heather Macnaughtan supported my adventure and endured months of my obsessing over "the book". She's used her creativity and intelligence to entertain herself better than I could have if I hadn't been working on this book.

Introduction

*P*erl 6 Now is the early adopters' guide to the Perl 6 language and its concepts. It demonstrates the Perl 6 language's concepts, ideas, and features and their roots in Perl 5. It uses the advanced features of Perl 5 that were generalized to serve as a basis for Perl 6's implementations. It demonstrates features new as of Perl 6 using modules. Using features from these sources, this book does the following:

- Shows how Perl 6 generalizes Perl 5 language facilities

- Introduces new ideas, their applications, and why Perl is adopting them

- Illustrates these new ideas using modules so Perl 5, so programmers can start using them now

- Concentrates on modern Perl, ignoring legacy baggage

- Solves real programming problems

- Introduces skills demanded of senior programmers

This book is for those eager to see where Perl is headed, Perl 5 programmers who want to know that their favorite tricks will still work in some form, and programmers wanting to open their minds to advanced programming topics taken from several of the most powerful and interesting languages running.

Improving Perl

Tom Christiansen, a famous Perl personality best known for coauthoring *The Perl Cookbook*, (O'Reilly, 1998), in his 1996 "Seven Deadly Sins of Perl" article, wrote the following:

> *Back in the Perl4 days I made a list of the greatest "gotchas" in Perl. Almost all of those have been subsequently fixed in current incarnations of Perl, some to my deep and abiding amazement. In that same spirit, here's of my current list of what's—um . . . let's be charitable and just say "suboptimal". . . .*

Tom Christiansen's listed sins have long been stumbling blocks for novice and intermediate Perl programmers, and fixing some of them required deep-seated changes to the language. All have been addressed in the design of Perl 6, though few of them have been fixed in the obvious way. Problems were fixed by generalizing the language rather than merely removing the unpleasant bits.

Convincing you to buy this book (if you haven't already) means convincing you that Perl 6 is interesting, and that means selling the idea that Perl 6 introduces features you want but may not have realized you want. Besides cleaning up rough edges, Perl 6 brings to Perl a host of the most sought after features previously lacking.

Saying that Perl could improve is not a slur against Perl. Perl 4 defined most of the Perl language, but it had plenty of room for improvement. Namespaces, data structures, lexical variables, and dynamically loadable binary extensions, added in Perl 5, make up only a small part of Perl, but they're now considered critical parts of the language.

Advanced programmers and programmers working on large or complex projects will reach a point where they'd benefit from features present in other languages but missing from traditional Perl 5. Novices and those learning Perl for casual use could be surprised less often by the language. The parts of Perl unique to Perl are now much easier to explain and teach.

Perl is unique in that it's developed primarily in the spare time of people who use the language for their day job. Pie-in-the-sky notions of how things "should be" are ignored in favor of pragmatic solutions to real problems. Perl 6 imports ideas from other languages not merely because the language has something Perl lacks but because these features are legitimately useful, at least in special circumstances.

Major Themes

Perl 6 is perlier Perl. Some themes repeated throughout Perl 5 come back with a vengeance in Perl 6. Here are places where Perl 6 builds on the accomplishments and design of Perl 5:

Stringification and numification: Objects communicate sets of data between operators internally, and user-defined logic in the object decides what the object should look like when used as a string or number. Perl 6 allows programmers to write their own rules for when data items should be considered true or false and makes stringification and numification easier.

Contexts: Hashes, arrays, function and method calls, references, and objects respond to the circumstances of how they're used. Perl 6 adds more contexts, a reference context allows expressions to serve as references without any special dereference syntax, and an object context allows function results to transparently encapsulate multiple return values using an object in a form that can also stringify or numify to present the same information in different forms.

List processing: Operating on sets of data is nearly as easy as operating on individual items of data. Sorting, searching, and iterating are Perl 5 primitives. Perl 6 adds *hyper operators* that operate on entire lists and arrays and setwise operations that compute intersections (and other set operators) on data. Reference context allows collections of data to be more easily handled—it's now almost never necessary to explicitly use the reference operator.

Compilation: Programs may be bytecode compiled and/or bundled for easy distribution. Perl 6 programs may be Just In Time compiled, where the program is compiled on demand, and Perl 6 designs in support for true compilation without any dependency on an interpreter.

Flow control: Meta information may be read from caught errors, and logic runs conditionally depending on the circumstances of a blocks exit. In Perl 6, expressions may be restructured to more easily move data between blocks. Continuations take snapshots of program state, and coroutines pipeline data between routines.

The default variable: The default variable, $_, is used by certain new flow control constructs, including a built-in `case switch` construct. It's the current object in method bodies, and method calls are performed on it by default when no other object is provided.

Extensibility: No design can anticipate the future in any meaningful way. Perl 5 left open many avenues for programmers to extend the language to meet their specific needs, and Perl 6 takes this idea further, allowing definition of operators, hooks into compilation, and better interoperability with other languages.

Stricture: Perl optionally helps verify your code, given meta-information. Better, safer, cleaner code is encouraged.

Perl 6 builds on the best parts of Perl 5. These themes manifest repeatedly through numerous features discussed throughout this book. For a detailed account of topics covered in this book, see the "Organization of This Book" section.

Who This Book Is For

Besides showcasing distinctly Perl innovation, *Perl 6 Now* also bridges Perl with ideas popularized by other programming languages such as Java, Ruby, C#, and Scheme. As a natural consequence, programmers of those other languages find in this book Perl equivalents to familiar ideas.

However, the primary audience is Perl 5 programmers who are curious (and in many cases, anxious) about Perl 6. Many Perl programmers pick up a few other scripting languages to expose themselves to new ideas, and learning Perl 6 is a nifty way to get this exposure, as Perl 6 borrows heavily from other languages.

Programming Novices

Perl 6 Now covers several university computer science topics such as graphs, recursion, compiler diagnostics, strong typing, and other concepts you're not likely to be exposed to outside of college. However, this book doesn't teach *programming basics*. This book could be considered a companion to *Beginning Perl* by James Lee (Apress, 2004).

Programmers of Other Languages

Larry Wall, the creator of Perl, has said that it's OK to speak a subset of Perl. This book *will* teach you a subset of Perl, but you must be aware you'll learn a subset not used by the mainstream. The *entirely new* parts of Perl are interesting, useful, powerful tools for Perl programmers, but they're not the most important features of the language. Conversely, Perl 6 drops problematic and hard-to-teach parts of Perl 5 in favor of cleaner interfaces, and this book simplifies the process of teaching Perl by avoiding these now deprecated features.

Perl Programmers

Until now, published knowledge on Perl 6 has come from only a few sources, the best known of which are the design documents themselves, the Apocalypses, written by the creator of Perl, Larry Wall. The Apocalypses are brilliantly written, but they're unreadable without an advanced knowledge of Perl and computer science lore. Damian Conway's Exegeses break down Larry's design so mere mortals can follow, and they admirably demonstrate practical uses for the new features, but the rationale behind the new features is largely lost in the absence of the required Perl and computer science lore.

Perl 6 Now was conceived as a hands-on, practical guide to Perl 6 concepts and features rather than syntax. This book gives the background necessary to understand the Apocalypses and the computer science lore necessary to understand the Exegesis.

Discussion of Perl concepts new to Perl 6 accomplishes little if you can't use the ideas. CPAN modules implementing Perl 6–like features for Perl 5 lay at the heart of this book. When I proposed this book, I had several modules in mind I thought to be nonobvious (as well as the obvious picks). By some fluke, I'd written one of them, and I've since written another. I've scoured CPAN in search of more modules to demonstrate the ideas from the Apocalypses, and I've talked to legions of Perl programmers. Herein lies the fruit of my labor.

Today's Perl 5

Ten years ago, Perl 5 was released, introducing objects, data structures, and lexical closures to the language for the first time. These nine years haven't been wasted. Perl has been repeatedly reinvented as threads, a compiler, a decompiler, weak references, `lvalue` subroutines, tainting of input data, data structure serialization, and other goodies were added to the language. Today's Perl 5 hardly resembles the Perl of yesteryear. Some chapters document underappreciated or imperfect features of Perl 5 slated for stability in Perl 6 (by virtue of being designed into the language rather than bolted on).

As it turns out, announcing Perl 6 was the best thing that could happen to Perl 5. That so many experimental Perl 5 features would be selected to be part of the core of the Perl 6 language was vindication to the people who thought of them. This encouraged further development and more widespread adoption. Undefined areas, such as `Switch`, were finally fully specified after being put off for too long. The community reached precious consensus that `Switch` should be done and on how to do it.

Adam Turoff best put light on the situation in the article "The State of Perl" that was published at `http://perl.com`. Adam has this to say about Perl 6 as the future of Perl:

> In 2000, Larry Wall saw Perl 6 as a means to keep Perl relevant, and to keep the ideas flowing within the Perl world. . . . Furthermore, backwards compatibility with thirteen years (now sixteen years) of working Perl code was starting to limit the ease with which Perl can adapt to new demands. . . . Today, over three years later, the Perl development community is quite active writing innovative software that solves the problems real people and businesses face today. However, the innovation and inspiration is not entirely where we thought it would be. Instead of seeing the new language and implementation driving a new wave of creativity, we are seeing innovation in the libraries and modules available on CPAN—code you can use right now with Perl 5, a language we all know and love.

> In a very real sense, the Perl 6 project has already achieved its true goals: to keep Perl relevant and interesting, and to keep the creativity flowing within the Perl community. One way to get a glimpse how Perl is used in the wild is to look at CPAN. I recently took a look at the modules list (`http://www.cpan.org/modules/01modules.index.html`) and counted module distributions by the year of their most recent release. These statistics are not perfect, but they do give a reasonable first approximation of the age of CPAN distributions currently available.

Table I-1 shows increased CPAN activity over time using Adam's counts of modules uploaded or updated and the percentage of the modules on CPAN those uploads and updates represent.

Table I-1. *Module Release Activity by Year*

Year	Modules Released or Updated	Percent of CPAN Added or Updated
1995	30	(0.51%)
1996	35	(0.59%)
1997	68	(1.16%)
1998	189	(3.21%)
1999	287	(4.88%)
2000	387	(6.58%)
2001	708	(12.03%)
2002	1268	(21.55%)
2003	2907	(49.40%)
CPAN	5885	(100.00%)

Adam points out that half of CPAN was updated in 2003 and concludes that Perl development is quite healthy. Adam also warns that these numbers don't tell the whole story. Modules are uploaded for numerous reasons, including bug fixes. On the other hand, some modules have been stable for years and merely haven't been updated because no bug fixes are required. Still others have been abandoned and won't be updated regardless of Perl developments that arise. Certainly not all of those 49.40 percent of modules updated in 2003 represent stimulation in the Perl 5 camp by the announcement of Perl 6, but they do indicate that the announcement of Perl 6 has done nothing to diminish Perl 5.

The previous quotes were taken from somewhere in middle of the article; the article talks about the realities of needing a new version, how Perl is actually being used today, and in what ways and to what degree Perl's user base is stable. Adam's article is available in full at http://www.perl.com/pub/a/2004/01/09/survey.html.

Announcing Perl 6

Perl 6's roots go back to 1999, when Chip Salzenberg announced the Topaz project to rewrite Perl's internals. (The announcement for Topaz is on the Web at http://www.perl.com/pub/a/1999/09/topaz.html.) The goal for Perl 6 was to make the interpreter easier to maintain, not to update the language. Code written for Perl 1 still runs on Perl 5.8.6 with little adjustment, and at that time, no one suggested breaking this line of compatibility. However, each feature added to Perl created bugs in far-removed parts of core, and many highly sought after features seemed impossible to add to the Perl 5 core at all. The internals were scaring away new developers. Topaz eventually fizzled—rewriting Perl proved far more time consuming than expected, and those using Perl were by and large oblivious to the plight of Perl's developers. Cleaning up the internals is still a high priority, and Chapter 2 delves into the perks of rewriting the internals (such as Just In Time compilation).

The seeds were sown in 2000 when Jon Orwant (the reserved, universally respected editor of the *Perl Journal*) walked into a Perl Conference meeting where Larry Wall and others were discussing reportedly mundane things. As Larry Walls tells the story at http://www.mail-archive.com/perl6-meta@perl.org/msg00409.html, this is what happened:

> Jon walks in and stands there for a few minutes listening, and then he very calmly walks over to the coffee service table in the corner, and there were about 20 of us in the room, and he picks up a coffee mug and throws it against the other wall and he keeps throwing coffee mugs against the other wall, and he says "we are ****** unless we can come up with something that will excite the community, because everyone's getting bored and going off and doing other things" . . . . He said, "I don't care what you do, but you gotta do something big". And then he went away.

Larry describes this as "the most perfectly planned tantrum you have ever seen". Consensus was that Jon was right, and Perl 6 was what had to be done. Mailing lists were set up. Soon thereafter, Damian Conway (who wrote many of the modules mentioned in this book) published a bold vision for improving Perl as a language by making the whole language more consistent, intuitive, extensible, and expressive. Current specifications for Perl 6 strongly reflect the basic goals of this document, a copy of which is archived at http://web.archive.org/web/20040207072905/http://www.yetanother.org/damian/Perl5+i/. (The Web site at http://dev.x.perl.org/perl6/talks/ further chronicles the early history of Perl 6.) Damian Conway's suggested plan for Perl 6 drew primarily on things programmers were trying to do with Perl 5 but were having trouble with, for one reason or another.

Because specifications for Perl 6 directly addressed the tasks programmers have trouble with in Perl 5, Perl 6 has a large amount of prior art to draw from in the form of Perl 5 modules. The bulk of the improvements for Perl 6 are formalizations of Perl 5 modules and idioms. Should Perl be found lacking in any serious way, at least one CPAN module would attempt to rectify the problem. In this way, much of what's new for Perl 6 actually started as a proof of concept in Perl 5. These attempts are sometimes badly implemented, sometimes are just impossible to do right, and sometimes lack nothing but being formalized as part of the language, included into core, and documented in books on the Perl language.

Damian Conway would later write an article on the relationship of Perl 5 and Perl 6 and publish it on the Web at http://www.linux.org.au/conf/2004/eventrecord/LCA2004-cd/papers/90-damian-conway_Perl6.pod. In part, the article reads as follows:

> First of all, Perl 5 ain't broke. Those of us who are working on the design of Perl 6 are doing so precisely because we like Perl 5 so much . . . . It's because we like Perl 5 so much that we want it to be even better . . . . Moreover, our love of Perl doesn't blind us to its flaws. Those $, @, and % prefixes on variables are confusing; some of its other syntax is unnecessarily cluttered; it lacks some basic language features (like named subroutine parameters, or strong typing, or even a simple case statement); its OO model isn't really strong enough for most production environments; and the list goes on. So the Perl 6 design process is about keeping what works in Perl 5, fixing what doesn't, and adding what's missing.

Reading This Book

Newly introduced, indexed terms appear in *italics*.

Monospace type is used for text typed at the keyboard, including URLs, code examples, program names, and commands to type at the shell. In this book, most commands to be typed at the shell are invocations of the perldoc command.

Should your system lack perldoc, the standard documentation is also available from http://www.perldoc.com, and documentation for CPAN modules is online at http://search.cpan.org.

The future is a risky business. While the specifications for Perl 6 have largely stabilized, they're subject to change. The Perl 6 examples are to be considered tentative; although I've made every effort to follow development and double-check them, they may or may not actually work when Perl 6 is finally released. The Perl 5 examples have, of course, been extensively tested by myself and by the technical reviewers.

Organization of This Book

Perl 6 and Perl 5 extensions offer new things for every part of the language, so I wrote this book in the style of a plain programming-language manual with basic concepts coming first and later chapters building on them. Each chapter in this book introduces an idea but also leads into the next chapter. For example, the chapter on the Switch module leads into the chapter on block control constructs, which leads into the chapter on subroutines. The chapter on multidimensional arrays leads into the chapter on data structures. Figure I-1 summarizes the relationship between chapters.

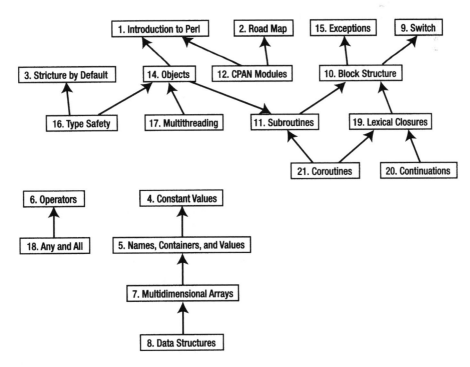

Figure I-1. *Chapter dependencies*

However, this isn't an ordinary programming book. The book is divided into four parts, and only the first two cover topics normally addressed in a traditional programming-language manual. The three parts correspond to the field of programming primarily responsible for the new Perl features documented. (Where ideas were new and had no field, I put the chapter where I thought best.) The book quickly moves onto cover features from functional programming, object-oriented programming, and ideas unique to Perl. The new parts of the language make strong use of existing concepts such as contexts, lexical variables, and symbol tables, so they're thoroughly covered in the first part.

This book spans the bottom of the intermediate well into the advanced. It was written with accomplished Perl programmers in mind, but the early chapters cover topics anyone can use.

Part 1

Parts 1 and 2 cover features implementing ideas that go back to the 1960s or 1970s. Compiler diagnostics, constants, variables, symbol tables, multidimensional arrays, data structures, control structures, and subroutines all fit this description. Part 1 also takes care of some pre-liminaries. Advanced programmers will find the first half of the chapters in the first part something of a rehash; the trickery and magic appears at least halfway through these chapters.

Chapter 1 shifts the introduction of Perl to a technical one from the social one. Perl 5 and Perl 6 are the result of originality and influence from other languages, and it's useful to examine which influences are new in Perl 6 and which are shared with Perl 5. After a brief overview of Perl's license, Chapter 1 instructs you on how to download, compile, and patch the latest development or production version of Perl. One module used heavily throughout the book requires a patch to the Perl core, so this is necessary.

Chapter 2 lists the parts of Perl 5 and Perl 6 you'll encounter in development and gives some resource pointers for projects to mix Perl 5 and Perl 6 in the same program. It also talks about other projects to migrate from Perl 5 to Perl 6. Chapter 2 talks about the technical agendas surrounding the project to replace the virtual machine for Perl 6.

Chapter 3 introduces compiler diagnostics, a feature that's largely optional in Perl, and how they relate to changes in the language. Perl 6 increases communication between the programmer and the compiler so the compiler is better able to help the programmer find and avoid bugs. The bugs Perl programmers struggle with most are exactly the ones that Perl is best able to check for and report on—when the options are enabled.

Part 2

Chapter 4 introduces literals and constants. It looks at numeric literals, string literals, and constant values such as system symbolic constants. It touches upon using string interpolation, treating data as files, and bundling files in literal data. Perl 6 expresses some constants differently, and the rules for interpolating hashes and arrays into strings have changed. Perl 6 standardizes code interpolation.

Chapter 5 introduces variables, arrays, and hashes, and then it takes a detour into variable innards. Perl 6 has the same four layers of abstraction variables exist in, but all levels are much more readily accessible to programmers. For instance, aliasing variables together allows multiple arrays and hashes to share data and present different views of that same data. Perl is a dynamic language, and a single variable may hold different datatypes at different times. Each datatype knows how to interpret itself in various contexts. Strings, numbers, arrays, and hashes all have different ways of deciding whether they are true in a boolean sense. Perl 5 and Perl 6 both allow programmers to meddle with how data is stored and how variables interpret the data they hold.

Chapter 6 examines Perl 6's truth testing operators, hyper operators, stacked file test operators, stacked comparison operators, and new mutating operators. The special undefined value is more widely recognized and supported, new operators and operator features save typing, and more expressive code is possible.

Chapter 7 introduces rectangular arrays. These are easier to explain than full-blown data structures and have the added benefit of being gentle on RAM. They're primarily useful for processing numeric data, images, audio samples, and other large sets of uniform data. Perl 6 introduces vectorized operators on sets of data as well as rectangular multidimensional arrays with minimal storage requirements.

Chapter 8 use references, arrays, and hashes to represent irregular arrays, linked lists, graphs, binary trees, and other structures. Data structures are essential for modeling data and problem solving with it. Perl 6 simplifies data structure construction, replaces weak references with garbage collection, introduces a reference context, and adds numerous other features.

Chapter 9 looks at simple conditionals, starting with if, and then dwells on given, Perl's switching construct. The dose of structured programming will make you feel like it's the 70s all over again, setting the stage for far more interesting control structures later in the book.

Chapter 10 shows how to break out of loops and how to provide code to run as blocks are exited in different ways, an idea introduced in Perl 6. It also takes a first look at the idea of variable scope.

Chapter 11 shows how to write and call subroutines, including the built-in functions that are always available. It examines argument processing, context, prototypes, and formal parameter lists. Subroutines may provide different contexts to their arguments, just as built-in functions do. Beyond formal parameter lists, Perl 6 introduces lexically scoped subroutine definitions, curried functions, and access to information about the number of types of results expected from a function call, all of which I have Perl 5 examples for.

Part 3

Part 3 is about ideas coming out of the software industry. Software shops have a love affair with object-oriented programming. Objects are a social institution that communicate to new programmers how to jump into a project and that establishes boundaries between programmers so that responsibilities and faults are clear. Objects are a technical institution that let the compiler help you by performing more sanity checks than any reasonable human would bother to write. There's little hand holding.

Chapter 12 introduces the Comprehensive Archive Network (CPAN) and ideas of code compilation, packaging, and distribution, with an eye toward rolling out desktop applications in the corporate setting or for download with the professional flourishes.

Chapter 14* discusses writing classes and objects in Perl. It examines the syntax for constructors, accessors, and inheritance. Perl 6 does most of the work for you, including processing arguments to an implied constructor—creating a class is as easy as creating a data structure. Notes on navigating interfaces that return object help programmers deal with the more complex modules available for Perl. Objects may present themselves as a string, number, boolean value, array, or hash when used as such. Objects may be given rules to define their

---

*There is no Chapter 13.

sorting order and to decide whether they're logically equivalent to another object. Methods called in object context should return objects, such as iterators, or bundles of data.

Chapter 15 looks at object-oriented error handling, which really has little to do with objects or object-oriented programming but does allow programs to understand what has gone wrong and deal with it accordingly.

Chapter 16 introduces a whole class of static analysis that object-oriented languages can perform on your program. Objects encourage the programmer to think about what the exact classes of problems are and work out what routines are capable of handling what data. Chances for reuse and problem cases both become evident when this is done. This continues the idea, introduced in Chapter 3, that if you give the compiler more information about what you're trying to do, it can help you do it.

Chapter 17 is a quick introduction to threads in Perl. It teaches the ideas of concurrency and its evil twin, race conditions.

Part 4

Part 4 looks at techniques out of academia. Popularized by applications such as artificial intelligence, they bring the most difficult problems down to earth.

Chapter 18 introduces two other kinds of data collection something like arrays: conjunctive sets and disjunctive sets. These let programmers ask easy questions of the data such as "do any match?" and "do all match?" Sets may contain other sets, not necessarily of the same type, allowing data to be structured in ways encapsulating the logic of a complex comparison.

Chapter 19 talks about subroutines that can be configured and customized and then passed as an argument or returned as a result.

Chapter 20 explains functional continuations. Continuations ease connecting pieces of code, lessoning the need to hard-code function or method names into a routine by letting multiple coexistent function calls pass data back and forth without knowing to whom they're talking.

Chapter 21 describes coroutines, which allow multiple subroutine calls to be made in parallel. Concurrent network connections represent well as coroutines.

Sales Support Perl Development and the Electronic Frontier Foundation

Twelve-and-a-half percent of the royalties from this book go to the Electronic Frontier Foundation (EFF). The EFF is a nonpartisan, nonprofit organization defending the rights of software programmers to innovate.

Twelve-and-a-half percent of the royalties from this book go to the Perl Foundation (TPF). TPF accepts donations with which to sponsor Perl developers working on key projects, such as some of those documented in this book.

Broad support is more important than my support; I'm donating primarily to make *you* aware of the work of these groups and to get you involved. To that end, I'd like to tell you a little about them.

The Perl Foundation

TPF oversees Perl public relations, heads up the Perl Mongers user groups, and manages the Perl 6 project. TPF puts on the Yet Another Perl Conference event around the globe, which is inexpensive to attend. The group maintains the http://perl.org Web site and works with creators of important Perl-related resources such as CPAN, in which it has an unofficial hand. It also accepts donations and uses the money to sponsor projects. In 2001 through 2003, TPF hired three core developers.

Larry Wall completed some of the hardest parts of the language design for Perl 6, including operators and subroutines, while funded by TPF. He also spent countless hours reading every post to the Perl 6 language mailing list and responds personally to many.

Damian Conway was hired for 18 months, and TPF flew him to 20 cities in the United States, England, Germany, Canada, and Australia, where he presented for companies and user groups. At the same time, he collaborated with Larry Wall on the design of Perl 6 and wrote 14 new modules, most of which are related to Perl 6 and are discussed in this book.

Dan Sugalski made considerable progress on Parrot, the virtual machine for Perl 6, while working under the TPF grant. The virtual machine has garbage collection, basic I/O, and a full complement of datatypes. Dan has more recently completed the first version of support for objects.

TPF has a Web site at http://perlfoundation.org where it accepts donations online. Most work done by these fine folks and the dozens of other people who actively hack on Perl is still done without compensation, but compensation certainly makes it easier to do the things you want to do. Donating to the TPF is one of the best ways to speed the development of Perl 6. Funding development of Perl is an excellent way to entice core developers to come to your college or user group and present (and ask for more money). Most of all, supporting TPF is a great way to say thank you.

The Electronic Frontier Foundation

In 1991, U.S. bill S.266 stated the following:

> *It is the sense of Congress that providers of electronic communications services and manufacturers of electronic communications service equipment shall ensure that communications systems permit the government to obtain the plain text contents of voice, data, and other communications when appropriately authorized by law.*

A couple years later, the National Security Agency (NSA) would unveil the Clipper Chip as a system of government-issued encryption. High-strength encryption would be made available with the understanding that the keys would be on file with the government. The physical encryption chip would be placed in specially equipped telephone handsets and PC expansion cards. Around the same time, the creator of PGP (Pretty Good Privacy, an encryption tool), Phil Zimmermann, and others involved in marketing PGP were sent a letter by the U.S. State Department informing them they'd need to register as arms dealers to distribute cryptographic tools, apparently a cue taken from Cold War politics.

A few short years later in 1997, people clung to the little yellow padlock icon in Netscape as their lifeline when confiding credit card numbers online. That little yellow padlock almost didn't happen.

The EFF subpoenaed details of the NSA's Clipper Chip project and testified before Congress, representing both future-minded businesses and privacy-minded citizens. The EFF helped fund Phil Zimmermann's defense in the interest of setting a precedent against regulation of cryptography. Government-provided encryption would have made the e-commerce revolution impossible. Had the Netscape browser required expensive hardware to conduct secure transactions, it's doubtful online shopping would have taken off. Remember, at the time, Netscape was a lark. No one predicted the e-commerce revolution.

This is one example. A sample of EFF victories include the following:

It coordinated the defeat of S.314, the Online Decency Act, which would make it illegal to transmit any "obscene" material, forcing ISPs to censor all communication. Of course, this was before ISPs were mainstream and large enough to take care of themselves, and most people who used computer networks were on "information services" not connected to the Internet.

It coordinated opposition to the eventually withdrawn UCITA bill. UCITA would make free software programmers unable to disclaim warranty against special and incidental damages of software distributed over the Internet. "Incidental damage" includes any money a user of the software is not able to make because the software fails, in some circumstance, to do something it tries to do. Commercial software has always disclaimed special and incidental damages.

It represented and successfully defended Jon Johansen in Norwegian court. Jon Johansen clean-room reverse-engineered the encryption on DVDs and used the knowledge to create a DVD player for Linux. Before this program, it was already possible to copy DVDs, but DVDs could be played only on Microsoft Windows, Apple Macintosh computers, and dedicated DVD players.

Details of past victories are available online at http://www.eff.org/effector/. Current battles are every bit as serious, and details of current litigation and legislation are news items at http://www.eff.org. Joining the EFF as a member is one of the best things you can do to protect everyone's right to innovate and use technology.

PART 1

■ ■ ■

Basics, Data Flow, and Program Flow

■ ■ ■

## CHAPTER 1

The Programmer's Introduction to the Perl Computer Programming Language

Perl is a technical creation as well as a social creation, and the license it's distributed under tells a good deal about what kind of social creation Perl is.

Perl 5 borrows heavily from other languages, most of which are procedural or special-purpose languages, and by far, the most powerful features come from special-purpose languages. Perl 6 also favors features from the object-oriented languages of industry and from the functional languages of academia.

You'll need the latest, unreleased version of the language to run the examples; this chapter will help you download, patch, and build a development version of Perl from sources. This book uses Perl modules heavily to demonstrate Perl 6 concepts, and in the interest of easily installing these, I'll show you how to set up `perl` to fetch CPAN modules automatically on demand, which is itself a Perl 6 concept. (CPAN is the Comprehensive Perl Archive Network.) Many of these modules tailor, or let you tailor, Perl's behavior to datatypes, so I summarize Perl 5 datatypes; this chapter also acts as a guide to the standard documentation for built-in functions.

The following chapters outline in detail the changes and additions to Perl 5 that create Perl 6, but this chapter first sets the stage for these changes.

Hello, World

`perl` is the program that parses and executes Perl programs.

```
$ perl -e 'print "Hello, world!\n";'
```

Run this at the command shell for the familiar greeting.

Dual License

Perl is a copyrighted work, but the owner of the copyright, Larry Wall, makes Perl available under two license agreements, as is the privilege of a copyright holder. Generally speaking, licenses grant others certain rights with a copyrighted work they otherwise wouldn't have under the terms of copyright law. Often, these licenses leave precious few rights; for example, licenses could state the following: one person at a time may use this software on one computer; the software may not be moved to another computer or sold with the computer; you may not reverse engineer the software to build utilities that work with it; and the copyright holder may revoke at any time your license to use this software, even though you paid money for it. This is in addition to not allowing you to make or distribute copies.

Perl's license is far less restrictive than these examples, but it keeps certain controls in place. You have the choice of two licenses, the Artistic License and the GNU General Public License (GPL). Under the terms of either license, you're not limited in how you may use Perl, and, provided you abide by the terms of the license, the license is nonrevokable.

The Artistic License, included with Perl in the file named Artistic, allows for the creation of commercial versions of Perl provided they don't conflict with, and are properly distinguished from, the community-maintained Perl. This preserves Larry Wall's creative control over the official Perl while allowing others to make improved and specialized versions. The Artistic License also grants programmers the right to embed Perl in commercial creations of their own (provided the primary selling point of that creation isn't that Perl is embedded in it). This lets you build a business around Perl and even make user extensibility with Perl a feature of products you create. Commercial interest may cause Perl to be ported to new platforms where the free software developers don't have the knowledge or inclination to do so.

Under the terms of the GNU GPL, the software community may modify and enhance Perl and may redistribute, and even sell, copies of Perl (as long as the license is perpetuated in copies). Because Perl can't be taken off the market by any single entity, you'll never find yourself helpless to obtain bug or security fixes, because any competent C programmer can, with some work, perform this service for you.

This section was a rough summary of Perl's license; read the file Artistic, included with Perl's source code, and the GNU GPL at http://www.gnu.org/copyleft/gpl.html for more details.

Perl's Influences

I can't think of a better introduction to the Perl language than listing the features it sports, much like an advertising brochure would.

It's widely known that Perl versions 1 through 4 borrowed from "C, sed, awk, and sh", and "language historians will also note some vestiges of csh, Pascal, and even BASIC-PLUS". (I'm quoting the perldoc perl manual page here.) Regular expressions originated in ed, the Unix line-mode text editor, of which sed is a noninteractive version intended for batch-processing text data. awk is a text-scanning and reporting language also possessing a decidedly C influence (which is little wonder as awk and C share creators). csh apparently contributed some notions of lists and list processing (including the $#arr syntax for counting the number of elements in an array, @arr), and the ideas of readily piping data to and from other programs and expanding variables in strings come from shell scripting languages such as csh and sh. (sh is the Bourne shell.)

Perl 5 Influences

Perl versions 1 through 4 took from procedural, special-purpose, text-processing languages and from scripting languages, but Perl 5 branched out into functional and object-oriented languages.

Perl 5.00, released in 1994, introduced objects, a feature first realized in Simula (1968), where it languished in academia for nearly 20 years before it was popularized by C++. Perl added support for overloaded operators soon after the first release of Perl 5, allowing programmers to create objects that behave as ordinary strings and numbers as far as the operators are concerned or even invent new meanings for operators when used on their objects. Perl 5.00 also took the idea of lexically scoped variables from Lisp. (*Lexical* is a functional programming concept that refers to a system of scope and reference counting where variables are limited in scope to the current block.)

From PL/I (1965), Perl 5.005 took multiple concurrent threads of execution.

Lisp also introduced the concept of code as data, which would later become known as *reflection*. Reflection allows a running program to inspect itself to learn about such things as functions defined and variables defined. Perl borrowed this idea, as well. (However, no languages outside the Lisp family of languages have truly completed and generalized this idea, because Lisp source code is just lists of data.)

Perl 6 Influences

Perl 6 continues in the footsteps of Perl 5, drawing from functional, object-oriented, and specialized languages.

Ada arguments may be passed into functions using parameter names rather than positions in a list. In other words, if a function had a variable named fred, a call to that function could supply a value for fred with an expression of the form function(fred = 10). Python brought this feature into the mainstream, and Perl 6 adopts it.

The Lisp folks have a saying about how all other languages slowly evolve toward Lisp. Perhaps this is true, if they don't mean evolve *exclusively* toward Lisp. Lisp macros are defined just as regular function calls are, but when called, the call executes immediately, stopping compilation momentarily to do so. The output of the macro may be code that's substituted back in the place of the call (which may be nothing more than a constant value or variable reference computed at compile time).

Also useful for extending the language is an idea from the ML family of languages: allowing programs to extend the language by introducing entirely new operators rather than merely overloading existing operators.

Perl 6 better rounds out Perl's reflection facilities, allowing inspection of the parameter names and types expected by subroutines and the ability to inspect lexical variables in other lexical contexts.

Perl 6 adopts Smalltalk's concept (from the early 1970s) of making everything an object to generalize the language and add flexibility to objectish tasks people wanted to perform. In Perl 6, for example, subroutines are objects and may be queried for information, such as the parameters they expect. Operators are a kind of subroutine and likewise may be queried for meta-information.

Python and C both have a concept of user-defined types beyond the character and numeric types included with the languages, and both languages attempt to check for consistent use of these types, because, unlike numeric types, they couldn't automatically be converted between. Object-oriented languages and functional languages alike ran with the idea of program validation, and Perl 6 optionally, on a variable-by-variable basis, performs this checking.

The Icon programming language introduced a combinational behavior, where logic tests are performed on sets of data, where each set may be composed of other sets. This overloads the meanings of the logic operators. For example, (1|2|3) = (0|1) is true because 1 exists in both sets. Perl 6 includes this feature.

Perl 5 implementations are available for most of the features mentioned here, including combinational logic, the idea of making everything an object, better type checking, and, to a degree, named parameters and reflection. This book also covers other topics.

Functional and Object-Oriented Languages

Object-oriented languages introduce a sense of multiplicity to programming, where instead of merely having one module with its own data and functions, you may have multiple independent copies of that module, and rather than having a single implementation of that module, multiple versions of it may be swapped out and used concurrently in a single program.

Functions in *functional languages* are guaranteed to return the same results given the same arguments, which implies a lack of global variables and a lack of side effects from expressions. For example, there are no special variables that alter the basic rules of pattern matching, and no built-in functions exist that change the working directory for the entire program. As a result of restricting the design of the language, functional languages developed powerful primitives for expressing solutions recursively and for pipelining lists of data through series of operations. Just as many languages are primarily, but not completely, object oriented, most functional languages are primarily, but not entirely, functional. Lisp, Scheme, Haskell, and the ML family of languages represent functional languages, with the last two being the most pure of these.

Many functional languages, such as Common Lisp and Ocaml (an ML language), have object systems and are thus hybrid languages. Because Perl 6 adds more list-processing built-in functions, it seems fair to call it a hybrid language as well.

Getting and Building Perl

Examples for this book require Perl 5.8.4 or later. Some features described require the "bleeding-edge" (unstable) version 5.9.2. One module used heavily throughout this book, autobox, requires patches to the Perl interpreter. The examples and discussion apply equally to Microsoft Windows and Unix-like systems, including Apple's Mac OS X, but Microsoft Windows users need to perform a few additional steps, which are outlined in the next section. Everyone else can skip to the "Building Perl" section.

Microsoft Windows Users

ActiveState Perl directly interfaces to the Microsoft Windows operating system and because of that is normally the preferred version of Perl for Microsoft Windows machines. However, it doesn't come with sources, and modules aren't built inside a full POSIX 2–compliant environment; therefore, this hobbles some of the more demanding modules documented in this book. You'll need the Cygwin environment to take advantage of this book; you can download Cygwin from http://www.cygwin.com. You'll get a small installer that automates fetching and installing potentially hundreds of optional software bundles. You'll also need a full compiler build environment, including make, gcc, and bash. After installing Cygwin and the appropriate bundles, you'll have a Unix-like system running on top of Microsoft Windows. Cygwin's command shell is bash, the GNU Bourne Again shell, which works with the command-line examples in this book. Modules install using the process shown in the "Installing Modules" section. Code examples in this book require no modification under Cygwin, but you should consult perldoc perlport for information about potential portability problems. If you don't have perldoc installed, the same documentation is available online at http://www.perldoc.com. Follow the instructions in the next section, "Building Perl", for the next steps in building Perl from source.

Building Perl

For POSIX 2–compliant systems with full build environments (such as Cygwin, Linux, FreeBSD, and Apple's Mac OS X), get the portable version of Perl 5 from CPAN at http://www.cpan.org. Fetch the latest source code from ftp://ftp.cpan.org/pub/CPAN/src. The following are two of the entries right now:

```
-rw-rw-r-- 1 ftp     ftp     11930764 Jul 19 21:57 perl-5.8.5.tar.gz
-rw-rw-r-- 1 ftp     ftp     11995887 Mar 16  2004 perl-5.9.1.tar.gz
```

Odd, minor-numbered versions are development versions. 5.9.1 is development (9 is the minor version), and 5.8.5 is stable (8 is the minor version). If you have the bunzip2 utility, get the bz2 version instead of the gz version to save bandwidth. You'll need to patch your copy of Perl, so don't do this yet. On a Unix-like system, the generic source build and install process goes as follows, assuming version 5.8.5:

```
tar -xzvf perl-5.8.5.tar.gz
cd perl-5.8.5
./Configure -de && make && make install
```

The -de arguments to Configure request defaults to all questions; you may want to go through the build process without -de once to see the options available.

After moving into the directory containing the sources and before running Configure, apply the autobox-0.xx/patch/perl-5.x.x.diff patch for your version of perl and your version of autobox. You'll first need to download and uncompress the autobox module from CPAN. Find it using the CPAN search engine at http://search.cpan.org.

```
tar -xzvf autobox-0.12.tar.gz
tar -xzvf perl-5.8.5.tar.gz
cd perl-5.8.5
patch < ../autobox-0.12/patch/perl-5.8.5.diff
./Configure -de && make && make install
```

Perl's install process will no longer replace /usr/bin/perl by default, so if you have a vendor-supplied version that you'd like to install over the top of, use the --prefix argument to Configure, like so:

```
./Configure -de --prefix=/usr && make && make install
```

After make install, run perl -v; you should see a message similar to the following:

```
This is perl, v5.9.4 built for i386-netbsd
(with 1 registered patch, see perl -V for more detail)

Copyright 1987-2004, Larry Wall
```

```
Perl may be copied only under the terms of either the Artistic License or the
GNU General Public License, which may be found in the Perl 5 source kit.

Complete documentation for Perl, including FAQ lists, should be found on
this system using 'man perl' or 'perldoc perl'.  If you have access to the
Internet, point your browser at http://www.perl.com/, the Perl Home Page.
```

Your version and host platform will likely differ from mine. If you do remove the version of Perl supplied with your operating system, scripts written in Perl that came with your operating system may fail to function; compared with previous versions of Perl, newer versions of Perl 5 are more aware of syntax errors, deprecated features, and grossly unsafe operations.

If you elect not to replace the version of Perl that came with your system, the default (for most platforms) is to install into /usr/local. Use #!/usr/local/bin/perl as the shebang line to use the new version you've installed. I like to reference specific versions of Perl in my scripts to ease upgrades. I can then change each script, one by one, to use the new version of Perl and test it. This way, no scripts brake completely and escape attention. You can reference specific versions of Perl explicitly as long as they aren't uninstalled:

```
#!/usr/local/bin/perl5.9.0
```

Modules dependent on a specific version of Perl will need to be installed for the new version of Perl. The old version of the module will stay installed for the old version of Perl. The cpan shell's autobundle command creates an installable bundle of modules for an existing version of Perl and places the bundle under the .cpan directory of your home directory (or wherever cpan was configured to place its data). This is useful if you've installed modules for the previous version of Perl and programs depend on those modules. After installing a new version of Perl, install this bundle as if it were any other Perl module.

■Red Hat's RPM package manager It's strongly recommended that Red Hat users doing serious development install Perl from source and not use rpm to install modules or updates. Perl does a lot of work to manage different versions of module dependencies, and RPM was never designed for this complexity.

Development Versions of Perl

Development versions include bug fixes as well as new features and usually work well. Use the rsync utility to download Perl (or update an already downloaded copy of it).

```
mkdir bleedperl
rsync -avz rsync://ftp.linux.activestate.com/perl-current/bleedperl/
```

To build a development version of perl, you'll need the -Dusedevel command-line argument to ./Configure.

```
cd bleedperl
./Configure -de -Dusedevel && make && make install
```

Module incompatibilities and errors with some expressions are common problems. If you don't mind dealing with and reporting these hiccups, running the development version helps the testing process.

Installing Modules

Perl is a user-extensible language. Modules are the means by which the language is extended. The most important features are the ones we haven't even thought of yet. This book heavily uses optional modules to extend Perl 5 into performing Perl 6–like tasks.

Perl 6 will fetch and install modules for you, should you attempt to use a module you don't currently have installed. You can also do this with Perl 5 with the Acme::Intraweb module and the CPANPLUS module. CPANPLUS also gives you an easy shell to use to install modules manually, invokable with the command cpanp. Once in the shell, use the install command with the exact name of a module, without the version number, and the module will download and install. Acme::Intraweb will likely fail on at least one module in this book, so remember that using cpan or cpanp are the traditional methods of installing modules. Fetch CPANPLUS from http://search.cpan.org/search?q=CPANPLUS, fetch Acme::Intraweb from http://search.cpan.org/search?q=Acme::Intraweb, and install them by hand. In the search results, the bolded name takes you to the documentation, and the smaller version with a version number takes you to a screen with a download link. Click Acme-Intraweb-1.01 in the search results for Acme::Intraweb, for example.

```
tar -xzvf CPANPLUS-0.048.tar.gz
cd CPANPLUS-0.048
perl Makefile.PL
make
make test
make install
```

This procedure is standard. Repeat the process for Acme::Intraweb.

Datatypes

Perl features true *lexical* variables. Lexicals are a rare treat for a language frequently used outside academia to write production code. Lexical variables are valid in any code until the end of the block. Even if a reference to a portion of that code is returned or stored and then executed later, those variables will still have their values. The values will be remembered even if the routine has since been called again. This feature comes to Perl by the way of Lisp. Declare lexical variables using the my keyword. Perl's basic datatypes are hashes, arrays, and scalars, any of which can be lexicals when declared with my.

```
# Lexical variables - Perl 5 and Perl 6
my $foo;    # declares a scalar - references are scalars
my @foo;    # declares an array
my %foo;    # declares a hash
```

Scalars can hold references to other things such as regular expressions, objects, and code.

■**Naming things** Variables traditionally have lowercase names with underscores separating words: $like_this. Constants traditionally are written in all capital letters with or without underscores: $LIKETHIS. Class names are written in mixed case with no underscores: SuchAsThis.

Typing perldoc perlfunc at the shell opens the documentation for the built-in functions. The Perl core is rich in functions that interface to the operating system and work on arrays and hashes. perldoc perlfunc uses a sort of shorthand when listing the functions. For example, chomp is listed with three forms: chomp VARIABLE, chomp(LIST), and chomp.

chomp will work on any variable, on a list of terms, or without an argument at all. Built-in functions such as chomp can do completely different things depending on how you use the result (which context they execute in) and what you pass to them. The possibilities for the kinds of things you pass to built-ins are as follows:

- SCALAR: A scalar variable, such as $foo, that holds a single string, number, or reference

- VARIABLE: Any variable, such as $scalar_var, @array_var, or %hash_var

- LIST: One or more values of arbitrary origin, all in a list

- ARRAY: An array variable, which looks like @foo

- HASH: A hash variable, which looks like %foo

- EXPR: An expression returning a string, number, array reference, filename, or whatever is equivalent to the type of constant expected

- NUMBER: A number

- FILENAME: A string representing the name of a file

- FILEHANDLE: The result of opening a file as well as STDOUT, STDIN, and STDERR

- BLOCK: A block of code, either right there or a reference to a subroutine

- Others: Other values with less formal meanings are also used

- None: Operates on the default variable, $_

Operations that require an ARRAY won't accept a LIST. An array can be modified in various ways where a list is read-only.

Summary

That's the penny tour. perldoc perlintro is another quick introduction to Perl that introduces Perl from the perspective of its basic syntax. You should have perl installed and built from source (though many examples will still work with only a reasonably modern but otherwise unmodified perl). You should know how to install modules and know where to go for the documentation for modules, for operators, and for built-in functions. I've tried to convey how Perl builds on the ideas of other languages and how the individual ideas are more valuable for being combined in a greater-than-the-sum-of-their-parts sort of way.

CHAPTER 2

■■■

Perl 6 Road Map

The freethinking of one age is the common sense of the next.

—Matthew Arnold (1822–1888)

Perl 6 is, obviously, the sixth incarnation of the Perl language. It has been in development for years, it breaks compatibility with Perl 5 source code, it has compatibility mechanisms, it's associated with the Parrot project, it was designed by open committee, it renames some operators, and it adds a lot of new ideas to the language.

This chapter primarily serves to answer questions surrounding what exactly Perl 6 is. It covers the individual parts that compose Perl 6, explains why so many parts are needed compared to Perl 5's monolithic design, and describes what this design accomplishes. Not every aspect of this design has a Perl 5 counterpart, but I'll provide examples for those that do.

Perl 6 is a language specification. It's a list of features and behaviors combined with a formal grammar definition. Perl 5, on the other hand, is a de facto standard. Perl 5, as a language, is defined by what the perl program from the perl-5.8.4.tar.gz (or whichever) source code distribution does. By contrast, the C language has numerous compilers and several interpreters. No single cc program defines the C programming language. Perl's creators and users with special interests ultimately hope that Perl 6 will run on all sorts of virtual machines and in all sorts of places that Perl 5 couldn't manage. They also want Perl 6 to run on multiple virtual machines, so no particular implementation may come to be recognized as the default Perl 6 implementation.

Backward compatibility is another major theme of both this chapter and the Perl 6 development process. The most important avenue for this between Perl 6 and Perl 5 is PONIE (which stands for *Perl on New Internals Engine*), which melds the Perl 5 and Perl 6 implementations, allowing Perl 5 and Perl 6 code to exist side by side in a program. This is a critical project for developers starting the long transition to Perl 6. Existing Perl 5 code will live on for a long time, and it's too much to ask that it all be rewritten or thrown away. Members in the community are undertaking other approaches concurrently in the form of Perl-related projects, and I'll cover how they came about and how they're useful (or potentially useful).

Programming languages, especially scripting languages, have been exploding in number, which has created an interest in reusing code written in one language in a program written in another. Also, pressure exists for language developers to provide migration paths from beginner-oriented languages such as BASIC. In fact, the proliferation of platforms such as GNOME, KDE, OpenOffice.org, Win32, and Mac OS X is making it hard for languages to keep up with language bindings. You're currently limited in your selection of languages to use for most applications because of this. Code reuse between languages using a common runtime rises to meet these challenges, too. All of this has created a market for language interoperability, and Parrot, the virtual machine being written by the Perl community to host Perl 6 and other languages, is heeding this call. Besides hosting the primary Perl 6 implementation, Parrot runs assorted other languages and attempts to support the needs of every language known to man. Perl 5 has a built-in interpreter, but Parrot is open, documented, reusable, and, most of all, designed to meet the needs of diverse languages. Gluing together different languages is the final theme covered in the context of the design and interface of Perl 6 and Parrot.

Parrot runs languages other than Perl 6, so it'd be incorrect to refer to Parrot as perl6. Perl 6, the language, partially runs on the Perl 5 virtual machine. The separation between the language and interpreter for Perl 6 is a major theme of this chapter. Many new Perl 6 features were also later implemented in the Perl 5 core or as Perl 5 CPAN modules. Therefore, this book will provide examples of Perl 6 concepts.

Introducing Some Lingo

This chapter documents the migration strategy between Perl 5 and Perl 6. To understand this strategy, you'll have to understand the technical stimulus for change. Here's what you need to know to follow this strategy:

A *virtual machine* is an abstraction of a computer. It can do anything that a real computer can do: read files, do math, process text, and so on. It's often closely modeled after how at least one real-world computer was designed. Virtual machines are traditionally written in C. This allows them to be easily ported to different operating systems and makes them virtually independent of the actual processor used.

Bytecode is a binary program in the instruction format of a virtual machine. It's the native, internal language that a virtual machine uses. Virtual machines are generally not bytecode compatible. In other words, code for one virtual machine will not run on another. This rule has rare exceptions. Several virtual machines will run code generated for Sun Microsystems' Java Virtual Machine (JVM).

An *obfuscated* language is one that's challenging, but rewarding, to write programs in. It's even more challenging to read programs written in such a language. These languages were added to the Parrot distribution to test it (and just for fun).

The Nebulous Perl 6 Language

Before delving too deeply into the discussion of what the various parts of Perl 6 are, I'll stress that Perl 5 runs on its own interpreter. Furthermore, Perl 6 and numerous other languages, covered in this chapter, run on Parrot as an interpreter, and PONIE is a confluence between the two of them (see Figure 2-1).

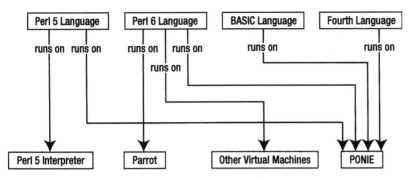

Figure 2-1. *While Parrot supports a large number of languages, PONIE is the current focal point of the Perl universe, supporting both Perl 5 and Perl 6.*

You should be aware that PONIE and Parrot exist but that this book is primarily about the Perl 6 and Perl 5 languages. After this chapter, the rest of the book doesn't mention PONIE or Parrot.

Language Specification

Perl 5, as a language, was never formally specified. No serious attempts were made to make compilers or interpreters for it using a separately written grammar. Perl 5 is a de facto standard; in other words, it's supposed to behave just like the official version of the language does (unless that's found to be wrong, and then the de facto standard is changed).

Perl 6, on the other hand, was built from design documentation and, with hope, unambiguous design documents at that), and it's open to reimplementation. A large base of programs written in Perl 6 isn't floating around right now. Large amounts of production code don't depend on the quirks of one particular compiler. The Apocalypses and Exegeses, published by Larry Wall and Damian Conway, respectively, specify the syntax and features of the language.

The Exegeses are based on the Apocalypses. The Apocalypses are based on requests for comment (RFCs). This acronym was borrowed from the Internet Engineering Task Force's community documentation process of the same name, where ordinary people propose new Internet standards in the form of proposals requesting feedback from the technical community. A good design is revised, clarified, implemented twice, voted on, ratified, and adopted. After Perl 6 was announced, Larry Wall asked the Perl community for RFCs. Each Apocalypse scores relevant RFCs on three criteria: whether the problem it attempts to solve even exists, whether it solves the problem, and whether it can be implemented as proposed. In contrast to the Internet Engineering Task Force (IETF) process, RFCs aren't implemented by the person who wrote the RFC. Discussion takes place on the various mailing lists to find weaknesses in the specifications. These clarifications, taken with the original specifications, should be enough for developers to implement an interpreter or compiler for the Perl 6 language.

Official Perl 6 Implementation

The reference Perl 6 compiler is perl6 and is included in languages/perl6 in the Parrot distribution. Building the code in languages/perl6 creates the perl6 program.

The perl6 program automates all the steps of going from Perl 6 source code to Parrot byte-code. Compiling and then running is a two-step process. This is in contrast to the single-step process of Perl 5, where the Perl source is fed directly to the perl program for parsing and then immediate execution.

Compiling and Executing

To compile and run a Perl 6 program using the official compiler, execute these commands at the command prompt:

```
perl6 file.p6
parrot file.pbc
```

It generates code in an intermediate format used by IMCC, the intermediate language compiler. IMCC in turn generates bytecode that parrot directly runs. IMCC is included with Parrot in the languages directory.

See perldoc perl6 and perldoc parrot for current documentation on these programs, or pick up a copy of *Perl 6 Essentials* (O'Reilly, 2003).

File Extensions

The official Perl 6 implementation, as built on top of Parrot, recognizes several file extensions. Perl 5 and its related tools use a few of the same extensions.

- .pl6 and .p6 are Perl 6 source code.

- .pl may be either Perl 5 or Perl 6—the interpreter or compiler will try to guess.

- .pm is a Perl module, either Perl 5 or Perl 6.

- .pmc is a bytecode-compiled Perl 5 module.

- .plx is a special extension that ActiveState Perl uses on Microsoft Windows to indicate that a console window shouldn't be opened. Use this when you've written your own graphical user interface.

- .pbc is Parrot bytecode. It's generated by the perl6 compiler and other Parrot compilers.

- .pasm files contain Parrot assembly. This is input to IMCC, and IMCC generates .pbc from it; it's usually deleted after the .pbc is generated from it.

If a .pm or .pl file has a class declaration or a use 6 line, it's Perl 6. Otherwise, it isn't (though these rules are subject to change).

Parrot

Parrot is a virtual machine designed to support the needs of dynamic languages such as Perl. It also caters to the special needs of functional languages; Chapter 20 will cover some of these features, with others covered in Chapter 21 and Chapter 12. Of course, it wouldn't be complete if it didn't cater to the needs of object-oriented languages.

Parrot is being developed by members of the Perl community, with input from Perl users. Supporting Perl 6 is the primary goal of Parrot, and the Parrot developers monitor the development of the Perl 6 language to watch for things that need special consideration.

I've taken care to distinguish between Parrot and Perl 6 in this book. This same care is taken during discussions on the development mailing lists. Simon Cozens took the Parrot development reigns originally, but now Dan Sugalski breaks ties and sets the agenda. Parrot has a home page at http://www.parrotcode.org.

Microsoft's Common Language Runtime (CLR) is the closest example of another virtual machine that supports multiple languages. Both CLR and Parrot were explicitly designed to suit the needs of diverse languages. Perl 6 is only one language that runs on Parrot. Lumping Parrot and Perl together would be misleading. Parrot runs BASIC and a number of other languages, and BASIC is never lumped together with Parrot.

Parrot is meant to allow developers to transparently mix objects written in numerous languages. Language implementers working on other languages are encouraged to support Parrot as a target of their language.

The languages/ directory in the parrot distribution has at least initial implementations of these languages:

- **Perl 6** is a reference Perl 6 language compiler.

- **Python** is a well-known, clean, object-oriented scripting language.

- **Ruby** is a clean, powerful, expressive, object-oriented scripting language.

- **Scheme** is a Lisp-derived language popular in college courses about artificial intelligence (AI) and language implementation

- **TCL**, the tool command language, is another popular scripting language often linked against other programs to add scripting and graphical user interfaces.

- **FORTH** is the famous reverse Polish notation stack language popular for embedded application programming (VCRs, microwaves, and such).

- **BASIC** is the Beginners All Purpose Symbolic Instruction Code, created at Dartmouth University, made famous by Microsoft, and accused of ruining novice programmers for life.

- **regex** is a compiler for regular expressions.

- **m4** is a popular Unix macro language.

- **cola** is a simple Java-like language extended with regular expressions and other Perlisms.

- **jako** is a simple language like Perl and C, and it was one of the first created to test Parrot.

- **befunge** is a fun language of the obfuscating variety.

- **ook** is another strange, minimal, obfuscated language.

- **bf** was originally a Commodore Amiga microlanguage with a compiler implemented in 256 bytes.

A Parrot-based version of the PHP language is also in the works.

Parrot itself is closely modeled after a register-based computer, which describes almost any modern computer. It adds objects and strings as native data types and defines semantics for building complex data structures out of these parts. It also lets the objects themselves define how operations work on them, which is unusual for a computer processor but typical of object-oriented programming languages.

Parrot includes a Just in Time (JIT) compiler for certain architectures. A JIT compiler attempts to blend the strengths of an interpreted language and a compiled language, giving you both portability and speed. Supported architectures are Intel's extremely popular x86 architecture, the PowerPC architecture used in Apple and big-iron IBM machines, the ARM processor used in many mobile devices, and Sun Microsystems' Sparc RISC architecture used in technical workstations and servers. Systems not supported by the JIT compiler should still be able to run the interpreter and slog along without the speed boost.

For the same processors, Parrot includes a regular compiler, which generates native binary executables for any language that runs on the Parrot virtual machine. This was an often-requested feature of Perl 5 that isn't mature (at the time of this writing).

▪**Compiling Perl 5**   See Chapter 14 for instructions on compiling Perl 5 to C or to portable bytecode.

▪**Perl 5's virtual machine**   Perl 5's virtual machine is what's known as a *stack machine* but is extended in a way that closely matches the semantics of the Perl 5 language. If you're familiar with Parrot but curious about Perl 5's virtual machine, I've written some documentation and included references at http://perldesignpatterns.com/?PerlAssembly. Contrasting the two is a fun exercise for the technically savvy.

▪**Mono's virtual machine and Parrot**   Parrot and Mono are locked in a healthy competition. Mono is a portable implementation of Microsoft's .NET runtime and virtual machine. PHP and Python are being ported to both virtual machines, and Parrot hopes to run the languages faster. You can get more information on Mono at http://www.go-mono.com.

PONIE

The PONIE project implements Perl 5 on top of Parrot. It's useful in allowing Perl 5 and Perl 6 code to be mixed in the same program and to share data, objects, methods, and functions with one another. You can use existing CPAN modules in Perl 6 programs, and you can add new modules, written in Perl 6, to legacy applications. PONIE's home page is at http://www.ponie.org/.

Other ideas were considered to solve the problem of backward compatibility, such as using a source translator to parse Perl 5 and spit out Perl 6, but the virtual impossibility of translating modules using the XS binary interface (that is, modules partially written in C or such languages) makes this infeasible. No matter how well the code translator worked, some code will always use the core in some unexpected way or will be partially written in a language not expected.

Piece by piece PONIE is replacing the Perl 5 core with Parrot native bytecode, creating an implementation of the Perl 5 language and interpreter that runs entirely on Parrot—just like the other language compilers and interpreters distributed with (or for) Parrot. The PONIE project ultimately plans to implement Perl 5 on top of the Parrot virtual machine, including the XS binary interface, Perl 5's grammar, and its virtual machine. This approach should make nearly any Perl 5 program or module run correctly on PONIE. Perl 5 and Perl 6 would intermingle just as Perl 6 and Python intermingle (or any other language with a Parrot implementation).

The great thing about this approach is that a usable Perl 5 implementation already exists today. PONIE works now—it merely hasn't reached its ultimate goal. To be able to share data between Perl 5 and Perl 6, the Perl 5 interpreter must use the Parrot implementation of scalars, arrays, hashes, and so on. This is where the current work (and progress) lies. The next step is to rewrite Perl 5's C internals in Parrot assembly (or something that compiles down to Parrot assembly).

PONIE doesn't attempt to translate the Perl 5 source code into Perl 6 source code—that's another project.

Migrating from Perl 5 to Perl 6

Perl 6 tries to be all things to all people, and Perl 5 programmers want it to be a natural continuation of the Perl line of languages. Three approaches to making this upgrade seamless are currently being explored. Each is at a different level of maturity.

Automatic Translation

The original strategy was a Perl 5 module closely related to the B::Deparse module. B::Deparse is a decompiler for Perl 5 bytecode. Something close to the original source code is reconstructed from the bytecode of the compiled program. The original plan called for using this same technique but output Perl 6 source code instead of Perl 5. This plan keeps using the existing Perl 5 parser to parse Perl 5, which makes things a lot easier to implement and easier to implement correctly. Not every Perl 5 construct easily maps to Perl 6, and this approach would likely fail to convert a lot of code for lack of a corresponding Perl 6 idiom. Larry Wall set a target that 90 percent of Perl 5 should be translated with 90 percent accuracy. This would leave a significant amount of manual cleanup left for humans to do, and many people prefer that the code not be translated at all; instead, they want to have the original Perl 5 continue to work unaltered. That's where PONIE comes in.

PONIE

PONIE will identify which version of Perl it has been fed by looking for a use 6 line or the telltale Perl 6 class declaration. Should Perl 6 be spotted, perl6 will compile the program; otherwise, PONIE's Perl 5 on Parrot implementation will. Currently, the code is assumed to be Perl 5.

Perl 6 Features Implemented in Perl 5

Individual elements of the Perl 6 language have been implemented in Perl 5. Others already existed in Perl 5, and Perl 6 ran with them, and yet others are a lucky coincidence or the effects of cosmic forces. When describing these features, *Perl 6* can only be used as an adjective. Calling them *Perl 6 inspired* or *Perl 6–like* is more accurate. I'm pretty sure that it isn't fair to pass a partial reimplementation of a language off as that language. They will be labeled *Perl 5* throughout this book even though they may vary radically from traditional Perl 5.

These features are implemented using one of several approaches. XS, the Perl 5 interface for extending the language and accessing internals from C, is used by coroutines, documented in Chapter 22. *Source filters* extend the syntax of the language by running the source code through a Perl module first before compiling it. For more information on source filters, see `Filter::Simple` on Comprehensive Perl Archive Network (CPAN) at `http://search.cpan.org`. The `given { }` statement, documented in Chapter 10, was implemented this way. "Hidden Treasures of the Perl Core, Part II" by Casey West, available at `http://www.perl.com/pub/a/pub/a/2003/06/19/treasures.html`, has a gentle introduction. Some modifications to the language have been implemented using only Perl and modules such as `B` and `B::Generate` that allow programs to inspect their internals. The `typesafety` module, documented in Chapter 17, was created using this. Other features are implemented in the core Perl 5 language rather than as extensions. The `//` and `//=` operators (pronounced *defined-or* and *defined-or-assign*, respectively) and `my $_` are now part of the Perl 5 core language after starting as specifications for Perl 6. See Chapter 7 for more information on the defined-or and defined-or-assign operators.

This book documents only this last plan, retro-implemented features, as it's the only available technique as I write this. I hope that future editions can give equal attention to all three techniques.

Summary

After reading this chapter, you should appreciate how interconnected everything on the Perl 6 road map is. Other languages take a high-road approach to design where committees make decisions based on speculation. Even the best planning lacks the benefit of hindsight. Perl is all over the road. Problems are being attacked from every angle. There are sure to be some spectacular successes and some spectacular failures, but the diversity of approaches increases the odds of finding the best routes to compatibility and interoperability.

Today, only Perl 5 implementations of these ideas may be considered for serious, production work (and then only some of them). This book concentrates on these Perl 5 implementations. The native `perl6` compiler is second on the list of tools suitable for production work, but this isn't expected to be ready for production soon. Code examples labeled *Perl 6* are intended to educate and amuse even though they aren't immediately useful: `perl6` can't actually run most of the Perl 6 examples in this book. Therefore, you should treat the examples as tentative.

CHAPTER 3
■■■

Stricture by Default

I'm breaking tradition. The first thing I'll talk about on the subject of writing Perl is stricture—the thing that Perl is famous for not having.

Stricture is any mechanism designed to make something stricter. A language with a lot of stricture is, of course, strict. Stricture is one of those sometimes annoying things that is "there for your own protection".

Perl does in fact offer lots of stricture in many varieties, but it's all optional. This book assumes you're writing Perl professionally, as a skilled trade, not merely for kicks. I'm assuming you and your client need the code to be free of subtle bugs and to be readable by others. Many other Perl books don't share this assumption; in fact, authors too often incorrectly assume that you'll be playing with their ideas on a private Web server that isn't attached to the Internet or you'll be writing unimportant code that no one depends on or maintains. It's true that programmers learn on real projects. On the other hand, Larry Wall, the creator of Perl, famously said that any program that gets the job done before you get fired is "correct".

It's fun to joke about how much a language lets you "shoot yourself in the foot" or how restrictive it is in the crusade to prevent foot-wounding incidents. Programmers not up to the task often cause themselves grief with language features they can't control. Advanced programmers using overly restrictive languages often find that useful tools have been confiscated.

The usual conclusion is that no languages are suitable for programmers of all skill levels and that not all languages are suitable for all types of people. Many advanced programmers love the safety afforded by restrictive languages.

Most Perl books fit in one of the following two mind-sets:

- You're a novice who can benefit from help from the language but don't want to be bothered with that right now.

- You're an advanced programmer who doesn't need any help from the language.

This book likes to think that one of the following is true:

- You're a Perl novice who should be warned when you're doing something inherently dangerous.

- You're an advanced programmer who already values the assistance of good programming tools and knows how to use them to maximize productivity and minimize frustration.

It just so happens that this matches the direction the world is going and the direction Perl 6 is going—with one notable exception. Perl tries, with an unquantified level of success, to be all things to all people. If you're an expert who hates having some executable henpecking his kamikaze programming style, or if you're a novice who absolutely refuses to listen to what more experienced programmers say is good for her, Perl lets you turn stricture off, either on a case-by-case basis or entirely.

Always use strict and warnings in your programs. They'll catch most of the semantic errors you make. perl by default doesn't report things that are *probably* errors—only things that *definitely* are errors.

In repeated debates about whether strict and warnings should be on by default, Perl programmers are constantly reminded that Perl is often used for quick "one-off" scripts that are used once and then thrown away or used infrequently for some utilitarian purpose by the programmer. This is no less valid than it ever was before, but Perl has been becoming increasing popular as a language for writing large programs, even if the programs become large only by accident. And programming culture has a lot to say about programs that become large by accident—specifically, that they should gracefully deal with this growth. Novice programmers make errors in very small scripts that warnings would have saved them from making. But I'm a hypocrite in saying this: I often write one-liners or dozen-line scripts without warnings or strict. Remember, a strong case exists for always using them.

Perl 6 adds more kinds of stricture than you could ever hope for, but the most noticeable difference is in the defaults. In Perl 5, the default is always to not have stricture. In Perl 6, for modules, this default changes: stricture is enabled by default. Table 3-1 compares the stricture in Perl.

Table 3-1. *Perl Stricture*

Scenario	Strict by Default?
Perl 5 main	No
Perl 5 module	No
Perl 6 main	No
Perl 6 module	Yes

This book assumes you're writing your code as a module or, if you're programming in the main namespace, you've turned on stricture. This assumption applies to both the discussion and the code examples.

It's good to be in the habit of using strict and warnings. You can explicitly enable them like this:

```
#!/usr/bin/perl
use strict;
use warnings;
```

strict and warnings are two pragmatic modules; *pragmas* alter the universe in some way, and *pragmatic modules* are modules implementing pragmas. The following sections outline how strict affects your code. This chapter also includes examples of things that will generate helpful messages when warnings are enabled (the warnings module is used). Users running your program probably won't report the output of warnings, and it may fill up Web server logs or cause other problems, so many people prefer to use warnings only during development. perl -c foo.pl checks the syntax of a program; you may want to check programs for syntax and for compile-time warnings with a command such as `perl -c -w foo.pl`. This won't, however, report run-time warnings.

Modern Debugging with Stricture

Back in the days when computers filled entire rooms and programs were written on punch cards, you turned in a deck of punch cards to the counter at the computer room and waited for the job to be run. When got your *abend* (abnormal end) log back, you had all the time in the world to ponder what went wrong and construct your next attempt with perfect care, double-checking everything. Compiler diagnostics were utterly unhelpful. Programs "messed" all over their data and the program code itself before being killed by the operator. Postmortem, the memory image was dumped to tape, and the programmer slogged through it, trying to account for the contents of each memory location. The chain of events leading to the catastrophic failure had to be followed in reverse order all the way back to the single error that caused the cascade failure. Unraveling the problem meant solving a mystery.

Nowadays, we count on rapid compilation, helpful diagnostics, run-time checking by the language, and compile-time stricture to off-load onto the language much of the brainwork of debugging.

After around 30 lines of code, depending on the programmer, more time is spent in debugging than cranking out the first pass. The final result seldom looks anything like the initial attempt. You're already spending so much effort compensating for flaws in initial assumptions and correcting mistakes. Giving the compiler a little help in helping *you* is perfectly reasonable. It's time well spent.

Everything that stricture asks is so that it can verify the consistency of your code. The following sections cover the things that use `strict` requires of you to this end.

Declare Variables

Declaring variables allows the program to verify that variables are used only within the scope where it makes sense to use them and that new variables aren't accidentally created by mistyping the name of an existing variable.

How do you declare variables? Using `my`, like so:

```
# Declaring variables - Perl 5 and Perl 6

my $color;

my ($name, $password) = split;
```

This avoids problems with global values, all of which boil down to ambiguous data flow. From where did the value come? Is it always valid in a given place in the program, or is it just coincidentally left over? Who else is going to be using it after it's left lying around? How much of the program uses it since the whole program can see it? With global variables, there's no way to know. Every variable is an accident waiting to happen.

Declaring a variable lexically makes it clear to humans where the variable is valid. It isn't valid anywhere in the program, only just for one small block (or more correctly, the part of the block after the statement that declares it—Perl 6 changes the scope to be from the start of the statement that declares it). Data should travel into a function via its parameter list so that you can trace the flow of data as you trace the order things are executed when `perl` runs the program.

■Note See Chapter 11 and Chapter 20 for more on this. Also, Chapter 12 covers this when it introduces the idea of parameters and arguments.

Soft References Are Bad

Don't write code to compute variable names. *Computed variable names* are a technique that many programmers stumble across while trying to work out how to store data in different slots according to the value of another variable. For example, if you wanted to set something equal to red but the thing you're setting to red could be any number of things, and another variable, $key, tells what's being set to red, you may write the following:

```
# set $color to 'red'
# don't do this - computed variable name in Perl 5

$key = 'color';
${$key} = 'red';


# don't do this either, but it is the same thing in Perl 5

$key = 'color';
${__PACKAGE__.'::'.$key} = 'red';
```

Use hashes instead. Computing a variable name using *symbolic references* is just looking the variable up in the current symbol table as if the symbol table were a hash. Perl 5 uses a specialized descendant of the hash table as a symbol table anyway—they really are closely related. Instead, keep collections of related data in hashes, like so:

```
# Use a hash instead

# use Perl6::Variables; # uncomment for Perl 5

my %hash;
my $key = 'color';
%hash{$key} = 'magenta';     # same as: %hash{'color'} = 'magenta';
```

Using the same key, such as color in this example, won't overwrite what you've stored there.

Without strict, computing variable names is something you can easily do accidentally when expecting something else to happen. Sometimes perl will silently do the wrong thing or do nothing when it expects a reference of some sort but instead you give it a plain scalar. For example, file handles must be references, but perl will silently fail if the file handle isn't. Using strict will catch this error. For example:

```
# Perl 5, accidental use of indirect object syntax because of missing comma
my $message = "Hello, world.";
print $message "\n"; # whoops, forgot the comma after $message
```

In this example, Perl thinks $message is an open file handle and tries to print to it. Without strict or explicitly testing for failure with or die, this silently fails. print isn't the only function that has this problem.

See Chapter 16 for how to make failed system calls raise exceptions by default. Also, Chapter 6 has some simple hash examples, and Chapter 9 introduces hashes that reference other hashes.

Prototype Bareword Subroutines

An attempt to call an undefined subroutine is purely a run-time error. The following code compiles and runs fine:

```
if(0) { test_signal_handlers() }
```

This happens because the following example is common:

```
# this is legal - Perl 5

test_signal_handlers();
sub test_signal_handlers {
    kill int rand 10, $$;
}
```

do_something() calls a function. sub do_something { } defines a function. It's legal to call a function before it's defined, as this example shows. Perl is better able to check the correctness of your code if it has already seen the function definition, though. This is documented in Chapter 12. Undeclared subroutines often take the form of constants, like so:

```
# Perl 5 - this code contains an error unnoticed without strict

use Fcntl;
use IO::Handle;

open my $fh, '+<', 'file.txt' or die $!;
seek $fh, 0, SEEK_END; # failed attempt to seek to end of file
$fh->print("Data to be appended to end of file\n");
```

This doesn't seek to the end of the file as expected. It seeks to the beginning, and the print statement overwrites potentially crucial data, corrupting the file. SEEK_END isn't imported from the Fcntl module as may be expected. To do that, you must write use Fcntl ':seek'; as Fcntl doesn't export those symbols by default. Perl 5 defines unknown symbols as strings that stand for themselves, or *barewords*, when they haven't been defined as a subroutine and use strict isn't in effect. seek attempts to use the string 'SEEK_END' as a number, and it parses to undef, which is functionally equivalent to 0 when used as a number. 0 is the same as Fcntl::SEEK_SET, which tells seek to seek to an absolute position, rather than one relative to the beginning or end of the file. The correct numeric value for the symbol SEEK_END is 2. After a use Fcntl ':seek', the symbol would correctly resolve to 2. use strict forbids barewords because of the confusion it creates in cases such as this. Barewords have countless times provoked novices into crying that perl has a bug. This chain of events isn't unusual without strict in force, and it's difficult to solve because the code *looks* like it should work. use strict has the unfortunate consequence of making Perl hostile to poetry.

Perl, the poetry language Barewords have made Perl famous as a language for writing English poetry. It's possible to write valid English that parses as Perl when unknown words stand for a string containing themselves. Look for "Black Perl" at http://history.perl.org/PerlTimeline.html under 1990 for a famous example. Indeed, the Perl timeline is fascinating reading.

No Strict

Need to do something dangerous? Don't turn strict off for the whole module, just the block, like so:

```
# Perl 5

use strict;

{
    no strict 'vars';
    # temporarily legal use of global variable here
}

# strict is back in effect here
```

You can specify 'vars', 'refs', and 'subs' as arguments to no strict. If no argument is specified, strict is disabled. Code that has to get under the hood must do this from time to time. Normal application code should never need this. These options to strict correspond to the previous three points in the "Modern Debugging with Stricture" section.

You can disable warnings in the same way, but you can enable and disable warnings individually for a large number of dangerous code constructs. Also, not all warnings are enabled when you say use warnings. To enable these optional warnings, you must request them explicitly. See perldoc perldiag for details.

The Code Police

It could be worse. You could be operating under Acme::Code::Police.

This is the Acme::Code::Police module. Provide this module to programmers who fail to use strict, and most of their coding errors will be instantly eliminated.

I don't want to give away the joke, but don't actually use Acme::Code::Police in your or anyone else's code. Just remember that stricture could be much worse. Also, see the Acme::Freedom::Fighter module on CPAN.

Warnings

YOU HAVEN'T DISABLED SET-ID SCRIPTS IN THE KERNEL YET! (F) And you probably never will, because you probably don't have the sources to your kernel, and your vendor probably doesn't give a rip about what you want. Your best bet is to put a setuid C wrapper around your script.

—perldoc perldiag

Warnings are generated by things that aren't necessarily errors, but they're close enough for alarm.

Warnings, enabled with use warnings or the -w command-line switch, are helpful messages in cases where you made what's probably a mistake. perl is extremely smart about probable problems in your code, but it doesn't share this information with you unless you ask for it. Unlike strict, warnings doesn't prevent you from doing dangerous things, though warnings may be made fatal with use warnings FATAL => 'all'. Many possible warnings exist. The diagnostics module will look them up in perldoc perldiag for you and report the full text of the error message. Use use diagnostics while developing, especially if you're new to Perl, and comment it out when putting the program into production, because it adds greatly to the startup time of programs.

The following two scenarios cause the most warnings:

- Compile-time warnings about syntax where you said something goofy but probably meant something else that isn't goofy

- Run-time warnings where your code is trying to do something goofy

Besides these typical cases, warnings may be generated by code trying to use a Perl feature that's being retired (also known as a *deprecated* feature) and by internals errors in Perl (that aren't your fault). Warnings classified in perldoc perldiag as "severe" are fatal errors by default. These tend to be syntax errors and are generated during compilation (if generated at all). Some of the more common warnings you'll see are as follows:

- Use of uninitialized value in print.

- Name "main::foo" used only once: possible typo.

- Global symbol "foo" requires explicit package name.

- Modification of a read-only value attempted.

- my variable $x masks earlier declaration in same scope.

The strings print, main::foo, foo, $x, and scope will vary, and the real messages will include the filename and line number on which the warning occurred.

Initialize variables to get rid of the Use of uninitialized value message. Assign either 0 or '', the empty string, to them. You can do this at the same time that you declare them, like so:

```
# Perl 5, avoiding the uninitialized warning

my $num = 0;
my $str = '';
print "$num people are going to $str.\n";
```

Certain operations won't trigger the uninitialized value warning. For example, my $num; $num++ isn't considered dangerous.

Newer Perls don't warn about empty arrays, because it's considered normal for arrays to contain no elements. An array created with my @arr isn't considered to be uninitialized. You'll never have a need to say my @arr = ().

See perldoc perldiag for a proper enumeration of the error types and information about getting fewer or more warnings. perldoc perldiag is a humorous read—and interesting, too— if you're the sort of person who enjoys learning all the ways things can go wrong.

Security Concerns

Perl offers stricture so that you can avoid specific kinds of bugs that attackers use to gain access to your system, steal other users' information, relay spam from your system, and other such things.

Tainting

The -t and -T command-line arguments enable *tainting*. Tainting tracks data flow at run time and complains if input is ever used in an insecure way without first performing input validation on it. -t makes using invalidated input a warning, and -T makes it a fatal error.

Insecure here means "likely to be abused". Each thing that taint catches is something that has historically been a real problem. Damage includes, but is not limited to, allowing malicious input that allows an attacker unlimited access to the database or to the shell as the user who the script is running as or that allows access to other site visitors' cookies. Any program run by untrusted parties (over the network or otherwise) should taint-check its input.

If the -t argument is specified on the "shebang" line, but wasn't specified when the program ran, then perl will die with the fatal error Too late for "-t" option.

This shouldn't happen on Unix-like systems under normal circumstances, save one scenario. For example:

```
perl -t tainted_program.pl   # okay
./tained_program.pl          # okay
perl tained_program.pl       # error!
```

The idea is simple: when data is read as input or taken from the operating system from a place that an external user could have influenced, the data is marked as tainted. Validating input is the act that causes the data to no longer be tainted. How it is untainted is a frequently asked question. The answer depends on your data, so you'll need an arsenal of validation routines, such as that provided by Regexp::Common.

Regexp::Common contains several regular expressions that match all sorts of different things. In most cases, you'll want to match your input to one of those and pick out what's matched. If nothing is matched, you have a problem. If something matched, the corresponding match isn't tainted and can be assigned back into the variable that held the tainted value, like so:

```
use Regexp::Common;
use CGI;

my $cgi = CGI->new;

print $cgi->header;

my $age = $cgi->param('age');

if($age =~ m/^($RE{num}{int})$/) {
    $age = $1;
    # $age is now no longer tainted because $1 isn't tainted
```

```
} else {
    print "Enter your age, not your shoe size.\n";
    exit;
    # kids these days...
}

# $age may be safely used here
```

This avoids all manner of attack, including *cross-site scripting*.

Cross-Site Scripting

`HTML::Scrubber::StripScripts` and `HTML::TagFilter` remove undesirable constructs in cases where a site accepts submissions formatted as Hypertext Markup Language (HTML). A class of security problems known as *cross-site scripting*, or XSS, occurs when a site mindlessly repeats input as output. If a site can be tricked into repeating and running malicious JavaScript, for example, an attacker has the ability to examine cookies, make requests, and do other things as the site itself. Therefore, a site should carefully filter input for both JavaScript and tags such as `<object>` that can include another uninspected document. In this case, use a module such as one of these two to remove everything not explicitly permitted.

Never display nonvalidated input from one user to another user. Don't store nonvalidated input in a database or file where it could confuse logic expecting clean data or be displayed to anyone.

If input from one user will display to other users, always validate input or else JavaScript can be abused to steal cookies or anything else. JavaScript coming from a site is trusted with cookies from that site and with the ability to perform form posts to other sites. User posts containing JavaScript get the permissions of that site. This is an XSS attack. Always filter out code, and remove all tags except those explicitly allowed.

Impossibility

Few things are impossible in Perl. Perl won't be teleporting your Roomba to Mars to collect soil samples for you anytime soon, but on a security note, don't consider anything programmatic impossible.

Specifically, the following are all technically possible:

- Data in one part of the program can be inspected by another part of the program, including private lexical data and class instance data.

- Most common problems found in Perl are syntax or features that cause core dumps and program termination when used in certain ways.

- Buffer overflows and other ways of breaking out of `Safe` sandboxes are rare but not unheard of.

In general, for anything mentioned in this book as being impossible, unlikely, or otherwise not what usually happens, don't count on it for any security-related purposes. If the book states that something is your best option, then don't trust it entirely, but distrust the alternatives.

Sandboxes created with the `Safe` module are useful for allowing execution of arbitrary untested Perl when combined with good backups, good logs, carefully considered permissions, user separation, and kernel sandboxing.

Never Run Perl setuid Root

perl running setuid root has a long and ugly history. setuid programs run with the permission of another user besides the one running them. Running C setuid root, too, has a long and ugly history. Privilege separation is founded on the idea of giving a process as little permission as it needs to do its job. This is a cornerstone of computer security. Consistent with this idea, make tasks that must be done as root separate programs that contain as little logic as possible, and use a utility such as sudo to invoke them with root privileges. sudo is available freely from http://www.courtesan.com/sudo/. If your Perl program itself must run as root, remove all user interface, argument processing, and other nonessential logic and place it in another script. Use interprocess communications to communicate between the two separate programs, and use authentication. Socket pairs are ideal. See perldoc perlipc for ideas.

Use Binary Clean Interfaces

Don't escape dangerous characters when you can use interfaces that don't interpret certain characters as special. Don't escape shell characters when you can use the two-plus argument version of system() and bypass the shell like this: system 'program', @arguments.

open(), when used to open a pipe, is similar. Write something such as this: open my $mail, '|-', '/sbin/sendmail', '-t', $username. Likewise, use placeholders in SQL rather than interpolating user-supplied data into the SQL. Don't write $sth->execute("update foo set bar = '$baz'") but instead write $sth->prepare("update foo set bar ?"); $sth->execute($baz);. See perldoc DBI for details on this last example, or pick up *Programming the Perl DBI* by Alligator Descartes and Tim Bunce (O'Reilly, 2000).

Avoid Reinventing Wheels

In the course of demonstrating how things work, this book "reinvents wheels", or solves problems that have already been solved. The easy ones have all been solved already, and solutions to large problems are themselves large. The point is to make sure you understand the work that went into creating a module, which is work you don't have to do. Don't construe it as encouragement to create your own versions of existing modules for any other purpose than self-education. Don't try to parse HTML or Extensible Markup Language (XML) yourself. Don't try to implement network protocols such as Hypertext Transfer Protocol (HTTP) or Internet Relay Chat (IRC) yourself. If you do set out to reinvent a wheel, write it off from the beginning as a learning exercise and don't expect stability, security, or reliability out of the project until it has been in production for a few years. See Chapter 14 for more.

▪**Build in security** Someone on your programming team should know the issues and keep an eye out for security. If that someone has to be you, get a good book on the subject. Your only exposure to security shouldn't be this little note.

Summary

This chapter makes specific cases for strictures, but you should have a general appreciation of them. I don't want to have to make cases for strictures later, each time I introduce them. All of the modules introduced in this book are designed to make your life easier, but a large chunk of them make the computer smarter through hints you feed it. Go ahead—throw your computer a bone.

You're far more likely to run into limitations and rough edges in Perl itself rather than suffering from some stricture. And you can always disable the stricture for the rest of the block.

PART 2

###

Variables, Arrays, and Control Structures

CHAPTER 4

■■■

Text, Numbers, and Other Constant Data

Constants are numbers, text, and other values that are special because they're part of the program itself. They're also called *literal data*, *hard-coded values*, and a number of other terms. If information doesn't come from the current program, the program must be told where to find it or who to ask for it via a filename or uniform resource locator (URL), both of which are also constant values.

Constants are prevalent in programming, and Perl pays special attention to them. A surprising number of ways exists to quote strings. Perl supports numbers that can be very large or precise. Perl allows for quoting blocks of text. Strings can contain variables that are substituted in at run time or can contain other Perl expressions. In this case, the quoted text isn't entirely constant, but these expressions look like constants.

New in Perl 6

Perl 6 adds several features and changes the syntax required to use other features. This section and the next concisely list them for the benefit of Perl 5 programmers. The full explanation of these features then follows.

Starting with Perl 6, hashes interpolate in strings just as arrays do, according to whatever *stringification* logic a hash picks. Method calls and functions interpolate, too. Arbitrary code including method calls can be more easily interpolated into double-quoted strings.

Changes for Perl 6

The following are some of the changes regarding constants in Perl 6:

Here documents have an amount of whitespace, equal to their indenting, stripped off. The rules for quoting using whitespace have changed. The terminating string must be quoted when it's specified.

0c prefixes octal numbers rather than merely 0. Hexadecimal constants still start with 0x, and this is more visually consistent.

Numbers may be written in any base, not just binary, octal, decimal, and hexadecimal.

Globs, or typeglobs, are gone. The is constant trait replaces glob tricks.

To interpolate in strings, hashes and arrays require bracketing on the end. To interpolate the entire hash or array, use empty brackets. @arr doesn't interpolate in strings in Perl 6, but @arr[] does, and @arr[1..3] interpolates a slice of @arr. %hash won't interpolate in Perl 6, but %hash{} does. &foo() interpolates a subroutine call, and $ob.meth() interpolates a method call. Neither works without the () on the end and the sigil in front.

Perl 6 no longer recognizes the backslash sequences to indicate uppercase, to indicate lowercase, to quote special characters, and so on. Instead of writing "\Ustuff" to put part of a quoted string in uppercase, you'll write "{ uc "stuff" }" using the code interpolation semantics.

Numeric Constants

Numeric values are the simplest constants. This section covers expressing, in various bases, numeric values in program source code, printing numbers out in different bases, and decimal numbers.

Numbers appear by themselves. They're used often enough that other means of quoting them or announcing them would be cumbersome.

```
# Numbers appear as themselves without quotes, Perl 5 or Perl 6
```

```
print 3, "\n";
```

Virtually every computer language follows this pattern. This rule means that function names, variable names, and so forth, can't start with a number. Numbers can be expressed in scientific notation, and they may be negative. They can have decimal points.

```
-1000
0.3
15e100
1.5e101
0.5e-3
```

You can break numbers up with underscores to make them more readable. The comma (in the English system) or period (in some European countries) is normally used for this purpose in written language. For example:

```
1_000_000.00 # 1000000.00
```

No requirement exists that the underscore breaks up digits into groups of three, but this is a common convention.

■**More than you wanted to know?** Don't worry if this is more information than you wanted to know. This chapter tries to thoroughly cover the topic of constants. Skim the tricks and features you don't need, and save them for later. Single-quoted strings, double-quoted strings, other quote characters with q and qq, and the basic premise of interpolation are key concepts for future chapters.

Decimal, Octal, Hexadecimal, and Binary Constants

Humans have ten fingers, and we count in base 10. But computers have no such number of fingers.

```
# Expressing numbers in various bases - Perl 5 and Perl 6
```

```
print 37;       # decimal - prints 37
print 037;      # Perl 5 octal - prints 31 (037 is 0c37 in Perl 6)
print 0x37;     # hexadecimal - prints 55
print 0b0100101; # binary - prints 37
```

The constructs in these examples are automatically recognized in your program source code. Perl's parser recognizes them and converts them to an internal representation. If you'd like to print out a number in a notation other than plain old decimal, use sprintf().

```
# Printing numbers in various bases - Perl 5 and Perl 6
```

```
printf "%x\n", 37; # convert to hexadecimal
```

See perldoc -f printf, perldoc -f sprintf, perldoc -f pack, and perldoc -f unpack.

Octal is base 8 and is useful for specifying Unix file permission bits and other bit-related things. An octal digit is a number between 0 and 7, which requires exactly 3 bits to represent (2 ** 3 = 8). You can express a byte using 3 octal digits with 1 bit left.

Hexadecimal, or *hex*, is widely used for representing addresses in memory. Two hexadecimal digits describe a byte, and 8 hex digits describe a 32-bit value. Attempting to print a reference gives you the hexadecimal memory address that the reference is stored at, plus some other information about the reference. Like addresses look alike when displayed in hex (but become scrambled when displayed in decimal). You can also use hex to express sequences of bits.

Automatic Decimal Parsing

Strings that happen to contain numbers can be used as numbers. When an attempt is made to use the string as a number, Perl automatically parses it in order to convert it to a number. For example, '37628x3' almost parses as a valid number, '3872' parses as a valid number, and 7422 is already a number. Quotes around characters, including numeric characters, construct a string from those characters.

Perl always reads input as a string; should you ever require a number to be input, you must convert the input string to a number. A string describing a decimal number is automatically converted to that number should it be used as a number.

```
# Strings are automatically parsed as numbers on demand - Perl 5 or Perl 6

print "5" * 2, "\n";  # same as: print 5 * 2, "\n"
```

It's preferable to *not* quote numbers as strings in your program source code, but an oct() or hex() function isn't needed to parse decimal numbers taken from input—Perl does this automatically.

Manual Hexadecimal, Octal, and Binary Parsing

Because the language parser automatically parses hex, octal, and binary, programs are often surprised that hex, octal, and binary aren't automatically recognized in input. Keyboard input, file data, and Common Gateway Interface (CGI) parameters are all sources of input. Input strings are parsed as decimal numbers when used as numbers, so the need to manually convert may not be intuitive.

The built-in hex() converts strings containing hexadecimal numbers into a numeric value.

```
# Converting input from a string containing hexadecimal notation
# into a number - Perl 5 or Perl 6

print "Enter a hexadecimal number:\n";
my $string = <STDIN>;
my $number = hex $string;
print "You entered the decimal number 55\n" if $number == 0x37;
```

The 0x37 read-in from input must be manually converted to a number using hex(), but the 0x37 that appears in the program is automatically recognized as hex and parsed as such. perl understands Perl source code, but it can't possibly know the syntax or meaning of data read in by a program.

Use the built-in function oct() to convert program input from octal notation. oct() pays mind to any 0b or 0x prefix on the number, recognizing it as binary or hexadecimal given the correct prefix. Need another conversion? Ask CPAN (search at http://search.cpan.org), or see perldoc for pack and unpack.

Numeric Constants in Perl 6

All the caveats still apply about the source code representation being converted to the internal representation when the program is compiled, and that data input needs to be explicitly converted by the programmer, rather than being part of the source code.

Remember that these bases and representations in ASCII using little pictures of symbols from the Roman alphabet exist purely for the sake of humans.

Perl 6 introduces a new syntax for constants that are part of the program source code. Any base may be used, but bases larger than 36 can't be represented with the numbers 0 through 9 and letters *a* through *z*. (This means that perl can't directly parse your base 64 Multipurpose Internet Mail Extensions [MIME] attachments.)

```
# Numeric constants in arbitrary bases - Perl 6

print 37;          # decimal - prints 37
print 8#37;        # octal - prints 31
```

```
print 16#37;       # hexadecimal - prints 55
print 2#0100101;   # binary - prints 37
```

Nonstandard bases are available.

The prefixes from Perl 5 have been adapted, except that 0c signifies octal rather than a bare 0.

```
# Numeric constant prefixes - Perl 6

print 37;         # decimal - prints 37 - same as P5
print 0c037;      # octal - prints 31 - was 037 in P5
print 0x37;       # hexadecimal - prints 55 - same as P5
print 0b0100101;  # binary - prints 37 - same as P5
```

As in Perl 5, use printf(), sprintf(), pack(), and unpack() to convert the internal representation into one of these notations. Use oct() and hex() to convert string input back into an internal binary representation of the number.

Perl 6 also introduces some metanumbers: Inf and NaN. Inf is infinity, and NaN means "not a number". NaN is the result of certain illegal or illogical operators. Inf represents infinity. All numbers are smaller than positive infinity, and Inf can be used to iterate, for example.

You use traits and types in Perl 6 to fine-tune the workings of variables, including removing limitations.

```
my Int $num is bigint = 10000000000;
```

In Perl 5, 10000000000 would overflow a 32-bit integer. Traits customize variables. I'll introduce them in the next chapter.

String Constants

Constant text that's part of a program is called a *string* (no, this isn't physics string theory).

```
# Simple constant string, Perl 5 or Perl 6

print "Hello, world!\n";
```

Perfectly mnemonically, text constants are text placed in quotes. The text is *mnemonic* because you're telling the computer to use it literally, and you're suggesting that it's data that came from elsewhere and is just reproduced in the program. It's copied or quoted in your program, so to speak.

The name *string* is a relic of the old days where a single character (letter, number, or symbol) could be stored in a memory location but several could be strung together in consecutive memory locations to spell words and make sentences. A *string* refers to a string of characters.

Perl offers numerous ways to quote strings. You can quote entire blocks of text. You can quote text with quote characters in it using other characters. You can mix constant text with values to be substituted in or with expressions to be replaced with their results, which I'll explain in the section "Interpolation".

Single characters are either a string that happens to have a length of one character or a numeric value holding the number assigned to a character according to some character set. Use chr() to convert such a number to a string containing one character, or use ord() to convert such a string to such a number, at least for the default character set.

User-Selected Quotes

So far I've used the most familiar quoting construct: double quotes.

```
print "Hello, world\n";
```

Quoting a string with double quotes is the most obvious and mnemonic way but can quickly become pathological in the wrong situation. HTML is one such situation. For that, the qq operator shines.

```
print qq{<p style="font-family:sans-serif">Hello, World!</p>};
```

Since the double-quote character isn't being used to quote the string in this example, it can be freely used inside the string without concern of having to escape it.

qq and other quoting operators allow you to select the character used to do the actual quoting. I've used matching *braces*, but that's merely my personal favorite. If you use a character that has an opposite closing counterpart, then you use its counterpart to end the string. Otherwise, you use the same character again to close it.

```
# Quoting strings with user-selected quoting characters - Perl 5 and Perl 6

print qq<Hola, World!\n>;
print qq[Hallo, World!\n];
print qq(Saluton, World!\n);
print qq#OHAYO, World!\n#;

print qq]Hello, World!\n[;     # Perl 6 only
```

Like other quoting operators, qq was modeled after the s and m operators used to quote regular expressions (for substitution and matching, respectively). You don't need to know that, but it may help everything fit together; this syntax isn't an anomaly in Perl but is instead a common and useful mechanism for quoting arbitrary data.

Strings can span several lines. If you fail to terminate something, or forget which character you used to start the string, perl will offer a helpful hint.

```
Might be a runaway multi-line (type) string starting on line (number)
```

Double-quoted strings and their equivalents have numerous special features that you may or may not want. The characters \, $, @, and % have special meanings within a double-quoted string. See the upcoming section "Interpolation" for more information.

Single-Quoted Strings

Single-quoted refers to the quoting character better known as the *apostrophe*. Singled-quoted strings are better known as *noninterpolated strings*.

```
print 'Hello World\n';                # bad - this won't do what you probably want
print '/\/\/\/\/\/\/\/', "\n";        # good - print an ASCII wavy line
```

You should use single quotes when you want to avoid the interpolation features of double-quoted strings.

The q operator works the same way as the single quotes, which is to say that it also disables the sometimes-undesirable features of double-quoted strings.

```
print q{Hello World\n};        # bad - the \n sequence isn't replaced with a newline
print q{/\/\/\/\/\/\/\/}, "\n";   # good - print an ASCII wavy line
```

A backslash (\) is special when the next character is a single quote (') or another backslash (\). It escapes the next character, making the next character literal instead of special. The backslash and the single quote or backslash after it are replaced by only the single quote or one backslash. The first backslash dies in the effort and vanishes.

```
\\   becomes   \
 \'  becomes   '
```

The ' and \ that get substituted in don't terminate the quoting or escape the next character—they're literal, not special.

In noninterpolated strings, the backslash makes a special character literal (makes it stand for itself and nothing more) and makes a literal character special—if a special meaning is to be had. When removing special meaning, you're *escaping* the value. The backslash is a sort of escape character; you break out of the normal rules and apply alternate rules. The forward slash has no special meaning when escaped in noninterpolated strings.

Interpolation

Interpolation means, among other things, to "alter or corrupt by the insertion of new or foreign matter". Perl recognizes requests to perform interpolation in strings in program source code.

Strings quoted using double quotes or the qq operator are subject to the rules of escape sequences and variable interpolation. Certain characters are *metacharacters*—characters that mean something other than themselves (see Table 4-1).

Table 4-1. *Metacharacters and Their Meanings*

Metacharacters	Meaning
$	Replaces name of variable with its value when prefixing a variable name
@	Same as previous, but for arrays
%	Same as previous, but for hashes (Perl 6 only)
&	Substitutes in the result of performing function call
\	Prevents any of the previous from being special, or introduces an escape sequence when used with other characters

Rather than taking only variable names, Perl 6 will interpolate the result of a parenthesized expression. $ may introduce an object in a method call in Perl 6 (this behavior isn't recognized in Perl 5). & introduces a function call in Perl 6 (function calls don't directly interpolate in Perl 5).

String Interpolation of Scalars

Variable interpolation substitutes in the value of variables in place of the variable name.

```
# Perl 5 or Perl 6 - simple interpolation:

my $message = "Hello, World!";
print "$message\n";
```

This works on the same principle as escape codes, such as \n, in strings. The following lines are all equivalent:

```
# interpolation is just fancy concatenation:

print "$message\n";       # Perl 5 or Perl 6
print $message . "\n";    # Perl 5
print $message ~ "\n";    # Perl 6
printf "%s\n", $message;  # Perl 5 or Perl 6
```

Interpolation best serves simple, natural-language text strings, but use it wherever it looks right. Interpolating a scalar variable such as $message into an otherwise constant string is a simple case. Other things may be interpolated, as you'll see.

Interpolation Happens at Run Time

Interpolation is recognized when the program is first parsed and the logic to perform the substitution is created. The actual substitution doesn't happen until the code actually runs. Otherwise, only constants could be substituted into other constants, which would be pretty useless. It's too useful to interpolate in a loop as a variable changes value and other such things.

Interpolation happens when the string is encountered in code during run time.

```
# Perl 5 or Perl 6 - interpolation uses current values for variables

sub who_called_us_when {
    my $foo = localtime;
    my $bar = caller;
    print "At $foo, $bar called us\n";
}
```

If the values change, the new values are used in the interpolated string.

```
# Perl 5 or Perl 6 - interpolation uses current values for variables

for my $color (qw(red green blue)) {
    print "The sky is a lovely shade of $color.\n";
}
```

This outputs the following:

```
The sky is a lovely shade of red.
The sky is a lovely shade of green.
The sky is a lovely shade of blue.
```

■**Interpolated strings work in closures** Code references created with sub { } hold references to any variable they use from surrounding code blocks. This is a *closure*. For the purposes of closures, interpolation of a variable into a string counts as a reference. Interpolated strings work correctly with closures. Chapter 19 covers closures.

Interpolation isn't a feature of strings. It doesn't happen when a string containing something such as $foo is evaluated.

```
# Perl 5 or Perl 6 - this INCORRECTLY tries to interpolate and fails:

my $foo = localtime;
my $string = 'The time is $foo.';
print $string, "\n";
```

Evaluating the double-quoted string with the interpolated variable triggers interpolation. Using data containing variables names alone doesn't. This is why I say that interpolation is recognized as the program is compiled and happens only in double-quoted strings and their equivalents. Every now and then someone wants Perl to interpolate variables contained in variables.

```
# Perl 5 - this approximates scalar interpolation:

use PadWalker 'peek_my';

my $foo = localtime;
my $string = 'The time is $foo.';

# added these lines to make this example work:
my $pad = peek_my(0);
$string =~ s/(\$\w+)/${$pad->{$1}}/ge;

print $string, "\n";
```

This is really a topic for Chapter 5, which has other PadWalker examples. Rather than simulating interpolation of scalar variables into a string, it's usually much cleaner to interpolate in values from hashes. This keeps like collections of values together and avoids the evils of symbolic references. A data structure should hold the values you're using rather than variables in the program. See Chapter 8 for an implementation. Implementation-wise, the requests to interpolate are identified in string constants when Perl parses the source code. The interpolated string is distilled down to a string concatenation between the variable parts and the constant parts. The string is scanned for interpolation constructs only once at compile time. It's just syntactical sugar for concatenation, which would otherwise be done with the . operator in Perl 5, the ~ operator in Perl 6, or the built-in functions sprintf() or join() in either Perl 5 or Perl 6. See perldoc perltie for variables that can perform tasks such as interpolating every time they're referenced.

Array and Hash Interpolation

Perl 5 interpolates arrays in strings, separating each array element with whatever value is specified in $".

```
# Array interpolation separators - Perl 5

do {
    @a = (1 .. 10);
```

```
    local $" = ' <> ';
    print "@a";
};
```

```
# Is Equivalent to
```

```
do {
    @a = (1 .. 10);
    print join ' <> ', @a;
};
```

If you set the value for $", don't forget to localize it to the block first so as not to affect other code in the program. This example does this correctly.

Perl 6 gives each array its own separator, skirting the issue that requires you to localize those funny variables in Perl 5. (Perl 6 reduces the number of variables with global effects, favoring traits and such.) This field is @array.sep for arrays and %hash.pairsep for hashes.

```
# Array interpolation separators - Perl 6
```

```
@a = (1 .. 10);
@a.sep = ' <> ';
print "@a()";
```

This explanation assumes the default stringification logic. You can attach custom stringification logic to arrays, hashes, objects, and so on, using traits, which are introduced next chapter. Traits may trump the value specified by .sep().

Hash interpolation is new in Perl 6. Hash variables appearing in double-quoted strings are stringified.

```
# Hash interpolation - Perl 6
```

```
my %things_that_go_bump = {
    goblins         => hungry,
    boogie_monsters => creepy,
}.pairsep(' ').separator(', ');
```

```
print "%things_that_go_bump are under my bed!{}\n";
```

This may print goblins hungry, boogie_monsters creepy are under my bed!. Perl 5 doesn't interpolate hashes, and without Perl 6's custom stringification logic, you don't have enough control over how the hash looks as a string for most cases.

Array and hash references work, too. "$hashref->{foo}\n" in Perl 5 and "$hashref.<<foo>>\n" in Perl 6 do what you'd want.

Code Interpolation

You can stuff arbitrary Perl inside strings. The resulting value replaces the code in the output. The Interpolation module from CPAN provides an implementation of this idea for Perl 5.

```
# Interpolated expression - Perl 5

use Interpolation E => 'eval';
print "$E{7+8} = 15... Adding up numbers!\n";

# Interpolated expression - Perl 6

print "{7+8} = 15... Adding up numbers is very uplifting.\n";  # Perl 6
```

Interpolation enforces a *scalar context* on the expression; that is, it asks the expression for a single value. Should the expression compute a list, Perl will flatten it into a string to make it a single value.

Expressions placed inside the {} block inside the double-quoted string can contain other strings, function calls, operators, and most other Perl features.

```
# Interpolated expressions may contain quotes - Perl 5

print "The following people have just been sacked:
    $E{join ', ', sort 'Mike', 'Thomas', 'Adrian', 'Alex'}\n";

# Interpolated expressions may contain quotes - Perl 6

print "The following people have just been sacked:
    {join ', ', sort 'Mike', 'Thomas', 'Adrian', 'Alex'}\n";
```

The Interpolation module provides escapes for formatting percentages, formatting dollar amounts with commas and two decimal places, correcting case on expression output, and performing numerous other cool and useful actions.

If you don't want all of that, you can trick Perl into evaluating code in the middle of a string as-is. This avoids a module dependency.

```
# Perl 5 - interpolation without using a module

 print "Head-count will be reduced by a factor of @{[$layoffs/$employees]}.
     Profits will be increased by a factor of
     @{[($employees+$layoffs)/$employees]}\n";
```

You can use Interpolation and @{[ ]} from within *here documents*, which are discussed later in the "Here Documents" section.

See also the Perl6::Interpolators CPAN module, which gives Perl 5 interpolation semantics closely resembling Perl 6's. This is accomplished with a *source filter*.

■Source filters are dangerous Source filters themselves have problems. Specifically, perfectly valid constructs may result in syntax errors. Attempts to use more than one source filter at a time can make things really blow up. And when things blow up, it's difficult to figure out why, as there may be no rhyme or reason to what exactly triggers the problem or how it manifests. Also, source filters dramatically add to the startup time of programs, which is inappropriate for CGI environments unless the code is first compiled or bytecode compiled. Source filters are great as an amusement, but when used to solve real problems, the cure is often worse than the disease.

Function and Method Call Interpolation

You can interpolate arbitrary expressions to place the values of scalar variables or the result of function calls into a string. Like scalars, method calls and function calls may be directly interpolated in Perl 6. Interpolating a method call is easy.

```
# Interpolated method call - Perl 5

use Interpolation E => 'eval';
print "It is going to rain $E{ $noaa->radar } this evening.\n";

# Interpolated method call - Perl 6

print "It is going to rain $noaa.radar() this evening.\n";
```

The parentheses on the end of the method call are required for Perl to pick up on the method call being a method call. Of course, you could place {} around the call to $noaa.radar(), but it isn't necessary as long as the trailing parentheses are there. You can place arguments, including arbitrary expressions, in the parentheses.

Function calls require the & sigil in front of the function to be called.

```
# Interpolated function call - Perl 6

print "It is going to rain &radar() this evening.\n";
```

The & sigil isn't normally required (or wanted) when making function calls.

Escape Sequences

Escape sequences are sequences of characters with special meanings when used inside strings. qq-quoted strings interpret the same escapes as plain old double-quoted strings; the backslash followed by a letter represents a useful character or character sequence. These escape sequences are sequences of several characters standing in for a character that can't be typed, can't be displayed neatly in your editor, or are otherwise problematic.

Common Escape Sequences

Escape sequences in strings start with a backslash, much like variable interpolation sequences start with $, @, or %. The most popular escape sequences are as follows:

```
\n   new-line
\r   carriage return
\t   tab
\b   backspace
\a   bell
```

Newer printer control languages have made other escape sequences obsolete. Yes, escape sequences have their origins in printer control. The vertical tab (\v) and some others are now gone. Table 4-2 shows some example escape sequences.

Table 4-2. *Example Escape Sequences*

Escape Sequence	Meaning
\045	ASCII character number in octal. The next character after \ is 0 or 1.
\x24	ASCII character number in hexadecimal. The character after \ is x.
\cM	Control character (Ctrl+M).
\x{263a}	Unicode hexadecimal wide char (SMILEY) from the perlop man page.
\N{REGISTERED SIGN}	Named Unicode character.

Escape sequences generated from the backslash aren't substitutions made by the print() built-in function or any other built-in function but instead are performed directly on the source code as it's read by perl's grammar. Escape sequences are decoded as the literal is parsed, and the decoded sequence becomes part of the program. substr() applied to the string returns the special character, not the escape sequence.

Other escape sequences look like the ones in Table 4-2 but actually result in code being generated rather than just literal data.

Perl 6 drops the Perl 5 semantics of \L, \l, \u, \U, \Q, and so on. Use lc(), lcfirst(), ucfirst(), and uc() inside a code interpolation block instead, or use sprintf().

```
# printf instead of interpolation and escape sequences - Perl 5 and Perl 6

printf "OHAYO %s %s!\n", uc $surname, ucfirst $name;

# Interpolating a code block - Perl 6

print "OHAYO { uc $surname } { ucfirst $name }!\n";
```

It may be useful to call CGI::escape(), call routines in Regexp::Common, and call various other routines to prepare strings before substituting them into a string. sprintf() is like printf() in that it recognizes %s as a placeholder to substitute a value into (as well as other % escapes), but sprintf() evaluates to a string rather than printing the result my $greeting = sprintf "OHAYO %s %s!", uc $surname, ucfirst $name;.

Newlines, Networks, and Operating Systems

The \n construct in strings is almost always what you want when reading and writing data on your own machine to end a line. It's translated to the local concept of the line-ending sequence.

Different systems have different ideas of line endings.

```
# What ASCII codes constitute a new line on this system? Perl 5

my $cr = "\n";
print join(", ", unpack "C*", $cr), "\n";
```

The local concept of a line ending shouldn't be trusted for network programming, where the local hosts idea of line endings may not agree with the remote hosts. When sending data over the network, be explicit.

```
# Internet standard line endings

"\015\012"
"\cM\cJ"
chr(13) . chr(10);  # Perl 5's . is ~ in Perl 6
```

Carriage returns and line feeds are actions that printers perform and terminals approximate.

Named Unicode Characters

To use the named Unicode characters, you have to load the names first.

```
# Perl 5 - UNICODE character escapes

use charnames ':full';
print "\N{REGISTERED SIGN}\n";
```

On my system, these come from /usr/local/lib/perl5/5.9.0/unicore/NamesList.txt. On Linux, drop the local part for most vendors' packaged versions of Perl. Or, do a perl -e 'print "@INC\n";', and look in those directories. On any system, adjust the version number.

Here Documents

Here documents elegantly quote large blocks of text. Identifiers—think variable names—delimit the blocks of text. Strings of letters with possible numbers and underscores, beginning with a letter or underscore, work fine as identifiers. You can easily choose the identifier as something that doesn't occur in the string. The MIME standard does something similar.

```
# Here documents, Perl 5 and 6:

print <<"SEYMOUR";
  <head><title>Hello, World!</title></head>
  <body bgcolor="chartreuse">
    Hello, World!
  </body>
SEYMOUR
```

Arbitrary data is easier to quote with arbitrary strings than arbitrary characters. For any given character, it's likely to occur in a sufficiently sized random chunk of data. MIME also uses unique strings to delimit data.

```
MIME-Version: 1.0
Content-Type: multipart/alternative; boundary="
----=_NextPart_000_00A3_01C2D230.34821A40"
Type:  multipart/alternative;

This is a multi-part message in MIME format.

-------=_NextPart_000_00A3_01C2D230.34821A40
Content-Type: text/plain; charset="iso-8859-1"
Content-Transfer-Encoding: quoted-printable
```

```
THIS WEEK AT PAPAGO - 02/11/2003 =20
...

------=_NextPart_000_00A3_01C2D230.34821A40
Content-Type: text/html; charset="iso-8859-1"
Content-Transfer-Encoding: quoted-printable

<!DOCTYPE HTML PUBLIC "-//W3C//DTD HTML 4.0 Transitional//EN">
<HTML><HEAD>
...

------=_NextPart_000_00A3_01C2D230.34821A40--
```

Generate and read MIME envelopes such as this one with `MIME::Lite` and `MIME::Tools`.

Here documents interpolate variables just as double strings were documented to do in the "Interpolation" section earlier in this chapter. Put single quotes around the identifier to avoid interpolation. This is mnemonic for the syntax for single-quoted strings that also refuse to interpolate.

```
# No interpolation in here documents - Perl 5

# "$path" is printed rather than the contents of the $path variable

print <<'SEYMOUR';
    $path must be set to the location of the data at the top of the script
SEYMOUR
```

Perl 6 allows the entire contents of the here document to be indented. Indent the contents of the here document to match the indenting of your code. An amount of whitespace equal to the indenting of the terminating identifier will be removed from each line in the here document.

```
# Here documents, auto-unindented, Perl 6:

{
    print <<"SEYMOUR"
        Stuff to print here
        That is indented
        According to the usual rules for code
        SEYMOUR
}
```

Perl 5 takes some syntax to emulate this and can't handle the terminating identifier being indented.

```
# Here documents, manually unindented, Perl 5:

do {
    print map "$_\n", map { (m/ {7}(.*)\n/g); } <<SEYMOUR;
        Stuff to print here
        That is indented
        According to the usual rules for code
SEYMOUR
};
```

The `perldoc perlfunc` entry for `<<EOF` suggests another syntax for doing the same thing. Use whichever you like best. This `perldoc` entry also enumerates features not mentioned here.

Whitespace as the quoting string is a supported special case. It matches the first blank line.

```
# Here documents, terminated by a blank line, Perl 5:

print << ;
        Stuff to print here
        More stuff to be printed here

# the first blank line terminates the quoting

# Here documents, terminated by a blank line, Perl 6:

print << '';
        Stuff to print here
        More stuff to be printed here

# the first blank line terminates the quoting
```

You can also use here documents in the middle of expressions; don't put anything else on the line with the terminator, don't indent the terminator in Perl 5, and don't forget the semicolon on the end. These examples place the line-ending semicolon before the contents of the here document. Either way is valid.

```
# Here documents in an expression with the semicolon placed after
# the terminating string - Perl 5

# This message will be printed entirely in upper case:

print uc <<SPAM
  100% free visit us now http://freestuff4u.ru no closing cost improve your
  love life you can't lose!!!!!! act now! save! half off!
  free free free!!!!111!!111
SPAM
;
```

This example places the semicolon on a line after the terminator. This is a Perl 5 requirement that Perl 6 drops.

Constant Data As Files

File operations perform lots of useful tasks. For example, you can seek to a position, read specific number of bytes, read a line with `readline`, keep reading where you left off, and truncate the file. Best of all, files easily hold binary data. No tedious process exists for escaping things.

Perl Archive

PAR, which stands for the *Perl ARchive* format, is another excellent module. Perl 6's method of distributing included files will almost certainly take a form closer to PAR. A program and all its dependencies are packaged into a single compressed file. See Chapter 12 for more information.

Strings As Files

Sometimes you need a file that contains constant data or data you've computed and put in a scalar. Writing the data out to disk using a temporary file is an option, but that's messy and has security considerations. Files can be constants, too. Perl has a special form of open that opens a scalar as a file: open my $new_file_handle, '<', \$scalar_that_contains_data or die $!;. Use this to hard-code small files inline in your programs.

Lists Are Constant

What looks like a string can be a list of strings.

```
# Simple constant list, Perl 5 or Perl 6

print 'Numbers: ', qw<one two three>, "\n";
```

A list is kind of like a constant array; you can use a list in many, but not all, places that an array is accepted. print(), and many other built-in and user-defined functions, happily accept more than one argument and operate on each. Perl makes it easy to construct these lists of values.

The operators << and >> quote words, returning a list of words. *Words* here means things separated by whitespace: newlines, tabs, spaces, and the like.

```
qw< :default ftsize entereval sort >;   # Perl 5 and 6
<< :default ftsize entereval sort >>;   # Perl 6 only
```

This example actually creates four string constants, but it's useful to think of qw as quoting a constant list.

The idea of quoting a list may sound strange, but Perl finds it natural to perform tasks in terms of lists. When using a module, you can import a list of keywords or provide the arguments.

```
# Quoting lists - Perl 5

use ops qw<:default ftsize entereval sort>;
use POSIX qw<:errno_h :fcntl_h>;   # adapted from the POSIX manual page
foreach my $color (qw<red green blue>) { print chr $pixel{$color} }
```

Perl 6 allocates << and >> to mean qw<>.

```
# Quoting lists - Fictitious Perl 6

use ops <<:default ftsize entereval sort>>;
use POSIX <<:errno_h :fcntl_h>>;
for my $color <<red green blue>> { print chr @pixel{$color} }
```

It's doubtful that Perl 6 will get a version of the ops.pm module, but if it does, using it may look like the previous listing.

The qw operator is an abbreviation of *quote words*. The word *words* has a special, specific meaning in Perl.

```
# Almost interchangeable - Perl 5

use ops qw<:default ftsize entereval sort>;
use ops split /\s+/, ':default ftsize entereval sort';

# Almost interchangeable - Perl 6

use ops <<:default ftsize entereval sort>>;
use ops ':default ftsize entereval sort'.split /\s+/;
```

The regular expression engine defines a word as \w+, which matches letters, numbers, and the underscore character (_). Well, I'm not using that meaning but instead approximating it. \s+ is a run of whitespace (newlines, tabs, spaces, and such), and qw<> looks for things broken up by that.

Declaring Symbolic Constants

Literal values should be represented with a symbolic name when that literal value is subject to changes in future versions of the program, especially when that value is referenced in more than one place. Naming values documents code. For example, $days_in a_week explains why you're using the value 7.

Symbolic Constants in Perl 5

Use the constant *pragmatic module*.

```
use constant WIDE => 64;
```

This is essentially the same as the following:

```
sub WIDE () { 64 }
```

Perl attempts to optimize away subroutines that generate constant values (using no variables that are referenced elsewhere). Such constant subroutines are replaced with the value they generate.

constant, when passed an anonymous hash, declares several values at once.

```
use Config;

use constant {
    BIT    => 1,
    NIBBLE => 4,
    BYTE   => 8,
    WORD   => $Config{intsize} * 8,  # 32 on my system
};
```

You can then use WORD in place of $Config{intsize} * 8 and use BIT in place of 1, and so on.

Symbolic Constants in Perl 6

Declare variables as constants using the is constant trait.

```
my $release is constant = 6;
```

A constant can be assigned a value only once. If the compiler finds another attempt, it reports it as an error.

Declaring something constant allows the compiler to optimize expressions using the constant. constant is a hint that the value will never change, so there's no need to recompute it in expressions. You could reduce the previous if to the following:

```
if( length($bitstring) * 8 <= WIDE)  # which is the same as:
if( length($bitstring) <= WIDE / 8)  # which is the same as:
if( length($bitstring) <= 8)         # optimized version: 64/8 = 8
```

Perl 5 too precomputes constant expressions but has no way of knowing whether a scalar is constant.

System Constants

Unix-like systems vary from one another and from other systems. Worse, they're field upgraded. A system shipping with support for only IPv4 may later have an IPv6 library installed. The only way to know what a given machine can do is to look at the header files and libraries installed on it. That isn't to say that nuances of the operating system don't affect the programmer, because they do.

You'd think that Perl may insulate you from this. Many languages try—they specify a feature set and then do whatever is needed to make that feature set work on each host. But Perl means too many things to too many people. In the early days, Perl performed two main functions to provide system resources to a programmer: it let you pipe input to and from other programs easily, and it let you call virtually any of the Unix kernel routines. This was seen as a huge improvement; rather than roping you off in an area thought to be useful, Perl let you swim in the deep end. This tradition fostered a new tradition: easily supporting libraries that weren't around when your version of Perl was written, supporting libraries that are on some platforms but not others, and supporting odd and out-of-the-way libraries that no language could be expected to come out of the box supporting.

To use these operating system features, you must provide the correct arguments to the right system calls and library calls. The programmer could attempt to find the numbers, special values, and formats required, but this would be tedious, error prone, and nonportable. The values are likely to be different between systems and versions of the library. Giving the constants and special values names makes code easier to read, write, and port.

Back in the old days, you'd use a program called h2ph to read C-style include files sporting the .h suffix and turn them into a perl program sporting a .ph suffix. Now days, h2xs generates the beginnings of a perl module starting from a C-style header file. Problems parsing C headers aside, the old h2ph gave you only constant values of symbols. This was wonderful for talking to the host operating system to use its idea of the Unix application programming interface (API) and for easily adding support for new and unheard-of libraries.

Perl supported the W3C's libwww program with open arms, creating LWP, or lib-www perl, and getting an early foothold on Web robot programming. Likewise with database interface modules, early adoption by Perl was important.

I want you to understand why you should turn to CPAN modules to get values from system symbolic constants and why they aren't and can't be defined in the Perl core. If you understand this, you'll know to look for the constants you need in the CPAN module, which provides the binary interface between perl and the library you want to use.

The POSIX module defines system error codes and flags used by system input/output (I/O) routines. Socket defines numerous network-related constants and routines to convert values. Fcntl defines constants for file operations such as seeking and locking. Although DBD::mysql heavily uses constants from /usr/local/include/mysql/*, few of them are made available to Perl programs. Instead, they're merely used internally. Searching http://search.cpan.org for the word *constants* gives interesting and numerous results. Table 4-3 lists some example constants and the module in which they're defined.

Table 4-3. *Example Constants and Modules Defining Constants*

Symbol	Module	Defined In
LOCK_SH	Fcntl	EWOULDBLOCK
POSIX	PF_INET	Socket

These are just examples. Each module implementing an interface to a library will define constants.

Regular Expression Constants

Regexp::Common, available from CPAN, provides all but the least commonly needed regular expressions. Subclasses provide specialized regular expressions for different purposes. Hundreds are available, so you have a good chance that one of them is the one you need.

Regular expressions are normally used inline, but those that are needed at multiple points in a program may be declared as a sort of constant. The qr// quote-like operator quotes a regular expression and returns a reference to it.

```
my $word = qr{[A-Za-z][a-z'-]*};
```

The qr{ } operator is documented in the "Regexp Quote-Like Operators" section of perldoc perlop, and regular expressions in general are documented in perldoc perlre and perldoc perlretut. See Perl6::Rules from CPAN for a Perl 6–style *rules* implementation for Perl 5. Rules are a more-readable, more-powerful system based on regular expressions, taking further the idea of the Perl 5 x regular expression flag for "extended" regular expressions. They're documented in Apocalypse 5, available from http://dev.perl.org, and in *Perl 6 in a Nutshell* (O'Reilly, 2004).

REFERENCES AND THANKS

This chapter was originally based on Apocalypse 2, Joseph F. Ryan's "String Literals", and Angel Faus's "Numeric Literals" posts to the `perl6-documentation` list, as well as the `perl6-documentation` and `perl6-language` lists themselves. The site at `http://cog.cognitivity.com/perl6/val.html` is another excellent resource. These sources are comprehensive and Perl 6 centric.

The numerous quoting operators are documented in the "Regexp Quote-Like Operators" section in the `perlop` manual and at `http://perldoc.com`. See "Gory Details of Parsing Quoted Constructs" in `perldoc perlop` for details on how Perl 5 identifies and interprets string literals.

Mark Jason Dominus wrote `Interpolation`, and Tom Phoenix wrote `constant`.

Not Covered in this Chapter

Interpolation, covered in this chapter, makes it easy to generate customized output from constant text, variable values, and expressions. More complicated tasks require a more sophisticated approach, and that's a *templating system*. These let you separate Structured Query Language (SQL), Hypertext Markup Language (HTML), and other kinds of code and encoding from your program where it'd increase the maintainability of the program. The templating system combines them in some way. This is especially useful when nontechnical people need to change the presentation of a program, such as is the case with graphic designers at Web development companies who need to customize the output of CGI applications. Each templating system has a different take on the problem; you should pick one that suits your purposes. However, using a templating system is beyond the scope of this book (if I gave you an example of one, I'd have to give you an example of all of them). See `HTML::Template`, `Mason`, `Template`, and other modules on CPAN (search at `http://search.cpan.org`), or roll your own if you must.

See `Template::Extract` for a module that does the opposite; it picks data out of a document that has a constant structure. `HTML::Parser` is a more powerful "untemplater" for HTML documents, and `HTML::TableExtract` distills the document to table cells.

Perl 5 builds in a kind of page-oriented report-style templater. This featured is called *formats*, and the documentation is in `perldoc perlform`. Formats are for printing forms where data needs to be presented neatly in rows and columns with headers and footers in plain text. Perl 6 moves this to a module, and Damian Conway thoughtfully and cleverly made the interface available to Perl 5 as the module `Perl6::Forms`. Formats are the subject of Apocalypse 7, available from `http://dev.perl.org`.

Summary

In this chapter, you learned about text, numbers, and other constant data. Numbers represent themselves and don't need quotes. Strings that contain numbers are parsed as numbers when used as numbers.

Single-quoted strings stand for exactly what they are, unless they contain \q, ', or some \ sequences. Single-quoted strings look like 'this here', q{this here}, or other permutations of the second example.

Double-quoted strings look like "this here", qq{this here}, or other permutations of the second example. Double-quoted strings stand for something computed from variable names and code in them combined with the textual data they contain. Sequences starting with $, @, and % introduce variables or expressions that interpolate into the string at run time. Perl 6's $() sequence and Perl 5's $E{} sequence with the Interpolation module run code. The other forms take data from a variable, which may trigger code being run in the case of tied variables or stringify methods in Perl 6, which is discussed in Chapter 14.

Here documents may be functionally equivalent to single-quoted strings or double-quoted strings, depending how you use them.

Use symbolic constants to represent constant values when the constant value is used several places in a program and is a hard-coded value. Perl 5 and Perl 6 both have idioms for doing this.

CHAPTER 5

■ ■ ■

Names, Containers, and Values

This chapter is the what, why, and how of variables in Perl. Perl variables interpret themselves according to the context in which they're used. How a variable behaves depends on the type of the variable, any traits they've been extended with, and the value itself. This system has three layers. Understanding these layers will help you integrate Perl with other languages, write cool hacks using Perl, write effective Perl, and, perhaps most important, understand the rest of this book.

We think of *names* when we think of variables. A name has meaning only within a given scope, and a name represents something. (It could represent just about anything, but variables, functions, and packages are the most common things to be named.)

Containers hold *values*. Containers store the data and information about how to interpret it. A name always points to a container, but a container doesn't always have a name.

Values are exactly what they sound like—an internal machine representation of data.

Perl 6 gives finer control over variables with a consistent, flexible system of *traits*. Traits control optimization, control error checking, and tell Perl how to interpret the data in a variable. Traits attach logic to values in order to add features or override implementations of existing features.

Properties extend values, filling in blanks in the meaning of the data.

Modules create *namespaces* that serve to divvy up functions and variables into *packages* when segregation is in order.

Classes build on modules, combining functions in a module with private data to create objects. This, and *exporting*, is how logic and data from one module is used in another.

Figure 5-1 shows the relationship between names, values, and containers.

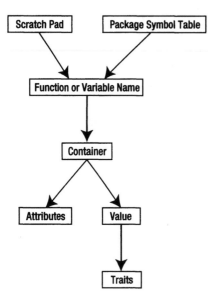

Figure 5-1. *The relationship between names, values, and containers*

Perl has two kinds of name tables—one specific to the block of code (the lexical symbol table, or *scratch pad*), and the package-wide symbol table. These name tables reference names, which reference containers, which reference values.

- Names exist in symbol tables and lexical scopes.

- Containers hold values.

- Values are assigned to containers and fetched from containers.

- Traits customize containers.

- Properties customize values.

This chapter uses Perl6::Variables. Unlike a lot of the source-filtering Perl6:: modules, Perl6::Variables is used (almost) consistently throughout the whole book. I don't want to confuse matters with both syntaxes. Neglecting the old way simplifies the examples and makes data structures a lot easier to explain.

Devel::Peek is brought in to dump out the internal state of variables, giving a glimpse of the raw values as well as the container implementation that backs up a variable name.

Math::BigFloat is used as an example of a container.

Data::Alias is an alternative to the stupid globbing tricks Perl 5 programs had to do.

Perl6::Export does what Perl 5's Export module does but with different syntax—one using traits.

Last but not least, this is the PadWalker chapter. PadWalker probes the otherwise private lexical variables of code references and the block of code that called the current routine (as well as the code blocks that called it). It gives access to variables that otherwise wouldn't be visible.

Chapter Objectives

This chapter lays some groundwork for future chapters, mostly serving those who aren't intimately familiar with Perl 5. It tries to establish a correct frame of mind for thinking about Perl variables. More complicated features of Perl are natural extensions of the three layers of abstractions; variables are composed of *names, containers,* and *values.*

Names have scope; in other words, they're valid only between certain points. Data structures, documented in Chapter 8, take advantage of the idea of multiple variables names referencing a single container. It's useful to understand the ways that a value may be customized and how the possible values are defined by what a container can hold. Names exist in symbol tables or lexical scopes. Modules exporting variables and functions must manipulate the symbol table, so you should understand how variable names are made visible to a program or block.

The structure of this chapter reflects the layered architecture of Perl variables; I'll cover names, containers, values, and then symbol tables, in that order.

This chapter also presents the basics of arrays and hashes. I'll present sample applications for customizing values, one of which shows how to attach additional data to a value. You'll develop a proper understanding of the relationship that packages, or namespaces, share with each other, which should clear up a confusing subject.

Changes for Perl 6

Typeglobs are dead, but a convenient binding syntax, using the `:=` operator, effectively replaces them. Exporting symbols to lexical contexts works in Perl 6, and it's easier to probe your caller and other contexts for the contents of their lexical variables.

You now export symbols with the `is export` trait, which can specify `is export(:default)` or other cases. No `Exporter` module is required to do this. Symbols may be exported to lexical scopes as well as to packages. This is useful for creating pragmatic style modules that temporarily change or extend the language, as well as for avoiding namespace pollution.

Variables have a selection of storage implementations. Perl 5 had this to a limited degree via modules such as `Math::BigInt`, but Perl 6 formalizes this. Programmers may specify the representation for each variable individually. This is the variable's *type*.

Values are extensible within the confines of their types. Perl 6 formalizes this, too.

Keywords That Introduce Variables, Traits, and Properties

For quick reference, this section outlines the Perl keywords that declare specific behaviors in conjunction with variables.

These keywords introduce the following variable names:

- `my` introduces a variable into a program block.

- `has` introduces an instance variable in an object definition.

For this chapter (and for most of the book), I'll declare variables with `my`, except where I demonstrate `temp` in this chapter.

has creates persistent variables used in methods within objects. Chapter 14 covers objects and instance variables.

my and has introduce names, and other keywords customize those names or the values they hold.

- is attaches a trait to a container. Traits are established at compile time.

- but attaches a property to a value. Properties are applied at run time.

Traits are attached to the my, our, or has declaration for a variable, such as with my $zero is constant = 0 or my constant $zero = 0.

Properties attach to any value, regardless of whether it's a constant, it's stored in a variable, or it's computed by expression. This looks like (5 + 3) but false or undef but true.

Names

Every programming language gives you some way of naming and referring to memory locations. These are *names*, *variable names*, or *symbols*. A name has meaning in a given scope such as in a loop, subroutine, package, class, or file. Outside the *scope*, the name is meaningless (or perhaps defined to mean something else).

Names have scope, reference a container, and exist in a symbol table. Properties extend them. The following sections cover the idea of scope and offer examples of using my to declare variable names.

Declaring Variables

Use the my keyword to introduce variables. They'll be valid until the end of the current block. Variables created with my are called *lexically scoped variables* or *lexical variables*. Perl variables start with funny symbols, called *sigils*. Scalar variables contain a single value and start with a dollar sign, like so:

```
# Declaring variables in a function - Perl 5

sub foo {
    my $bar;
    my $baz;
    # ...
}

# Declaring variables to hold parameters - the common case - Perl 5

sub add_two_things {
    my $first_arg = shift;
    my $second_arg = shift;
    return $first_arg + $second_arg;
}
```

```
# Declaring function parameters - Perl 6

sub add_two_things (int $first_arg, int $second_arg) {
    return $first_arg + $second_arg;
}
```

Scalars store numbers, strings, or references, and they're the simplest datatype.

Chapter 11 covers more about reading arguments, and there I'll introduce Perl6::Parameters for Perl 6–like parameters in Perl 5. Chapter 19 talks more about lexical variables and the implications of these scoping rules.

my is also used to declare array variables and hash variables.

```
# Lexical variables - Perl 5 and Perl 6

my $foo;    # declares a scalar - references are scalars
my @foo;    # declares an array
my %foo;    # declares a hash
```

This declares three variables: $foo, @foo, and %foo. The symbol in front, the sigil, specifies the type of the variable but is also part of the name of the variable.

Declaring Lists of Variables

You can declare multiple variables, but you need to use parentheses.

```
# Declaring multiple variables at once - Perl 5 and Perl 6

my ($foo, $bar, $baz);
```

my defaults to operating on a single variable name. This is to make constructs such as open my $filehandle, '<', $filename or die $! work.

Failure to declare a variable will win you the following prize:

```
Global symbol "$ddata" requires explicit package name at test1.pl line 100.
```

This cryptic error message means that strict is on and the variable hasn't been declared. It assumes you really want a package-scoped variable and suggests using syntax that's out-of-date with current practice and style. I'm not sure why this error message doesn't say Global symbol requires declaration with my instead. You can avoid this warning in numerous ways, but the easiest is to declare the variable using my.

■Global variables I've neglected to mention our variables. They work like my, but our references the *same* variable each time rather than creating a new variable. our variables are package-scoped variables, stored in the package's symbol table. Later in this chapter, I'll talk about how Perl 6 makes lexical scopes powerful enough to replace the package symbol table. I personally discourage using our unless you really, really know what you're doing. Chapter 11 explains why you should pass data to subroutines and return values from subroutines rather than stuff data into global variables.

Hashes and Arrays

Arrays and *hashes* both store numerous values in a single variable. They offer multitudes of containers accessible by a single name. They're related in that they're Perl's two fundamental, built-in datatypes that are capable of storing multiple values. Arrays and hashes are utterly unlike arrays in terms of the problems they solve. Arrays naturally map to sequences of things that have an order and may be processed in a loop. Hashes are natural in cases where associations need to be made between two sets of data or two representations of the same data.

Storing Data in Arrays

Arrays store an assortment of related values, organizing the values by position in the array. The position is a number, called an *index* or *subscript*. Indexes can store values at only positive whole numbers.

Each of the following lines accesses a different container. If you're using Perl 5, use the Perl6::Variables module from CPAN to play with this syntax. The array and hash examples in this section, and indeed in this book, require it.

```
# Arrays represent many data items with just one name - Perl 5 and Perl 6

# use Perl6::Variables;    # Perl 5 requires this for these examples

my @arr;

@arr[0] = rand;
@arr[1] = time;
@arr[2] = -s $0;

print @arr[0], "\n";
print @arr[1], "\n";
print @arr[2], "\n";
```

Each slot in an array is essentially a distinct variable with a compound name composed of the variable name and the subscript in brackets. @arr is the base variable name, and the part in the [ ] after the name is an array *subscript* or *index*. Both work together to point at a specific container. The value in subscript can be computed by an arbitrary expression.

Perl's arrays grow as needed—you'll never need to preallocate space. Numerous built-in functions work on arrays. See perldoc perlfunc for an exact list.

Array Lengths

The first element of an array is in the 0 position.

```
# Arrays start at zero - Perl 5

use Perl6::Variables;
use Perl6::Contexts;
use autobox;
use autobox::Core;
```

```
my @array;

print 'last element: ', @array->last, ' number of elements: ', @array->elems, "\n";

@array[0] = int rand 100;

print 'last element: ', @array->last, ' number of elements: ', @array->elems, "\n";
```

This prints the following:

```
last element: -1 number of elements: 0
last element: 0 number of elements: 1
```

In Perl 6 and in Perl 5 while using Perl6::Contexts, array variables (just the variable name alone without a subscript) evaluate to a count of things in the array when used with numeric operations. When a value automatically turns into a number when used as a number, it's said to *numify*. This saves having to call a method on an array to get its length when you're using the length in a math operation.

```
# Array variables may be used as a number in numeric operations
# and evaluate to the count of elements in the array - Perl 5 and Perl 6

# Uncomment for Perl 5:
# use Perl6::Contexts;
# use Perl6::Variables;

my @arr = ( 1 .. 100 );
for my $element ( 0 .. @arr - 1) {
    print "The value at position $element is @arr[$element]\n";
}
```

The .. operator builds a list of numbers starting at the number on the left, 0 in this case, and counting to the number on the right. The - operator also coerces the values (or results of expressions) on both sides into being numbers. This isn't the most elegant way to write a loop; it merely illustrates how to use an array as a number to get at its element count. print "$_\n" for @arr is much more elegant.

Perl 6 and Perl 5 with Perl6::Contexts also recognize cases where string operations (and other operators) are performed on arrays, and in these cases, the array *doesn't* evaluate to a count of the things it contains. In these cases, the array instead stringifies according to the rules outlined in Chapter 4's "Interpolation" section.

The count of elements in an array, queried with elems(), is always one more than the index of the last element, queried with last(). Confusing the count of elements with the index of the last element is a classic programming error. Chapter 8 provides background on the problem and gives rules of thumb for thinking about the situations that arise.

Lists Aren't Arrays

Arrays are a sort of container type (they implement storage for variables and may or may not have names). Being variables, they can be modified. Lists aren't variables and can't be modified. (Lists can, however, contain variables and other expressions that may be modified.)

Perl happily deals with multiple values as readily as it does single values. ( ) or something equivalent is used in other languages to initialize arrays. It does that and much more in Perl. It means essentially "there are a few of these puppies here". Rather than only initializing arrays, the list constructed may be returned, subscripted, iterated over, and subjected to other actions.

Lists built with ( ) are an entirely different beast than you get with array variables (and array references). Lists can't be modified by functions. Items in a list may be indirectly used to modify variables and expressions in the list, but the list itself is never lengthened, shortened, or replaced piecewise. Lists may not have references taken to them. (Though you may get a list of references—one reference to each item in the list, in which case, you probably want to construct an anonymous array using a list, which looks like [(1, 2, 3, 4)] or just [1, 2, 3, 4]). You can build lists with ( ) any place that a list is accepted. The parentheses establish that a list is being built where it would otherwise be ambiguous. In places where a list is always assumed, you don't need parentheses. my defaults to expecting a single variable name, so parentheses are required to declare several variables with a single my. User-defined functions, unless prototyped otherwise, accept a list of values, so parentheses aren't needed around the argument list. Perl 6 extends this rule of optional parentheses to method calls as well as function calls. Chapter 8 has the exact rules with examples.

▪Assigning lists and arrays to scalars Funny things happen when lists or arrays are assigned to a scalar. (Technically, lists don't exist in scalar assignments or other scalar operations, but the comma operator combined with parentheses make it look like a list is being created.) What happens depends on whether you're running Perl 5 or Perl 6. See the section "List Context Assignment" in Chapter 8.

▪Creating variables to pop, shift, chomp, or splice Many built-in operations require a variable to work on because they modify the contents of the variable as part of what they do. A list isn't a variable, but an array is. This is the one case where you'll often need to create a variable to be used just once. Perl normally avoids these scenarios. The anonymous array construction syntax, [ ], and the anonymous hash construction syntax, { }, both create nameless variables. Use these to avoid declaring a variable to be used once. Chapter 8 documents them. You can use my in the middle of an expression. For example, it's valid to say push my @new_array, 5;. The name is immediately available in Perl 6 though Perl 5's grammar doesn't recognize the name until the next statement. The variable lives until the end of the block.

▪Brackets have multiple purposes This introduces one use of the brackets—subscripting. They're subscripts when they appear immediately after a variable name, such as with @foo[1]. But the [ ] symbols have other purposes; they also construct nameless array variables, bypassing the my syntax. See Chapter 8 for information on this meaning of [ ]. This happens when a term (*expression*) is expected, such as where a variable name may appear.

▪Perl6::Variables and slices Some examples that call for Perl6::Variables may appear to work without it. This is sometimes a syntax error in Perl 5 and sometimes means something else entirely. See "Array and Hash Slices" for an explanation.

Storing Data in Hashes

Hashes are similar to arrays in that one name provides multiple containers. They start with the % sigil and are subscripted with the curly braces, { }. Rather than being subscripted or indexed by a positive number, they're subscripted by a string.

```
# Hashes represent many data items with just one name - Perl 5 and Perl 6:

# use Perl6::Variables;   # Perl 5 requires this for these examples

my %hash;

%hash{'fred'} = 10;
%hash{'mike'} = 20;
%hash{'john'} = 30;

print %hash{'fred'}, "\n";
```

Just as with arrays, each slot in the hash is essentially a distinct variable. The value in the subscript can be computed by any arbitrary expression and is called the *hash key*. References, such as references to objects and other hashes and arrays, can be used as a subscript because references work as strings. Chapter 8 has details on using datatypes other than plain strings as hash subscripts.

Many built-in functions work on hashes. See perldoc perlfunc's "Perl Functions by Category" section for a complete list.

Braces have multiple purposes The braces, { }, have several purposes. They're hash subscripts when they appear immediately after a variable name, such as with %foo{'one'}. (Perl 5 allows whitespace after the variable name, but Perl 6 takes the whitespace as a hint that the braces introduce a code block.) The braces also construct nameless hash variables when used where an expression is expected. Bypassing the my syntax, { } also creates blocks of code. See Chapter 10 for information on this meaning.

Arrays Are Ordered, Hashes Aren't

Values in arrays exist in a certain order. Values in hashes don't. Iterating over the elements in an array will always start at the element in position 0 and go up to the last one. Iterating over the elements in a hash will go in no particular order at all. If you have keys for fred, alex, and mike, mike may go first, then alex, and then fred. My perl does something else. It's a common idiom to sort the hash keys when iterating on hash keys to give some kind of order to the output.

```
# Sort hash keys when iterating on them to provide a non-arbitrary ordering

# use Perl6::Variables; # uncomment for Perl 5

my %hash = ( alex => "march", mike => "april", fred => "september" );

for my $name (sort keys %hash) {
    print $name, ' ', %hash{$name}, "\n";
}
```

Because hashes have no natural ordering, it doesn't make sense to add values to the "beginning" or "end". There's no beginning or end. When a value is pushed onto the end of an array, a new index is allocated for it. For an array that has five elements, stored in positions 0 through 4, position number 5 would be allocated to store something pushed onto the end. When a value is unshifted onto an array, all the indices are renumbered to a value one more than their current number, freeing up the 0 index to store the new value. This is what happens conceptually. In actuality, the numbering is implicit and is inferred from the position.

Variable Name Sharing

You may think that Perl wouldn't let you give three different variables the same name. Well, it does let you. Each foo can be a completely separate foo. Data-processing idioms in Perl perform actions such as creating hash representations of arrays. When two variables have the same name, differing only in the sigil, convention dictates that they're different representations of the same data. For example, the following counts the number of occurrences of strings in an array using a hash:

```
# Perl 5 - representing the same data in an array and hash of the
# same base name

use Perl6::Variables;

my @people = qw<fred john mike paul mary mike alex bill dave john>;
my %people;
foreach my $person (@people) {
    %people{$person}++;
}
print qq{There are %people{'mike'} people named "Mike".\n};
```

To use the same base variable name for two different sets of data would be confusing and is best avoided. This use of a hash is called a *counting hash*.

Array and Hash Slices

Slices extract a chunk of a hash or array. More than one value is fetched at the same time.

```
# Array slices subscript multiple array indices at the same time

# use Perl6::Variables;  # uncomment for Perl 5

my @square_roots = map sqrt, 1 .. 100;

my @roots_one_through_six = @square_roots[1, 2, 3, 4, 5, 6];

print "$_\n" for @roots_one_through_six;
```

This outputs the following:

```
1.4142135623731
1.73205080756888
2
2.23606797749979
2.44948974278318
2.64575131106459
```

These may be slightly different thanks to variations in floating-point hardware and chip manufacturers' attempts to redefine the number system.

Compare @square_roots[1, 2, 3, 4, 5, 6] to a normal array subscript that looks like @square_roots[16]. It becomes a slice because I've fed it multiple subscripts to look up. The result of looking up each subscript is returned as a list of each value in the same order as the subscripts. It will always return one value for each subscript.

```
# Obtaining multiple elements from an array - these three are equivalent
 # use Perl6::Variables; # uncomment for Perl 5

@square_roots[1, 2, 3, 4, 5, 6];

 map { @square_roots[$_] } 1, 2, 3, 4, 5;

my @results;
 for(1, 2, 3, 4, 5) {
     push @results, @square_roots[$_];
 }
@results;
```

The hash slice syntax is similar.

```
# Slices fetch multiple hash elements from a hash

# use Perl6::Variables;  # uncomment for Perl 5

my %cubes = map { (sqrt $_, $_) } (1 .. 100);
# my %cubes = map { (sqrt $_, $_) }, (1 .. 100); # Perl 6 requires this comma

my @roots = %cubes{'2.64575131106459', '2.23606797749979', '1.4142135623731'};

print "$_\n" for @roots;
```

Hash subscripts in Perl 5 are strings. If you stringify the float and then attempt to use it as a number again, it may not translate to exactly the same floating number. This is because of the nature of translating between binary numbers (especially floating-point binary numbers) and decimal numbers. Your results may vary.

■**Slices may return** undef Any result value of a slice operation may be the special value undef. The defined built-in function detects the undef value. Getting undef as a value may indicate that the requested key doesn't exist, or the undef value may actually be associated with that key.

The result of slices may be assigned to the following:

```
# use Perl6::Variables;  # uncomment for Perl 5

%makes_maximum_use_of_24_hour_computer_lab{'john', 'scott'} = (1, 1);

print join ", ", keys %makes_maximum_use_of_24_hour_computer_lab; print "\n";
```

Expressions, such as array and hash slices, that can be assigned to are known as *lvalue* expressions. The *l* is for left, suggesting the expression is valid on the left-hand side of an assignment or similar operator.

Perl6::Variables is easily confused by slice syntax. For reliable results, use autoboxing and push, pop, and slice (documented in Chapter 14) when slicing with something other than a list of constant numbers.

In Chapter 11, I'll cover methods of manually processing the parameter list. This technique isn't in the subroutines chapter, Chapter 11, but some folks use slices this way to process parameters.

```
# Perl 5 - simulating named parameters using a hash slice

sub foo {
    my %args = @_;
    my($bar, $baz, $quux) = %args{qw(bar baz quux)};
    # do stuff with $bar, $baz, $quux here
}
```

This is used with a call something such as this:

```
foo(baz => 10, bar => 35, quux = 55);
```

my %args = @_ builds a hash from the parameter array. The my() expression creates a list of lexical variables that may be assigned to (the lexical variables are assigned to, not the list). %args is sliced for the names of the parameters desired. The same logic, written out without using a slice, is as follows:

```
# Using a slice from above example - Perl 5

my($bar, $baz, $quux) = %args{qw(bar baz quux)};

# Same thing without a slice - Perl 5:

use Perl6::Variables;
my $bar = %args{bar};
my $baz = %args{baz};
my $quux = %args{quux};
```

Every now and then, a slice will let you write a really concise expression that saves a bunch of repetitious code.

Values

Numbers and strings are simple values. Values may also be permutations of the idea of numbers and strings. Numeric values include not a number (NaN), infinity (Inf), positive and negative zero, and floating-point values. Bit fields may be implemented as integers or as strings. Reference types include objects, file handles, compiled regular expressions, and many other things. Perl 6 also features the special undef value, which is similar to null in other languages.

Values themselves are information rich, but what information is available depends on the container. An integer is composed of the whole number and the sign, and an unsigned integer is merely the whole number. A string contains length information, where the memory for the string was allocated, the length of the string, and other housekeeping information. Other datatypes have different details, but collectively these details make up the value.

Programmers often wish to convey more information than a simple string or integer holds. Attributes attach to values to provide more detail, and the rest of this section is about that. The original Perl 5 version of this idea revolves around a single scalar that behaves differently when used in different contexts. *Zero but true* scalars behave differently as numbers than as boolean values. *dualval* scalars behave differently as strings and as numbers. Perl 6 continues this tradition but in an open-ended, systematic way.

Perl 6 introduces a new concept to the language to extend the possibilities of the context system. Built-in functions and user-defined functions can return objects that encapsulate a collection of information. localtime(), when used in list context, returns the raw numbers representing the hour, minute, second, day, date, year, and so on. When used in scalar context, an object is produced and returned. This object may be queried for specific fields, such as with localtime.day, or the object may be used as a number, in which case it'd produce a number of seconds since an epoch, such as midnight, Dec. 31, 1970. (This moment in time is widely used as a reference when storing time as a number of seconds, though other epochs are used as well.) Or, the object may be used as a string, and the object would be asked to present itself as a string, such as with print localtime. The optimizer may optimize away the creation of an object and subsequent extraction of a single field or stringification of the object if the object is used only once.

Internal Number Representation

Numbers are stored in an internal format that's probably binary and depends on the hardware. When Perl parses numbers from program input or program source code, Perl converts the numbers to this internal representation. (The original data representing the number is lost unless you do some trickery with the overload module.) This internal representation may be a Perl integer, a Perl floating-point value, or something else, such as an arbitrarily large integer implemented by the Math::BigInt class.

When stored internally, numbers have no information stored about what number base you'd like them to be printed in, or even what base the number was in when it was parsed as a number. If you read in a string containing a decimal number, and that decimal number is converted to a Perl floating-point value, the fact that it was originally expressed as a decimal number is forgotten.

You can verify this with the excellent B::Deparse module that comes with Perl.

```
# Decompiling Perl source at the shell to see that 0x37 and 55 really
# are the same thing to perl - Perl 5

$ perl -MO=Deparse -e 'print 0x37, "\n";'
print 55, "\n";
-e syntax OK
```

B::Deparse takes compiled bytecode and turns it back into Perl source code. The result is usually slightly different from the original. This is useful for understanding what perl considers to be equivalent and what it considers to be different.

Perl 5 represents floating-point numbers and integers differently internally but promotes integers to floating-point numbers as needed.

```
# Automatic promotion to floating point from integer - Perl 5 or Perl 6

my $num = 5;
$num /= 2;
print $num, "\n";    # prints 2.5, not 2
```

A floating-point number can be converted back to an integer with the int built-in. This drops everything after the decimal point and may completely mangle large numbers in order to force them into the internal representation of an integer, which isn't equipped to hold very large numbers. Perl 5 also offers three packages for holding arbitrarily large numbers without loss of precision or limitations of the maximum or minimum values: Math::BigInt, Math::BigFloat, and Math::BigRat for very large integers, very large or very small floating numbers, and very large or very small rational numbers. Merely use the module at the top of your program.

How does one prevent Perl from mangling large numbers such as 82729437849278472? Use Math::BigInt, use Math::BigFloat, or quote it as a string if you only need to repeat it back in output and you're not ever going to use it as a number, such as in arithmetic statements or as an array subscript.

Truth

Perl 6 adds a boolean context, and function results and other values may present themselves as being either true or false when tested as boolean values. Perl6::Contexts attempts to simulate boolean context for Perl 5.

To inspect the truth of a value, boolean context is provided by the if() statement, the unless() statement, the and operator, the or operator, and several other operators, statements, and built-in functions.

undef is false, and so is 0, 1, 0.1, and -1. Any other nonzero number is true.

A string is true if it doesn't contain exactly '0' and isn't the null string, ''.

Strings may be parsed as numbers, such as with 0 + $str in Perl 5 or just + $str in Perl 6. In this case, signed values, floating-point values, and values in scientific notation are recognized. '9e5' means nine multiplied by ten taken to the fifth power. (Ten is always ten; this way, the e5 just means to move the decimal place over five places.)

Strings tested with numeric operators such as == are first parsed as numbers. The string '0e1' and strings like it parse as the number 0, as zero multiplied by ten to the first power is still zero, but this string doesn't meet the requirements for being a false string when not first parsed as a number. This inconsistency between how strings and numbers are tested for truth allows for the infamous Perl 5 *zero but true* hack.

```
# Infamous zero-but-true hack - Perl 5

my $a = "0e1";

print "true\n" if $a;
print "zero\n" if $a == 0;

# outputs:
# true
# zero
```

There's no single "zero but true" value. Any string other than the empty string and the string "0" will test true as a boolean. Scientific notation has a huge number of possible representations of zero other than the obvious "0". This example used zero with an exponent of one—a value that's still zero when parsed as a number but doesn't match the "0" stringwise.

Don't make a habit of comparing values to zero to test if they're true. To do so is to confuse numeric equality with boolean truth, and Perl has magic for handling booleans. "Zero but true" in Perl 5 is one case; while(readline $fh) is another. Code and datatypes are both aware of boolean context and act to support it. Using == 0 defeats this machinery.

```
# Booleans logic tests - Perl 5

if(keys %hash) {
}

if(! keys %hash) {
}

if(not keys %hash) {
}

unless(keys %hash) {
}

# Booleans - Perl 6

if %hash.keys {
}

unless %hash.keys {
}

if ! %hash.keys {
}
```

Later chapters in this book examine the various statements and operators providing boolean context.

Overloaded Variables (Perl 5)

Functions and methods need a clear way to signal failure, and Perl 5 features help with this. Detecting failure should be simple, requiring little code to implement, and shouldn't cause more breakage than it avoids.

Exceptions require programmers to write relatively large amounts of code to deal with failure, and even then they may consider them to cause more grief than they solve. Exceptions are available if you want them; see the discussion of Fatal.pm in Chapter 15.

Most commonly, Perl routines return undef in exceptional cases and set some prescribed variable to communicate the details of the error. The $! variable holds system error codes, and $@ holds user error messages unless some other special place is created for them, such as $DBI::errstr.

It isn't always possible to return undef to signal failure. system() returns 0 on success or an error code on failure to be compatible with the POSIX interface. Built-ins such as delete() return the value of the element they've deleted, which may already be undef.

Many built-ins and user-defined routines will return undef to signal failure. Detect this case with the err keyword.

```
read $fh, my $buffer, -s $fh err die $!;
```

Another Perl 5 trick involves storing data in both the numeric and string parts of a scalar and marking both of them valid to prevent perl from automatically converting one into the other. Scalar::Util exposes this functionality with its dualvar() function.

```
# dualvar - separate int and string values - Perl 5

use Scalar::Util 'dualvar';

my $foo = dualvar 15, "Hi boys and girls! ";
print $foo + 5, "\n";
print $foo . "Do you know what time it is? ", "\n";
```

This generates the following output:

```
20
Hi boys and girls! Do you know what time it is?
```

The existence of dualvar() is harder to justify than zero, but the concept of allowing variables to present themselves in different ways in different contexts is a useful one. By the way, you could also have achieved either of these with the overload module.

See Chapter 15 for more on signaling exceptional conditions with special return values.

Overloaded Variables Using Attributes (Perl 6)

Perl 6 uses the but keyword to introduce attributes.

Attributes are especially useful in solving the problem of how to return complex information that behaves differently in different contexts without resorting to overloading operators or throwing operators away entirely and returning objects full of methods. Values that behave in complex ways keep the language expressive, allowing programmers to write natural code that just does what you mean. It's the job of the programmer writing the subroutines that generate the values to decide how the value may be used and what the value should do when it's used that way.

Perl 6 introduces more contexts. Chapter 11 covers them in some depth, and so do Chapter 6 and Chapter 8. This chapter deals only with the boolean context, the numeric context, the object context, and the string context. The error value $!, set by built-ins that do input/output operations, behaves differently in each context. In boolean context, it returns true if there was an error (that hasn't been dealt with). In numeric context, it returns the system errno value for that error, should one exist. In string context, it returns a textual description of the error for human consumption. In object context, it provides an object-oriented interface for clearing the error, getting more details, comparing it to other error objects, and rethrowing the error. Whether an error is a subclass of another kind of error is a common test to perform when trapping errors. Chapter 10 and Chapter 15 cover this in depth.

Traits alter any value, not just strings.

```
# Zero but true - Perl 6

if 0 but true {
    print "This will always run\n";
}

# Zero but false - Perl 6

if 6 but false {
    print "This won't ever run\n";
}

if "Yes" but false {
    print "This won't run either\n";
}
```

Perl still automatically converts between internal types, but simple scalars can now store both integer and boolean information about themselves at the same time. This makes automatic conversion unnecessary and undesirable when the programmer has specified a boolean value. (User-defined types, or objects, are asked to convert themselves to the requested type; see Chapter 14 for more information.)

Attributes modify the value stored in the container. You can modify a value and reassign it into its container.

```
# Attach attributes to a value and copy it back to a container
# Perl 6

$foo = $foo but true;
$bar = $bar but false;
```

Built-in functions, operators, and keywords provide context in much the same way that values can be cast in other languages.

```
# provide context explicitly - Perl 6

if(bool $foo) { }   # boolean context
if(not $foo)  { }   # boolean context
if(num $foo)  { }   # numeric context
if(str $foo)  { }   # string context
```

Note that after these examples coerce $foo into one of the example contexts, the result is then coerced back into boolean context for if to operate on. This isn't a no-operation. Different results occur rather than testing the value directly. Each datatype has different rules for conversion to boolean truth, as discussed previously, so this if(str $foo) forces $foo to be tested for truth according to the rules for strings.

Chapter 4 gives the rules for converting to boolean for a truth test. You're working only with a small part of the picture until you've read Chapter 11. Operators either enforce or propagate context as well. For details on at least a few operators, see Chapter 6.

Undefined Value Warnings and Errors

Perl 5 throws you a Use of uninitialized value warning when you try to use a variable that contains undef, at least for most operations. use strict; use warnings; my $i; $i++; is acceptable; it was decided that trying to increment undef obviously means that undef should be interpreted as 0 and is common enough not to require explicitly declaring the variable. String operations, bitwise operations, and most math operations will throw this warning.

Can't call method "foo" on an undefined value is the result of use strict; use warnings; my $i; $i->foo();. Trying to call a method in something other than an object reference is a special case; perl couldn't fall back to some default behavior if it wanted to, short of silently doing nothing. With something other than an object or package name and with strict and warnings off, you'll get this other error message: Can't locate object method "foo" via package "string" (perhaps you forgot to load "string"?). Both of these are fatal but catchable.

Try to dereference a variable that contains undef, and Perl will chirp Can't use an undefined value as a symbol reference. They assume the scalar they're given is a reference to an I/O object. This too is fatal but catchable.

Use warnings to report on the accidental use of undef, and see Chapter 15 for how to trap these "reports."

Containers

A *container* encloses a value and is identified by a name or referred to by a reference. Containers fit between a name and a value. One container can be shared by several variables, and those variables can be a mix of hashes, arrays, and scalars. A scalar can store values in a container that's also part of an array or hash. Simply put, two variables may refer to the same data storage.

Perl attaches information to the container that the name represents. Each value held by a hash or array is held in a container of its own, even though the hash or array may have only one name. Anonymous variables, introduced in Chapter 8, are containers that don't have names at all—a reference to the nameless container is stored in a variable or is an intermediate value in an expression.

Containers Understand Their Contents

Containers know how to answer questions about the data they contain—is it true, in a boolean yes or no sense? Is it negative? What does it look like when represented as a string?

Perl 5 keeps this in a black box but isn't entirely inaccessible. The Devel::Peek module dumps internal information such as the number of references held to a variable (how many data structures reference this variable—variables can appear in more than one place when multiple references are in circulation), whether it's currently valid as a number, string, or both, whether it's floating point or integer if it's a number, whether it's blessed into a package, and other information.

```
# Peeking at containers and values - Perl 5

use Devel::Peek 'Dump';
use Scalar::Util 'dualvar';

my $foo = dualvar 15, "Hi boys and girls!";
print Dump $foo;
```

This generates output such as the following:

```
SV = PVNV(0x81e8350) at 0x814c218
  REFCNT = 1
  FLAGS = (PADMY,IOK,POK,pIOK,pPOK)
  IV = 15
  NV = 0
  PV = 0x814d368 "Hi boys and girls!"\0
  CUR = 19
  LEN = 20
```

15 and "Hi boys and girls!" are the values themselves, but a certain amount of metadata appears in the FLAGS, CUR, and LEN fields. This is part of the value, too. The container itself tracks how many data structures, aliases, and so on, can see the container. That's the REFCNT = 1. PVNV is the name of the container. A PVNV can hold both a numeric value and string value at the same time. This is used to cache numeric translations of strings and vice versa.

```
# Peeking at containers and values, take 2 - Perl 5

use Devel::Peek 'Dump';
use Math::BigFloat;

my $pi = Math::BigFloat->new(
    '3.14159265358979323846264338327950288419716939937510582097494944592'
);
print Dump $pi;
```

The output of it is too long to reproduce here, but understand that $pi is an object.

See Chapter 7 for an array storage implementation for Perl 5 that uses only one container to hold all the values in the array.

See Chapter 14 for information on objects, including objects that overload operators.

Assignment Copies Values

The assignment operator, =, copies a value from one container to another.

```
# Perl 5 or Perl 6 - the assignment operator, =, copies values from
# container to container
```

```
my $foo = 10;
my $bar = $foo;
$bar++;
print "foo: $foo bar: $bar\n";
```

This prints foo: 10 bar: 11.

Should the wrong kind of container be associated with a variable, it'll be thrown away and replaced, except in Perl 6 where the container type is specified, which looks like my Int $foo. This specifies that $foo's storage is implemented by the Int class, which just happens to be an object wrapper around integer numbers.

Binding Variables

Usually assignment does exactly what you want, but sometimes you want an alias, not a copy. Perl 6's new binding operator, :=, makes one variable temporarily synonymous with another.

```
# Perl 6 - binding one variable to another

my $foo = 10;
my $bar := $foo;
print "foo: $foo bar: $bar\n";
$bar++;
print "foo: $foo bar: $bar\n";
$foo++;
print "foo: $foo bar: $bar\n";
```

This generates the following output:

```
foo: 10 bar: 10
foo: 11 bar: 11
foo: 12 bar: 12
```

$foo got incremented at the same time that $bar did, because both variables are using the same data storage; that is, they share the same container. Assigning to $foo effectively modifies $bar for the same reason. $bar may later be aliased to another variable.

:== is another Perl 6 operator that aliases two variables together, but it's used at the time the aliased variable is declared and it's effect is permanent.

Data::Alias accomplishes the same thing, aliasing variables, in Perl 5. Operations in an alias block operate under altered semantics, where variables are aliased instead of copied wherever possible.

```
# Perl 5 - binding one variable to another

use Data::Alias;

my $foo = 10;
alias my $bar = $foo;
print "foo: $foo bar: $bar\n";
$bar++;
print "foo: $foo bar: $bar\n";
$foo++;
print "foo: $foo bar: $bar\n";
```

This generates the same output as the previous example. Contrast alias my $bar = $foo; with my $bar := $foo; from earlier in the chapter. alias may take an expression or a block. Here, I've intentionally not placed the expression in a block so that $bar will be declared in the present scope.

Binding into Data Structures

Arrays are often initialized using lists of scalar values, which are often other variables. This may not do what you want.

```
# Perl 5 - initializing an array using a list of scalar variables copies the
# values from the scalars into the array

use Perl6::Variables;

my $john = 5;
my $mike = 10;
my $fred = 15;
my @arr = ($john, $mike, $fred);
$john++;
print @arr[0], "\n";
```

This prints 5. Incrementing $john didn't change the corresponding value in the array. Perhaps there's a need to perform several operations on the same list of scalars. In Perl 6, := could have been used to alias @arr to a list of things. In Perl 5, you can create such an alias with Data::Alias.

```
# Perl 5 - initializing an array by aliasing to a list of scalar variables

use Data::Alias;
use Perl6::Variables;

my $john = 5;
my $mike = 10;
my $fred = 15;
alias my @arr = ($john, $mike, $fred);
$john++;
print @arr[0], "\n";
```

This prints 6. Incrementing $john changed the corresponding value in the array. Altering the array likewise affects the scalars. The array is just a view of the scalars composing it, or vice versa; the scalars are just a view of the array they compose.

Binding with Data::Alias aliases slices as well.

```
# Perl 5 - alias two scalars to a two array elements using the slice syntax

use Data::Alias;
use Perl6::Variables;

alias my ($foo, $bar) = @arr[0, 1];
```

```
# Perl 6 - alias two scalars to a two array elements using the slice syntax
```

```
my ($foo, $bar) := @arr[0, 1];
```

This makes it easy to create algorithms independent of the data structures on which they operate. Should the representation of data change, only the bindings need to change.

```
# Perl 5 - customer data is stored in alternating positions in one array
```

```
use Data::Alias;
use Perl6::Variables;

my @customers = (
    'Fred', '1234 Robin Lane', '515-4132',
    'Mike', '314 Pie Court', '515-7382',
);
while(my $i < @array) {
    alias my ($name, $address, $phone) = @customers[$i, $i + 1, $i + 2];
    # lots of logic here using $name, $address, and $phone
    $i += 3;
}
```

Should the data structures later change, only the binding and the loop need to change, not the logic that operates on the data.

```
# Perl 5 - customer data is stored spread across parallel arrays
```

```
use Data::Alias;
use Perl6::Variables;

my @customer_names = ('Fred', 'Mike');
my @customer_addresses = ('1234 Robin Lane', '314 Pie Court');
my @customer_phones = ('515-4132', '515-7382');
while(my $i < @customer_names) {
    alias my $name = @customer_names[$i];        # changed from above
    alias my $address = @customer_addresses[$i]; # changed from above
    alias my $phone = @customer_phones[$i];      # changed from above
    # lots of logic here using $name, $address, and $phone
    $i += 1;                                     # changed from above
}
```

Just as you can slice an array and bind to the slice, you can also bind to a hash slice.

```
# Perl 5 - initializing a list of scalars by aliasing to a hash slice
```

```
use Data::Alias;
use Perl6::Variables;

my %hash = ( foo => 10, bar => 20, baz => 25, quux => 35 );
alias my ($foo, $bar) = %hash{'foo', 'bar'};
```

Aliasing hash values works correctly.

Using the hash reference syntax introduced in Chapter 8, you could create the bindings from a data structure.

```
alias my ($name, $address, $phone) = @customers[$i]{'name', 'address', 'phone'};
```

You could later alter a program written with parallel arrays to use references, and bindings simplify that change.

Traits

Traits are introduced with the is keyword. Traits modify containers, the storage associated with a variable. Traits are compile-time operations. Everything about a container must be known when it's created. They're part of declarations and prototypes. They control the optional typing system, which is introduced in Chapter 16.

Having an effect only at the time the program is compiled, the compiler is able to use them as hints or mandates. As mandates, the compiler verifies they're always used consistently with their declaration. Chapter 11 mentions that parameters must be marked either is rw or is copy, or else the compiler will enforce that they be read and never written to. As hints, the compiler knows that it can take shortcuts that wouldn't otherwise be safe. If you try to cheat and use it against how it's declared, the compiler may complain, or you may just get incorrect results.

Remember that multiple variables and data structures can share a single container. You may think of a variable as synonymous with a container for now. You may be using a complex value but you're telling the compiler you're going to use it in only one simple way. Traits let you do that.

Traits (Perl 5)

Type information is a trait of the container.

```
# Attach optional type information to a container - Perl 5

my Int $age;
```

Int corresponds to the Int class, which is an object wrapper around integers. When Int is used this way, it describes the *kinds* of values that will be stored in the container.

No is keyword exists to modify the container.

The core Perl 5 language allows these type specifications, such as Int in my Int $age, but doesn't do anything with them. External modules can use this information, though. See Chapter 16 for details of using types with Perl 5.

This code sequence doesn't create an object; it merely communicates information about it. To actually create an instance of an object and store it in a variable, you'd write something such as this:

```
# Store an object in a typed container - Perl 5

use CGI;
my CGI $cgi = CGI->new();
```

See Chapter 14 and Chapter 16 for more information and examples.

Traits (Perl 6)

Perl 6 allows type information as in Perl 5 but goes on to define other built-in traits.

```
my $credit_card_number is private;
```

You can specify type information with attributes.

```
# type information can be specified with traits
# these two lines are equivalent - Perl 6

my Int $age;
my $age is Int;
```

Types on arrays describe their contents.

```
# type information can be specified with traits
# these two lines are different - Perl 6

my Int @ages;            # an array of things that are Ints
my @ages is Int;         # @ages itself is an Int - error
my @ages is Array of Int; # that's better - same as first
```

Specifying the type of an array itself lets you associate it with a package or add logic to it.

```
my Lockable @ages;     # an array of Lockable things
my @ages is Lockable; # @ages itself is Lockable
```

Usually you won't want to give an array a type, just its elements, but traits are useful for extending an array in order to add features that are useful for an array to have.

Traits are used for many things, so the discussion in this book is spread around by use. Chapter 7 uses them to declare rectangular arrays. Chapter 16 uses them to specify type information. Chapter 11 attaches them to subroutine parameters and to subroutines as well.

Symbol Tables

This section introduces basic and advanced symbol table wizardry. The key point is that objects are the way to get at logic in other packages, and exporting is the way to get at constant values and utility routines defined in another package. To this end, the section "Sharing Symbols Between Packages" is useful. The rest of this discussion is here for the sake of completeness. You'll want to know that your old tricks are still possible in Perl 6, and indeed they are, as are new tricks. The trickery is easier, too. Globs are dead, but the things people actually used them for are available in a convenient binding syntax by using the := operator. Exporting symbols to lexical contexts works in Perl 6, and it's easier to probe your caller and other contexts for the contents of their lexical variables.

Symbol tables are also known as *name tables* or *stash*es. Stashes are *symbol table hashes*. Symbol tables store names of variables and subroutines and associate those names with a reference to the variable or subroutine. Symbol tables are used at both run time and compile time to find the container associated with a name. Each place in your program that a name appears, perl does a lookup in the symbol table to find the container. Sometimes perl does this as it parses the program; other times it waits until that line of code actually runs to do the lookup.

Perl has always had a main symbol table, even before it was named `main::`. One symbol table is associated with each `package` statement in Perl 5 or `class` statement in Perl 6, plus a `main::` symbol table exists for code not explicitly placed into another class.

Perl 5 introduced symbol tables private to a block of code. These private symbol tables are called *pads*, or *scratch pads*. At any given time, there is one pad that's the current pad. These little symbol tables are separate from each other and separate from the main symbol table. They're a useful way to store intermediate values without making a mess.

Every symbol defined is defined into either the stash for the current class or into the pad for the current code block.

Perl 5's `local`, `our`, and `sub` (when `sub` is used with a name) keywords create entries in a symbol table for the current package. Perl 6's `temp`, `our`, and `sub` (when used with a name) keywords also create entries in the symbol table for the current package. Perl 5 and 6's `our` and `my` keywords create entries in the lexical scratch pad associated with the current block of code. Yes, `our` creates entries in both tables—the lexical pad and the symbol table for the current package.

Pads are a vast improvement over having just one huge classwide symbol table, but the big, old package-wide symbol tables are still in demand. Perl 6 adds features to pads to make them useful in cases where people were holding out.

Some features are exclusive to pads, and some are exclusive to stashes. Perl 6 unifies this and introduces lexically scoped subroutines, importing from pads, exporting to pads, looking up values at run time in the pad list, and the ability to pass references to the pad list. These are each formerly things that could be done only with the package-wide symbol table.

For more information on scratch pads, read `perldoc perlguts` and `perldoc perlhack`.

Sharing Symbols Between Packages

People frequently ask how to share symbols between two programs. You should either create an instance of the class or export symbols, depending on the application.

```perl
# Use simple objects to share value and code between two namespaces
# Perl 5

package Foo;

sub new {
    my $package = shift;
    my %data = @_;
    bless \%data, $package;
}

# Your code here:

sub something {
    my $self = shift;
    # use $self->{bar} and $self->{quux} - the values passed to new()
}
```

```perl
sub set_bar { my $self = shift; $self->{bar} = shift; }

package Bar;

use Foo; # if package Foo and its code is in another file, which it should be
my $foo1 = Foo->new( bar => 'baz',    quux => 1000 );
my $foo2 = Foo->new( bar => 'blurgh', quux => 300 );
```

Here's the same example, this time in Perl 6:

```perl
# Use simple objects to share value and code between two namespaces
# Perl 6

class Foo {
    has $.bar;
    has $.quux;
    method something {
        # your code here or in other methods
        # do something with $.bar and $.quux and any parameters the method takes
    }
    method set_bar ($bar) { $.bar = $bar }
}

class Bar {
    use Foo; # if package Foo and its code is in another file, which it should be
    my $foo1 = Foo->new( bar => 'baz',    quux => 1000 );
    my $foo2 = Foo->new( bar => 'blurgh', quux => 300 );
```

Code written this way makes $self->{bar} or $.bar available, indirectly, to other classes through the set_bar() methods. You should write this kind of glue to make code from one package or class available to scripts and other packages and classes.

Each object, $foo1 and $foo2, shares the same code but operates on different values. This allows the code to be reused. Code that can be "reused" only once can't be reused at all but merely used once as far as any single program is concerned. Note that $.bar is the instance variable, and $bar is the parameter in the Perl 6 example. When this example calls Foo->new(), it uses what looks like the Perl 5 list syntax but is actually the new Perl 6 named parameters syntax. See Chapters 8 and 14 for more on named parameters.

Exporting is another option. It's preferable when logic is being shared that doesn't have any persistent state. Utility routines that take all their information as arguments and use it to compute a value to return fit this description. Exporting logic simulates adding new built-in functions to the language.

```perl
# Exporting subroutine definitions to whomever uses us - Perl 5:

package My::List::Utils;

use Perl6::Export;
```

```
sub sum is export(:DEFAULT) {
    my $ret = 0;
    $ret += $_ foreach @_;
    return $ret;
}

sub zip(\@\@) is export {
    my $arr1 = shift;
    my $arr2 = shift;
    my @ret;
    while(@$arr1 or @$arr2) {
        push @ret, shift(@$arr1), shift(@$arr2);
    }
    return @ret;
}
```

Here's a program that uses this toy module:

```
package main;

use My::List::Utils ':ALL';

print sum 1, 5, 9;
print "\n";

my @one = ( 1 .. 10 );
my @two = ( 20 .. 30 );
print join ', ', zip @one, @two;
print "\n";
```

Modules using My::List::Utils will get a definition for the sum() function by default, but they must specify the :ALL tag or zip's name to get the definition for zip() as well. The documentation of Perl6::Export also mentions mandatory exports.

Because Perl6::Export is a source filter, you shouldn't use it for serious work. See the note in Chapter 4 for an explanation of source filters and their inherent problems. See the documentation on the standard, included Exporter module instead, which serves the same purpose using a different syntax.

Pads As Symbol Tables

It's possible to compute variable names and use the computed variable name to access a variable, but this is bad style and almost never necessary or desirable. Instead, use hash variables and turn the computed name into the hash key.

Computed variable names are interesting to module authors who write modules that extend and enhance Perl and to satisfy Perl 5 programmers that Perl 6 can do all the evil things that Perl 5 can, just more cleanly. Just as variables may be found by name in the package symbol table, variables may be found in the symbol table for the lexical block (or *pad*). See "Soft References Are Bad" in Chapter 3 for a specific example of the trouble that computed variable names cause.

The Exporter module's simple interface for one package to add features and keywords to another is the reason that the stash symbol table is still favored. Features supporting it, such as computing variable names, are now part of pads. That is, you can find pad entries by lookup at run time. Subroutines may be lexically scoped (entries in the pad), not just variables. See the section "Lexically Scoped Subroutines" in Chapter 11. The pseudo-class %MY works like other symbol tables in Perl 6, but it's an alias for the current pad.

```
# Perl 6
# the %MY package is an alias for the current pad
# Like Perl 5, symbol tables have :: on the end of their name as part of their
# name

my $my_scalar;

# these next two lines reference the same variable:

$my_scalar;
%MY::{'$my_scalar'};
```

This syntax is likely to change, but we've been promised that it will exist.

This example comes from Chapter 4:

```
# Perl 5 - this approximates scalar interpolation:

use PadWalker 'peek_my';

my $foo = localtime;
my $string = 'The time is $foo.';

# added these lines to make this example work:
my $pad = peek_my(0);
$string =~ s/(\$\w+)/${$pad->{$1}}/ge;

print $string, "\n";
```

Like the previous example, this looks up symbols in the current pad, where the names of the symbols aren't known until run time. $string could have been from user input, for example, but this would be horribly insecure. Chapter 8 has an example of substituting values into a string but from a hash rather than from the pad. Do that instead.

The Exporter module for Perl 5 takes advantage of these package-qualified names and the Perl 5 glob syntax to create additional references to subroutines and variables in other namespaces. By exporting, you're causing subroutines and variables to appear in two or more places. Each module that uses an exporting module gets its own reference to the variables and subroutines being exported. The Perl 6 exporter could be implemented in terms of the following logic:

```
# Addresses names in other packages - Perl 6:

%OtherPackage::{'$my_scalar'};
%OtherPackage::{'@my_array'};
%OtherPackage::{'%my_hash'};
```

Here, OtherPackage would be the name of a package created with the package statement.

Lexicals are still relatively inaccessible from the outside, unlike a package symbol table. To access the lexicals of a routine, they must call you. Your caller's %MY name table then becomes available as %CALLER.

```
# Perl 6 - %CALLER contains an alias for your caller's pad

sub foo {
  %CALLER.{MY}.{'$bar'};
}

my $bar;
foo();
```

Besides stuffing a symbol into, %CALLER is handy for debugging.

```
# Perl 6
# print out the value of all of the current variables of the routine that
# called us

sub dump_variables {
    foreach my $var_name (sort keys %CALLER.{MY}) {
        print $var_name, ' contains: ', %CALLER.{MY}.{$var_name}, "\n";
    }
}
```

Perl 5 can export only new symbols to stashes. Unlike pads, these are named. This means that entirely new variable and function names can't be exported to a lexical context, creating new my variables or my subs. Whether the symbol is passed into a routine that defines it in Perl 5, or PadWalker is used to discover the symbol without it having been passed to it, it still must have already been defined in that scope. Perl 6 aims to be able to export to lexical symbols that haven't been created. Something such as this may be valid.

```
# Perl 6 - hypothetical exporting of symbols

{
    use Some::Module;
    print $foo, "\n";      # Some::Module exports $foo
}
print $foo, "\n";          # error - $foo doesn't exist in this lexical scope
```

In a sense, use can do the work that my does, as could macro subroutines. This creates the possibility of user code creating new keywords that define things that are lexically scoped.

This example simulates exporting to pads by populating a symbol that's passed in. The previous Some::Module could be implemented in terms of the following, if a Perl 5 implementation were required:

```
# Passing in a reference to have it defined -
# example of the need for the ability to export
# Perl 5
```

```perl
package Some::Module;

sub import {
    $_[0] = sub {
        return $_[0] + $_[1];
    };
}

package main;

Some::Module::import(my $add_logic);
print $add_logic->(5, 6), "\n";
```

import() is normally called automatically when a use is performed, so the code in main would be written as use Some::Module my $add_logic in a more plausible example. This requests the importation of logic but first creates a lexical variable to contain the logic. use can't create the variable when a lexically scoped variable or subroutine is required (at least not without nasty source filter trickery). This has the problems of knowing in advance exactly what subroutines a module is going to export and explicitly asking for them. This mechanism breaks down when built-ins are redefined as wrappers for themselves or new functions are added that behave like keywords. It'd be silly to ask for a try() function from a module. It's thus desirable to have symbols defined without passing them in.

This is in contrast to the Exporter logic in Perl 5 that's able to create entirely new variables and subroutines—but only package-wide ones, not lexically scoped ones.

This example doesn't require the variable to actually be passed to be modified; it merely requires that it be already declared.

```perl
# Not passing in a reference to have it defined
# example of the need for the ability to export
# Perl 5

package Some::Module;

use PadWalker 'peek_my';

sub import {
    ${peek_my(1)->{'$add_logic'}} = sub {
        return $_[0] + $_[1];
    };
}

package main;

sub test {
    my $add_logic;
    Some::Module::import();  # no explicitly passed references
    print $add_logic->(5, 6), "\n";
}

test();
```

add_logic must be invoked as $add_logic->() rather than add_logic(), because Perl 5 doesn't natively offer lexically scoped subroutines, but see Sub::Lexical and the discussion of it in Chapter 11 for an implementation.

REFERENCES AND THANKS

The site at http://cog.cognitivity.com/perl6/val.html explains this complex topic clearly. It rocked my world. Apocalypse 2 and Exegesis 2 by Larry Wall and Damian Conway, respectively, first documented this and were referenced heavily as this book was written.

Various nice people wrote the various nice modules I've talked about in this chapter, and the credit is theirs that these tricks work. Robin Houston wrote PadWalker. Damian Conway wrote Perl6::Export and Perl6::Variables. Ilya Zakharevich wrote Devel::Peek. Mark Biggar, Ilya Zakharevich, and Tels wrote Math::BigInt and Math::BigFloat, with patches from others. Matthijs van Duin wrote Data::NoCopy. Each of these modules can do far more than I've demonstrated, except Perl6::Variables, which I've pretty much pushed to its limit. Please consult their respective documentation for details.

Summary

Variables are composed of data storage and names where the name is valid in a certain scope. my creates names that are valid within a lexical scope—that is, from where they're declared to until the enclosing brace or to the end of the file, whichever comes first. Multiple names may be associated with a single container.

Know the scope of variables you declare. Use strict and warnings to double-check your work. Keep the scope of a variable as small as possible. Rather than making everything global, pass arguments between functions. See Chapter 19 for ways of making this less tedious in extreme cases.

The arrangement of data structures is sure to change in a program as the requirements change. Bindings free programmers to make these changes with a minimum of work.

The special namespace %MY in Perl 6 lets you export names into other lexical scopes that represent blocks outside the current block. It also lets you inspect data that's visible lexically only in other scopes. This power lets you get around needing to use global data.

Use Perl 6 traits to customize or specialize how data storage is implemented for a variable. This includes defaults and even extending objects. This restricts what kind of container will be used to hold a value. That is, it restricts the type of data it holds. It also extends the specification of what's held in the case of user-defined objects. You do this in Perl 6 with the is keyword. Chapter 14 has some examples of using operating overloading to allow containers to control the presentation of data they contain, performing such tasks as responding to context.

Use Perl 6 attributes to customize values. Values travel from container to container and take properties with them. This kind of traveling includes being returned from functions, being stored in arrays, being passed to functions, and so on. Properties can tell a container more about how to interpret a value for certain fixed criteria. That is, values are rich and complex, and all the complexity is under user control using the but keyword. Taintedness is an attribute conceptually in Perl 5 but in Perl 6 is a proper attribute.

CHAPTER 6

■■■

Operators

A language that doesn't have everything is actually easier to program in than some that do.

—Dennis Ritchie

Perl is expressive: a little code gets a lot done. Any expressive language has a syntax more complicated than just being able to call methods and assign the results. It makes the language look messy at times, but many prefer to look at a screen full of operators than ten screens full of method calls and temporary variables.

The first section in this chapter, "New for Perl 6", covers the features new for Perl 6, which are primarily operator-related features rather than actual new operators in Perl 6. Some of these features create new classes of operators as versions of existing operators. This is a check-list of features without Perl 5 counterparts that consequently don't belong in the main text. For this I'll assume a working knowledge of Perl 5. I placed this information at the beginning of the chapter to satisfy the curiosity of Perl 5 programmers who are interested to know what Perl 6 adds to the language.

Next, the section "Changes from Perl 5 to Perl 6" concisely lists changes between Perl 5 and Perl 6. This is for Perl 5 programmers curious about the habits they'll have to break. Between Perl 5 and Perl 6, several operators have been renamed. This is usually the first change Perl 5 programmers notice about Perl 6, so I'll cover changes to operator names and behaviors. Perl 6 introduces several other new features related to operators that aren't available in Perl 5, and I'll summarize those features.

Operators covered in this chapter perform the following kinds of operations:

- Truth tests

- String operations

- Arithmetic

- Bitwise operations

These aren't hard-and-fast distinctions, though. Several operators straddle categories.

The truth-test operators perform logical tests on two or three expressions. These get special attention in this chapter because Perl has a large assortment of them and because they have many useful properties. The perldoc perlop documentation—specifically the sections "Relational Operators", "Equality Operators", and "Conditional Operator"—contains lots of details.

Numeric operators such as + and < automatically convert into numbers the results of the expressions they're fed. Perl has the standard suite of arithmetic operators plus a few handy extras. The standard module Math::Trig defines additional functions for working with numbers.

Operators with names made out of letters are still operators. For example, ne, gt, and . operate on strings. They take expressions on their left and right just like normal operators. String operators coerce their string arguments into being strings, if they aren't already. Perl isn't like some languages where + concatenates strings and also adds numbers. The . operator in Perl 5 and the ~ operator in Perl 6 join strings, freeing + to always make numeric addition work. Perl operators are (almost) always explicit, even though this results in more operators. This allows Perl to know when it must convert between numbers and strings. Adding values automatically parses strings as decimal numbers, but concatenation will happily join two numbers. Some buggy programs would append a two-digit number to 19 and print the result as a date, for instance. Of course, plenty of legitimate reasons exist to concatenate numbers to strings and to each other.

Most string operations are built-in functions (and of course CPAN modules), not operators. String operations performed by operators include stringwise comparison, concatenation, repetition, bitwise operations, and regular expression binding. The Perl 6 designers haven't said much about which built-in functions Perl 6 will have, but I have reason to believe this won't change much from Perl 5.

Bitwise operations shift values, test individual bits, and perform logic operations between sets of bits.

Many things you may expect to be functions are actually operators. Novices are well advised to skim through perldoc perlop and perldoc perlfunc. This will give you a feel for what functionality operators provide and what functionality built-in functions provide.

The following operators are interesting enough to have their own chapters:

- Reference operators (Chapter 8)

- Quote-like operators (Chapter 4)

- Set operators (Chapter 18)

- Binding operators (Chapter 9) and assignment operators (Chapter 5)

Other operators read lines from files, force contexts, bind regular expressions to strings, and perform other tasks. The "Neglected in this Chapter" section tries to round this chapter out by listing operators documented elsewhere in this book. Examples in previous chapters have already used at least two operators unique to Perl: the range operator, .., to create lists of numbers and the <$filehandle> syntax to read lines from file handles.

Finally, this chapter shows the idiomatic usage of various operators, compares string and numeric operators, and gives the rules for context as they apply to operators (or as operators apply context).

New for Perl 6

Perl 5 introduced the ability to overload operators. Perl 6 introduces the ability to create entirely new operators in much the same way that you can define functions. Operators require additional meta-information, such as relative precedence compared to other operators. Chapter 11 has a brief example of the Perl 6 syntax used to define operators. At this time, you can't define operators in Perl 5.

Lists (aggregates of values) now get the same preferential treatment that scalars do, thanks to *hyper operators* that work on one or two entire lists at once. undef too is more widely recognized in the Perl core, as new versions of existing operators assign back to the expression on their left, saving redundant mentions of variable names.

Perl 5 versions of the new Perl 6 operators are in short supply. Only err, //, and perhaps stacked file tests made it back (plus the dot operator, implemented by the Acme::Dot module). No Perl 5 equivalents exist for most of these operators.

Hyper Operators

Hyper operators work on lists of values. An operator may be made hyper toward the expression on its left, the expression on its right, or both. As is usual in Perl 6, references are automatically dereferenced.

```
# Spreadsheet-like operators in Perl 6 using hyper operators

@income_and_expenditures = @credits >>-<< @debits;
$balance = $balance +<< @adjustments;
```

The >> and << operators—when used to mean "greater than" or "less than"—require spaces between them and other operators.

Hyper operators save you from having to write for loops.

```
# Evolution of iterator variables in Perl, Perl 5, assuming Perl6::Variables:

for(my $i; $i < @things; $i++) { $count += @things[$i] } # uninspired
for my $thing (@things) { $count += $thing }             # better
for (@things) { $count += $_ }                           # better yet
$count =+<< @things;                                     # amazing
```

The for loops require an iterator variable. This example used $i, $things, and $_.

Something hyper on both sides looks like this:

```
# Hyper on both sides - Perl 6

@income_and_expenditures = @credits >>-<< @debits;
```

Hyper operators allow the computed result to be immediately used rather than merely stored in an array.

```
# Using hyper operators in larger expressions - Perl 6

for my $running_balance (@credits >>-<< @debits) {
    # ...
}
```

You can't use for loops in the middle of a larger expression. If the intent of the for loop is to build a list of values, then that list must be stored in an array.

```
# Same as previous but without hyper operators -  Perl 5

use Perl6::Variables;

my @running_total;
for my $i (0 .. @credits) {
    push @running_total, @credits[$i] - @debits[$i];
}
foreach my $balance (@running_total) {
    # ...
}
```

See the discussion of Perl6::Gather in Chapter 10 for an alternative to for that you can use in a larger expression.

Mutating Operators

Mutating operators change a variable (or any other lvalue) rather than merely compute a new value.

```
# Mutating operators - Perl 5

$i += 5;
$output .= "\n" . "-" x 79 . "\n";
```

Mutating operators aren't new in Perl 6, but they're ubiquitous in Perl 5. The /=, *=, -=, %=, and other mathematical operators mutate the variable to which they're applied. This is the same in Perl 6, but many new ones have been added.

```
# Mutating operators as in previous example - Perl 6

$i += 5;
$output ~= "\n" ~ "-" ~ xx 79 ~ "\n";

# A few of the new Perl 6 mutating operators

$obj.=bar();  # call a method in $obj and assign the result back into $obj
$foo \=;      # take a reference to ourself (proposed syntax)
```

$obj.=bar() could also be written as $obj = $obj.bar().

perldoc perlop's "Assignment Operators" section includes a chart of all these operators. These operators are available in Perl 6, but you should assume that a mutating version of an operator is available in Perl 6 until you discover otherwise.

Hyper Mutating Operators

Mutating operators may be hyper. Or hyper operators may mutate—depending on how you want to look at it. Hyper mutating operators operate on each element of a list (which may be on one side or on both sides), and they change each element of the array, scalar, or lvalue expression on the left of the operator.

```
# Hyper mutating operators - Perl 6

$population++;
@population_intelligence >>-= (1 / @population_intelligence);

my @temperature_deltas = map { rand 30 }, 1 .. @level_temperature;
@level_temperature >>-=<< @temperature_deltas;
print "Frozen over\n" if grep { $_ < 32 }, @level_temperature;

@current_nodes >>.=<< next_node();
```

In Chapter 8, I talk about how Perl deals as comfortably with multiple values as it does single values. Hyper mutating operators further level the playing field between single and multiple values.

Any and All

The & and | operators create sets composed of strings, numbers, objects, references, and other sets.

These operators are synonyms for any() and all().

```
# Perl 6 and Perl 5 Quantum::Superpositions superposition operators

all(1, 2, 3) # same as 1 & 2 & 3
any(1, 2, 3) # same as 1 | 2 | 3
```

Sets are useful for comparisons. Comparisons done on a set take place on each element of the set (or on as many elements as needed). The two kinds of sets have different requirements. The comparison must be true for each element of the set if the set is of the all variety. The comparison must be true for one element of the set if the set is of the any variety. Use hyper operators for performing operations on several values in parallel. See Chapter 18.

References to Operators

Perl will take references to user-defined routines.

```
my $subref = \&a_routine_that_does_something; # Perl 5
```

```
my $subref = &a_routine_that_does_something;  # Perl 6
```

Perl 6 also lets you refer to built-in functions—but wait, there's more. You can take references to operators, too. References taken to operators are code references. This is useful when writing routines that take part of their logic as an argument and when using such routines.

```
my @sorted_stuff = sort &infix:<=>, @unsorted_stuff;    # Perl 6
my @sorted_stuff = sort { $a <=> $b }, @unsorted_stuff; # Perl 5
```

The &infix:<=> expression applies the Perl 6 code reference sigil and syntax, &functionname, to an operator (in this case <=>). <=> does a three-way comparison between two numbers, indicating whether the number on the left is less than, equal to, or greater than the number on the right. infix, prefix, and postfix prefix the operators, differentiating various kinds of operators that otherwise look the same. A single operator may exist with different prefixes. For example, + may be an infix operator when it comes between two expressions, or it may be a prefix operator when it comes before an expression.

```
$3 + $7;    # infix +
+5;         # prefix +
$num++;     # postfix ++
```

Apocalypse 12, published at http://dev.perl.org, mentions prefix, infix, postfix, circumfix, and term as possible operator types.

<=> is prototyped to take two arguments, as are all binary operators, or *binops*, which are usually infix. Perl 6's built-in sort is smart enough to pass in each set of values being compared as arguments in this case where it's given a code reference prototyped to take two arguments. It's also smart enough to take one value as an argument, as you'll see in Chapter 8.

Semicolon As a Fat Comma

You may or may not be able to use ; to build lists of lists when used in list- and array-building constructs.

```
# These two may or may not be equivalent in Perl 6

[1, 2, 3; 4, 5, 6];
[ [1, 2, 3], [4, 5, 6] ];
```

The jury is still out on this possible meaning of the semicolon. This uses the [ ] anonymous array constructor introduced in Chapter 8.

Pipeline Operators

The <== and ==> operators collect lists and provide those lists as arguments to expressions. They can be chained one after another. This gets rid of parentheses in common usages of maps, greps, and sorts, where the output of one is used as input to the next. User-defined routines are likely to expect a few fixed arguments, and the data to be operated on is provided in a big, old list.

```
%hash.keys ==> sort ==> reverse ==> print;  # Perl 6 - pipeline operator
```

This changes the direction of data flow from the normal right to left to an exquisite left to right. It's more useful when some arguments are supplied and some are taken from the pipeline. This is the case where parentheses are averted.

```
# Autonumber rows of data, output HTML
# Perl 6

print '<tr>';
print join '</tr><tr>'  <==
    map "<tr>$_</td>"  <==
    zip 1 .. + @data, @data;
print '</tr>';
```

Think of <== as a superfat comma. No Perl 5 implementation is currently available.

Chained Comparisons

To test if one number is less than another, you'd write something like the following:

```
# Simple use of a numeric comparison operator, Perl 5 or Perl 6

if($number < 10) {
    # $number is less than 10
}
```

The result of < and > is a boolean value in Perl 5 and almost any other language. This prevents code such as the following from working:

```
# Comparison operators cannot be "stacked" in Perl 5

if(5 < $number < 10) { ... }     # between 5 and 10 - syntax error
if((5 < $number) < 10) { ... }   # between 5 and 10 - logic error
```

The first of these two doesn't compile at all—perl knows better. The second tests that 10 is less than the result of 5 < $number. As 5 < $number is numerically 0 or 1, depending, this will *always* be less than 10, and the body of the if() statement will always run. To do this in Perl 5, you'd need to write the following:

```
# Multiple comparison operations to check ranges in Perl 5

if(5 < $number && $number < 10) { ... }
```

Perl 6 uses the rules introduced in the "Values" section of Chapter 5. Rather than <, >, gt, and lt always evaluating to a boolean value, they evaluate to an object that encapsulates both the boolean truth of the comparison and the numbers involved in the test. Writing 5 < $number < 10 does the right thing in Perl 6.

Changes from Perl 5 to Perl 6

Operators were moved around in the design of Perl 6. These changes are sure to be a stumbling block for Perl 5 programmers. The following sections summarize the changes from Perl 5 to Perl 6 and assume knowledge of Perl 5's operators. I'll explain the purpose and use of each operator in detail in the "Context" section.

String Concatenation

The ~ operator replaces the . operator as the string-joining operator. The ~ operator means "stringwise" in general. Many Perl programmers prefer to write join '', "foo", bar(), $baz.

Dereferencing and Pointy Subroutines

The . operator replaces the -> operator as the method call and dereference operator. Perl 6 dereferences references automatically, so the . operator is required only for method calls. The -> operator is now one syntax for declaring argument lists to subroutines. Chapter 11's "Pointy Subroutines" section documents this use, which looks something like the following:

```
# -> $day, $sunshine { ... } is the same thing as
# sub ($day, $sunshine) { ... }
# Perl 6

for zip @day, @sunshine -> $day, $sunshine {
    die "day without sunshine" unless $sunshine;
    print $day, " is a nice day.\n";
}
```

If this is confusing, imagine parentheses around zip's two arguments, @day and @sunshine, and remember that -> is just one way of creating a block. for wants a list and a block, and that's exactly what it gets here.

Dot Operator

The dot operator, ., dereferences references. Perl 5 uses -> for the same purposes. Perl has many references, but . is immediately useful with code references, object references, hash references, and array references. When given an array or hash reference, the dot operator subscripts (or *slices*) the data structure. This looks like $foo.{bar} or $foo.[10], though the dot may be implied. (That is, if you don't type it, perl can usually figure it out and logically put it there.) Perl 5 won't imply the -> operator when subscripting arrays and hashes. Chapter 8 explains how references are used.

The dot is required when calling methods in objects, which looks like $obj.method, $obj.method $arg1, $arg2, or even $obj.method($arg1, $arg2). Perl 5 requires parentheses around the method arguments. See Chapter 14 for more on this.

You can also use . to invoke code references, which might look like $foo.(), $foo(), &foo.(), or $foo.($arg1, $arg2). The dot is implied in $foo(). Here, $foo holds a reference to the code to be executed. Contrast this with foo(). Perl 5 can't imply the -> in $foo->(). Chapter 14 explains this usage.

Bitwise Operators

Perl 5's & and | operators perform bitwise and and or operations in Perl 5. They work on either two strings or two integers. Perl 6 replaces them with the following four operators—two versions of the bitwise and operator and two versions of the bitwise or operator:

- +& is the bitwise *and* operator that operates on two integers.

- ~& is the bitwise *and* operator that operates on two strings.

- +| is the bitwise *or* operator that operates on two integers.

- ~| is the bitwise *or* operator that operates on two strings.

Stringification and numification are now explicit. This avoids problems where numbers and strings are used together with unexpected results when the string numifies or the number stringifies.

& and | have a new purpose in Perl 6: disjunction. Disjunction was selected by a panel of chimpanzees and lotto judges, against all odds, to be the next section.

Disjunction

& now means all(), and | now means any(). any() and all() work on numerous values at once to perform set operations between values. See Chapter 18 for more on these.

Ternary

?? :: is the Perl 6 equivalent of ?: in Perl 5.

```
push @numbers, $ready_for_an_odd_number    ??
               $number +|    0x01           ::
               $number +& +~ 0xfffffffe;
```

This is more consistent with the use of &&, ||, and // for flow control operators, and it frees : up to be used for referring to operators and other purposes.

Obsessive indenting By the way, I expect psychologists to name a new neurosis, *disjunctcolumnphobia*, where programmers obsessively reformat code into neat columns of operators, literals, and variables. This is also known as being *anal indentive*. Perl programmers are perhaps more productive only because they tend not to do this. Although I've obsessively indented in this text, don't feel you need to do so in your own programs. Correct indenting is another matter; it's essential to spotting logic errors in flow control constructs. Neatly formatting initialization data for hashes and arrays is also recommended practice.

---

x, the Repeat Operator

x in Perl 5 builds both strings and arrays. To build either, it gets its context from its left value; if it's an array or list, the output is a list, and the output is a string otherwise. In Perl 6, x enforces string context on its left side and numeric context on its right. This lets value stringify on command, and it's part of Perl 6's move toward operators dictating context and having separate stringwise and numeric operators. In the case of x, there needs to be a separate listwise version, and that's exactly what xx is.

```
'-' x 80;   # built a string of dashes, Perl 5 and Perl 6
(0) x 80;   # built a list of 0's, Perl 5
(0) xx 80;  # built a list of 0's, Perl 6
```

Because x and xx provide context in Perl 6, arrays may be repeated.

```
"@arr" x 80; # stringify an array and repeat, Perl 5
@arr x 80;   # stringify an array and repeat, Perl 6
```

In most cases, though, x will be used on something that's already a string.

Stacked File Tests

File test operators, such as -w (is this file writable by this user?) and -s (how large is this file in bytes?) can now take each other as arguments. The result of the chain is a boolean value indicating whether *all* the tests were successful. This replaces the use of *_ in Perl 5; see perldoc -f -X if you're curious.

Context

Something treated as a number is a number. Something treated as a string is a string. Perl doesn't take hints of the data type from the data itself. That would make automatic conversion between strings and numbers impossible. Instead, the clue comes from the operator used.

```
# Scalars are used as strings or numbers depending on the operator used.
# Any value in the variable is automatically converted (or at least an attempt
# is made).
# Perl 5 or Perl 6

my $string = '4-x';
if($string != 0) {
    print "Perl is weird.\n";
}
```

Confusing == and eq is one of the most common mistakes new Perl programmers make. Use ==, !=, <=, and >= when doing a numeric comparison. Use eq, ne, gt, and lt when doing a stringwise (sorting order) comparison.

■String vs. numeric operator rule of thumb String operators are themselves composed of lower-case letters. eq operates on strings. Numeric operators are composed of symbols. == operates on numbers.

Not all operators impose a predefined context on their arguments. Some impose the same context on their arguments that are imposed on them. That is, they propagate their context, just as a function evaluates in the same context in which the function was called. The ? : operator in Perl 5 and the ?? :: operator in Perl 6, for example, provide the same context to their two possible result values as was provided to the operator.

You can use context to decide whether subroutines should perform expensive computations. Scalar context wants one value—why compute more? Void context wants none—why compute any?

Operators that start with + apply numeric context to all the values (usually two) on which they work. ==, <=, >=, and != apply numeric context to both sides. Operators that start with ~ apply string context. You can place ~ in front of an expression to force string context on that expression. Note that bitwise operators can apply either numeric or string context depending on whether you're using strings or integers to store the bits. Placing ? before an expression requests boolean context. As Chapter 11 and Chapter 5 show, this can completely alter how truth is determined or interpreted.

Precedence

perldoc perlop contains the operator precedence chart for Perl 5. This tells which operators group more tightly than others. (The tightest are on the bottom, and the weakest are on the top.) Conceptually, the weakest binding operators (low precedence) run last in a statement, running only after all other operators have executed, but that's conceptually. The obvious corollary is that if you get it wrong, the code won't work as intended. Use Deparse to decompile Perl 5 source code back at you.

```
perl -MO=Deparse,-p -e 'open my $f, "<", "tmp.txt" || die $!;'

# outputs: open(my $f, '<', 'tmp.txt');
```

In this example, the || die $! got optimized away. The || attached to "tmp.txt", not the whole open ... expression; further, since tmp.txt is always a true value, the die would never run, so perl optimized it away. The || operator has much higher precedence than or. It will run early in the program. or and and were created as an alternative to parentheses for just this kind of thing.

Flow Control Operators

Besides if, unless, while, for, and so on, Perl uses operators to control flow. Table 6-1 lists Perl's conditional operators.

Table 6-1. *Conditional Operators*

High Precedence	Low Precedence	Description
&&	and	If left is true, run right.
||	or	If left isn't true, run right.
//	err	If left is undefined, run right.
!!	xor	Run both and return true if only one is true.

&&, ||, // and !!, the high-precedence logic operators, are for use in the middle of expressions. The low-precedence logic operators (and, or, err, and xor) join expressions.

or, and, err, &&, ||, and // *short circuit*. Based on the truth value of the expression on their left, they decide if the expression on the right should even be run. This is useful for *not* running code *unless* a condition is met, which is useful for code that has side effects, such as terminating the running program.

```
# when the left value meets expectations the right value isn't
# even considered, Perl 5 and Perl 6

0 and die;    # never dies
1 or die;     # never dies
0 err die;    # never dies
```

Use these in place of if where they make the statement more readable.

Low-Precedence Logic Operators

and, or, err, and xor join expressions. Being low precedence, they run as late in evaluation as permitted. The truth value of the expressions joined by and, or, err, and xor depends on both sides.

```
# When the left value doesn't meet expectations, the right value
# is evaluated, Perl 5 and Perl 6:

0 and 0;        # false
0 and 1;        # false
1 and 0;        # false
1 and 1;        # true

0 or 0;         # false
0 or 1;         # true
1 or 0;         # true
1 or 1;         # true
```

and and or are self-explanatory. err checks that the left side is undefined and, if so, executes the right side.

```
0 err 1;        # false
undef err 0;    # false
undef err 1;    # true
1 and die;      # always dies
0 or die;       # always dies
undef err die;  # always dies
```

I/O operations often return 0 as a nonerror value. Reading a nonblocking socket may come back with zero bytes read, but that doesn't mean anything other than no data happens to be available at the moment. Perl distinguishes this case from error cases, such as a closed connection, by returning undef instead of any numeric value. err checks for this error value.

```
# err checks for undef

undef err die;                          # always dies, Perl 5 or Perl 6

open my $fh, '<', 'file.txt' err die $!; # dies conditionally, Perl 5

my $value = <STDIN> err                 # dies conditionally, Perl 5
    die "Controlling terminal went for a hike! $!";
```

err is interesting because 0 is considered defined. <STDIN> could bring back a 0, and the last example wouldn't die. In fact, it's impossible to input an undef any other way than by an exceptional condition on the file handle.

See Chapter 15 and Chapter 5 for more information on signaling and handling error conditions.

xor asserts that exactly one of its arguments is true. The x stands for "exclusive," so xor is an or operation that asserts that any true value can be the exclusive (only) true value.

```
($cake xor $eat_it) or die "You can't have your cake and eat it too";
```

Here, they may be trying to have both $cake and $eat_it, or they can have neither. Both cases trigger the die. The only acceptable situation is that you have either $cake or $eat_it!

and, or, err, and xor are most often used to conditionally execute code for its side effects, but they're also useful for computing boolean values when used inside the parentheses. As with ||, &&, //, and !!, the side of the expression that satisfied the condition is the actual value that drops through, but this feature is most often used with ||, &&, and company.

High-Precedence Logic Operators

||, &&, !!, and // provide the actual value that satisfied the condition.

```
10 || 0;      # evaluates to 10
5 && 15;      # evaluates to 15
undef // 20;  # evaluates to 20
10 !! 0;      # evaluates to 10
```

The value may come from either the left side or the right side, depending on the operation and the values. If the condition isn't satisfied, 0 results. && is the high-precedence version of and. It returns its second argument if both are true, and it returns 0 or false otherwise.

|| is the high-precedence version of or. It returns the first of its two arguments (on the left and right) that's true.

//, pronounced "defined or" and also known as the *defaulting operator*, is the high-precedence version of err. It returns its first argument unless it evaluates to undef, in which case it evaluates its second argument. // is useful for providing defaults in cases where 0 is a valid value.

```
# Default argument with manual argument processing, Perl 5 or Perl 6,
# Perl 5 style

sub draw_cards_from_deck {
    my $cards_to_draw = shift() // 3; # draw 3 unless specified otherwise
    my @result;
    while($cards_to_draw--) {
        push @result, shift @top_of_deck;
    }
    return @result;
}
```

// can be chained to pick out the first defined value.

```
# Pick out the first defined value - these two examples are equivalent:

$one // $two // $three // $four;           # Perl 5 or Perl 6

use Scalar::Util;
first { defined } $one, $two, $three, $four; # Perl 5
```

|| can be chained, too, and it picks out the first true value.

Use !! or xor to check that only one of the arguments is true. !! returns the solitary true value or else 0 or returns logical false if both or neither is true. Use it to pick which of two exclusive options have been set.

err, //, and xor were specified for Perl 6 and then later added to Perl 5. !!, the high-precedence version of xor, is unavailable in Perl 5.

Comparison Operators

Perl has the standard complement of numeric comparison operators but has corresponding stringwise operators that compare lexigraphically as well. Table 6-2 summarizes these operators.

Table 6-2. *Numeric and Lexical Comparison Operators*

Less Than	Greater Than	Less Than or Equal To	Greater Than or Equal To	Equal To	Not Equal To
<	>	<=	>=	==	!=
lt	gt	le	ge	eq	ne

Perl defines two operators designed to work with sort. They return -1, 0, or 1 to indicate that the left value comes before, is identical to, or comes after the value on the right.

```
<=>   # 3 way numeric compare
cmp   # 3 way lexigraphical compare
```

You can use these as such:

```
@values = sort { $a cmp $b } @values;    # Perl 5 - sort lexigraphically
@values = sort { $^a cmp $^b }, @values; # Perl 6 - sort lexigraphically
```

See Chapter 8 for a whole lot more on sorting.

Boolean Context Operators

not is the low-precedence version of !. Both are pronounced "not", and both negate logical boolean values. Use not to avoid parentheses in the standard cases, such as in the conditional of an if statement where the value of the entire expression rather than merely the first term should be negated. ? is like ! in that it forces a boolean context, potentially alternating what information variables and routines provide, but it doesn't negate its argument. You'll seldom have to force boolean context; if() and such statements impose boolean context on the conditional already.

The Ternary Operator

and, or, xor and err affect the flow of execution. So does ?? ::, the ternary operator. The name *ternary* means "having three parts". It's the only operator that works on three values rather than one or two. ?? ::, and ? : in Perl 5 are inline versions of the if statement. If the first part is true, the operator evaluates to the value of the second part. If the first part is false, the operator evaluates to the value of the third part.

```
($acute_angle ? $right_fielder : $left_fielder)->dive();   # Perl 5
($acute_angle ?? $right_fielder :: $left_fielder).dive();  # Perl 6
```

?? :: and ? : expressions are valid on the left side of an assignment or other mutating operation. In other words, ?? :: and ? : are valid as lvalues.

```
# Conditionally modifying a variable

($acute_angle ? $right_fielder : $left_fielder) += $ball;    # Perl 5
($acute_angle ?? $right_fielder :: $left_fielder) += $ball;  # Perl 6
```

Depending on the truth of $acute_angle, either $right_fielder or $left_fielder will get $ball added to it. Perl 6's ?? :: works correctly with arrays because context is correctly propagated, avoiding premature array flattening.

```
# Perl 6 - pushing onto one of two arrays

push $acute_angle ?? @right_field :: @leftfield, $ball;
```

push wants an array, and it gets an array rather than a list of its contents. This isn't easily done in Perl 5; it involves taking references to the arrays, then dereferencing them after the ? : operation, and finally doing the push.

```
# Perl 5 - pushing onto one of two arrays

push @{ $acute_angle ? \@right_field : \@leftfield }, $ball;
```

You can alternate between (and use as a condition) expressions more complicated than variable names and references.

Bitwise Operators

The | and & operators in Perl 5 and +|, ~|, +&, and ~& in Perl 6 shouldn't be used in most conditional expressions. && and || are bad enough, binding too tightly, but these operators work bitwise. Among other things, this means that 1 & 2 is false.

```
# Bitwise operation versus boolean operation, Perl 5:

print "Yup\n"    if 1 & 2;
print "Uh huh\n" if 1 and 2;

# Bitwise operation versus boolean operation, Perl 6:

print "Yup\n"    if 1 +& 2;
print "Uh huh\n" if 1 and 2;
```

These output Uh huh but not Yup, even though 1 and 2 are both true. & doesn't consider the absolute truth value of its two arguments but instead the individual truth values of each corresponding bit.

```
# Bit operations test, Perl 5

my $input1 = 0b00001111;
my $input2 = 0b01010101;

my $result = $input1 & $input2;
```

```
printf "0b%08b\n", $result;

# Input1:  0b00001111
# Input2:  0b01010101
# Outputs: 0b00000101
```

Change the & to +& for Perl 6.

One logic operation is performed for each bit. A 32-bit machine will do 32 logic operations with one instruction when working on integers. This example defines 8 bits—the rest default to 0. With strings, as many operations take place as are needed to compare each bit.

Pattern Operators

The purpose of ~~ is first and foremost to return a reasonable boolean value in boolean context.

—Larry Wall

~~ is the smart match operator and, despite being composed entirely of tildes, works on anything and everything, including strings and nonstrings. !~ works the same way but returns an inverted logic value. like and unlike may or may not be low-precedence aliases for ~~ and !~ (the language designers haven't made a commitment yet). Chapter 9 is all about ~~.

Pipeline Operators

<== and ==> collect lists and provide those lists as arguments to expressions. They *pipeline* data between expressions. The output of one expression is the input to the next. This gets rid of parentheses in the common case where a list is filtered through a number of maps, greps, and sorts. They can be chained.

File Tests

Operators starting with a - and continuing with a letter are file test operators. Collectively, these return the size of a file, its modification date, whether it exists, whether it's a directory, and other juicy bits of information. Perl 6 returns a file status buffer object that "booleanifies" and numifies a value, indicating whether all the tests on it have been successful.

```
# Check for files that are executable by us but setuid someone else - Perl 5

use File::Find;

File::Find::find(sub {
    -u -x $_ and try_to_exploit($_);
}, '/');
```

This feature is available in a development version of Perl 5 and may not make it into a release version. See perldoc -f -X for the general description of file test operators and a table of available tests.

Neglected in This Chapter

Some operators are part of a larger concept and are documented in detail elsewhere in this book. Rather than duplicate the explanations, the following is where these topics are documented:

Chapter 8 and Chapter 11 cover \, the reference operator.

Chapter 11 covers *, the list-flattening operator. You'll also see it in the examples in Chapter 8.

Chapter 8 covers dereferencing data structures using the dereferencing operator (the dot in Perl 6 or the arrow operator in Perl 5). Chapter 11 covers the dereferencing operator as it relates to invoking code references. Chapter 14 covers the dereference operator as used to invoke code methods in objects. By the way, you can use a toy module to make the dot operator the dereferencing operator in Perl 5. It's called Acme::Dot, and you'll find it on CPAN.

++ and -- increment numbers and strings and deincrement numbers, respectively. Other than ++ also operating on strings to count in base 26, they work like their C namesakes. This feature may not be available in Perl 6. You'll find details in perldoc perlop.

.. generates a list when used in list context and when given two numbers. Examples in this book use this form of ... Bear in mind that .. is an entirely different operator in scalar context, where it emulates the sed operator of the same name. Used in the scalar context, .. is the "*bistable latch*" operator. It returns false until the expression on the left becomes true and then returns true until the expression on the left becomes false. This is useful for extracting the middle portion of some list using two conditional expressions. For details on scalar .. and information on ..., see perldoc perlop.

Some operators are also built-in functions. The zip function, introduced in Chapter 11, is also available as an operator using the yen symbol, ¥, which looks kind of like a little zipper.

Chapter 5 covered := and ::=, the variable-binding operators. Those temporarily or permanently make variables, hash slots, or array elements synonymous with each other.

The <=> operator performs a three-way comparison between two numbers and is useful in conjunction with the sort built-in function. Chapter 8 documents it along with cmp, the string equivalent.

Quote-like operators were the subject of Chapter 4. These quote strings, regular expressions, lists of strings, and other things.

Reference operators create references and access values by reference; Chapters 8 and 11 cover them.

You can overload Perl operators to perform user-defined functions on objects when the operators are used on an object. Chapter 14 has a few examples, but discussing operator overloading is beyond the scope of this book. perldoc overload has detailed instructions and examples.

ACKNOWLEDGMENTS

Mike Lazzaro's operator chart, posted to the `perl6-language` list, served as a starting point for this chapter and a checklist as it progressed.

Mark Lentczner created a graphical table of Perl 6 operators in the motif of a periodic table of the elements. The site at `http://www.cafeshops.com/perl6periodic` has for sale swag that sports this cool design. A PDF version is freely available, but this really deserves to be hung on a wall.

Summary

Most of the changes in Perl 6 regarding operators were to ideas already distinctly Perl. Changing the string concatenation operator from . to ~ and changing the dereference operator from -> to . are the most visible changes to the language.

In Perl 6, much more often than in Perl 5, context comes from the operator, and more operators and more permutations of operators exist to deal with all situations. The updates are bittersweet, though, because precious few have been retroimplemented to Perl 5.

Further, you can more easily avoid common pitfalls, such as mixing string and numeric values in bit tests. Distinguishing between string repetition and array repetition with x vs. xx is another case of clarifying semantics.

Almost any operator can have = prepended to it to modify the variable (or lvalue expression) on its left. Additionally, you can wrap almost any operator in sets of greater-than and less-than signs to make it hyper. These are the new rules for conjugating operators.

Pipelining as an alternative to deeply nested parentheses is new in Perl 6, as is the ability to call and define operators as subroutines. The ability to refer to operators as if they were code references, complete with prototypes, is nifty, as is the ability to define new operators as if they were subroutines.

Although you can still program Perl as if it's some sort of odd C dialect, there's more incentive than ever to delve into Perl-specific alternatives, such as using or or err in place of || to detect error return values.

CHAPTER 7

■ ■ ■

Multidimensional Arrays

Corresponding to at least some of these [type names], there will also be lower-case intrinsic types, such as int, num, str, and ref. Use of the lowercase type name implies you aren't intending to do anything fancy OO-wise with the values, or store any run time properties, and thus Perl should feel free to store them compactly. (As a limiting case, objects of type bit can be stored in 1 bit.)

—Larry Wall, Apocalypse 2

Perl 5 arrays hold sequences of scalars, which can be strings, numbers, references, or the special undef value. The scalar variable is rich in metadata and has the right amount of power for normal use, but it isn't a good fit for representing individual pixels or samples in a large data set. It's just too much metadata, and it's metadata that isn't needed. This chapter covers an alternative for Perl 5 that works better in these cases. I'm calling the alternative a *multidimensional array* to distinguish it from Perl's built-in single-dimensional arrays, though it'd be just as correct to call it a *lightweight array*.

Perl 6 arrays can contain scalars, just like Perl 5, but they're also able to directly hold a list of numbers. An *array of numbers* saves memory as opposed to Perl 5's *arrays of scalars containing numbers*.

Perl 5 accomplishes this with the Perl Data Language (PDL) module, called PDL. (See the "Perl Data Language" section for a lot more details on this.) Perl 6 uses the normal array syntax combined with traits. Lightweight types are variables declared with the ints and nums type traits in Perl 6 or created using the PDL module in Perl 5. In both cases, the effects are the same; both do the following:

- Efficiently store large data sets

- Store multidimensional information

- Efficiently perform operations on all members of a multidimensional array

Image data is notoriously large when uncompressed, and of course it must be uncompressed to perform any meaningful operation on it. Data for sounds, data sets for statistics, and data from hardware data-capture boards are other applications that have in the past required programmers to drop down to C or step up to a specialized platform.

Perl eschews optimizations that save a little memory and require programmer attention. In Perl 6, lightweight arrays require very little programmer awareness, and they can save quite a lot of memory. Perl 5 takes some work, but either way, they open up worlds to Perl.

Besides efficiently storing large data sets, math and logic operations quickly consider the entire set of data. Working in parallel, standard operators, such as addition, work on each element of both sets, but other operators and methods exist to perform operations that are useful only on data sets, such as averaging.

New for Perl 6

Perl 6 offers lightweight and normal scalars, arrays, and hashes. Lightweight types may not have properties, but they require far less storage. Simple types have names in all lowercase letters.

```
# Lightweight storage, Perl 6
# simple values:
my int $scalar;
# Arrays
my int @array is Dim(1000, 1000);
# or:
my @array of int is Dim(1000, 1000);
```

Compare this to my Int $array is Dim(1000, 1000), with Int having an initial capital letter.

■Naming variables Please don't actually name your scalars $scalar or your arrays @array. Also, don't name them $data unless you're really unsure what they're going to hold, and then you've got larger problems to worry about than variable naming. Few programs are smart enough to process raw, typeless, free-format data in any meaningful way. Thank you.

Chapter 5 documented new features for the standard, nonlightweight variables. This chapter is about lightweight variables as used in arrays. You can use Perl 6 lightweight variables as scalars, but there's little reason to do so unless your program declares millions of scalar variables (in which case it has larger problems). However, if you did want a lightweight scalar, you'd declare it in Perl 6 with the syntax my int $foo or my $foo is int.

Lightweight types in Perl 6 don't accept properties or additional traits. The variables can't remember anything except their value according to the limits of the storage type. Specifically, they can't remember any meta-information about themselves, but the compiler tracks a certain amount while compiling (such as their datatype and scope). However, arrays containing lightweight types do accept traits, and the datatype being stored in the array is specified using them, such as with my int @foo or my @foo is array of int. Note that my int @foo means that @foo stores ints, not that @foo itself is an int; hence, it's the same as my @foo is array of int.

■**PDL and undef** PDL Arrays don't recognize the special undef value in that they don't return it, and assigning it is equivalent to assigning in 0. However, PDL has optional bad value support with a similar purpose to undef. Unlike operations between undef and valid values, any operation between a bad value and any other value always results in another bad value. Bad values occupy individual positions in an array. Unless things go horribly wrong, an entire PDL array won't be a bad value, but it may contain several. See perldoc PDL::Bad for details.

Perl Data Language

In any event, it is absolutely my intent that the built-in array types of Perl 6 support PDL directly, both in terms of efficiency and flexibility.

—Larry Wall, to the perl6 language mailing list

PDL stores numbers compactly in RAM and operates efficiently on them. Arrays are composed of elements, and each element is the same size. Elements may be bytes, short integers, long (regular) integers, floats, or double-precision floats. Integers, short or long, may be signed or unsigned. Unlike normal Perl arrays, PDL arrays don't contain references, strings, or "tieable" (using Perl's tie feature, documented in perldoc perltie) values. None of the standard scalar metadata exists for elements of a PDL array.

Arrays created with PDL may have multiple dimensions. Whereas a standard Perl array accepts only one subscript, such as with @arr[10], an array created with PDL can have any number of subscripts, such as with $array->at(10, 5, 37). A one-dimensional array takes a single subscript and can be imagined as a single row of values. A two-dimensional array takes two subscripts and can be visualized as a square, with the first index traversing one axis and the second index traversing the second axis. A three-dimensional array is a cube, and so on.

Beyond a small amount of fixed overhead, the memory requirements of a PDL array are easy to compute: multiply each of the dimensions together, and then multiply the result by the number of bytes in each cell. A long integer is either 4 or 8 bytes depending on your hardware. A 1,000 by 1,000 array (a two-dimensional array) of long integers would be just short of 4 megabytes of memory, for example. An array of regular Perl scalar variables holding numbers would be at least eight times as large. They could grow much larger if used as strings, as Perl caches the string rendering of numeric values when non-PDL scalars are used.

Lightweight numeric types in Perl 5 and Perl 6 don't cache string representations of themselves. In Perl 6, strs don't cache numeric representations of themselves. In Perl 5 and Perl 6, normal scalars, including array subscripts, do cache numeric and string renderings of themselves for speed. Perl still automatically converts between integer and string representation for you, but applications that repeatedly use a single variable as a string and then as a number will suffer a performance hit compared with scalars. Lightweight variables can't store special values such as undef. These lightweight types do work with autoboxing, a feature introduced in Chapter 14. In Perl 5, multidimensional arrays can't have aliases or references taken to individual elements.

Some operators are *matrix operators*, which operate on two arrays according to the rules of matrix algebra. Some built-in methods, such as average(), *collapse* a PDL array by performing some operation on each array in the last dimension of the PDL array and by replacing the last dimension with the results of that operation.

Operators *vectorize* on PDL arrays. Adding one to a PDL array with $pdl + 1 adds one to *every element* of the array. When an operator is used on two PDL arrays, the operation is performed on each *corresponding element* of the arrays.

A logic test operator, such as <, tests every element of a PDL array, either against a single value or against another PDL array. The any() method is defined to test whether some operation is true for at least one element of an array. The all() method is defined to test whether some operation is true for all elements of an array.

■**Hyper operators** Perl 6's hyper operators, documented in Chapter 6, perform an operation on each element of an array. Normal operators used on PDL arrays cause that operator to behave as a hyper operator.

■**Any and all** any() and all() in the PDL sense are similar to Perl 6 junctions, implemented in Perl 5 by Quantum::Superpositions. See Chapter 18 for more on this stuff.

PDL-Bundled Documentation

The perldoc PDL manual page lists the dozen or so other PDL manual pages available. Included and external modules operate on the data structures, doing statistical, arithmetic, and image-processing operations. Interfaces exist to windowing toolkits, such as Tk and Prima, that use PDL::PrimaImage.

PDL::Impatient is the best starting point to get a feel for PDL. Also see PDL::Indexing, PDL::FAQ, and PDL::Indexing.

The following are all the modules loaded by default when you use PDL:

PDL::Core documents the constructor and routines, providing meta-information such as dimensions and index sizes. Type conversion routines are also in PDL::Core. Type perldoc PDL::Core at the command shell to pull up the documentation.

PDL::Basic is noncore PDL array creation and reporting logic. Consider it an extension of PDL::Core.

PDL::Ops documents the overloaded operators and their method call equivalents. This tells what happens when you use +, *, <, and so forth, on two PDL arrays.

PDL::Ufunc contains routines that "reduce" PDL arrays. Information from two dimensions (one dimension may hold a huge number of parallel arrays) are totaled, multiplied, averaged, or subjected to other logical or mathematical operations and compiled into a single dimension. This is like adding columns in a spreadsheet. See also PDL::Reduce for writing your own functions to reduce data.

PDL::Slices lets you slice a multidimensional subarray to create a new PDL array from an existing one and has the routines to modify indexing. In its own words, it's "stupid index tricks." One PDL data structure, or *PDL array* (pronounced *piddle array*), may be a view of another, not requiring memory of its own. Most of this is beyond the scope of this chapter, but slicing is useful for getting data into and out of PDL arrays. See also perldoc PDL::NiceSlice for a source filter that provides a simplified syntax for slicing PDL arrays.

PDL::MatrixOps performs operations on matrices. This is done in signal processing and 3D graphics, among other things. By the way, if you have a processor with "multimedia extensions," it has a small matrix engine built in.

PDL::Math imports trigonometric functions such as sin(), old standards such as ceil(), and operations for polynomials.

PDL::IO::Misc reads and writes various scientific data formats, as well as raw and ASCII.

PDL::Primitive has an assortment of routines built by other operations or used to build other operations. If you can't find something you're looking for elsewhere, try here.

PDL has a Web site at http://pdl.perl.org with some excellent screen shots of 3D plots that are easy to do with a few commands and the right modules installed.

Creating a PDL Array

Use the Dim trait in Perl 6 or the PDL->zeroes() class method in Perl 5.

```
# These two are equivalent for creating a single-dimensional array
my int $array is Dim(1000);              # Perl 6
my $array = PDL->zeroes(1000)->long;     # Perl 5 with use PDL
# These two are equivalent for creating a two-dimensional array:
my int $array is Dim(1000, 1000);        # Perl 6
my $array = PDL->zeroes(1000, 1000)->long;  # Perl 5 with use PDL
```

For the two-dimensional array, indices from 0, 0 through 999, 999 are valid, though PDL wants you to fetch data with $array->at(999, 999) rather than the more familiar $array->[999][999] syntax. You can get more dimensions by adding numbers to the list (and installing additional sticks of RAM to keep up with the exponential memory requirements of the additional dimensions).

You can build PDL arrays from existing data structures as well.

```
# Building a PDL array from an existing data structure
use PDL;
my $array = PDL->pdl( [ [ 0 .. 2 ], [ 3 .. 5 ], [ 6 .. 9 ] ] );
my $array = PDL->pdl( $perl_array_reference );
```

From here on in this chapter, everything is Perl 5 unless marked otherwise. Starting here, the examples also omit use PDL;. It's assumed to be there.

Type is one of byte, short, ushort, long, longlong, float, or double. If you're not familiar with C, double is a double-precision float, and a longlong is usually a double-wide long, but the smaller versions may be the same as the larger versions. Things are guaranteed to be of *at least* a certain size but are permitted to be larger.

A PDL array may be converted to any of the following types by calling a method of the same name as used to construct a type:

```
$array = $array->short(); # make into an array of shorts
my $new_PDL array = PDL->short( [1, 200, 1000, 15000] ); # new a PDL array of shorts
```

A short is a *short integer* that's usually 16 bits (half of what's required for a long), but it's quite possibly 32 bits (the same size as a long) and may be other sizes on truly bizarre systems. PDL's 32-bit long corresponds to Perl 6's int.

■**zeroes vs. pdl, long, short, and company** zeroes, ones, and sequence initialize a PDL array to be of a certain dimension. The arguments are the desired dimensions. pdl, short, long, ushort, longlong, and so forth, expect the data itself to be passed in, and the resulting dimensions of the PDL array depends on the dimensions of the data. All of them construct PDL arrays, but the two groups take different information as arguments. Want empty space of a certain datatype? Do something such as PDL->zeroes(100, 100, 100)->short(), creating the empty space and then changing the datatype. Or, to avoid allocating memory twice, write PDL->zeroes('short', 100, 100, 100);. Just remember that pdl and company don't create empty PDL arrays.

■**Namespace pollution alert** These examples pretend that PDL doesn't export any functions into your namespace, but PDL *does* export hundreds of symbols. If two modules try to export the same symbol, you get the one defined by the last module used. It's best to explicitly specify the package, writing PDL->sequence() or $pdl->sequence() instead of sequence(). If all your code is written in this object-oriented style, you may request that PDL, like most modules, *not* export symbols to your namespace. To do this, write use PDL (); instead of use PDL;. The empty list, (), is the list of symbols requested from the PDL module. While the various PDL operations are available as both methods and functions, I'm referring to them as *methods* under the assumption they'll be used as such.

Handy for debugging and experimenting, sequence() initializes a PDL array with a numeric sequence that keeps counting as it crosses rows. This creates easy-to-recognize data.

```
# sequence() creates easily recognizable data to test with
my $zero_to_ninety_nine = PDL->sequence(10, 10);
print $zero_to_ninety_nine;
```

This outputs the following:

```
[
 [ 0  1  2  3  4  5  6  7  8  9]
 [10 11 12 13 14 15 16 17 18 19]
 [20 21 22 23 24 25 26 27 28 29]
 [30 31 32 33 34 35 36 37 38 39]
 [40 41 42 43 44 45 46 47 48 49]
 [50 51 52 53 54 55 56 57 58 59]
 [60 61 62 63 64 65 66 67 68 69]
 [70 71 72 73 74 75 76 77 78 79]
 [80 81 82 83 84 85 86 87 88 89]
 [90 91 92 93 94 95 96 97 98 99]
]
```

Several examples in this chapter initialize PDL arrays using sequence() for simple demonstrations of other features.

Getting Data In and Out of a PDL Array

set stores a value at a given coordinate.

```
$array->set(int rand 1000, int rand 1000, 3);
```

This stores the value 3 at some random coordinate. A coordinate value is required for each dimension of the array with the value coming last on the argument list. The PDL-computed assignment operator, .=, writes in a way that modifies, rather than entirely overwrites, another PDL array. Here it's used with the slice syntax to assign into the middle of PDL. Use = to assign the result of PDL operations to a variable, ignoring the previous contents of the variable. Use .= to assign data into the lvalue result of other operations or replace data in a PDL that a variable contains a window into.

■**Computed-assignment operator** The concatenation operator in Perl 5 is ., and .= is the mutating (assigning) version of that operator. When used with PDL, .= doesn't concatenate but replaces data. (The .= operator had to be used instead of the = operator for technical reasons related to operator overloading in Perl, and Perl 5 doesn't allow for the creation of entirely new operators.) This example happens to be using it to concatenate data, in a sense, even though it's really just assigning data into the middle of an existing buffer. See the cat(), append(), and glue() PDL methods for other concatenate-like behaviors.

---

at returns a scalar that holds a number. Note that PDL arrays contain only numeric data and never contain string data (short of encoding characters as bytes). A PDL array is usually zero initialized (as in the initialization example) or one initialized (useful for matrices).

at takes one argument for each dimension to traverse. The following picks a random element out of the PDL array just created:

```
my $random_element = $array->at(int rand 1000, int rand 1000);
```

This is equivalent to my $random_element = @array[int rand 1000][int rand 1000] in Perl 6 or Perl 5 using normal arrays and Perl6::Variables. Had I created a three-dimensional array, picking a random element would instead look like this:

```
my $random_element = $array->at(int rand 1000, int rand 1000, int rand 1000);
```

Each additional dimension means another argument. The first argument to at() traverses the first dimension, the second argument to at() traverses the second dimension, and so on. The dimensions are numbered *from the inside out*. When a PDL array is printed, the first dimension corresponds to values inside the innermost set of brackets, the second dimensional is the set of brackets just outside that, and so on.

```
# PDL coordinates are numbered inside out respective what is printed
# to the screen
use PDL;
my $pdl = PDL->zeroes(3, 3, 3);
$pdl->set(0, 1, 2, 100);
$pdl->set(0, 1, 2, 100);
print $pdl;
```

This outputs the following (without the comments):

```
[
 [
  [0 0 0]
  [0 0 0]        # This would read [0 0 100] if dimensions were
  [0 0 0]        # numbered reverse of what they are
 ]
 [
  [0 0 0]
  [0 0 0]
  [0 0 0]
 ]
 [
  [  0   0   0]
  [100   0   0]  # Here's the 0, 1, 2 coordinate
  [  0   0   0]
 ]
]
```

The coordinates 0, 1, 2 correspond to the 0th value in the first set of brackets in the second block. This arrangement is backward from what you may expect.

If you wanted to generalize the process of randomly subscripting an arbitrarily sized PDL array, use the dims() method without an argument, which returns the number of dimensions an array has. dim($dim) returns the size of any given dimension. You could map { } through a rand call, like so:

```
# Extract a random element from a PDL array using dims() and dim(n)
my $random_element = $array->at(
    map { int rand $_ }
    map { $array->dim($_) } 0 .. $array->dims()
);
```

This loops from 0 to $array->dims(). On each iteration, it fetches the size of that dimension using $array->dim($_) and builds a list of those dimensions. These sizes are mapped through rand. The result of this is used as the list coordinates of the actual random element.

■Indexing multidimensional PDL arrays While set() and at() use lists of values to index a multidimensional array, many PDL methods (specifically those with names ending in ND) don't. The "Indexing Flattened PDL Arrays" section near the end of this chapter contains details.

---

print or anything else asking for a string representation of a PDL array gets data out in a way that's useful for debugging. Merely print the PDL array, like so:

```
# Dump a nicely formatted, human-readable rendering of a PDL array
print $array;
```

list sends back a nice, normal Perl array containing all the data in the PDL array. You'll want to do this with small PDL arrays, data sets after you've finished performing operations, or, more typically, a slice of a PDL array.

```
# Collapse all dimensions into one and return it as a plain Perl list
my $array = PDL->sequence(10, 10);
my @array = $array->list();
print "@array\n";
```

That's a roundabout way of writing my @array = (0 .. 100); print "@array\n";.

The list() method This method flattens multidimensional arrays. Perl 6 adds an operator for explicitly flattening arrays, *, introduced in the next chapter. The PDL list() method is similar. A flattened array has no structure (it's no longer organized into rows and columns) but is useful anywhere a list is accepted.

---

set() and at() are useful for experimenting with PDL to get a feel for the coordinate system (which was the point of this previous example), but they're not particularly useful for actually moving data into and out of a PDL array. For that, slice() and range() are used in conjunction with the .= operator to get data in, and slice() and range() are used with the list() method to get data out.

Let's say you wanted to work on a small piece of a larger PDL array.

```
my $array = PDL->sequence(10, 10);
my @array = $array->slice('1:8,1:8')->list();
print "@array\n";
```

A slice() creates a window into a PDL array, returning another PDL array. Except for the slice() method, this example is identical to the previous example. This slice() example shaves off the top row, bottom row, left column, and right column, cropping a border off from around the data. The slice is built from positions 1 through 8 in the first dimension and positions 1 through 8 in all the rows in the second dimension. A sliced-out PDL has the same dimensions as the PDL from which it was extracted. The format of the previous slice could be read as follows:

```
# Meaning of slice fields in the simple example
# This is not valid PDL
slice('dimension 1 start:dimension 1 end,dimension 2 start:dimension 2 end');
```

Slicing before taking a list() is an important idiom. I want to draw special attention to it, but it may be helpful to see what the slice actually looks like before it's flattened.

```
print PDL->sequence(10, 10)->slice('1:8,1:8');
```

These are simple examples of slice(). It has its own little metalanguage passed as its sole argument that describes *how* to take the slice. If you had a tile-based game with a large world map but wanted to show only a small portion of it at a time, slice() would be perfect.

When slicing off a multidimensional part of a PDL array, use the flat() method to create a single-dimensional PDL array. This is similar to list() except it returns a PDL array instead of a plain old list. This is the first part of an idiom for assigning a block of data into the middle of an existing PDL array.

```
print PDL->sequence(10, 10)->slice('1:1,:'); # needs to be flattened
print PDL->sequence(10, 10)->slice('1:1,:')->flat(); # that's better
```

Now that you know how to take a slice, the assignment operator, .=, will overwrite data in that slice with new data.

```
# Flattened slices allow easy assignment into a "window" into a PDL array
my $pdl = PDL->sequence(10, 10);
$pdl->slice('1:1,:')->flat() .= PDL->sequence(10);
print $pdl;
```

This assigns one single-dimensional sequence right into the middle of a multidimensional one. Rather than write out '1:1,0:9' in the argument to slice(), I've dropped the 0 and the 9, and slice() defaults to picking an entire dimension where it sees a bare :. If you extract a PDL array of the dimensions (3, 3, 3), you may assign another PDL array of the dimensions (3, 3, 3) into it without needing to flatten either PDL array.

The range() method generalizes the idea of slicing to accept the criteria of values to splice out as two PDL arrays.

```
# range() also extracts a PDL out of the middle of another PDL
my $pdl = PDL->sequence(10, 10);
print $pdl->range(PDL->pdl(2, 3), PDL->pdl(5, 5));
```

This generates the following output:

```
[
 [32 33 34 35 36]
 [42 43 44 45 46]
 [52 53 54 55 56]
 [62 63 64 65 66]
 [72 73 74 75 76]
]
```

The first argument to range() is the coordinates of the top-left corner of the area to extract, and the second argument is the number of elements required from each dimension. In this example, the first argument is (2, 3), indicating two rows should be skipped and three columns should be skipped to seek to the desired block of data. The second argument is (5, 5), indicating five rows and five columns should be returned. Rather than PDL arrays, you could use anonymous arrays, created with [ ], to specify the location and size of the window to create. For dimensions greater than two, add more numbers, just as with set(), at(), and other PDL methods. Both arguments to PDL arrays could be single dimensional, and if they're multidimensional, the operation is repeated for each row. If the second argument is neglected, a PDL array containing a single value is returned, which has the same effect as if the second argument was passed and contained all 1s. range() also takes an optional third argument that indicates how boundary conditions are to be handled. See perldoc PDL::Primitive for details. Various other PDL methods, such as whichND(), return coordinates, and you can use their output directly as input to range().

Craig DeForest gave me an example of using range() to splice icons onto a larger image. If you're rendering a bunch of spacecraft icons onto a bitmap of Earth and its environs, for example, you can write the following:

```
$image->range($locations, $iconsize, 'truncate') .= $icon;
```

This places onto the image a copy of $icon at each location listed in $locations. In the simple case, $locations contains a single-dimensional PDL that holds the coordinates of where a single copy of $icon should be placed. 'truncate' as a boundary condition tells PDL to ignore the situation of an icon placed partially off the image $image.

Processing Data in a PDL Array

The MOD file format (files with the extension .mod) was popular before Internet music went mainstream. Several music genres thrived in the MOD file scene, and the community surrounding the format has influenced several in turn. These files were originally associated with the SoundTracker program for the Commodore Amiga, but other programs on the Amiga and other systems were created to compose and play them. They're normally about a tenth of the size of an MP3 file. However, extremely large ones may be half the size of an equivalent MP3 file, and extremely tiny ones (a few kilobytes) were created as an amusement. They're composed of a music score, much like MIDI files, but they include their own samples, and MOD file authors love inventing new instruments and sampling things. The length of the file has little bearing on how long it plays for; it affects only the quality and the number of instruments. Play rate lets a sample be adjusted to different keys, and looping on the middle of a sample allows for different attack, sustain, and decay times to create realistic notes when a sample is used as an instrument. Numerous other effects can be applied to samples as they're played. Virtually all MOD files are licensed to be freely redistributed. Since they're composed of samples, it's easy to remix a track, change instruments, or even steal instruments you like from other MOD files. Some groups collect obscure and antique keyboard samples for this purpose. None of this is possible with MP3 files, so there's still an underground where MOD files thrive.

At the beginning of this chapter, I mentioned processing audio data as an example of where a program would need to deal with a large quantity of numeric samples. Throughout the rest of this chapter, I'll use operations on sound data as examples for PDL.

Representing Data in Memory

It's hard to implement a good MOD file player, or *tracker*, but it's easy to implement a bad one. Ultimately four channels of digital audio are scaled and mixed. The Commodore Amiga did this in hardware, but I wanted to mix it down to a WAV file.

```
# Compute the playing time of a mod file and multiply that by the sample rate to
# decide how much memory is required to hold the audio data.
my $wav_length = int(scalar(@positions) * (64 / (60/10)) * $sample_rate) + 1;
# Create four tracks of byte resolution data
# large enough to hold the entire wav file.
my $audio = PDL->zeroes(4, $wave_length)->byte();
```

This program fragment allocates four tracks, each as long as what I'm computing the MOD file to be, taken from the number of bars of music, the number of positions in each bar, how many bars a second played, and the number of samples per second. Since I'm writing a plain old WAV file, I picked 44,100 as a good standard sample rate. So, 44,100 times a second, the speaker will be asked to move into a new position. That new position should be very near the last one, unless something goes horribly wrong (such as when a data CD is put in a stereo by mistake). The result is a smooth, continuous sound wave. The sound wave itself is composed of lots of tones, high and low.

▪Samples *Sample* means both a chunk of audio data and an individual value from such a sample. It's also both a noun and a verb. Someone recording audio data takes samples of air pressure using a microphone. Data can be taken only at a certain rate (though it may be very high). Each time the air pressure is measured, it's a sample. To record sound data by sampling air pressure is *to sample* (the verb form of the word). From the verb form came the name for the result of taking samples: a *sample*.

Splicing in Data

The mod format reuses not only sample data but also musical score data. Each position specifies which frame is to be played. (A *frame* is similar to a bar of music.) Each frame has 64 ticks. Each tick, a new note can be started on a channel. If a note is already playing and no new one starts, the note continues playing. Ticks happen ten times a second. Four channels exist, and any may get a new note at each tick. The song structure amounts to several nested loops. The variable $offset keeps track of where the program is in the output PDL array, $audio.

```
# Loop over the MOD file data structures, splicing each note encountered into
# the wav data
use PDL;
use Perl6::Variables;
my $offset = 0;                          # Output wav data offset
my $offset_step = $sample_rate / 10;  # 10 times a second notes may change
for my $position (@positions) {
    for my $frame ( 0 .. 63 ) {
        for my $channel ( 0 .. 3 ) {
            my $note = @patterns[$position][$frame][$channel];
            if($note->{sample}) {
                # the note for this channel changed
                my $scaled_sample = scale_sample($note, \@samples);
                my $scaled_sample_length = $scaled_sample->dim(0);
                $audio->range(
                    [$channel, $offset], [0, $scaled_sample_length]
                ) .= $scaled_sample;
            }
        }
    }
    $offset += $offset_step;
}
```

This demonstrates using the PDL-computed assignment operator, .=, to modify data through a window in a PDL array. In this case, it's used to insert a block of data into the middle of a PDL array where the window into the array was created with range(). =sample_rate is the number of individual samples (bytes) generated per second for output. $offset_step is the number of sample values needed to fill one-tenth of a second at the current sampling rate. Every frame, the program advances this much in the audio file. Notes always start on a frame boundary.

$scaled_sample->dim(0) returns the size of the first (0th) dimension, which is the length of the sample, as it's one dimensional. A following routine generates $scaled_sample. As one instrument sample is used to generate different notes, you must scale the sample up and down to change the pitch. $scaled_sample_length is the length of the sample being spliced in.

@patterns is a data structure representing the MOD file song structure. It's an ordinary Perl array of arrays (array of array references, technically), not a PDL array. When subscripted as @patterns[$position][$frame][$channel], it returns the number of any note to be played at that moment in the song. The syntax of data structures or the structure of this data structure isn't important to this example.

Scaling and Oversampling Data

Part of this work is scaling samples. Since the samples in MOD files are usually sampled at a low rate, sampling them up is the normal case for this program. Samples are scaled to change the *pitch* (which is the primary frequency audible in a sample). Scaling the sample creates different notes from just one sample of an instrument, so they're not even scaled by a fixed rate. The amount of scaling changes with each note played.

This example, after obtaining the song data it needs, computes a number to scale the sample by ($stretch_factor), computes an interval with which to subsample the sample to shrink or expand it to the desired length ($inverted_stretch), builds an array of these subsample positions (@sample_indices), and then uses the PDL interpolate() method to interpolate values for the subsample positions from the audio sample data.

```
sub scale_sample {

    my $note = shift;
    my $samples = shift;
    my $period = $note->{period};  # speed to play at
    my $waveform = $samples->[ $note->{sample} ]->{waveform}; # audio data
    my $sample_khz = $amiga_constant / ( $period * 2 );
    my $stretch_factor = $sample_rate / $sample_khz;
    my $inverted_stretch = 1 / $stretch_factor;

    my $sample_index = 0;  # current subsample position
    my @sample_indices;    # compiled list of subsample positions

    while($sample_index < $samples_requested) {
        push @sample_indices, $sample_index;
        $sample_index += $inverted_stretch;
    }

    my $zero_to_a_lot = PDL->sequence($waveform->dim(0));
```

```
(my $stretched_wav, my $err) =
    PDL->float(\@sample_indices)->interpolate($zero_to_a_lot, $waveform);

return $stretched_wav;
}
```

The variable $amiga_constant is a constant known to MOD file players and editors. It's the clock speed of the Amiga's sound chip. Samples in the MOD file are set to be played at multiples of this speed.

Samples in MOD files are sampled at a pretty low rate, and it must scale these up—or perhaps down if it's playing a high-quality sample for a low-pitch note. $stretch_factor is a multiplier by the size of the sample. This number times the size of the input sample is the size of the desired output sample.

$inverted_stretch is the inverse of this. When stretching, it will be a floating-point number less than one. When shrinking a sample down, it will be a floating-point number greater than one. Since you advance through the input sample this amount each loop and it's less than one, you wind up partway between samples.

Truncating the values in @sample_indices (rather than using floating-point values and interpolating) would work. This would find the nearest sample, but a trick called *oversampling* can improve the quality of the low sample rate input sample by approximating the sample value between two actual samples. This example uses interpolate() to oversample. This technique isn't specific to audio processing. It's used in all fields of data analysis as well as computer graphics (for example, to smooth out image maps and texture data in 3D graphics). It uses some mathematical method to guess where a true waveform would go given the limited resolution of the sample data.

Figure 7-1 shows the effect supersampling has on audio data.

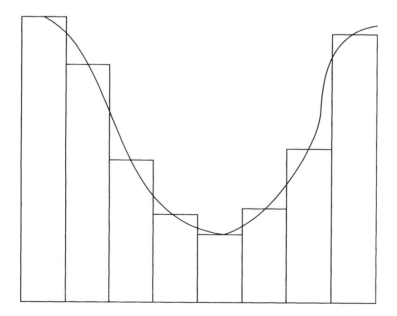

Figure 7-1. *Sine wave interpolated from discrete samples*

The rectangles are limited-resolution samples (the input). The line going through their tops is a *spline* that approximates the probable sound wave from which the sample was recorded. Some data is lost and there's no way to recover it, but this interpolated waveform avoids the buzzing noises, static, and speaker pops associated with low-resolution samples.

The following is a simple example of interpolation, based on the previous example:

```
# Interpolation smooths out data when the sampling rate is changed
use PDL;
# Subsample positions: output sample will have this number samples (6)
# from these places in the input sample (0.3, 0.6, 1.1, 1.5, 1.9, 2.0):
my @sample_indices = (0.3, 0.6, 1.1, 1.5, 1.9, 2.0);
# Common case is the input data represents a series of evenly spaced
# samples starting at 0 counting up to the number of samples in the
# input data.
my $waveform = PDL->pdl( [ map { int rand 10 } 1 .. 3 ] );
my $zero_to_a_lot = PDL->sequence($waveform->dim(0));
print "zero to a lot: ", $zero_to_a_lot, "\n";
print "waveform: ", $waveform, "\n";


(my $stretched_wav, my $err) =
    PDL->float(@sample_indices)->interpolate($zero_to_a_lot, $waveform);
print "stretched wav: ", $stretched_wav, "\n";
```

$waveform is randomly generated data. (It was three samples long in this example, and in the previous example it was a PDL array containing the low-resolution-input sample data.) In Figure 7-1, that's the blocky data that would sound crummy coming out of a speaker.

The floating-point values in @sample_indices subscript $waveform. interpolate() takes two arguments: the X coordinate data of subsample positions and the Y coordinate data PDL array of sample data. $zero_to_a_lot serves as the X data in these examples, and $waveform serves as the Y data. The interpolate() method is called as a method on the PDL array containing the subsample positions, which serves as X positions at which to subsample.

In both these examples, $zero_to_a_lot communicates to PDL that $waveform is a series of evenly spaced samples starting with the index 0 and counting up to however many samples you have (six in this case). The sequence() method computes this sequence as a PDL array. If the samples in $waveform weren't evenly spaced, $zero_to_a_lot would contain floating-point values describing the exact spacing between them, and a plain old sequence couldn't be used. If you were plotting temperature throughout the day, and you got up to log the temperature whenever you remembered, the values in $zero_to_a_lot would be the time of day you took a reading. Regardless, the values in $zero_to_a_lot must be in numeric order. This isn't really a handicap, but the Y data must be kept with the X data in case the Y data needs to be sorted.

interpolate() returns a PDL array with the cleaned-up, smoothed-out, higher-resolution waveform. This data also has limited resolution, but it's based on the infinite resolution of the waveform approximated through interpolation. You also get a flag telling you if any of the values were out of bounds. I'm ignoring this in the example.

Merging Multichannel Audio to One Track

After building the data structures and then going through the score and rendering the samples into the different channels, scaled and looped as needed, the last step is to mix them, and the average() method does just that. I've mentioned that operators and methods will perform an operation on each element of an array, perform operations on corresponding elements of two arrays, perform matrix operations between two arrays, and remove a dimension from an array. The collapse() method is a case of the latter: it removes a dimension.

```
# Average together four parallel tracks into one track and dump it as bytes
$wav->write( $audio->xchg(0, 1)->average()->list() );
```

$wav is a wav file opened with Audio::Wav. list() dumps that as Perl data. xchg() swaps the dimensions (logically, without actually moving any data). The following is the heart of that statement again, with comments:

```
# Average together four parallel tracks into one track and dump it as
bytes $audio              # 4 by 100,000 array two-dimensional array
    ->xchg(0, 1)    # 100,000 by 4 array two-dimensional array
    ->average()     # 100,000 element long single-dimensional array
```

Assuming the decompressed song is 100,000 samples long (it'd actually be much larger), $audio would be four long, narrow tracks with the dimensions (4, 100000). The xchg(0,1) call rearranges the dimensions to be (100000, 4), where there are thousands of arrays, each containing only four elements, with each element a single sample from each track. That gets it ready to invoke average() on. average() removes the last dimension of an array, leaving an array of the dimension (1000000). In the simplest case, averaging a single-dimensional array, average() yields a zero-dimensional array (a single scalar). On a two-dimensional array, as in the MOD player example, it yields a single-dimensional array, containing a list of averages. The data must be averaged instead of totaled, or else the poor 8-bit bytes will overflow and the audio will buzz badly. This example dumps the entire PDL array all at once, first to Perl memory as a plain old list and then to file. This is unacceptable in cases where the PDL array is large, because the native Perl representation of the data is several factors larger than the PDL representation and both representations are kept in memory at the same time. Process the data incrementally; otherwise, when possible, use one of the PDL::IO methods (something I'll cover in the section "Comparing PDL Arrays").

Autoleveling

The MOD format was designed to be played easily by hardware. The Amiga has four-channel digital sound, and the sound chip will stream audio from memory at a variable rate and mix the four channels into stereo. Since I'm mixing in software, not hardware, I could use something larger than a byte to hold data for each channel and add notes, using addition, rather than assign over the top what's there. This strategy mixes as it goes. This approach doesn't require four separate audio tracks at all; it requires merely a datatype large enough to hold the numbers without overflow. A 32-bit signed integer can hold the sum of 8 million bytes.

```
# Demonstrate that 31 bits can hold the sum of 8 million bytes
use Math::BigInt;
print(0x7fffffff / 256, "\n");
```

That's plenty, and a short (16-bit integer) may be too little, safely holding only 256 overlapping notes, each note being 8 bits large. Any number of notes may be playing at the same time, and their values are all summed up, easily overflowing an 8-bit value, but you're supposed to be writing an 8-bit value. Even if I write a 16-bit WAV file, 32 bits could overflow it, but on the other hand, it would be barely audible as a 16-bit wave file. That presents something of a problem. When the data was on four tracks, you knew you could just average those tracks together, but now an arbitrary number of tracks have been merged with no count of how many were merged at the point where the most notes were playing at once. Autolevel to the rescue! The waveform, at its highest point, should be exactly the largest value in the output data, and the rest of the waveform should be relative to that. (However, the average volume could be raised if the tops of some of the largest waveforms were clipped off, but I'll leave this as an exercise for the reader, major record labels, and radio stations.) Autoleveling consists of two things: identifying the maximum value and scaling the rest of the data relative to that value. In PDL, this is easier done than said.

```
# Autolevel a single track of audio data
use Math::BigInt;
my $max_int = 0x7fffffff;    # 31 bits
my $max_level = $audio->max();
my $scale_factor = int($max_int / $max_level) - 1;
$audio = $audio * $scale_factor;
```

Take another max() reading on $audio after this scaling operation. It should be close to what use Math::BigInt; print 0x7fffffff, "\n"; prints. You can create some sample data with something such as use PDL; my $audio = PDL->sequence(1000); to test this example. $scale_factor is the ratio between the largest value found in the data stream and the largest value you can represent with an unsigned 32-bit value. If unsigned shorts had been used instead of unsigned ints, then you'd have to use 0xffff as the maximum constant. As always, judiciously using print statements will help you understand what's happening.

This approach requires changes to the other example. $audio is a one-dimensional array rather than two, and data is added to the $audio track rather than replaced into it. += is used instead of .=.

```
# Modification to the "Loop over the mod datastructure" example to accommodate
# a single, scaled track
$audio->range( [$offset], [$scaled_sample_length] ) += $scaled_sample;
```

As previously, this creates a window into the data that's the size of the scaled note. Instead of assigning the scaled note in, it adds (with arithmetic addition) each sample. You no longer have to merge the tracks before writing the data file, because the code merges them as it goes.

Comparing PDL Arrays

PDL plots to numerous graphing libraries you probably don't have. It also writes the NetPBM formats (bitmapped, grayscale, and true color). NetPBM includes compressions and converters to generate GIF, JPEG, PNG, MPEG, TIFF, and numerous other formats. This makes sense because PBM is a go-between format. Rather than having GIF-to-PNG conversions, TIFF-to-GIF conversions, and so on, you need only converters to and from PBM.

```
my $audio_length = $audio->dim(0);
my $pbm = PDL->zeroes(255, $audio_length)->long;
my $steps = 254;
my $chunk = 0x7fffffff / $steps;
for my $i (reverse 0 .. $steps) {
    my $range_start = PDL->long(($chunk * $i) x ($audio_length - 1));
    my $range_stop = PDL->long(($chunk * $i + $chunk) x ($audio_length -1));
    $pbm->range([$i], [$audio_length]) .=
        (($audio > $range_start) & ($audio < $range_stop));
}

$pbm = $pbm->xchg(0, 1);

$pbm->wpic("piddle.pbm");
```

$steps sets the Y resolution of the output image. The possible range of values is divided by this number. Each line of graphic output encompasses $chunk values. In other words, the image is drastically scaled down from the resolution of the actual data. You make $steps pass through the data, each time identifying everything in range. Two PDL arrays are created: $range_start and $range_stop. $range_start contains a PDL array as long as the audio data that contains the lower-range value repeated through its whole length. $range_stop is the same, except it contains the cutoff value for the line of graphic output. Using comparison operators, you can find everything that's between the two ranges.

```
$pbm->range([$i], [$audio_length]) .=
    (($audio > $range_start) & ($audio < $range_stop));
```

This draws in a row of the image where each pixel is off unless the wave data is in range. Remember that PDL arrays always operate on all their values at once, so no loops are required to do a single line of graphic output. $range_start and $range_stop are the same length (have the same size in their first dimension) as $audio. < and > each return a PDL array as long as their two input PDL arrays. The returned PDL array is composed entirely of 0s and 1s. Each output value is 1 if the corresponding input values have the described relationship. & also takes two PDL arrays of the same length and returns a PDL array, but the bitwise *and* operation is performed, not the logical *and* operation. This works exactly like the boolean *and* when input values are 0 or 1. PDL::Ops describes logical, less-than, and greater-than operations, as well as others.

The following are some easier examples to help understand what's happening:

```
# Simple demonstration of vectorized logic operators in PDL
my $garbage = PDL->long(map { int rand 10 } (1 .. 20));
my $range_start = PDL->long((3) x 20);
my $range_stop  = PDL->long((7) x 20);
print 'garbage contains:    ', $garbage, "\n";
print 'garbage above start: ', $garbage > $range_start, "\n";
print 'garbage below stop:  ', $garbage < $range_stop, "\n";
print 'intersection:        ',
    ($garbage > $range_start) & ($garbage < $range_stop), "\n";
```

Since it's random, your data is almost certain to be different, on the first run at least, but the following is the first run for me:

```
garbage contains:    [0 9 1 7 8 5 8 2 9 5 3 0 9 9 2 3 8 9 7 4 9]
garbage above start: [0 1 0 1 1 1 1 0 1 1 0 0 1 1 0 0 1 1 1 1 1]
garbage below stop:  [0 0 1 0 0 1 0 1 0 1 1 1 0 0 1 1 0 0 0 1 0]
intersection:        [0 0 0 0 0 1 0 0 0 1 0 0 0 0 0 0 0 0 0 1 0]
```

The intersection line is where the garbage above start and garbage below stop lines both have true values. For a bit to be set in the graphical output, the audio at any given X point must fall between the upper and lower bounds for the current Y line being drawn. Figure 7-2 shows a nice bass wave for your viewing pleasure.

Figure 7-2. *Example audio data plotted as an image*

NetPBM is a family of formats: PBM, PGM, and PPM. The wpnm() method takes one of those three strings as its second argument. PBM stands for *Portable Bit Map* (1 bit that's black and white), PGM stands for *Portable Gray Map* (black and white), and PPM stands for *Portable Pixel Map* (true color, 8 bits per channel, 24 million colors). perldoc PDL::IO::Pnm has more information on reading and writing PNMs. Get more information on the PBM family of filters from http://netpbm.sourceforge.net and http://acme.com.

■**Signed and unsigned waveforms** Mixing signed and unsigned data causes the speaker to pop between samples, as zero is in a different place. This chapter uses unsigned data. Signed data is normal for the PC, but the Amiga uses unsigned. In the name of oversimplification, the examples here are unsigned.

Swapping Dimensions

PDL has an assortment of methods for exchanging dimensions, removing dimensions, and remapping dimensions. None of these is easily or quickly possible with normal arrays in Perl 5. perldoc PDL::Slices and perldoc PDL::Core document the methods.

transpose() swaps the rows into columns, rotating the data 90 degrees. This isn't what actually happens, but it's what effectively happens. The data doesn't actually move, but the metadata in the PDL array that contains information about the indices is updated, so transposing arrays is extremely quick in PDL.

```
# Transposing an array effectively rotates as columns and rows are swapped
my $zero_to_ninety_nine = PDL->sequence(5, 5);
print $zero_to_ninety_nine;
print $zero_to_ninety_nine->transpose();
```

This example, when run, outputs the following:

```
[
 [ 0  1  2  3  4]
 [ 5  6  7  8  9]
 [10 11 12 13 14]
 [15 16 17 18 19]
 [20 21 22 23 24]
]

[
 [ 0  5 10 15 20]
 [ 1  6 11 16 21]
 [ 2  7 12 17 22]
 [ 3  8 13 18 23]
 [ 4  9 14 19 24]
]
```

xchg() swaps one dimension with another.

```
# Data may be reshaped by swapping dimensions
my $zero_to_ninety_nine = PDL->sequence(5, 5);
print $zero_to_ninety_nine;
print $zero_to_ninety_nine->xchg(0, 1);
```

Arguments are the numbers of the two dimensions you want to swap. They can be any two dimensions. If you have 100-dimensional data, you can swap dimensions 37 and 58, for instance. For a two-dimensional array, exchanging those two dimensions has the same effect as transpose().

reorder() lets you specify the order of the dimensions, potentially moving all of them around. reorer() is from PDL::Core.

clump() merges several dimensions. It's documented in PDL::Core.

dummy() adds a new dimension to data after the fact. Use it to repeatedly to aggregate existing data with new data for use with collapsing operators such as average(). Dummy dimensions use no memory.

Indexing Flattened PDL Arrays

Indices in multidimensional arrays may be single values rather than lists of coordinates. The at() and set() methods take one argument for each dimension of the PDL array, but methods ending with ND, such as whichND() and indexND(), operate on a flattened PDL array, which may have been any number of dimensions before being flattened. whichND() and other functions return PDL arrays full of indices, and it's far easier to operate on flattened copies of a PDL array and represent each element's position as a single value rather than as a variable-sized list of indices. flat() makes a logical copy of the original that shares memory but merely has a different coordinate system, so there's no need to permanently throw away dimensions. The operation is extremely efficient. This is an advanced usage of PDL.

Earlier in the chapter, I gave the following example for selecting a random element from a PDL array with exactly two dimensions, each with a size of 20:

```
# Previous example
use PDL;
my $array = PDL->sequence(20, 20);
my $random_element = $array->at(int rand 20, int rand 20);
print $random_element;
```

The following is a version that works on PDL arrays with any number of dimensions:

```
use PDL;
my $array = PDL->sequence(20, 20);
my $random_element = $array->flat->indexND(int rand $array->nelem());
print $random_element;
```

The indexND() method, documented in perldocPDL::Slices, operates on a PDL array and takes as arguments indices of values to return from the PDL array. This behavior resembles regular Perl array slices. indexND() also accepts a PDL array of positions to look up, in which case the PDL array returned contains multiple items.

Not Covered

PDL is worthy of a whole book. This chapter picks and chooses what *kinds* of things about PDL are most interesting.

One PDL array may serve as a window into another. The slice() syntax, among many others, can create a data structure shaped to provide a specialized view of the data while storing it in a format that another algorithm requires. You'll find this covered in the PDL documentation but not here.

PDL has built-in data persistence as it dumps to numerous formats used by other systems. See PDL::IO::FastRaw and PDL::IO::Pnm. PDL::Impatient mentions other I/O interfaces.

PDL::MatrixOps documents matrix operations. PDL::Impatient has a good, quick introduction to them as well. These are specialized in applications, and people who need them generally know they need them.

PDL::Graphics::TriD renders data as 3D objects using OpenGL or MesaGL in a window and lets the user rotate it in real time. See its documentation for details.

The PDL CPAN distribution installs a command shell, perldl. perldl interactively accepts commands, executing them immediately, features a history facility, and defines shortcuts. See perldoc perldl for information.

The PDL method where() allows operations to be performed on a subset of items from a PDL array. where() works with <, >, ==, and other logic operators. It returns a PDL composed of items for which the logic condition is true, and the resulting PDL may be modified using operators and methods to alter the corresponding values in the original PDL array. See perldoc PDL::Primitive's synopsis of where() for a code example that finds values over a certain value and caps them at that value.

Resources

Apocalypse 9 at http://dev.perl.org covers the mixture of lightweight storage and arrays as it fits into the Perl 6 world. PDL has its own site at http://pdl.perl.org with documentation and screen shots. CPAN's search tool at http://search.cpan.org lists page after page of modules that work with PDL, interfacing the graphics packages, file formats, statistical systems, and other things. If something doesn't come with the main PDL distribution, CPAN is the next stop. Finally, `perldoc PDL::Math` has an excellent example you can try that plots a 3D graph using GL, OpenGL, or MesaGL.

This chapter was written to complement `perldoc PDL::Impatient`, not replace it, so I also strongly recommend reading that documentation. The examples on using overloaded operators alone are worth cracking the cover.

The PDL `any()` and `all()` methods work with matrix operators to allow the programmer to compute a large number of possibilities and then verify that all of them meet some criteria (for example, checking that nothing can go wrong and that all tolerances are within specification) or checking that one of them meets some criteria (for example, if done correctly, the goal is possible). While Chapter 18 deals with these ideas in depth, remember that you can use PDL for a similar sort of mass computation and evaluation of possibility sets.

PDL vectorizes operations, which fits with Perl 6's concept of hyper operators. Speed benefits aside, hyper operators simplify working on sets of data. An expression that can otherwise be written as loops nested two, three, four, or twenty deep becomes simple expressions involving an operator and two PDL arrays. Chapter 6 explains hyper operators.

Summary

PDL is a bit like a closet that's full of toys and in that way is a bit like Perl itself. Chances are good that you can find what you need, and even if you don't, you'll find a lot of other features you'll use later. It's evident that a huge amount of work went into PDL. I've outlined in the chapter's introduction a few domains that PDL helps with: digital signal processing, processing audio and graphic data, and statistics. But that's a simple-minded view. PDL's arrays complement Perl's native arrays perfectly and naturally have boundless uses in day-to-day programming. Any application processing batches of numbers is a candidate for PDL.

Interpreted languages such as Perl 5 aren't suitable for processing large batches of audio and video data directly. The virtual machine is suited to executing high-level, complex operations with good speed. Perl 5's virtual machine isn't suited to executing billions of tiny, low-level operations at blazing speed. Compiled languages, and to a lesser degree Just In Time–compiled languages, are perfect for this, and PDL is an XS Perl extension written in C. This enables PDL to do the tiny, low-level, repetitious number crunching quickly and frees Perl to do the high-level, complex operations.

You can consider PDL to be a language built on top of Perl. Commercial number-crunching environments offer many of the same primitives, but building an environment on top of Perl allows Perl's expressive syntax to shine through, and that's to say nothing of CPAN.

PDL is production-quality software and is widely deployed; it's used for research, data processing, and visualization.

CHAPTER 8

■■■

Data Structures

Show me your flowchart and conceal your tables, and I shall continue to be mystified. Show me your tables, and I won't usually need your flowchart; it'll be obvious.... Smart data structures and dumb code works a lot better than the other way around.

—Fred Brooks, The Mythical Man Month

Sigils and references confuse new Perl programmers. The most visible change in Perl 6, the rethinking of sigils and context, chases the horrors associated with data structures out from under the bed. With a few ideas of when you'd want to use references, you'll be applying them with ease and liberty.

Programming is about algorithms, not functions. Don't get trapped a in mind-set of thinking work gets done by calling the right function, or you'll find yourself clutching a reference book, eternally helpless to solve programming problems. Algorithms, both existing ones and ones you devise, are computer intelligence. Fundamentally, algorithms transform data. Computers are able to perform work because they process data. Whether work gets done by calling a function or by using a module, an algorithm is used either way. By understanding how to represent problems and apply algorithms to the representation, you'll be able to solve problems, not just apply existing solutions that have been bundled with the language. This is important in Perl, as surprisingly few reusable algorithms are built into Perl, and this isn't likely to change. sort() is a notable exception, and math functions such as sqrt() are, of course, algorithms. Perl does offer built-in functions, operators, and syntax to ease writing algorithms. This is a far superior, more general solution to a hard problem. No number of built-in reusable algorithms would ever be enough, but making writing them easier is much more effective than applying a small library of algorithms.

Certain information has little structure. A list of names, for instance, is just a series of items you can lump together in the same mental "bucket". The names are just a collection of items that are alike in more ways than not. By contrast, a list of a person's vital statistics requires some structure. You can't lump all people's names, street addresses, e-mail addresses, cell phone numbers, and locations of tattoos together in an array. If you try, you'll spend an obscene amount of effort trying to force an array to have structure it just doesn't have with rules such as "Every sixth item is a person's name". You can better represent this natural pattern to data by grouping it into units and connecting the units. The arrow, ->, in Perl 5 code and the dot, ., in Perl 6 code represent the logical traversal of the connections between these units of like data. An eye for structure in data will go a long way toward effectively representing it.

This chapter covers Perl6::Contexts, yet another module created on a lark while writing this book. (My project manager wasn't pleased.)

Tom Christiansen's 1996 article, "Seven Deadly Sins of Perl", listed the duality between references and nonreference types as the fourth sin. Programmers expect a reference to work anywhere that a normal array or hash would work, but Perl 5 treats references as second-class citizens. Perl 6 repairs this. References still start with scalars as their sigil, but they dump their contents when used in list context (but not necessarily when used with the list-building operator, ,). The push built-in function can push values onto references without special dereference tricks. They interpolate into double-quoted strings as a hash or array would. As part of the same deadly sin, Tom also cites confusing sigil rules for reference vs. nonreference types, but Perl6::Variables largely clears this up.

Chapter Objectives

First-year computer science students at a popular midwestern university learn C, learn Scheme, and then move onto a class on algorithms. By the time they get to the algorithms class, they already know how to represent real-world objects and structures in memory in various ways so that various algorithms can work on them. When representing the real world in memory, students don't consider only how it can be represented but also how it must be represented to perform the desired operations on it. That is, the algorithm dictates the form the data must take. The structure required for the algorithm may be completely different from what you think the data *is*. Most of this chapter details ways to move data from one representation to another. The process is surprising when you're not used to it.

Data in Perl is represented using hashes, arrays, arrays of arrays, arrays of hashes, hashes of hashes, hashes of arrays, and so on. These are the building blocks of trees, linked lists, doubly linked lists, and graphs, and I'll demonstrate each in this chapter.

This chapter heavily uses the sort built-in function, which extracts lists of keys and values from hashes using the keys and values functions (which are methods in Perl 6). This chapter also introduces a small selection of algorithms, including depth-first recursion and multikeyed sorting.

Chapter 11 is largely about context as it relates to subroutines. This chapter is largely about context as it relates to variables.

Chapter 5 introduced arrays and hashes in their basic form of storing collections of data; refer to that chapter for the basics. You should already understand the relation between lists and arrays. (Arrays hold lists of values, but arrays are variables and lists aren't.) Further, you should understand how to add data items to arrays and hashes.

As noted in Chapter 5, using two variables of different types with the same name is perfectly legal. When this happens, one will usually be a representation of another, but that's just a convention.

Changes for Perl 6

Sigils follow their variable names. A hash named %foo is always referred to as %foo, never $foo, not even when subscripting it. Perl6::Variables accomplishes this in Perl 5.

Built-in operators such as push work on references to arrays as well as on arrays. You no longer need to dereference any reference before using built-in functions on it.

Arrays and hashes turn into references to themselves in scalar context. Hashes didn't have a widely useful scalar context behavior in Perl 5. Arrays in scalar context formerly always returned their length. Their length is available in Perl 6 via `@array.elems,` but a bare array such as `@array` still returns its length in numeric context, meaning it usually does the right thing on its own. `Perl6::Variables` changes Perl 5 to match these new rules.

The `kv` method of hash objects performs several hash manipulations that are commonly done in Perl 5 code. Hashes are initialized using { } rather than ( ).

Hashes can no longer be subscripted with barewords. You must quote the key if it's a constant. A new syntax quotes one or more keys.

Hashes

Hashes associate values. The association is formed with a key and a value. Given the key again, the hash reproduces the same value. Think of a hash as a grouped set of variables.

Changes to Hashes for Perl 6

When an identifier appears in a hash subscript in Perl 5, Perl 5 assumes it's a string constant rather than the name of a function. This is inconsistent with the rest of the language, but it's usually the right thing to do. Sometimes it caused confusion, though.

```
# These two are the same - Perl 5
my $foo = $bar{shift};
my $foo = $bar{'shift'};
```

Many people, myself included, are used to writing `shift` without any parentheses to read the next argument from the function or program argument list, and then they have a hard time remembering that the parentheses are actually required in this case. Perl 6 changes the default to the following:

```
# These two are the same - Perl 6
my $foo = %bar{shift};
my $foo = %bar{shift()};
```

Two basic ways exist to use a string as a hash key in Perl 6.

```
# These two are the same - Perl 6
my $foo = %bar{'baz'};
my $foo = %bar<<baz>>;
```

That last syntax, `%bar<<baz>>`, borrows from the Perl 6 syntax of list quoting. Chapter 4 documents the list-quoting syntax.

Perl 5 hashes dump their key and value, intermixed, into one big, flat list. Perl 6 hashes dump their key-value pairs as a list of pair objects. To get the Perl 5 behavior in Perl 6, use the `kv` method of hashes: `%hash.kv`.

Hashes As Data Structures

Perl doesn't exactly have an equivalent to the C language's `struct` keyword. Perl programmers use Perl hashes for the same purposes, or else they step up to objects.

```
# Hashes store related bits of information
# use Perl6::Variables; # uncomment for Perl 5
%person{'name'} = 'Fred';
%person{'age'}  = 42;
%person{'transportation'} = 'Harley';
```

The `Hash::Util` module's `lock_keys()` function prevents errors where Perl would otherwise silently let you mistype a hash key.

```
use Perl6::Variables;
use Hash::Util 'lock_keys';
%person{'name'} = 'Fred';
%person{'age'}  = 42;
%person{'transportation'} = 'Harley';
lock_keys(%person);
if(%person{'anme'} eq 'Fred') {
    %person{'age'}++;
}
```

This dies with a helpful `Attempt to access disallowed key 'anme' in a restricted hash` message. Use `lock_keys()` on a hash after first initializing which fields it's supposed to have. Values associated with the keys can still change, but keys can't be added, intentionally or accidentally, until the hash is unlocked with `unlock_keys()`.

Hash Size

Hashes don't really have a size, but they can tell you how many items they hold. It's common to count the number of keys.

```
# Number of keys in a hash
keys %hash;      # Perl 5 used in scalar context
int %hash.keys;  # Perl 6 - int is usually optional as context is implied
```

The keys function, when used in numeric context in Perl 6 or in scalar context in Perl 5, returns the number of keys in a hash.

It also makes sense to count the number of defined values if a possibility exists that not every key holds a non-undef value and the distinction is important.

```
# number of non-undef keys in a hash:
my $number_of_non_undef_keys = grep defined, values %hash;      # Perl 5
my $number_of_non_undef_keys = grep { defined }, %hash.values; # Perl 6
```

Nothing in the Perl core will tell you how much memory a hash has consumed.

Iterating Over Hashes

It's often necessary to process, in turn, each key-value pair stored in a hash.

```
my %hash = ( foo => 10, bar => 20 );

# Perl 5 and Perl 6 - common idiom
for my $key (keys %hash) {
    print $key, ' => ', %hash{$key}, "\n";
}

# Perl 6 - suggested idiom
for %hash.kv -> $key, $value {
    print $key, ' => ', %hash{$key}, "\n";
}
```

The Perl 6 idiom resembles the Perl 5 approach using the each built-in.

```
# Perl 5 - iterating over a hash with each()
for((my $key, my $value) = each %hash) {
    print $key, ' => ', %hash{$key}, "\n";
}
```

This never really caught on, probably because the keys arrive unsorted. You can use autobox to iterate over a hash as a method call on the hash.

```
# Perl 5 - iterating as a method on hashes
use Perl6::Variables;
use Perl6::Contexts;
use autobox;
use autobox::Core;
my %hash = ( foo => 10, bar => 20 );
%hash->each(sub {
    my $key = shift;
    my $value = shift;
    print $key, ' => ', $value, "\n";
});
```

This probably won't, and shouldn't, catch on either. I suggest using the common idiom for Perl 5 and the suggested idiom for Perl 6. The following is the common idiom again with a call to sort strategically placed:

```
# Perl 5 and Perl 6 - common idiom with sorting
for my $key (sort keys %hash) {
    print $key, ' => ', %hash{$key}, "\n";
}
```

Sorting a hash gives it the appearance of order.

Parallel Hashes and Simple Data Structures

Anywhere that a program creates multiple arrays and stores data in corresponding elements of arrays, it should probably use an array of hash references or an array of array references instead. Separate arrays where elements are intended to match are *parallel arrays*. For example, given parallel arrays composed of one @names array, one @addresses array, and one @phone_numbers array, you're better off creating one @people array that holds hash references, each with a name, address, and phone field. Structuring this as a data structure composed of an array of hash references lets you sort the data, pass around references to individual records, and add new fields without having to rewrite other parts of the program. Parallel arrays make these operations difficult. You should avoid parallel hashes for the same reasons.

This section uses the problem of parallel hashes to introduce simple data structures. The pieces are chess pieces from a logic puzzle. (Apologies to the author of the puzzle.) They have names: K, B1, B2, Q, and T1 are the king, first bishop, second bishop, queen, and first tower (rook), respectively. When you want to know where a chess piece is on the board, you look in %figs. When you want to know what image is used to draw a chess piece, you look in %images. In this puzzle, the pieces for only one side are on the board, and no pawns exist.

```
# One hash stores piece locations, the other piece images - counter example
# Perl 5
use Perl6::Variables;
my $kings_location = %locations{K};
my $kings_image =    %images{K};
```

These two hashes both have the same fields. You wouldn't create 32 individual little hashes, one for each piece, each with a location key and an image key. That would be silly. What if you had 32 attributes to remember for each of the 32 pieces? What if you had 200 attributes to remember for each of the 32 pieces? Then you'd start seriously thinking about creating 32 individual little hashes, one for each piece. A better way exists. You can remove redundancy by rearranging how things are stored, nesting hashes inside each other (see Figure 8-1).

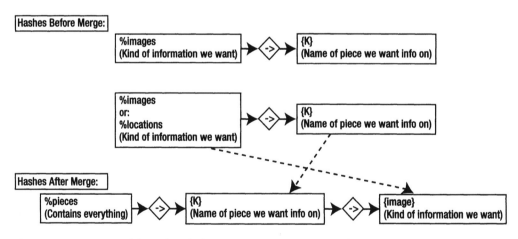

Figure 8-1. *Structure of chess data before and after merging parallel hashes*

The arrows (or dots, in Perl 6) navigate a path to what you're looking for—such as directories and files on a file system. Nesting hashes lets you reuse names. Each name means something different depending on how you navigated there, just as the file /etc/passwd is something other than /home/scott/passwd.

Using this structure looks like the following:

```
# One hash stores all information - Perl 5
use Perl6::Variables;
my $kings_location = %pieces{'K'}{'location'};
my $kings_image    = %pieces{'K'}{'image'};
```

This is a hash of hashes. (More correctly, it's a hash that's full of references to other hashes.) Think of this as a tree (see Figure 8-2).

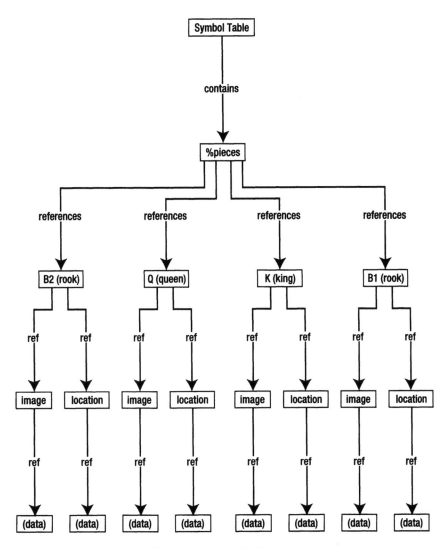

Figure 8-2. *Tree structure of the chess example data structure*

Showing how to construct these data structures is getting ahead of myself, but I've included Listing 8-1 for the sake of completeness, quick reference, and future reference.

Listing 8-1. *Initializing a Hash of Array References vs. Initializing Parallel Hashes*

```
# Counter example - adapted from the amba.pl example included with Prima
# Apologies to Prima
# Perl 5
my %locations = (
    K  => [0, 0],
    B1 => [0, 1],
    B2 => [0, 2],
    Q  => [0, 3],
    T1 => [0, 4],
    # and so on...
);
my %images = (
    K  => $images[1],
    B1 => $images[0],
    B2 => $images[0],
    Q  => $images[3],
    T1 => $images[4],
    # and so on...
);
# These two hashes merged - Perl 5:
use Perl6::Variables;
my %pieces = (
  K => {
      position => [0, 0],
      image    => @images[1],
  },
  B1 => {
      position => [0, 1],
      image    => @images[0],
  },
  B2 => {
      position => [0, 2],
      image    => @images[0],
  },
  Q => {
      position => [0, 3],
      image    => @images[3],
  },
  T1 => {
      position => [0, 4],
      image    => @images[4],
  },
  # and so on...
);
```

```
# Those two hashes merged - Perl 6:
my %pieces = {
  K => {
      position => [0, 0],
      image    => @images[1],
  },
  B1 => {
      position => [0, 1],
      image    => @images[0],
  },
  B2 => {
      position => [0, 2],
      image    => @images[0],
  },
  Q => {
      position => [0, 3],
      image    => @images[3],
  },
  T1 => {
      position => [0, 4],
      image    => @images[4],
  },
  # and so on...
};
```

Again, this is here for the sake of completeness only. See the "References" section later in the chapter for a discussion of how to initialize arrays and hashes. Basically, nested names are used in data structures to get at buried bits. %pieces{'K'}{'location'}, from this example, first goes into %pieces, then looks up K in that, and then expects another hash, and finally looks up location in there.

Exists, Defined, True, and False

As Chapter 4 explained, a value may be true, false, or undefined. Arrays and hashes are slightly more complex, because an array subscript or a hash key may not exist at all. Then the value isn't only undefined, but the undefined value isn't even there. The exists built-in provides this test. To be true, a value must exist, be defined, and contain a true value.

If you initialize the hash and then lock the keys, you'll always know what keys are in it. However, most hashes are built in an ad-hoc style. Which keys a hash contains depend on the data set. The %ENV hash contains the current user's path, home directory, and a wealth of other information provided by the operating system and dependent on the operating system and configuration. It's impossible to guess what keys may be in there.

```
# Possible states of a value stored in a hash by a key - Perl 5
use Perl6::Variables;
my $key; my %hash;
```

```
# Uncomment one of these to trigger the corresponding test
# $key = 'test'; %hash{'something_else'} = 'hi there'; # doesn't exist case
# $key = 'test'; %hash{$key} = undef;                  # undef value case
# $key = 'test'; %hash{$key} = 0;                      # false value case
# $key = 'test'; %hash{$key} = 'hi there';             # true value case
exists  %hash{$key} or print "$key doesn't exist\n";
defined %hash{$key} or print "$key indexes an undef value\n";
%hash{$key}         or print "%hash{$key} is a false value\n";
%hash{$key}         and print "%hash{$key} is a true value\n";
```

These same operations, exists() and defined(), work on arrays and perform similar tests. exists() can tell you whether an array element ever had a value even if it contains undef.

```
# Does an array element exist?
# use Perl6::Variables; # uncomment for Perl 5
my @arr;
@arr[0] = undef;
# no value for @arr[1] is specified
@arr[2] = 1;
print '@arr[0] ', exists @arr[0] ? 'exists' : 'does not exist', "\n";
print '@arr[1] ', exists @arr[1] ? 'exists' : 'does not exist', "\n";
```

This outputs the following:

```
$arr[0] exists
$arr[1] does not exist
```

People don't like to think about whether an array index exists and instead assume that everything between 0 and @array.end or $#array is valid. This assumption is fine, because Perl makes it just work, but this meta-information is available to anyone who cares.

Although this example just works, you may have noticed that $arr[0] is printed instead of @arr[0]. This glitch is a side effect of Perl6::Variables being implemented as a source filter. Perl6::Variables munged @arr[0] and @arr[1] in the single quotes back to Perl 5 native style, where $arr[0] is the correct syntax for subscripting a single element from an array and @arr[0] is used only to take slices (multiple subscripts) from an array. Altering the contents of literal strings is one of the more innocuous ways source filters can go wrong. In this case, you may safely pretend you didn't see this little slip-up.

The Perl standard documentation for exists, available from the shell as perldoc -f exists, has a far better table of the possibilities.

Arrays

Chapter 5 introduced arrays, and Chapter 7 revisited them. An index, rather than a key as in hashes, is used to look up items in an array. Indexes must be numbers, but they can be numbers computed by arbitrary expressions. Arrays are faster than hashes and use less memory when the indices are small and nonsparse. Using a very large number as an index allocates an array large enough to hold elements from 0 to that element. Hashes do no such thing.

Jagged Arrays

Perl grows arrays as needed, and *jagged arrays* naturally result.

```
  my @datastructure = (
    [0, 1, 2],
    [3, 4],
    [5, 6, 7, 8, 9, 10],
);
```

[0, 1, 2] constructs an entire array without having to name it and returns a reference to that new array. Assuming Perl6::Variables, @datastructure[0] contains a reference to an array with three elements, @datastructure[1] references an array with two elements, and @datastructure[2] contains a reference to one with six elements. This isn't one array with multiple dimensions but instead an array that's full of references to other arrays. Each array has one dimension. In other words, native Perl 5 arrays and Perl 6 arrays not declared with is dim are arrays that can hold other arrays by reference. To subscript an array of arrays, you'd write @arr[$x][$y], not @arr[$x, $y], unless you created a Perl 6 array with is dim and provided sizes for two dimensions. This knowledge isn't critical to using arrays, but it may help you conceptualize what's happening.

Even if you start with a perfectly rectangular array, it's possible to modify it into something that isn't rectangular.

```
# Add a random element to a random array in an array of arrays - Perl 5
use autobox;
use autobox::Core;
@datastructure[int rand @$datastructure]->push(int rand 10);
```

This invokes the push() method on a random element of the @datastructure array. The ARRAY class contains the push() method, and the ARRAY class is created and specified by autobox and autobox::Core. Calling methods in primitive datatypes such as arrays is called *autoboxing*; this example uses the autoboxing syntax to avoid having to explicitly dereference Perl 5 references in order to use them with built-ins such as push(). (Chapter 14 introduces the autoboxing syntax properly.) Autoboxing allows you to push onto an array reference (and otherwise use references) without having to first dereference them.

Unless you're using the Perl Data Language (PDL) in Perl 5 or using is dim in Perl 6, your arrays will grow as needed. (Chapter 7 introduced PDL.)

Array Length

The last element of an array is always one less than the number of elements in the array. Perl doesn't use two different numbering systems in an attempt to confuse you. This is an age-old problem that's well-known to ranchers. It's widely known that to put up a length of fence, you need one more fence post than you do lengths of fence, because something has to secure the last length. So, to put up 100 lengths of fence, you'll need 101 fence posts. Whenever you're thinking about arrays, be explicit about whether you're counting the lengths of fence (the index of the last thing in the array) or the fence posts (the number of things in the array). Getting this wrong results in an "off-by-one error". Falling into this trap can yield incorrect results by failing to process the last element of an array. It can cause the program to abort with a fatal error when it attempts to work on a nonexistent array element by doing something such as trying to dereference undef (but see the example at the end of Chapter 16 about calling methods on undef for a way to safely trap even this error).

```
# Finding the index of the last element of an array and the number of elements
# in an array

use Perl6::Contexts;
use autobox;
use autobox::Core;

# Index of the last element in an array:

@array->last;      # Perl 5, using autobox and company
@array.last;       # Perl 6 tentative method name

# Number of elements in an array:

scalar @array;     # Perl 5
int    @array;     # Perl 6

0 + @array;        # Perl 5 with Perl6::Contexts
  + @array;        # Perl 6

@array->elems;     # Perl 5 using autobox and company
@array.elems;      # Perl 6 tentative method name
```

An array such as @array, used in a numeric context, evaluates to its number of elements. This applies to both Perl 5 under Perl6::Contexts and Perl 6. You can request numeric context in Perl 6 with the num keyword. The Perl 5 way to find the last element of an array, @array, is $#array, but @array->last is more mnemonic. @array->last in Perl 5 requires Perl6::Contexts, autobox, and autobox::Core. You're better off writing $#array for applications to be distributed or to run on servers you don't control, because autobox requires a patch to the Perl interpreter.

Iterating over Arrays

It's easier to iterate over an array than to figure out how many elements it contains.

```
# Successively better idioms for iterating over array elements:

use Perl6::Variables;
use Perl6::Contexts;
use autobox;
use autobox::Core;
my @array = ( 1 .. 10 );

# Error prone and verbose, but familiar to C programmers.
# Provides the current index which is sometimes needed.
# Perl 5:

for(my $index; $index < @array; $index++ ) { print @array[$index], "\n"; }
```

```
# Error prone and verbose but familiar to C programmers - Perl 6:

loop(my $index; $index < @array; $index++ ) { print @array[$index], "\n"; }

# Useful for when both the index, $index, and the element, @array[$index],
# are needed - Perl 5 and Perl 6:

for my $index (0 .. @array->last) { print @array[$index], "\n"; }

# Idiomatic - using the autobox idiom:
@array->foreach(sub { my $element = shift; print $element, "\n"; });

# Best - requires none of the above modules:

for my $element (@array) { print $element, "\n"; }
```

The last of these is the standard idiom for iterating over each element of an array. $element is an alias to the current element of @array, which allows the easy modification of the array elements in a loop.

@array->foreach() gives the code block only the current element.

@array->for()'s first argument to the code block is the current index, the second argument is the current element, and the last is a reference back to the array being iterated over. This is more complex and more powerful than the other autoboxed idioms, and it follows the design of the loop statement in Perl 6.

Negative Indexes Are Relative to the End of the Array

@array[-1] is the last element of any array that has elements. @array[-2] is the second-to-last element, and so on. You could query the last index of the array and use it as a subscript to perform the same task, but this is neater.

As a side effect of @array[-1] indexing the last element of an array, the following code creates a ring buffer using doubly linked lists:

```
# Build a circular doubly linked list - Perl 5
use Perl6::Variables;
my @row = map {}, 1 .. 10;
for my $i (0 .. $#row) {
    @row[$i - 1]{'right'} = @row[$i];
    @row[$i]{'left'} = @row[@i - 1];
}
```

A circular doubly linked list is a list where each node links to the next node and to the previous node. @row holds your nodes while you work on them. The last element in @row links to the first as its right, and the first element in @row links to the last for its left. Essentially the two ends are connected, like an extension cord plugged into itself.

map {}, 1 .. 10 builds a list of ten hash references, though you can change this number, and it will just work.

The expression @row[]{} combines an array subscript with a hash subscript. Whatever @row[$i] evaluates to gets used as a hash reference.

```
# Build a circular doubly linked list - Perl 6
my @row = map hash {}, 1 .. 10;
for my $i (0 .. @row.size) {
    @row[$i - 1]{'right'} = @row[$i];
    @row[$i]{'left'} = @row[@i - 1];
}
```

{} looks like an empty block in Perl 6, so the hash keyword is used in this example to force it to be a hash constructor.

Lists

Perl works with multiple values as easily as it does with single values. Lists can be function call arguments, and they can serve as values to initialize an array with, as values to iterate over in a for statement, as lists of values to assign to, and, in Perl 5, as ways of hinting that an expression should return multiple values. Hyper operators, mentioned in Chapter 6, are part of this same trend.

■**Lists aren't arrays** You can use lists to initialize arrays. Both arrays and lists represent multiple ordered values. Arrays are variables and can be modified by operators and functions that alter arrays. Remember, you can't modify lists. I outlined this distinction in the section "Lists Aren't Arrays" in Chapter 5 and the section "Lists Are Constants" in Chapter 4.

Commas and Parentheses Build Lists

(3) is a list of one thing. Parentheses, whether around an expression or around a variable an expression is assigned to, build up a list—assuming that a list is expected (that is, assuming list context). List context is how Perl knows it's working on more than one value at once. The following are both lists:

```
# Examples of lists:
somefunction 1, 2, 3;    # list of arguments
(1, 2, 3);               # parentheses signal a list is being built
```

Perl 6 retires the comma from separating expressions; do { } does that just fine. Instead, commas only build lists. Parentheses are still useful for clarifying otherwise ambiguous constructs.

```
# Parentheses with lists clarify what is being done - ambiguous:

my $a, my $b = somefunction;

# Which of these two did the programmer intend?
(my $a, my $b) = somefunction;    # somefunction() returns two values
(my $a, (my $b = somefunction)); # somefunction() returns one value
```

Perl picks the second of the two cases, which often isn't what's intended.

In Perl 5, parentheses are required to build a list when initializing an array.

```
# Doesn't do what it might look like in Perl 5 nor probably Perl 6
my @arr = 'foo', 'bar', 'baz';
```

The prize from this beauty is the following:

```
Useless use of a constant in void context at - line 3.
Useless use of a constant in void context at - line 3.
```

This happens because the previous is the same as the following:

```
# Silly - Perl 5:
(my @arr = 'foo'), 'bar', 'baz';
```

Remember to use parentheses when building lists or accepting lists.

The only other time you can build lists without parentheses in Perl 5 is during a function call.

```
# Function calls expect lists
some_function 'foo', 'bar', 'baz';
```

Perl 6 method calls also relax the requirement for parentheses.

List Flattening

You can build one list from other lists.

```
# These two lists are the same - Perl 5 and Perl 6
(1, (2, 3, (4), (5, 6), (7, 8, 9)))
(1, 2, 3, 4, 5, 6, 7, 8, 9)
```

Test this with print $_, "\n" for(1, (2, 3)).

The first is actually a list that contains other lists, but when perl evaluates it, perl builds a single list. That is, perl *flattens* it.

Arrays included in the list flattened in the same way.

```
my @two_through_five = (2, 3, 4, 5);
my @one_through_nine = (1, @two_through_five, 6, 7, 8, 9);
print $_, "\n" for @one_through_nine;
```

Perl doesn't stand for anything, but Larry Wall later decided perhaps it should stand for Pathologically Eclectic Rubbish Lister, or perhaps the Practical Extracting and Reporting Language. CPAN stands for the Comprehensive Perl Archive Network. Pretending that PERL stands for one of those and supposing that CPAN really stands for the Comprehensive PERL Archive Network, the *P* in CPAN stands for four letters, not one word. Some hypothetical acronym purists could argue that CPAN should properly be CPERLAN. After all, the statements my @PERL = qw(Pathologically Eclectic Rubbish Lister) and my @CPAN = ('Comprehensive', @PERL, 'Archive', 'Network') when printed clearly support the hypothetical acronym purists' ideas.

```
# According to Perl's list-flattening rules, CPAN should really be CPERLAN
# Perl 5:
my @PERL = qw(Pathologically Eclectic Rubbish Lister);
my @CPAN = ('Comprehensive', @PERL, 'Archive', 'Network');
print map( { substr($_, 0, 1) } @CPAN), "\n";
```

Perhaps it's better for Perl not to stand for anything after all.

According to Perl's concept of lists, items in lists in lists don't vanish or abbreviate when the list is evaluated.

The Null List

'' is the null string. (That's two apostrophes right next to each other, not a double quote.) If you add the null string to the end of a string, the string remains unchanged. () is the null list. If you push it onto the end of an array, the array is unchanged. You can flatten numerous arrays into a list with a result of fewer values than arrays from which it was built. This isn't surprising if you realize that null lists vanish.

```
# Countdown is "1, 2, 3, 4, 5" except for King Arthur, in which case it is
# "1, 2, 5".
# Perl 5:
my @countdown = (1, 2, $name eq 'Arthur' ? () : (3, 4), 5);
# Perl 6:
my @countdown = (1, 2, $name eq 'Arthur' ?? () :: (3, 4), 5);
```

Chapter 11 introduces the null list as a useful return value, and Chapter 4 talks about truth and falsehood, including that the only false array is the array that contains only the null list.

Initializing Hashes and Arrays

You can use lists in Perl 5 to initialize both hashes and arrays.

```
# Lists initialize hashes and arrays in Perl 5
my %numbers = ( one => 1, two => 2, three => 3 );
my @numbers = ( 0, 1, 2, 3, 4, 5, 6 );
```

It's important to remember that ( ) doesn't construct an array. It merely builds an aggregation of data that's used to initialize @numbers or %numbers. That data is copied into an existing array or hash. The same happens when an array is assigned to another array, when an array is assigned to a hash, and so on.

[ ], besides subscripting arrays, builds arrays. { }, besides subscripting hashes, builds hashes. Both return references to the thing they've built, as that's the only way to refer to something that doesn't have a name. Obviously you're not going to talk about something by name if it's anonymous.

```
# Arrays may be initialized from anonymous array references or lists - Perl 6
my @numbers = ( 0, 1, 2, 3, 4, 5, 6 );    # init an array from a list
my @numbers = [ 0, 1, 2, 3, 4, 5, 6 ];    # init an array from an anon array


# Hashes may be initialized from anonymous hash references or a list of pairs -
# Perl 6
my %numbers = ( one => 1, two => 2, three => 3 ); # init hash from pairs list
my %numbers = { one => 1, two => 2, three => 3 }; # init hash from hash ref
```

Perl 5 isn't capable of initializing hashes and arrays directly from anonymous hashes and arrays constructed with { } and [ ], so you must use ( ) instead. (Otherwise, you must first dump the contents of the hash or array built with { } or [ ] as a list, or, alternatively, you must make an alias.) This last Perl example, %numbers = { }, yields a fatal warning in Perl 5, giving the message Reference found where even-sized list expected. @numbers = [ ] isn't a warning in Perl 5 because it does something that may be useful, but you almost certainly mean @numbers = ( ) instead.

When you see a list and an assignment, remember that it means to copy in the list of values. For Perl 6, when you see a hash or array anonymous constructor ({ } and [ ], respectively), the constructed array or hash gets stored directly into the variable and isn't copied.

```
# Preferred method of initializing arrays and hashes in Perl 6
my @numbers = [ 0, 1, 2, 3, 4, 5, 6 ];    # init an array from an anon array
my %numbers = { one => 1, two => 2, three => 3 }; # init hash from hash ref
```

Perl 5 always initializes arrays and hashes from a list.

```
# Initializing arrays and hashes in Perl 5
my @numbers = ( 0, 1, 2, 3, 4, 5, 6 );               # init an array from a list
my %numbers = ( one => 1, two => 2, three => 3 ); # init hash from list
```

Perl 5 and Perl 6 both create references the same way—by using the anonymous array and anonymous hash syntax.

```
# Creating references to anonymous hashes and arrays
# Perl 5 and Perl 6
my $numbers = [ 0, 1, 2, 3, 4, 5, 6 ];     # init reference with an anon array
my $numbers = { one => 1, two => 2, three => 3 }; # init with hash ref
```

I'm not initializing a reference here, just creating it. $numbers wasn't a reference before I stored something in it. @numbers, on the other hand, was an array before I stored something in it.

Perl 6 will usually do the right thing when it sees a set of { }, whether the right thing is to create an anonymous subroutine or to construct a hash. Should you feel the need to clarify, use the hash context–generating keyword.

```
# Hint to the Perl 6 compiler using context that we're creating a hash
my $numbers = hash { some_function_that_returns_pairs() };
```

Without the hash, Perl 6 would create an anonymous subroutine.

You can build pairs from lists in Perl 6.

```
# Building hashes from lists in Perl 6 - these lines are equivalent
my %numbers = { one => 1, two => 2, three => 3; };       # normal case
my %numbers = { pair 'one', 1, 'two', 2, 'three', 3; };
my %numbers = { pair qw/one 1 two 2 three 3/ };
my %numbers = { pair <<one 1 two 2 three 3>> };
my %numbers = hash { pair <<one 1 two 2 three 3>> };
```

The pair keyword takes a list and returns pairs. { } turns these into a hash.

The Perl developers have hinted that lists may also create references when used in that context, but they've given no final word.

Both lists and arrays can be subscripted. (Actually, lists, arrays, and array references can be subscripted.) You can use both lists and arrays as arguments to grep, map, for, and numerous other statements and built-ins that don't (necessarily) modify their arguments.

The for statement is a borderline case. The iterator is an alias to each item in the list in turn. If you attempt to modify the iterator when iterating over a list, you'll get a nice Modification of a read-only value attempted message.

```
# Items stored in a variable may be modified by an iterator
my $thing = "horse";
my @numbers = (1 .. 20);
```

```
for my $i ($thing, @numbers, qw(30 31 32 33 34)) {
    $i++;
    print $i, "\n";
}
```

This gets all the way through the items in @numbers before failing to modify the items from the qw().

Initialization Saves Repeated Assignment

Anything you do with the initialization syntax you can also do with repeated single assignments. The initialization syntax just saves you some typing. Note that *the initialization syntax* isn't really a special phrase in Perl jargon; it's just a term I'm using here to describe the process.

```
# Assuming %foo{'bar'} is empty, these two lines perform the same
# initialization - Perl 5 or Perl 6
%foo{'bar'} = ["fred"];
%foo{'bar'}[0] = "fred";
```

These lines are interchangeable *only* when nothing is already stored at %foo{'bar'}, because the first of the two complete replaces the value stored there, possibly obliterating an array reference stored there. This is fine if you're initializing a new data structure. The second inserts "fred" into an existing array (by reference), creating the array if no value is already there.

More verbosely, it's true that the following two sets of statements are equivalent ways to initialize:

```
%foo{'bar'} = ['fred', 'mike', 'alex', 'john'];

%foo{'bar'}[0] = 'fred';
%foo{'bar'}[1] = 'mike';
%foo{'bar'}[2] = 'alex';
%foo{'bar'}[3] = 'john';
```

When initializing a new data structure, use the concise syntax.

Variables and Context

An @array in scalar context returns a reference to itself.... This is the big change. It's what allows us to treat arrays as objects and call methods on them like @array.length. I don't think anyone will argue that's not a good thing.

　　　　　　　　　—Michael Lazzaro of cognitivity.com in a post to the perl6 language list.

Context boils down to expecting a value of a certain type and magically getting it. Expressions both provide context and respond to context.

▪Note http://cognitivity.com hosts an excellent resource on the Perl 6 language.

As Mark Jason Dominus puts it, "Context always comes from the left". The variable, or the list of variables, being assigned to dictates the context. An enclosing expression dictates what kind of return value from a function is expected (though it may not always get what it wants).

Scalar context has been subdivided into boolean context, numeric context, integer context, string context, reference context, and others. List context is the opposite. List context is the generic case where more than one value is expected.

List Context Assignment

Perl 6 introduces the splat operator, *, for explicitly flattening arrays. Perl 5 flattens arrays implicitly (unless Perl6::Contexts is in use). Perl 6 also introduces hyper operators that will happily assign element by element—oblivious of whether its arguments are references, lists, or arrays. This bypasses the powerful but sometimes troublesome context semantics of Perl 6. * forces a list to be expanded at run time and necessarily defers any consideration for context or prototype until the expression is actually evaluated.

Arrays and hashes always act differently depending on context. This section introduces context rules using assignment as a simple case to start.

Two basic cases exist: array assignment and scalar assignment. Scalar assignments look like $foo = ... Array assignments look like @arr = ...

The following are some examples of list context assignment, where the expression being assigned to is either a list or an array, and the expression being assigned from is either a list or an array:

```
# Examples of assignment in list context

# Typical boring list context assignment - this copies one array to another

@one_array = @another_array;

# Initializing an array from a list built of scalars

@array = ($foo, $bar, $baz, $quux);

# Initializing a list of variables from an array

($foo, $bar, $baz, $quux) = @array;      # Perl 5
($foo, $bar, $baz, $quux) = * @array;    # Perl 6
```

Lists are normally constant, but Perl builds a list of individual things that can be assigned to in this last case. Assigning the array to the list doesn't modify the list but instead modifies the scalars that compose the list.

It's equivalent to the following:

```
# Initialize a list of variables from an array, the long way
# use Perl6::Variables; # for Perl 5
$foo = @array[0];
$bar = @array[1];
$baz = @array[2];
$quux = @array[3];
```

Note that any of these cases could have used variable binding rather than assignment. You do this in Perl 6 with the binding operator, :=, or in Perl 5 with the alias keyword from Data::Alias.

In Perl 6, you must specify * when something should flatten. In Perl 5, you must specify \ when something *shouldn't* flatten.

Perl6::Contexts changes Perl 5's semantics to match Perl 6's. Because no splat operator is available in Perl 5 (as it previously wasn't needed), the flatten() method needs to be called on an array to flatten it.

Without the splat operator in the Perl 6 example, ($foo, $bar, $baz, $quux) = * @array, $foo would get a reference to @array, and $bar, $baz, and $quux would remain unmodified.

Assigning to a list provides list context to the expression on the right of the assignment. The following two lines are equivalent:

```
# Using a single variable in a list as a way of providing list context
# and picking out the first return value - Perl 5
(my $first_match) = $str =~ m/(\w+)/g;
my $first_match = ($str =~ m/(\w+)/g)[0];
```

Assigning to a list of one scalar is easier on the eyes than putting the parentheses around (or, in Perl 6, placing the list keyword before) the expression to be executed in list context.

Most people (but not myself) use array assignments to read subroutine and method parameters in Perl 5.

```
# List assignment to read function parameters, Perl 5
sub foo {
    my($bar, $baz, $quux) = @_;
}
```

I like to shift my arguments one at a time, because I find lots of bracketing characters unsightly, and reading one per line leaves room for comments. Write what feels good to you.

Note that my can operate on a list at once, but the parentheses are required.

```
# Perl 5 - these two lines are equivalent
my($bar, $baz, $quux) = @_;
(my $bar, my $baz, my $quux) = @_;
```

@_ is the list of parameters inside a function or method call in Perl 5 and is the list of arguments to the program outside a function or method.

The following is another example of assigning to a list of variables:

```
# Read a pbm/ppm/pnm file - Perl 5
# The first 3 lines look something like this:
# P3
# 492 402
# 255
# The rest is image data, which may be binary or ASCII formatted
open my $ppm, '<', 'foo.ppm' or die $!;
(my $version, my $dimensions, my $color_depth, my @image_data) = <$ppm>;
close $ppm;
```

Here it is again, this time in Perl 6:

```
# Read the headers of a pbm/ppm/pnm file - Perl 6
my $ppm = open '<', 'foo.ppm' or die $!;
(my $version, my $dimensions, my $color_depth, * my @image_data) = <$ppm>;
close $ppm;
```

You can assign to any list of lvalues. Some built-in functions are valid lvalues and can be assigned to as part of a list or otherwise. perldoc perlfunc lists the built-in functions that are valid as an lvalue, and the "Lvalue Subroutines" section of perldoc perlsub documents the concept.

$version gets the first line of the file (P3 in this case), $dimensions gets the second line, $color_depth gets the third line, and @image_data gets all the rest. Each remaining line of the file becomes an element in @image_data. <$ppm> executes in array context because of the parentheses around the variables on the left of =. In scalar context, it returns a single value: the next line. In list context, it returns the entire file as a list, each line its own value. PBM (which stands for *portable bitmap*) is a widely supported, noncompressed, easy-to-read, easy-to-write format. See http://netpbm.sourceforge.net and http://www.acme.com for more information.

Again, contexts are universal in Perl, but assignment is an easy scenario with which to start.

Scalar Context Assignment

Scalar context assignment is the act of assigning a value to a scalar. Without Perl6::Contexts, arrays in scalar context in Perl 5 return their number of elements. Perl 6 subdivides scalar context into string context, boolean context, reference context, numeric context, and others. The default scalar context in Perl 6 is reference context—something that doesn't exist in Perl 5 before Perl6::Contexts's approximation of it.

```
# Reference and numeric context - Perl 6
$foo = @array;      # Perl 6 - $foo becomes a reference to @array
$foo = + @array;    # Perl 6 - $foo gets the number of elements in @array
```

Here, + forces numeric context, changing @array's scalar context behavior. @array % 4 will evaluate to zero if the number of elements in @array is a multiple of four. if(), and, and others force boolean context, and string operations such as join and Perl 6's ~~ force string context. For most operations, @array will interpret itself in the way that you happen to desire and, when it doesn't, use a context modifier such as str, int, bool, num, or so on. Reference context is provided by push and . (the method call operator and subscript operator in Perl 6), and it's assumed during scalar assignments where no evidence exists to the contrary, as in the previous example.

Perl6::Contexts rewrites the rules for Perl 5, approximating Perl 6's numeric, string, and reference contexts.

```
use Perl6::Contexts;
$foo = @array;      # Perl 5 - $foo gets a reference to @array
$foo = 0 + @array;  # Perl 5 - $foo gets the number of elements in @array
```

->, the method call and subscript operator in Perl 5, provides reference context, as does the default assignment case. For technical reasons, the zero is actually required in Perl 5 but is redundant in Perl 6.

Both Perl 5 and Perl 6 recognize the backslash character, \, as the reference creation operator. Explicitly asking for a reference during assignment sure doesn't hurt.

```
$foo = \@array;        # Perl 5 and Perl 6 - take a reference to @array
```

Assigning a hash or array to a subscript of an array or hash produces reference context.

```
# Perl 5 and Perl 6 - store an array in an array
# use Perl6::Contexts;  # uncomment for Perl 5
# use Perl6::Variables; # uncomment for Perl 5
use Data::Dumper;
my @laundry;
my @shirts = ('the green retro t-shirt', 'red button up one with patterns');
my @socks = ('black nylon one', 'black cotton one', 'white jogging sock');
@laundry[0] = @shirts;
@laundry[1] = @socks;
print Dumper @laundry;
```

Reference context makes building data structures much easier. Because this is done with references, remember that @laundry[0][0] and @shirts[0] refer to the same value. Changing one affects the other. In this example, @shirts and @socks evaluate in reference context. To make a copy during assignment, do @laundry[0] = [@shirts] instead.

In Perl 5, before the world was graced with Perl6::Contexts, code such as this wouldn't do the right thing. @laundry would be an array of the number of shirts and socks to be washed, not an array of the actual names of the articles of clothing to be washed.

These rules apply to hashes as well. A hash can be stored inside another hash using only assignment, thanks to reference context.

Lists and Hyper Operators

Operators can provide context, too. Hyper operators provide list context to the expressions on either side of the operator. Hyper operators start with two greater-than signs and end with two less-than signs but otherwise appear the same as other operators. This is the hyper add:

```
>>+<<
```

And you use it like so:

```
my @sums = @column_a >>+<< @column_b;
```

Chapter 6 introduced hyper operators, but I want you to know that hyper operators are an alternative to flattening with the splat operator. Since a hyper operator expects lists on either side, it will turn an array reference into an array or a list reference into a list.

```
# Using hyper assignment to force list context on both side and store return
# values in a list - Perl 6
my string @strs >>=<< get_a_bunch_of_strings();
```

While unavailable in Perl 5, this is likely to become the preferred method of assigning lists of values to arrays.

References

References let you store a hash or array inside another hash or array. They also let you pass entire data structures to subroutines.

The "Parallel Hashes" section contains an example of storing a hash inside a hash. The previous "Lists" section contains examples of simple initializations. The previous "Scalar

Context Assignment" section contains an example of storing an array inside an array. The following sections spell out the specific rules and give more complex examples of dealing with nested data structures.

{ }, [ ], and \ all produce references. References are the keys to building data structures. They let two different sections of code access the same data structure where scoping rules wouldn't permit it otherwise, without having to store the data globally. This allows you to efficiently make large data structures available to subroutines by passing a reference to the data rather than making a copy.

Data Structures, References, and Stricture

strict and warnings help immensely when learning and using data structures. strict will stop you if you try to use something as a reference that isn't a reference. warnings recognizes and complains about many expressions that lack useful behavior or are almost certainly mistyped. This is invaluable when navigating complex data structures. See Chapter 3 for more information.

Scalar Variables as References

So far I've demonstrated using hashes to store hashes and using arrays to store arrays, which is the normal, natural thing to do.

```
# Basic hash and array usage, for contrast
# use Perl6::Variables # uncomment for Perl 5
my %hash_var;
my @array_var;
%hash_var{'ten'} = 10;      # %hash_var is a hash
@array_var[10] = 10;        # @array_var is an array
```

The following is the same thing again but with scalar variables containing the hash and array variables:

```
# Storing arrays and hashes by reference in scalars
# Perl 5
my $hash_ref;
my $array_ref;

$hash_ref->{'ten'} = 10;    # $hash_ref is a hash reference
$array_ref->[10] = 10;      # $array_ref is an array reference
```

Notice that both variables look the same in that they start with $. They have the same sigil, and that's the sigil of a scalar. Using a scalar as a hash or array reference causes it to become a hash or array reference. This is called *autovivication*. The hash or array springs into life automatically. This happens when the scalar is assigned to or otherwise modified, such as with push, and it doesn't already contain a different kind of value or reference.

The following shows the same thing again, this time in Perl 6:

```
# Storing arrays and hashes by reference in scalars
# Perl 6
my $hash_ref;
my $array_ref;
```

```
$hash_ref.{'ten'} = 10;    # $hash_ref is a hash reference
$array_ref.[10] = 10;      # $array_ref is an array reference
```

The dot, ., replaces the arrow, ->, but is optional in this case. Perl 6 can usually tell when a dereference is needed.

A reference is a scalar. Taking a reference to a hash or array means indirectly storing the hash or array in a scalar. The scalar stands in for the array or hash. It's usable in any way that the array or hash is, but it's only a bit of indirection. It's only a stand-in, not a copy.

Because a scalar can contain a hash, an array, an object reference, a regular expression (rule) reference, or a reference to a number of other things, you may accidentally try to use one reference as two different things at two different points in your code. This is an error.

```
# Illegal - uses $foo as a hash reference and then as an array reference
# Perl 5

my $foo;
$foo->{'ten'} = 10;    # $foo is a hash reference
$foo->[10] = 10;    # can't use $foo as an array reference - already a hash ref
# Output:
# Not an ARRAY reference at - line 4
```

Since $foo holds a hash reference after the $foo.{'ten'} = 10 line runs, $foo->[10] = 10 tries to do an array operation on a hash reference. This dies with an error message.

Interpolating References in Doubled-Quoted Strings

In Chapter 4, I gave examples for interpolating scalars, arrays, hashes, and expressions, but I said nothing about references. Here's how to interpolate a reference:

```
# Interpolating and subscripting hash references
"Hi, $person->{name}\n"; # Perl 5
"Hi, $person{'name'}\n"; # Perl 6

# Interpolating and subscripting array references
"It's $days->[1] today\n"; # Perl 5
"It's $days[1] today\n";    # Perl 6
```

Under Perl6::Variables and in Perl 6, regular nonreference array and hash interpolations look like "It's @days[1] today\n" and "Hi, %person{'name'}\n", respectively.

References Share Data

Any number of references can point to the same data.

```
# References may be copied but the data is shared - Perl 5 and Perl 6
my $e = CGI->new();
my $f = $e;
```

Both $e and $f hold the same value, but they're separate containers. This value happens to be an object reference. Even though the reference was copied, it still references the same object, and any methods called using the reference affect this shared object.

Often you'll build an array of references in a loop.

```
# Build a data structure from a file, Perl 5
use Perl6::Variables;
open my $f, '<', 'file.txt' or die $!;
my @records;
while(<$f>) {
    chomp;
    my @columns = split /\|/, $_;
    push @records, \@columns;
}
```

Then, you can use @records[$line][$column] to fetch a value from a given column of a given line. Be careful not to declare @columns outside the loop, or else a reference to the same variable will be added to @records for each iteration. Every line will appear to contain the same data, which is the data from the last line of the file.

Don't worry about a speed penalty from creating a new lexical each pass-through. The same memory will be reused each time unless a new lexical needs to be allocated. Failing to get a new array each pass-through is a common "gotcha". Remember that my, when executed, makes sure you have a truly private, unique variable, even though the primary behavior of my is to allocate a variable at compile time. Using [ ] and { } avoids the lexical scope problem, as they always construct a new array or hash.

```
# Build a data structure from a file, Perl 5
use Perl6::Variables;
open my $f, '<', 'file.txt' or die $!;
my @records;
while(<$f>) {
    chomp;
    push @records, [ split /\|/, $_ ];
}
```

Nothing is special about enclosing an expression inside [ ]; the result of the code is used as the list of values from which to build an array.

Built-in Functions and References

The syntax for pushing onto an array pointed to by a reference has changed between Perl 5 and Perl 6.

```
push @{$array}, $something;       # Perl 5
push $array, $something;          # Perl 6
```

This is an area where Perl 6 does the right thing, automatically assuming you want to access the contents of a reference when a reference is used where an array or hash is expected. (Conversely, using a hash or an array as a reference automatically produces a reference.) I don't have a Perl 5 implementation of this syntax to offer you. Perl6::Contexts automatically takes references only to hashes and arrays; it doesn't make references directly usable everywhere hashes and arrays are.

Use autobox in Perl 5 to avoid the @{ EXPR } syntax. The autobox syntax works in Perl 6 as well.

```
# Pushing onto an array reference, Perl 5
use autobox;
use autobox::Core;
$array->push($something);
```

```
# Pushing onto an array reference, Perl 6
$array.push($something);
```

Note that you may also do @array->push($something) in Perl 5 when Perl6::Variables is in force, as Perl6::Variables recognizes the reference context provided by ->.

Building Data Structures with the Backslash Operator

The backslash operator creates references out of existing hashes, arrays, and scalars in both Perl 5 and Perl 6.

```
my $a;        # yields a scalar
\my $a;       # yields a reference to a scalar
```

You'll seldom need the backslash operator in Perl 6 and in Perl 5 with Perl6::Contexts in effect. The anonymous array constructor, [ ], and the anonymous hash constructor, { }, are easier and cleaner (in most cases) than creating an array or hash and then taking a reference.

[ ] is a shortcut over declaring a variable and then taking a reference to it.

```
# [ ] and { } simplify creation of array and hash references

# These two accomplish the same thing:

\my @arr;
[ ];

# These two are the same:

\my %hash;
hash { };
```

The my versions have the additional effect that a variable name is created in the current scope. [ ] and { } don't do that. More correctly, do { \my @arr } is equivalent to [ ].

\ operates on the thing to the right of it, which may be an expression, such as a code block, that evaluates to a hash, array, or scalar. The hash keyword is usually required in Perl 6 to construct a hash when no pairs are inside. hash isn't available in Perl 5, because this will always construct a hash when used as a value.

These examples concentrate on references to hashes and arrays, though it's possible to take references to strings, numbers, and a wild assortment of other things. In most cases where you'd take a reference to a scalar, variable binding with the := operator in Perl 6 or Data::Alias in Perl 5 is neater.

Taking a reference to an array or hash is useful in building data structures from existing hashes and arrays. The result of \ is a scalar that can be passed around as a single argument, stored where scalars are stored, and blessed into object hood. The primary goal of taking a reference to something, though, is to lump a bunch of arrays or hashes into another array or hash, keeping each of the original arrays or hashes separate from each other.

```
# @array_of_arrays will always contain exactly 5 array references after this,
# assuming @array_of_arrays and @array1 through @array5 have been declared

# Perl 5
my @array_of_arrays = (\@array1, \@array2, \@array3, \@array4);
push @array_of_arrays, \@array5;

# Perl 6
my @array_of_arrays = (@array1, @array2, @array3, @array4);
push @array_of_arrays, @array5;
```

Without the backslashes (reference operators), there could be five items in @array_of_arrays; there also could be a lot more, or there could be fewer, subject to the rules of list flattening. Each element of each array would get dumped into @array_of_arrays, possibly creating one big mess (depending on your intentions). Perl 6 requires *, the list-flattening operator, to override the default behavior of taking a reference.

Fed a scalar that's already a reference, the reference operator faithfully takes a reference to the reference. Yes, this is somewhat pointless. Fed a list, it returns a list of references, one for each item in the list. This is also pointless. You probably want to save the reference operator for real arrays, hashes, and, in Perl 5, subroutines.

Sorting

Perl's built-in sort function sorts lists of data, including lists of references. You'll usually do sorting as part of reporting, where data stored in data structures is formatted nicely for output. sort returns a sorted list. It doesn't sort in the list or array provided as an argument in place. A for statement, a call to map, or any other operator or subroutine that accepts a list can use the result of sort directly.

Sort's Criteria Block

You must tell perl what criteria to use when sorting. Perl provides two operators that implement two common criteria. For lists of numbers, use the numeric comparator, <=>, and for strings, use the lexical comparator, cmp.

```
# Sorting numeric data
@sorted_data = sort { $a <=> $b } @data_to_sort;      # Perl 5
@sorted_data = sort { $^a <=> $^b }, @data_to_sort;   # Perl 6

# Sorting alphanumeric data lexically
@sorted_data = sort { $a cmp $b } @data_to_sort;      # Perl 5
@sorted_data = sort { $^a cmp $^b }, @data_to_sort;   # Perl 6
```

$a and $b in the Perl 5 examples are special built-in package variables created just for the purpose of quickly and efficiently getting sort parameters to the criteria blocks. The names are predetermined; $a and $b aren't example names. You must use these names unless you're using another subroutine that has been prototyped to take two scalar arguments.

```
# Perl 5 - sorting using a comparator prototyped to take two arguments
sub numeric_sort ($$) {
    my $left = shift;
    my $right = shift;
    return $left <=> $right;
}
my @rand_numbers = map int rand 100, 1 .. 100;
@rand_numbers = sort \&numeric_sort, @rand_numbers;
```

And then you can shift them off the argument list and call them whatever you like. The ($$) in sub numeric_sort ($$) { } prototypes the numeric_sort() function to expect two scalars as parameters.

$^a and $^b, on the other hand, are just emulating the Perl 5 style using *placeholders*. Placeholders are Perl 6 parameters automatically read and added to the prototype. This is shorthand syntax for writing a parameter list. { $^a cmp $^b } could have been written as sub ($a, $b) { $a <=> $b } or -> $a, $b { $a <=> $b }. Chapter 11 documents placeholders and prototypes.

Built-ins in Perl 5 that directly accept a code block don't expect a comma after the code block. A comma is required after a sub { } or other code reference and is required after blocks in Perl 6.

Perl 6 allows operators to be used as function references.

```
@sorted = sort &infix:<=>, @data_to_sort;  # Perl 6 only - numeric sort order
@sorted = sort &infix:cmp, @data_to_sort;  # Perl 6 only - alphanumeric sort
```

An operator used this way works just like a function reference in Perl 6 and is prototyped to take as many arguments as the operator normally works on. An infix operator takes two, and postfix and prefix operators take one. This is a shorthand way of writing the previous code. cmp is considered to be an operator.

The comparator function (the sort criteria) returns -1, 0, or 1 to indicate the relative order of the two values. -1 means the left comes before the right, 0 means they're lexically identical, and 1 means the one on the right comes first. This behavior is a requirement of the two-argument sort criteria.

Sorting Hashes and Data Structures

With a criteria block, sort will sort references in addition to just strings and numbers. The references to be sorted can come from anywhere, including references stored in an array or values taken from a hash with the values built-in.

```
# Process a hash in numeric order of a field in a referenced array
# Perl 5
use Perl6::Variables;
my %addresses = (
    Heather => [1234,  "Robin Lane"],
    Scott   => [692,   "Mill Ave"],
    Sherry  => [16231, "Timbucktoo Court"],
);
```

```
for my $address_record (
    sort { $a->[0] <=> $b->[0] } values %addresses
) {
    print $address_record->[0], ' ', $address_record->[1], "\n";
}
```

This outputs the following:

```
692 Mill Ave
1234 Robin Lane
16231 Timbucktoo Court
```

In the criteria block, { $a->[0] <=> $b->[0] }, values from the hash are subscripted as array references. These array references are the parts of the %addresses data structure that look like [1234, "Robin Lane"]. The first element, such as 1234, of each array reference is compared to at least one other first element. $address_record takes on the value of each array reference in turn for the body of the for loop.

Sorting Hashes of References

sort operates on lists of data, including hash keys and lists of references. Sort the hash keys to get both the key and the value, because the key may easily be used to obtain the value.

```
# Process a hash in numeric order of a field in a referenced array
# Perl 5
use Perl6::Variables;
my %addresses = (
    Heather => [1234,  "Robin Lane"],
    Scott   => [692,   "Mill Ave"],
    Sherry  => [16231, "Timbucktoo Court"],
);
for my $name (
    sort { %addresses{$a}[0] <=> %addresses{$b}[0] } keys %addresses
) {
    print %addresses{$name}[0], ' ', %addresses{$name}[1], ' ', $name, "\n";
}
# outputs:
692 Mill Ave Scott
1234 Robin Lane Heather
16231 Timbucktoo Court Sherry
```

This example changes values %addresses from the previous example to keys %values. It also changes the criteria block and body of the for loop to accommodate references stored in the hash values rather than the hash keys as in the previous example. This approach has the advantage that the hash keys—such as Heather, Scott, and Sherry—are available.

The line reading sort { %addresses{$a}[0] <=> %addresses{$b}[0] } keys %addresses is the sort criteria.

$a and $b each take one of the hash keys computed by keys %addresses. The hash keys are immediately used to index the hash, %addresses. This picks out the array references held as values and then picks out the first element of the array. The first position of each array contains the street number.

Using %addresses{$a}[1] and %addresses{$b}[1] instead, sort would sort on street names. (And then you should use the cmp operator instead of the <=> operator.) Any other technique that returns consistent values would work as sorting criteria. For instance, the criteria block could call methods in objects as long as those methods returned the same value for the same set of arguments. The behavior is undefined if the criteria block is indecisive as to whether one item should come before another.

Single-Argument Comparators

Perl 6 needs to know only how to convert a given member of the list into a number that can be used to sort the list. It doesn't require a block that compares the two numbers to each other, because it can do that itself. It does still accept blocks that compare two numbers. To support this, sort takes blocks or subroutine references that are explicitly or implicitly prototyped to take either one or two arguments.

The following is the address sorting example from previously in the chapter, with the body of the for loop removed for brevity:

```
# Sort our %addresses hash, replicated dereference, Perl 5
use Perl6::Variables;
for my $name (
    sort { %addresses{$a}[0] <=> %addresses{$b}[0] } keys %addresses
) { ... }
```

The following is the same example but with the redundancy of the two %addresses subscripting expressions replaced by a subroutine:

```
# Sort our %addresses hash, factored out dereference, Perl 5
use Sub::Lexical;
use Perl6::Variables;
sub criteria { %addresses{$_[0]}[0] };
for my $name (
    sort { criteria($a) <=> criteria($b) } keys %addresses
) { ... }
```

Perl 6 helps you factor out repeated array and hash subscripts. Its sort criteria block may accept one or two arguments. Written to accept one, it uses that subroutine to fetch the value that should be used to sort the data structures. If it accepts two, then you must write the logic to compare the values. The following shows the previous example modified to take advantage of this feature:

```
# Sort our %addresses hash, factored out dereference, Perl 6
my sub criteria ($address_key) { %addresses{$address_key}[0] };
for sort &criteria, keys %addresses { ...  }
```

Since criteria() is prototyped to take one argument, Perl 6 knows exactly what it must do. Note that &criteria is a subroutine reference. The Perl 5 equivalent is \&criteria.

This can be written as one expression without an external subroutine definition.

```
# sort our %addresses hash, factored out dereference, inline block, Perl 6

for sort { %addresses{$^a}[0] }, keys %addresses -> $name { ... }
```

Perl 6's criteria function may return a string or an int. Perl will sort lexically if the function returns a string and numerically if it returns an integer. The result of numeric operations, string operations, and boolean tests has predictable type information, and perl will use this if available. The value may also be numified explicitly.

```
# Sort our %addresses hash, factored out dereference, inline block, numified
# Perl 6

for sort { + %addresses{$^a}[0] }, keys %addresses -> $name { ... }
```

Likewise, ~ stringifies a value, so perl knows the result of ~ is always a string.

Descending and Case-Insensitive Sorting

Perl 6 defines the descending and insensitive traits to be applied to the criteria. Append is descending after the closing brace of the sort block or the subroutine reference.

```
# Sort our %addresses hash, factored out dereference, inline block, traits, Perl 6

for sort { %addresses{$^a}[0] } is descending, keys %addresses -> $name {
... }
```

If you're doing the comparison yourself using a two-argument sort criteria, the descending and ascending code traits are meaningless, as it's then your responsibility to perform the comparison in reverse. descending is logically the same as the following:

```
# Sorting descending, numerically
sort { $^a } is descending, @data_to_sort;   # Perl 6
sort { - $^a }, @data_to_sort;                # Perl 6
sort { $^b <=> $^a }, @data_to_sort;          # Perl 6
sort { $b <=> $a } @data_to_sort;             # Perl 5
reverse sort @data_to_sort;                   # Perl 5 and Perl 6
```

Use whichever seems most intuitive to you.

You can make sorts case insensitive by folding case. Usually case is folded to lowercase to avoid confusion with Unicode character sets that understand different kinds of uppercase letters, such as title case.

```
# Sorting case insensitive, lexically
sort { $^a } is insensitive, @data_to_sort; # Perl 6
sort { lc $^a }, @data_to_sort;              # Perl 6
sort { lc $^a cmp lc $^b }, @data_to_sort;   # Perl 6
sort { lc $a cmp lc $a } @data_to_sort;      # Perl 5
```

Again, use the one that makes conceptual sense to you.

Sorting on Multiple Fields

With the street address sorting routine, I've sorted by street number and I've sorted by street name, but what if you want to sort by both of them?

```
# Sorting a data structure on multiple fields - Perl 5
use Perl6::Variables;
my %addresses = (
    Heather => [1234,  "Robin Lane"],
    Scott   => [692,   "Mill Ave"],
    Sherry  => [16231, "Timbucktoo Court"],
    Fred    => [1234,  "Infinity Drive"],
);
for my $name (
    sort {
        %addresses{$a}[0] <=> %addresses{$b}[0]
        ||
        %addresses{$a}[1] cmp %addresses{$b}[1]
    } keys %addresses
) {
    print %addresses{$name}[0], ' ', %addresses{$name}[1], ' ', $name, "\n";
}
```

I added a clause to the sort criteria: || %addresses{$a}[1] cmp %addresses{$b}[1]. Should the %addresses{ ... }[0] fields match exactly, <=> will evaluate to 0, and || will then evaluate and return the value of %addresses{$a}[1] cmp %addresses{$b}[1]. In other words, this first compares the street number, and if the street numbers are the same, it compares street names. You could do it the other way, too, and sort first by street name and then by street number. Just swap the order of the %addresses{$a}[0] <=> %addresses{$b}[0] and %addresses{$a}[1] cmp %addresses{$b}[1] expressions. This requires the two-argument version of the sort block. You could also sort on three or more fields, but around four or so fields, I'd look for a way to generalize the comparison. Something such as first { $^c <=> $^d } zip %addresses{$^a}, %addresses{$^b} would work in Perl 6.

Sort Speed

Perl currently uses the Mergesort algorithm. Older versions used Quicksort. These algorithms don't compare each element to every other element; both sort in *n log n* time. In other words, the number of comparisons they must make (which is the primary basis of how fast they are) scales linearly to the number of elements times a small factor that depends on the number of elements. With 20 elements, that small factor is about 3. In other words, sorting is extremely fast.

```
# How many comparisons does it take to sort a list of 20 things using
# Mergesort? Perl 5
my $comparisons;
my @random_numbers = map { rand 1 } (1 .. 20);
@random_numbers = sort {
    # print "debug: $a vs $b\n";
    $comparisons++;
    $a <=> $b;
} @random_numbers;
print "Comparisons required: $comparisons\n";
```

Running this a few times, it performs 55–65 comparisons.

Running the comparator function on each argument even three times may be unacceptable if the function is very slow. If the comparator function performs database queries or accesses the file system and you have more than a dozen things to be sorted, consider using the classic Schwartzian Transform, conceived by Randal Schwartz, author of numerous fine books, articles, and hacks. No book on Perl would be complete without the Schwartzian Transform.

```
# Schwartzian Transform to efficiently sort files by date, given a
# list of file names. Perl 5.
my @sorted_file_names =
    map  { $_->[0] }
    sort { $a->[1] <=> $b->[1] }
    map  { [$_, -m $_] }
    glob '*';
```

The following is the same, this time in Perl 6:

```
# Schwartzian Transform to efficiently sort files by date, given a
# list of file names. Perl 6.
my @sorted_file_names =
    map  { $^a.[0] },
    sort { $^a.[1] },
    map  { [$^a, -m $^a] },
    glob '*';
```

Working from the bottom upward, glob runs first, generating a list of filenames in the current directory. This produces a list that the map reads in and performs a single -m operation on. Once for each filename, the map builds an anonymous array containing the modification time and the filename and returns a reference to that array. This builds the list that the sort block works on. sort sorts each array reference by the second thing in it, which happens to be where I've stored the modification time. The next map up takes the output of the sort, which is a list of sorted array references, and extracts the first field from the array reference, which is where I've stored the filename. This throws away the modification time information. This is worth some thought. If you don't understand it, stare at it for a while and play with it.

Graphs

The data structures you've looked at so far are all trees of sorts. They branch outward from a central trunk, and they end in a scalar. A graph is more like a highway system, where the references lead this way and that, forming a tangle.

The following examples generalize and illustrate the principles outlined in this chapter. Graphs bring up a special set of considerations, and Perl has features and modules that answer those considerations.

Graph Example: Navigation

The example shown in Listing 8-2 creates several arrays, each named after a Phoenix, Arizona, metro-area highway. These arrays are created and used as references. Each array holds several of the other references.

Listing 8-2. *Graph Construction and Random Navigation*

```
# Arizona highway navigation, Phoenix metro area
# a graph example for Perl 5, version 1

use Perl6::Variables;
use autobox;
use autobox::Core;

my %ref_to_name;
my $i101n = [];  %ref_to_name{$i101n} = 'Interstate 101 North';
my $i101s = [];  %ref_to_name{$i101s} = 'Interstate 101 South';
my $i10   = [];  %ref_to_name{$i10}   = 'Interstate 10';
my $i202  = [];  %ref_to_name{$i202}  = 'Interstate 202';
my $us60  = [];  %ref_to_name{$us60}  = 'U.S. Route 60';
my $sr51  = [];  %ref_to_name{$sr51}  = 'State Route 51';

$i101n->push( $sr51, $i202, $i101s );
$i101s->push( $sr51, $i202, $i10, $i101n, $us60 );
$i202->push( $sr51, $i101s, $i101n );
$us60->push( $sr51, $i101s );
$sr51->push( $i101s, $i101n, $i10, $us60 );
$i10->push( $sr51, $i101s, $i202 );

my $location = $i10;
my $destination = $i101n;

while($location ne $destination) {
    $location = $location->[int rand $location->elems];
    print "Take the ", %ref_to_name{$location}, " exit.\n";
}

print "And you're there!\n";
```

Run this about a dozen times to get a feel for what it does. This random approach to navigation won't work reliably for every city. In many places, it would often fail to get you to your destination.

All the lexicals, such as $i101n and us60, are declared in advance and populated with array references so references may be taken to them. Each of these lexicals holds references to several others of themselves. Each reference is full of references to other references. %ref_to_name gives these references nice names that may be printed and understood by humans.

The references to the roads must be pushed onto the array references. If this example tried to replace them by assigning a newly constructed array reference, it'd replace the other arrays that hold references and break the chain.

Hash Keys As References

I'm using array references such as $i101n as keys in the %ref_to_name hash. In Perl 5, this works by stringifying the hash references into something textual such as ARRAY(0x8122170). This string uniquely identifies the reference. These stringifications of references start with the type of thing it references, ARRAY in this case, though it could be HASH, CODE, SCALAR, or the name of a package into which the reference was blessed. The number in parentheses is the memory location to which the reference points. Because hash keys are stored as strings, you use string operations such as ne to compare them to each other.

I have constant $destination and starting $location values so you can see the different routes it comes up with between two fixed points. If you wanted to randomize them, you could do something such as the following:

```
# Pick a random list element - bad - Perl 5 or Perl 6
my $location = ($i101n, $i101s, $i10, $i202, $us60, $sr50)[int rand 6];
```

You now have to add names such as $i101n both to the line where you initialize it and to the array from which you initialize $location. This makes the program harder to change; being hard to change makes the program prone to breaking when it's changed. You can't use the keys of the hash %ref_to_name as references to pick from, because perl turns the references into (unique) strings when it stores them. Perl 6 changes this, allowing references to remain references when used as hash keys. Then, to pick a random reference, you could have simply said the following:

```
# Pick random starting location, or, in general, pick a random hash key
# Perl 5
my $location = (keys %ref_to_name)[rand keys %ref_to_name];
```

Remember that ()[] is a subscript on a list. That picks one value from a list of values. The list itself is built from the keys stored in the %ref_to_name hash. These keys are array references to the highway arrays.

Tie::RefHash has a hash implementation that doesn't mangle references when they're used as keys. Using Tie::RefHash, this example for picking a random starting point works. In the previous example, simply add use Tie::RefHash to the top, and change the %my ref_to_name; line to read as follows:

```
tie my %ref_to_name, 'Tie::RefHash';
```

It's possible to look up keys in a hash by value (the opposite of the normal case) but only by either building a reverse index, which looks like my %ref_to_name = reverse %name_to_ref, or iterating through all the keys and values looking for the desired key-value pair. Building a reverse index is faster than traversing all the key-value pairs more than a few times. Tie::RefHash allows reverse indices to be built on hashes holding references as values. If the example data had started in a hash, %name_to_ref, that mapped names to references, you could build a mapping of references to names using Tie::RefHash.

```
# Exchange keys and values on a hash where values are references - Perl 5
tie my %ref_to_name, 'Tie::RefHash', reverse %name_to_ref;
```

Thanks to Tie::RefHash, %ref_to_name's keys remain valid as references after this.

Solving Graphs with Recursion

This highway navigation program gets you where you want to go eventually, but Phoenix's highway system can always loop you back to where you came from. The Minneapolis/St. Paul highways can trap you. Random navigation such as this is extremely painful where dead ends appear.

A *recursive function* is one that calls itself. Each time it calls itself, it gets a little closer to solving the problem. If it reaches a dead end, it stops calling itself for a while and starts returning to a point where it isn't stuck anymore. Then it starts calling itself again, taking a new direction. If this sounds like maze exploration to you, you're right. And is a highway system not a maze of sorts? See Listing 8-3.

Listing 8-3. *Recursive Depth-First Graph Navigation*

```
# Insert code from above to define and initialize both
# %highways and %ref_to_name here
my $location = $i10;
my $destination = $i101n;
my %already_did = ($location => 1);


sub solve_maze {

    my $location = shift;
    my $destination = shift;

    for my $exit ($location->flatten) {
        next if exists %route{$exit};
        return (@_, $exit) if $exit eq $destination;
        %route{$exit} = 1;
        my @ret = solve_maze($exit, $destination, @_, $exit);
        return @ret if @ret;
    }
    return ();
};


# And finally, test this:

my @res = solve_maze($location, $destination);

for my $i (@res) {
   print %ref_to_name{$i}, "\n";
}
```

solve_maze() implements a simple depth-first recursion algorithm. solve_maze() takes three items as arguments: the current node it's examining, the destination node, and a list of nodes from the starting node crossed to get to the current node. The first call passes only the current node and the destination node that implies a null current path.

If the destination node is immediately reachable, the current path is returned as the solution. If the destination node isn't immediately reachable, the current path plus the next untried exit is fed back into the same function, and it recurses. When the function calls itself, the current invocation keeps all its state. Should it be returned with anything but a success, it may try other exits. Several function calls (or hundreds, in a more complex application) may exist on the stack, each a snapshot that may be returned to. %already_did tracks already examined nodes to avoid pointless loops. Should recursion run into an exit already taken, it'll ignore it. Should recursion run out of new exits to try from any given place, it'll return the empty list, signaling the failure of the current path of exploration. Should solve_maze() take a wrong turn while exploring, it will figure it out and return to a point where it can try another exit.

Listing 8-3 won't always find the shortest route, given any data set. See Chapter 21 for an implementation of breadth-first recursion. Breadth-first recursion always finds the shortest route.

This listing would cleaner and easier to follow if %already_did and $destination were lexical variables in a block around the subroutine. Lexically scoping the subroutine definition would avoid having %already_did in scope for the rest of the file. solve_maze() wouldn't need to pass $destination back to itself as an argument each call, and it wouldn't have to break the rule of style that says variable data should be communicated to functions only as parameters. Chapter 11 has examples of creating lexical scopes apart from the file scope for subroutines to run in.

Circular References, Weak References, and Garbage Collection

Both versions of the highway navigation program have *circular references*. Being a graph implies having circular references (see Figure 8-3).

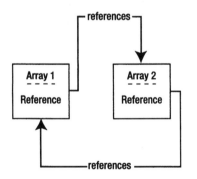

Figure 8-3. *Circular references*

Circular references are fun and useful, but they have a problem in Perl 5: they leak memory. Perl 5 uses a system called *referencing counting*. As long as there are references to an array, a hash, an object, or any other thing, perl keeps that thing around. Normally this works fine, but circular references maintain references to data structures that the program proper can't see anymore.

```
# Noncircular references are reaped, Perl 5
while(1) {
    do {
        my $thing_one = [rand 10];
        my $thing_two = [rand 10];
    };
```

```
    # $thing_one and $thing_two are no longer in scope at this point
    # and nothing has references to either, so perl takes the memory back
    # from them
}
```

This is a horrible waste of CPU power, but it should run for a good long time. The following shows how reference counting goes wrong:

```
# Circular references aren't reaped, Perl 5
# Danger! Do not run on a production server!
while(1) {
    do {
        my $thing_one = [];
        my $thing_two = [];
        $thing_one->[0] = $thing_two;
        $thing_two->[0] = $thing_one;
    };
    # $thing_one and $thing_two from the last loop both still have references
    # to them so they aren't reclaimed
}
```

I don't know how this will end on your machine. On mine, I get a segmentation fault as perl tries to use stack space that it wasn't able to allocate (or something colorful like that). In any case, sooner or later, the program will stop running. It'll probably take all the virtual memory with it, denying other programs the ability to allocate memory and possibly causing them to exit suddenly.

Parrot, the primary Perl 6 virtual machine, goes one step further than counting references; it makes sure each reference is visible from the active program somehow. It must be able to trace a route from the current data set of the program to each data item; otherwise the data item is considered dead.

Perl 5 can mark references as being *weak*. *Weak references* don't count toward the total reference count for a data item.

```
# Circular references reprimanded by weakening the offending circular
# references, Perl 5
use Scalar::Util 'weaken';
while(1) {
    do {
        my $thing_one = [];
        my $thing_two = [];
        $thing_one->[0] = $thing_two; weaken $thing_one->[0];
        $thing_two->[0] = $thing_one; weaken $thing_two->[1];
    };
    # $thing_one and $thing_two have no nonweak references and they've
    # gone out of scope, so perl reclaims them
}
```

This too will soak up CPU time, but like the first example, it doesn't soak up RAM.

Objects As Data Structures

There's no such thing as a perfectly designed data structure for a program with evolving requirements. Avoid replicating complex sequences of dereferences around your code.

```perl
# Something like this is fine a few times, but avoid littering too many
# around your program - Perl 5

my $kings_location = %pieces{'K'}{'location'};
```

Create a class to represent the data structure being navigated. Create methods in the class to perform the complex deference operations.

```perl
# The above could be written instead as this - Perl 5
my $kings_location = $pieces->piece('K')->location;
```

Objects centralize the dereference logic. Should the shape of the data structure change, you need to change this logic in only this one central place. This could save you from manually editing hundreds of lines or more and from introducing the associated potential of bugs. For example, the chess pieces in a future version of the example software may not link to their locations but instead have a board of locations that link to the chess pieces. The object method location() could search the entire chess board for the piece and return that as the location.

Files and Data Structures

An earlier example used a simple fixed format, readable with the following logic, to build an array that's full of array references:

```perl
# Simple file format - Perl 5
use Perl6::Variables;
open my $f, '<', 'file.txt' or die $!;
my @records;
while(<$f>) {
    chomp;
    push @records, [ split /\|/, $_ ];
}
```

Perl programmers often must parse existing file formats over which they have no control, so they write code such as this. That's fine.

CPAN has modules to parse just about any format you'd like: Web access logs, the system wtmp file, Rich Text Format (RTF), Hypertext Markup Language (HTML), and too many others to count. Use these when you can. MIME::Parser and HTML::Parser come to mind. Image formats are popular, too.

Parse::Date and Text::Balanced are extremely useful when dealing with strange formats. To write your own grammar for a complex format, use Perl6::Rules or Parse::RecDescent.

Those techniques are fine if the only data you read and write is the same data another application stores. Applications fitting this description include report generators, filters, and viewers.

Programmers wanting to save general state or invent a new format should consider two technologies: Extensible Markup Language (XML) and the Storable module.

XML and Data Structures

XML both exchanges data with other programs and saves the state of objects and data structures for your programs to use.

The little chess puzzle example from the end of the "Parallel Hashes" section may look something like Listing 8-4, written as XML.

Listing 8-4. *Dumping the Chess Puzzle Example's Data*

```
# Dumping the chess puzzle example's data, Perl 5:
use XML::Simple;
print XMLout(\%pieces);
# outputs:
<opt>
  <T1 image="8196828737276">
    <position>0</position>
    <position>4</position>
  </T1>
  <Q image="9276728297743">
    <position>0</position>
    <position>3</position>
  </Q>
  <B1 image="4828929672927">
    <position>0</position>
    <position>1</position>
  </B1>
  <K image="3828472821749">
    <position>0</position>
    <position>0</position>
  </K>
  <B2 image="4828929672927">
    <position>0</position>
    <position>2</position>
  </B2>
</opt>
```

Or, to send this data to a file, write the following:

```
# Dumping the chess puzzle example, Perl 5:
use XML::Simple;
use IO::Handle;
open my $fh, '>', 'pieces.xml' or die $!;
$fh->print(XMLout(\%pieces));
```

To read the data back in, use the XMLin() function.

```
# reading the chess puzzle data structure back in, Perl 5:
my $pieces = XMLin(IO::File('pieces.xml'))->{'opt'};
```

$hashref = XMLin($fh) and $hashref = XMLin($string_full_of_xml) are the general cases. The XMLout() method takes a reference, and XMLin() returns a reference. Hash keys must conform to the XML naming specifications that prohibit most punctuation. Hashes and arrays may not contain binary data. Data structures with circular references or anything other than trees may not be stored or may take large amounts of disk to store. See the documentation included with XML::Simple for more examples, caveats, and options.

When information is written in a cross-program standard format, a document type definition (DTD) is used. This is the XML-based set of rules for validating documents in that format. SOAP and XML-RPC are two protocols for writing network services (Web services) using XML. Rather than receiving HTML from the Web server and then submitting a form POST back, XML is sent as an HTML form submit or HTTP POST operation. XML makes the data easily understandable by programs; it removes JavaScript form validation in favor of the DTD, gets rid of HTML tables that have nothing to do with the data, and presents the data in a structure that communicates its meaning rather than suggested visual rendering. See the excellent Soap::Lite and XMLRPC::Lite modules by Paul Kulchenko.

The new features in Perl 6 don't make Perl more effective with XML, and it's doubtful such a feature is needed. *Programming Web Services with Perl* (O'Reilly, 2002), written by Randy J. Ray and Pavel Kulchenko, is an excellent book on the subject.

Storable

Storable, which comes with perl, is the preferred alternative to XML for Perl programs that don't need to share their saved data with other languages. Storable correctly handles binary data, circular references, and objects, and it even has experimental support for dumping code references via the excellent B::Deparse module. Storable gives Perl true object persistence. A program can maintain the internal state of objects between runs, making it almost as though the program wasn't stopped and restarted. Storable defines several functions to work directly to and from files and to lock files with which it's working. Use these when writing to and reading from disk. freeze() and thaw() are the best known functions, though.

```
# Saving data structures to disc with Storable, Perl 5:
use Storable 'freeze', 'thaw';
my $binary_data = freeze(\%pieces);
my $pieces = thaw($binary_data);
```

Just like with the XML example, the result of encoding the data may be written to disk. That's $binary_data here. Also like the XML example, this encoded data can't directly be manipulated. It's encoded. Unlike the XML example, the reference I give freeze() may be a reference to an object.

REFERENCES AND THANKS

Gurusamy Sarathy and Ed Avis wrote Tie::RefHash. Tuomas J. Lukka wrote Scalar::Util. Gurusamy Sarathy wrote Data::Dumper. I wrote Perl6::Contexts and autobox::Core. Chocolateboy wrote autobox. Michael Schwern, Nick Ing Simmons, and Jeffrey Friedl wrote Hash::Util. Matthijs van Duin wrote Data::Alias.

This chapter moved quickly and covered a lot of ground. Programmers not in the habit of creating and using data structures may benefit from a tutorial that slowly covers the basics. perldoc perlreftut is included with perl and will help you understand the topics that this chapter glossed over. *Learning Perl Objects, References & Modules* (O'Reilly, 2003), written by Randal L. Schwartz with Tom Phoenix, goes step by step, establishing the basics and showing how to perform progressively more complex tasks with references. Without being presumptuous and assuming you have a burning desire to join the object-oriented camp, it shows exactly when and why you'd want to use these language features.

Summary

Advanced Perl programmers will want an intimate knowledge of references, but programmers no longer need be preoccupied with references. Instead, they can think about data structures in terms of arrays of arrays, hashes of arrays, hashes of hashes, and so on. This simplification is a testament to Perl 6 and the Perl 5 modules covered in this chapter. References working as keys in hashes are one simplification, being able to push values onto a reference is another, and implied dereferences are yet another.

To understand the examples in this chapter, or to keep your own code straight in your head, print the data structures often. Print them as often as you need in order to understand what they contain and what the logic in the code is doing to them. You can deduce the effect of anything in this chapter with this golden rule. It's critical to know what your data structures look like. To view the structure and contents of a data structure, place use Data::Dumper; at the top of your program, feed the Dumper() function a reference to your data structure, and carefully inspect the result. If you're into that sort of thing, strong typing (documented in Chapter 16) can track this for you if you provide perl with type meta-information.

## CHAPTER 9

Switch

Briefly, there's no official case statement, because of the variety of tests possible in Perl (numeric comparison, string comparison, glob comparison, regex matching, overloaded comparisons, ...). Larry couldn't decide how best to do this, so he left it out, even though it's been on the wish list since Perl 1.

—From "How do I create a switch or case statement?" in `perldoc perlfaq`

Unfortunately, the problem of how each type would compare to every other type prevented a clear plan for a `switch` statement in Perl 5. But the `Switch` module by Damian Conway solved this problem, and the solution is what's standardized into Perl 6, with a few modifications and additions.

Innovations in 1970s-era languages gave special attention to two areas: flow control and data structures. Language designers strongly thought data structures that organize data into fields in records would prevent programmers from misusing data and flow control constructs would prevent programmers from using goto. But the future is a risky business. Neither worked out exactly as planned, but the new way of doing things made a lasting impression.

The `switch` statement was one advancement. `switch` is faster than a series of `if()` statements and is a more controlled alternative to the *jump tables* popular in assembly language. With a `switch` table, you're branching to small, inline routines rather than a place far away, and execution continues after the `switch` statement rather than some place in the program far away.

This chapter introduces conditional execution in Perl, concentrating on `Switch.pm`, which is the basis of the `given` statement in Perl 6. It also introduces *smart matching*, where different datatypes are compared in a reasonable way that depends on the datatypes. Perl's `switch` construct is built around the idea of smart matching.

Changes for Perl 6

`given` blocks topicalize a parameter as `$_`, the default variable, for `when` blocks to test against. In topicalizing its parameter to `$_`, `given` behaves like the `for` statement. `when` is a specialized version of `if` that knows how to compare different types to each other and executes the equivalent of a `last` when a match is found. These were previously available only with the `Switch` module bundled with Perl. Switching on class names is new in Perl 6, where it tests class membership. Regular expressions are anchored to the current parse location (the position in the string where the last match left off when the `gc` flags are used and what `pos` returns). This default makes it easier to implement grammars using switches. The default case in a switch statement is now default rather than else. In both versions of Perl, code may be left inline, and default is equivalent to just leaving inline code at the bottom of the switch statement.

Switch Workarounds (Perl 5)

The Switch module for Perl 5 offers a given implementation that's close to the Perl 6 one. The Switch module isn't right for serious implementation work, as it's implemented as a source filter.

Chained if Statements

Novices are told to chain if statements together.

```
if($a == 0) {
    # ...
} elsif($a == 1) {
    # ...
} else {
    # ...
}
```

This is because of the following considerations:

- Alternatives evaluate the cases sequentially anyway. The performance is the same.

- Alternatives use obscure features.

- Alternatives misuse common features.

- Any datatype can be compared to any other datatype using standard Perl expressions.

Other alternatives to given are more idiomatic.

for Blocks and Topicalizers

When chained if statements repeatedly test the same variable, the statement may be written more concisely using for's *topicalizing* feature. for aliases each of its arguments in turn to $_, the default variable. The default variable is said to be the *topic*. It's a sort of implied subject of the code. Many built-in functions default to $_ when no other argument is provided.

Table 9-1 lists some other topicalizers in Perl.

Table 9-1. *Other Topicalizers*

Topicalizer	Description
for	Iterates over an array
map	Iterates over an array, translating and building a result array
loop	Perl 6-like C's for (;;) statement
while	Topicalizes when sole argument is readline or <$fh>
grep	Iterates over an array, building a result array from select elements
given	Perl 6 switch statement

Methods in Perl 6 also topicalize the current object (passed as the first argument in Perl 5) as $_. if and unless don't topicalize.

Perl programmers often use for in place of if because for topicalizes.

```
# Simple case/switch workaround using for() as a topicalizer - Perl 5

for(scalar readline STDIN) {
    /yes/   and do { remove_all_files(); last; };
    /no/    and exit;
    /maybe/ and rand(10) < 5 and remove_all_files(), last;
    die "invalid input '$_'";
}
```

Pattern matches default to $_ in Perl 5, but Perl 5's equality tests don't. You can easily say /yes/ to attempt a pattern match on $_, but you can't implicitly test $_ for equality using ==, eq, or other comparison operators. Perl 6 and Switch remedy this with the when block. A lone constant value in a when block implies equality testing.

Dispatch to Methods

You should use objects in place of switch statements (or equivalents) in many, perhaps most, cases (see Listing 9-1). (Some folks argue you should use them for all cases.)

Listing 9-1. *Object Methods Can Replace Switch Cases (Perl 5)*

```
# Dispatch to object methods - Perl 5

package SiteCom::HTML::Color;

sub new {
    my $package = shift;
    bless { }, $package;
}

package SiteCom::HTML::Color::Red;
use base 'SiteCom::HTML::Color';

sub print_tag { print qq{<font color="red">} };
sub get_hex   { '0xff0000'; };

package SiteCom::HTML::Color::Green;
use base 'SiteCom::HTML::Color';

sub print_tag { print qq{<font color="green">} };
sub get_hex   { '0x00ff00'; };

package SiteCom::HTML::Color::Blue;
use base 'SiteCom::HTML::Color';
```

```
sub print_tag { print qq{<font color="blue">} };
sub get_hex   { '0x0000ff'; };

package main;

my $color = shift;

my $colorob = SiteCom::HTML::Color::Red->new();
$colorob->print_tag();
```

Listing 9-2 shows that the same example again, this time in Perl 6.

Listing 9-2. *Object Methods Can Replace Switch Cases (Perl 6)*

```
# Dispatch to object methods - Perl 6

class SiteCom::HTML::Color {
}

class SiteCom::HTML::Color::Red is SiteCom::HTML::Color {
    method print_tag { print qq{<font color="red">} };
    method get_hex   { 0xff0000 };
}

class SiteCom::HTML::Color::Green is SiteCom::HTML::Color {
    method print_tag { print qq{<font color="green">} };
    method get_hex   { 0x00ff00 };
}

class SiteCom::HTML::Color::Blue is SiteCom::HTML::Color {
    method print_tag { print qq{<font color="blue">} };
    method get_hex   { 0x0000ff };
}

class main;

my $colorob = SiteCom::HTML::Color::Red.new();
$colorob.print_tag();
```

When print_tag() is called, the correct print_tag() method will be invoked for the case. This one call replaces a switch that may otherwise look like this:

```
# Perl 5 - explicit type case analysis - counter example (don't do this)

for($color) {
    print_blue_tag()  if $_ eq 'blue';
    print_green_tag() if $_ eq 'green';
    print_red_tag()   if $_ eq 'red';
}
```

As more cases are added and the value is switched on in more places in the program, the savings of using method indirection in place of switch grows.

Create new subclasses of the base class to create new possible cases. The exact subclass of an object in which a method is called determines which case executes.

Not having to search through existing code to make changes minimizes the risk of breaking existing code with new features. Avoiding breakage is the primary point of object-oriented attempts to correlate code blocks, and this is a prime example of just that.

I threw in get_hex() methods to illustrate how all logic related to a given instance is compiled in one place. This makes the information more easily reusable, but the real virtue is in organizing it in a group of related logic pertaining to a given case.

Chapter 14 formally introduces objects.

Other Perl 5 Switch Constructs

Like many things in Perl for which no standard is supplied, there are as many homebrew switch constructs as there are programmers. Or so it seems.

See perldoc -q switch for the perlfaq entry on switchlike constructs.

Switch (Perl 5)

Larry Wall felt Perl's version of switch diverged enough from other languages' implementations (C being the famous example) that Perl's version should be separated conceptually and given a different name. While I call it the switch construct, the keyword is given in Perl 6 and in Perl 5 when the Switch module is used with the 'Perl6' option. Likewise, the individual case statements are given statements.

Getting at Switch

In Perl 6, switch is given, and case is when. This is the syntax documented in this chapter. To get at it, do this:

```
use Switch 'Perl6';
```

Load this near the top of the program as a quasipragmatic module.

Switching on Scalars

Scalars are numbers, strings, references to data structures, references to objects, references to subroutines, references to regular expressions, and other sorts of references and single values.

You must place scalar variables such as $foo in parentheses when used in a when clause.

```
when($regexpref) { }
# same as: if grep { /$regexpref/ } @$arrayref is true
```

If you neglected the parentheses, you'd get the following error message:

```
Missing opening brace or semi-colon after 'when' value near - line 6
```

The exact method for testing if any given when clause is true depends on the type of the expression in the when clause and the type of the expression fed to given (see Listing 9-3).

Listing 9-3. *The Test Performed in a Switch Depends on the Datatype Switched On*

```
# Switching on a scalar - Perl 5

use Switch 'Perl6';

my $val = 1;  # for example
my $other = 10;
sub func { };
my %hash;
my @array;
 given($val) {

    when 1          { }  # numbers are equal
    when "a"        { }  # strings match exactly
    when ($other)   { }  # numbers are equal
    when [1,2,3]    { }  # $val is in this list of numbers
    when (@array)   { }  # $val is in this list of numbers
    when /\w+/      { }  # regular expression matches $val
    when qr/\w+/    { }  # dereferenced regular expression matches $val
    when (%hash)    { }  # %hash has an entry for the value in $val
    when (\%hash)   { }  # a hash reference has an entry for the value in $val
    when (\&func)   { }  # executing a code reference returns a true value
    print "default\n";   # default case

}
```

Listing 9-4 shows the same example but with Perl approximations of when the condition is true.

Listing 9-4. *The Test Performed in a Switch Depends on the Datatype Switched On*

```
# Switching on a scalar - Perl 5

use Switch 'Perl6';

given($val) {

    when 1          { }  # $val == 1
    when "a"        { }  # $val eq 'a'
    when ($other)   { }  # $val eq $other
    when [1,2,3]    { }  # grep { $_ == $val or $_ eq $val } (1, 2, 3)
    when (@array)   { }  # grep { $_ == $val or $_ eq $val } @array
    when /\w+/      { }  # $val =~ /\w+/
    when qr/\w+/    { }  # $val =~ /\w+/
    when (%hash)    { }  # exists $hash{$val}
    when (\%hash)   { }  # exists $hash->{$val}
    when (\&sub)    { }  # sub($val) returns true - takes any code reference
    print "default\n";   # default case

}
```

Because it's unclear whether the block after a variable is a hash subscript or the body of the condition, expressions of the form $var { ... } are illegal in Perl 5.

Perl 6 uses whitespace to break the tie, so it's legal. $var { ... } in Perl 6 is a test against a variable followed by the code block for that condition. If whitespace separates variables from the block, the block is a code block. If there's no space, the block is actually a hash subscript.

■Parentheses and flow control statements Switch.pm for Perl 5 doesn't require parentheses around the expression after the when keyword. This is the norm for Perl 6 but an exception in Perl 5. for, while, if, and other *statements* require the parentheses. Braces, { }, are always required after a statement's expression and its body. The C form with one statement and no braces isn't available. Its use is discouraged in C anyway.

The braces can contain any arbitrary expression, just like any block can. Comments at the end of the line approximate the method Switch uses to decide if the code block should be run. These comments summarize how truth is decided when Switch compares the two expressions.

The Switch documentation recommends using an else for the default case. Perl 6 renames this to default, but both versions allow code to be mixed in. Both versions execute code that's inside the given { } block but outside any when { } block. The when { } blocks execute in order, and any other Perl statements between the when { } blocks are considered when (and if) they're encountered. There need not actually be any when { } blocks at all in a given { } statement.

when takes a scalar, but so far the examples are for nonreference types. References can be tested for truth as well.

Switching on Array References

Switching on an array reference performs various array-related tests.

```
# Switching on an array reference

my $arrayref = [1, 2, 5];

given($arrayref) {
    when 3            { }    # defined $arrayref->[3] assuming element exists
    when [3]          { }    # if grep { $_ == 3 } @$arrayref is true
    when [1, 2, 3]    { }    # any element from one array exists in the other
    when($other_aref){ }    # any element from one array exists in the other
    when qr/foo/      { }    # if grep { /foo/ } @$arrayref is true
    when($regexpref) { }    # if grep { /$regexpref/ } @$arrayref is true
}
```

Array references are produced automatically when arrays are passed to a subroutine when Perl6::Contexts is in effect or when the subroutine is correctly prototyped. They're also created by placing a reference operator, \, in front of an array, such as with my $arrayref = \ @array;. You can directly construct array references with [ ].

when 3 asks if the array element exists and is defined (not undef). The test is the same as what you'd do with the exists and defined built-ins. If both conditions are met, then the code block is run.

when [3] asks if there's any intersection between the array fed to given() and the set provided to when.

when [1, 2, 3] is the same as the previous case. If any element matches between $arrayref and [1, 2, 3], the test evaluates true and the associated block is run. This example has two matches: 1 and 2 both appear in both arrays. One match would have been enough. Rather than place the anonymous array constructor, [ ], directly in the when statement, you also could use a scalar holding a reference to an array. The when($other_aref) example does this.

when qr/foo/ and when($regexpref) are synonymous. qr// returns a regular expression reference. Both tests are true if the regular expression matches any element of $arrayref. $regexpref in the previous example would hold a value returned by qr//.

Chapter 8 formally introduces references.

Switching on Hash References

When given() is fed a hash reference, when { } conditionals test for the existence of keys in that hash.

```
# Switching on a hash references

my $hashref = { foo => 'bar', baz => 'qux' };

given($hashref) {
    when 'baz'      { }   # if exists $hashref->{'baz'}
    when($scalar)   { }   # if exists $hashref->{$scalar}
}
```

Perl produces hash references, like array references, when hashes are passed to subroutines while Perl6::Contexts is in effect or when the subroutine is correctly prototyped. You can also create them by placing a reference operator, \, in front of a hash, such as with my $hashref = \ @hash;. You can directly construct hash references with { key => value, key => value, ... }.

Switching on Code References

When given() is fed a code reference, parameters to the when { } conditionals are used as arguments to invoke the code reference. If the code reference returns true, the test is considered true, and the block associated with the when is executed.

```
# Switching on a code reference

my $coderef = sub { ($_[0] + $_[1]) % 2 };

given($coderef) {
    when 3           { }   # if $coderef->($3)
    when 'fred'      { }   # if $coderef->('fred')
    when($scalar)    { }   # if $coderef->($scalar)
    when [2, 4]      { }   # if $coderef->(2, 4)
    when($arrayref)  { }   # if $coderef->(@$arrayref)
}
```

when 3, when 'fred', and when($scalar) all perform the same test: the value provided to when is fed directly to $coderef as an argument.

when [2, 4] and when($arrayref) are the same: given a reference to an array, the array is dereferenced and the elements of the array are passed as the arguments to $coderef.

I've left some of the more esoteric cases for the documentation in the perldoc Switch page.

Switch Usage Scenarios

Rather than mix and match wildly like these example unintentionally imply, you'll probably find yourself picking one matching style for a given block and using that exclusively.

```
given($num) {
    when [0, 1, 2]  { $fan->speed('low') }
    when [3, 4]     { $fan->speed('medium') }
    when [5, 6, 7]  { $fan->speed('high') }
    else            { $fan->emit('smoke') }
}
```

Regular expression matching makes for some nice quick parsers, too.

Pros of Switch in Perl 5

Code using the Switch module will translate almost directly to Perl 6—not that you'll ever try to run your Perl 5 under Perl 6, but it may be fun to get in the habit of writing in the style of Perl 6.

Programmers are more readily able to grasp the meaning of code written using Switch. The code is shorter. Many of the constructs are powerful and systematically eliminate large amounts of code.

Switch.pm is included with newer versions of Perl 5.

Cons of Switch in Perl 5

Older versions of Perl 5 don't come with the Switch module.

Switch.pm uses a Perl feature called *source filters*, which have problems. Perfectly valid constructs may result in syntax errors, and attempts to use more than one source filter at a time can make things really blow up. When things blow up, it's very difficult to solve what the problem is—it seems like there's no apparent rhyme or reason behind the failure. Source filters dramatically add to the startup time of programs, which is inappropriate for CGI environments where the code isn't first compiled or bytecode compiled.

Switch (Perl 6)

Perl 6 builds in support for the switching construct with the keywords given and when. Some things have changed, and some things have been added, but most stay the same.

As if it weren't enough to compress all these semantics into a case switch–like construct, Perl 6 uses the same semantics for its new *smart-matching operator*, ~~. The binding operator, =~, in Perl 5, attempts matches between regular expressions and scalars. Smart matching attempts to match regular expressions against arrays, attempts to match arrays against arrays, attempts to match scalars against hashes, and attempts the rest of the cases already presented in this chapter.

All Blocks Are Given Blocks

You can place when { } statements in any block, or even outside any block, to get smart-matching behavior against $_. Think of it as a hot-rodded if statement or another way to write ~~. The given { } statement serves primarily to topicalize its argument to $_.

Package Names Mean Something

Perl 5 has long recognized package names as a special kind of symbol that can appear anywhere a term does.

```
# Package names are recognized as such - Perl 5

CGI->param();
'CGI'->param();

My::Object->my_method();
'My::Object'->my_method();
```

The ~~ operator and when statements test these mentions of classes against objects to see if the object belongs to that class. Subclasses of classes count as far as this test is concerned. This class membership test is the same test performed by ->isa( ) in Perl 5.

```
# Test $creature to see if its derived from Octaparrot or a subclass
# of Octaparrot - Perl 5

warn "Poly shouldn't be" if $creature->isa('Octaparrot');

# Test object to see if its derived from Octaparrot a subclass - Perl 6

warn "Poly shouldn't be" if $creature is Octaparrot; # or..
warn "Poly shouldn't be" if $feature ~~ Octaparrot;
```

Perl 6's given { } statement also tests an object's type for class membership.

```
# Perl 6 - testing an object to see if it has been derived from one
# of a few classes

given $objectref {
    when AI::FuzzyLogic   { .classify(new BotSnack) }
    when AI::NeuralNet    { .recognize(new BotSnack) }
    when AI::Sentient     { .pat_nicely() && back_away() }
}
```

Switch.pm for Perl 5 doesn't recognize this construct as anything special.

The following is the same example but translated to Perl 5:

```
# Explicit type case analysis - usually bad - Perl 5

for($objectref) {
    if   ($_->isa('AI::FuzzyLogic')) { $_->classify(BotSnack->new) }
    elsif($_->isa('AI::NeuralNet'))  { $_->recognize(BotSnack->new) }
    elsif($_->isa('AI::Sentient'))   { $_->pat_nicely() && back_away() }
}
```

The isa() method in Perl 5 is defined in UNIVERSAL, from which all packages silently inherit. (It's logically but not actually in their @ISA array.)

You're asking, given $objectref, whether it's one of those classes (or a subclass of any of those classes—subclasses work just as well). Object-oriented programming rhetoric forbids doing this kind of testing against a list of class names. In most cases where you may be tempted to use this, move the logic instead to the object and let the objects distinguish between themselves. Don't distinguish between them.

The previous logic should be moved into object methods, and the given statement should be reduced to calling this method. For example, $objectref should always contain a deal_with() method, and each subclass would define this method differently, with AI::FuzzyLogic defining deal_with() in terms of a call to .classify(new BotSnack), AI::NeuralNet as the logic .recognize(new BotSnack), and so on. Each possible class for $objectref should be a subclass of a common (possibly empty) parent class. That parent class should establish which methods can be counted on always being there, and it should be impossible for objects of that class to find their way into places they don't belong.

Despite this sage advice, Java, a relatively pure object-oriented language, uses this technique of matching objects according to their type to decide how to handle thrown error objects. If error objects weren't tested against types, each error object would require a catch() method that knows to how handle the error situation. Not using the switch construct would organize the code against what makes sense.

Perl 6 exception handling with the CATCH { } block uses the same semantics. When an object is thrown as an error, $! contains the error object and is used as the thing to switch on. It's provided automatically in the place of an argument to where. Chapter 15 has more information on exception handling.

Another use for switching on an object's class membership is to create methods that respond differently to different kinds of arguments. Perl 5 doesn't overload method names based on the types of the arguments passed in, so programmers need to write a single method that explicitly tests arguments against the different types it knows how to handle. You can use the previous example to do this. Using switching constructs to examine an object's class membership is part of a larger pattern where two pieces of code must be wired together.

Switch Style

The C language's cases fall through by default. C's break keyword prevents fall-through. Perl's cases don't fall through by default. Use a batch of if statements for that behavior.

```perl
# Attaining fall-through - Perl 5

for($file) {
    if(-f) { print "$_ is a file\n" }
    if(-r) { print "$_ is readable by you\n" }
    if(-f) { print "$_ is plain file\n" }
    if(-T) { print "$_ appears to contain text\n" }
    if(-B) { print "$_ appears to contain binary\n" }
    if(-z) { print "$_ is empty\n" }
}


# Attaining fall-through - Perl 6

given $file {
    if -f { print "$_ is a file\n" }
    if -r { print "$_ is readable by you\n" }
    # ...
}
```

Since when statements are evaluated sequentially in Perl, using a series of if statements in place of when statements doesn't result in a performance loss.

given is a specialized version of for that keeps arrays intact and doesn't iterate on them. when is a specialized version of if that knows how to compare different types to each other and executes the equivalent of a last when a match is found. There's no reason you can't mix and match, using given blocks with if statements and using for blocks with when statements.

```perl
# Mixing 'for' and 'when' - compare each element of @arr to other scalars
# Perl 5 and Perl 6

# use Switch 'Perl6'; # uncomment for Perl 5 source

for(@arr) {
    when "west"  { $x-- }
    when "east"  { $x++ }
    when "north" { $y++ }
    when "south" { $y-- }
}

# Mixing 'given' and 'if' - Perl 6
# 'when' statements may be mixed with the 'if' statements
```

```
given($something) {
    if($_ < 10) { $i++; }  # falls through
    if($_ < 25) { $i++; }  # falls through
    if($_ < 35) { $i++; }  # falls through
}

# Mixing 'given' and 'if'-like conditionals - Perl 5

use Switch 'Perl6';

given($something) {
    when sub { $_ < 10 } { $i++; }   # falls through
    when sub { $_ < 25 } { $i++; }   # falls through
    when sub { $_ < 35 } { $i++; }   # falls through
}
```

Using the sub keyword in front of blocks when code blocks are used as conditionals works in both Perl 5 and Perl 6.

Summary

Use given to avoid redundant code in chains of if statements.

given infers which test to use by the datatype of the variable being switched on and the expressions in the when statements. Some of the tests are extremely handy, cover common cases, and save typing. Others seem to be there for the sake of completeness.

given blocks may have regular Perl code intermingled with the when statements, just as for blocks full of if statements can.

for blocks in Perl 5 were the starting point for Perl 6's given blocks. In both cases, the $_ variable contains the thing being switched on. for blocks always fall through unless you explicitly do a last. given blocks implicitly do a last when a condition matches.

CHAPTER 10

■■■

Block Structure

Assembly language, COBOL, and old versions of BASIC don't indent code to distinguish the code run in a loop or run conditionally from the normal flow.

Block structure defines *scope*. Scope is the area (approximately the starting line and ending line or the file or the package) in which a variable, method, or subroutine is valid. Outside that scope, the variable (or whatever) virtually doesn't exist. Scope concentrates dependencies. Concentration is the opposite of scattering, and scattering dependencies is bad, so it follows that this concentration is a good thing.

Tom Christiansen's 1996 article, "Seven Deadly Sins of Perl", listed the global nature of special variables, such as $_, as the third sin. Global variables bypass use strict's checking.

Global variables have the entire program as their scope, meaning any code, anywhere, can muck the variable up, and the only way to find it is to trace the execution of possibly the entire program. Perl 6 drops the global nature of $_ and makes it lexically scoped by default. No longer can a subroutine halfway across the program clobber its value where you least expect it. Recent versions of Perl 5 allow $_ to be made lexical with the my keyword.

This chapter gives Perl programmers numerous tools for controlling program flow. Various types of blocks execute under different circumstances to simplify a program's logical design. These include looping constructs, blocks that execute according to success or fail conditions, and hooks into program compilation. Keywords control loop execution. This chapter also serves as a reference for various styles of blocks that may appear in a Perl program (other than user-defined control structures).

Changes for Perl 6

The do keyword is required only when the pair-building operator, =>, appears after a word it quotes as the first item in a block. That is, if a block doesn't look like it's merely building a hash, then it's a sub { } block.

Semicolons aren't required on the end of do { } blocks, anonymous sub { } blocks, or any other kind of block, provided that the closing brace is alone on its own line. Semicolons are required for do { } blocks, named subroutines, sub { } blocks, if statements, and any other kind of block when the closing brace isn't alone on its own line. User-defined functions, closures passed to user-defined functions, and built-in control statements such as while and if all play by the same rules now.

When they aren't used in the middle of an expression, blocks must be marked with some keyword, such as hash, sub, or do. Bare sets of blocks at the statement level aren't allowed.

You can use BEGIN { } blocks in the middle of expressions, and they can evaluate to values that are used in those expressions. Like Perl 5's BEGIN { } blocks, they execute only once.

for(;;) is now loop(;;). Plain old for() is the Perl 5 foreach(). for() just iterates over a list of values.

my no longer needs to be used on $_ to make it lexically scoped, as lexical scope is now the default for $_. Likewise, @_ is lexically scoped by default. Anything that topicalizes $_ introduces its own $_ independent of the $_ already in scope. Other global variables that are traditionally localized in a block, such as $/, have been replaced with traits and properties. The file handles, strings, arrays, and so on, that they affect have methods that specify behaviors for that particular file handle, string, or array.

New for Perl 6

You can place KEEP { }, UNDO { }, and CATCH { } blocks in another block to execute when that other block exits under various circumstances.

You can apply traits to variables to specify how that variable should be handled in various events revolving around the terms of the current block's exit.

A new control structure, gather { }, loops and builds a return value under program control. It's usable as a term in an expression rather than merely as a statement.

Indenting Blocks and Correctness

Carefully indenting your blocks makes the structure of the code apparent at a glance. Incorrectly indented code makes the code appear, at a glance, to do something other than what it does. Perl won't get confused, but you will. Everything after an open brace, {, up until the matching closing brace, }, should be indented. Always indent the same number of spaces so that when it comes time to close several blocks, you can tell at a glance whether you've missed any closing braces. (Four is a good number, but two and eight aren't uncommon.) Also consider the Emacs cperl mode, which nicely indents; Vim has a Perl mode as well.

Code Blocks

A *code block* is a section of code starting with a brace, {, and ending with a matching brace, }. These are the *brace* characters, or *squiggly braces*. One code block can contain other code blocks.

Braces group statements together. When executed, they execute the first statement, and then the next statement, and then the next, and so on. Any last executed will transfer control to just after the current code block.

Numerous statements use code blocks, including if, unless, for, foreach, while, do, sub, and loop in Perl 6; method in Perl 6; macro in Perl 6; and rule in Perl 6.

Various built-in functions accept blocks; for example, eval in Perl 5, map, and grep do. Some uses of code blocks don't run when encountered by program flow but rather define logic that's to be run later. User-defined functions can also accept code blocks as arguments, later invoking them, possibly repeatedly.

You can assign code blocks to variables, which saves the logic for later execution. For example, the variable a code block has been assigned to may be passed as an argument to a function, and that function may later trigger the logic in the code block to run.

Certain all-capital names before blocks designate them to run under specific conditions. BEGIN { } runs immediately, pausing the program's compilation. CATCH { } runs when its enclosing block throws an error. KEEP { } runs when its enclosing block exits without an error. These are *named blocks*, not statements. I'll discuss others in this chapter as well, but these are the most significant of the named blocks.

Sample Blocks

Here are a few sample blocks:

```
# A few blocks - Perl 5
sub foo {
    print "This runs when called by name - foo()\n";
}
my $coderef = sub {
    print "This runs when requested to do so later on.\n";
};
do {
    print "This runs now.\n";
};
if(rand > 0.5) {
    print "This runs when it wants to.\n";
}
```

Again, here are some sample blocks, this time for Perl 6:

```
# A few blocks - Perl 6
sub foo {
    print "This runs when called by name - foo()\n";
}
my $coderef = {
    print "This runs when requested to do so later on.\n";
}
{
    print "This runs now.\n";
}
if rand > 0.5 {
    print "This runs when it wants to.\n";
}
```

You'll most often see code blocks defining subroutines, bodies of if() statements, and bodies of for() loops.

Code blocks are intimately related to variable scope. my variables are valid in all the code up until the end of the block in which they were declared.

A bare set of { } in the void context (statements that aren't last in the block are in void context) in Perl 5 is also a do { }, not a hash constructor, but Perl 5 requires that either do or sub be specified in the majority of cases. The void context occurs when the result of an expression isn't used.

Semicolon Rules

It's never an error to put a semicolon on the end of a block that doesn't require one. In Perl 6, built-ins, user-defined functions, and control structures all have the same rules for semicolons. If the closing brace is alone on a line, the semicolon is implied and optional. Any block that ends on a line with other code requires an explicit semicolon. Under the new rules, no distinction exists between statements and control structures.

```
# Perl 6 must have a semicolon on the end of blocks even with built-in
# statements unless the block ends alone on a line
foo { code(); };
foo {
    code();
}
foo({
    code();
});
if rand > 0.5 { print "This runs when it wants to.\n"; };
```

Blocks are always allowed to end with semicolons, but in Perl 6, blocks ended by a brace alone on a line don't require them.

The value computed by the last expression in a code block is the return value of that code block when it's executed.

```
# These two examples are the same - Perl 5
my $color = join ' ',
    rand > 0.5 ? 'light' : 'dark',
    rand > 0.5 ? 'reddish' : 'bluish',
    rand > 0.5 ? 'green' : 'orange';
my $color = join ' ',
    do { rand > 0.5 ? 'light' : 'dark' },
    do { rand > 0.5 ? 'reddish' : 'bluish' },
    do { rand > 0.5 ? 'green' : 'orange' };

# These two examples are the same - Perl 6
my $color = join ' ',
    rand > 0.5 ?? 'light' :: 'dark',
    rand > 0.5 ?? 'reddish' :: 'bluish',
    rand > 0.5 ?? 'green' :: 'orange';
my $color = join ' ',
    { rand > 0.5 ?? 'light' :: 'dark' },
    { rand > 0.5 ?? 'reddish' :: 'bluish' },
    { rand > 0.5 ?? 'green' :: 'orange' };
```

The code blocks created in the preceding examples are frivolous. Parentheses should have been used instead, unless lexical variables were created to be visible for the duration of the block or unless the block actually contained multiple statements. In Perl 6, { } also creates references to code besides just grouping expressions. This happens automatically in reference context. Since { } isn't used in reference context here, its contents run immediately when it encounters the running programming, exactly like a do { } block. Conceptually, { } in Perl 6 always creates a code reference, but the code reference numifies or stringifies by evaluating itself.

do Blocks

do blocks immediate execute their contents when encountered in a running program. last can't be used to quit a do block. Use a do block to group code when it'd be ambiguous to have a bare set of braces in an expression. In Perl 5, this is any case where the block is used within a statement, rather than being a statement unto itself. In Perl 6, this is when the block would otherwise turn into a reference to itself, such as when assigned to a variable or passed as an argument to a function. In Perl 6, do is also desirable if the block appears to contain hash pairs, constructed with the => operator.

do blocks can have a while or unless clause attached to them to turn them into a loop or an if or unless to turn them into a conditional, just as any expression can.

```
# Perl 5 and Perl 6 - if and while used as clauses on a do block
do { something(); something_else() } if $cond;
do { something(); something_else() } while $counter--;
```

This makes loop construction easier in certain cases. For example, the eof function doesn't return a meaningful value until after an attempt to read from the file handle it tests.

```
# do { } while loops execute their body before ever testing the conditional
# Perl 5
open my $fh, '<', 'somefile.txt' or die $!;
do {
    my $line = <$fh>;
} until eof $fh;
```

while(my $line = <$fh>) { } is a better idiom for the same purpose. It builds in the logic of the previous example but is more concise and readable. < > is the operator version of the readline() built-in function. When either is used as the condition in a while loop, the while loop terminates when no more data is available to read (but not when blank lines or 0s are read).

In Perl 5, next doesn't work as expected in do { } while blocks. do { } while blocks need an extra set of { } inside the first set to make it function correctly.

```
# Work-around - Perl 5 do blocks can't use next directly
# Adapted from "perldoc perlsyn"
my $i;
do {{
    my $line = readline STDIN;
    chomp $line;
    next unless $line;
    # process $line
}} until $i++ > $10;
```

This is an accepted idiom.

Anonymous Subroutines

Code blocks created with the sub { } syntax can be stored in variables or passed to built-in or user-defined functions. In Perl 6, the sub keyword is optional except when the block otherwise looks like a hash or appears alone as a statement. Code blocks created with sub { } return a *code reference* for later execution of the code in the block. A code reference created directly from { } or sub { } is said to be an *anonymous subroutine*. If this anonymous subroutine references lexical variables from its enclosing block, it's said to be a *lexical closure* and is also said to *close over* those variables.

```
# Perl 6 - using a bare block as a code reference
my $coderef = {
    foo('bar', $baz, $^quux);
}
$coderef.(10); # calls foo('bar', $baz, 10)
```

Assignment doesn't automatically create reference context in any case, but this behavior is consistent with how Perl 6 handles the assignment of arrays and hashes to scalars.

```
# Perl 6 - other cases where assignment creates references
my $arrayref = @array;   # same as my $arrayref = \@array;
my $hashref = %hash;     # same as my $hashref = \%hash;
```

If $coderef is intended to contain the return value of foo(...), then the do keyword is required to break the tie.

```
# Perl 6 - avoiding generation of anonymous subroutines
my $coderef = do {
    foo('bar', $baz, $^quux);
}
```

This puts the result of calling foo() into $coderef, just like in Perl 5.

BEGIN Blocks

BEGIN blocks execute just as soon as the compiler encounters them while compiling the program. Compilation stops, the code is executed, and then compilation continues.

```
# Perl 5 and Perl 6
# Print HTTP headers as soon as possible, before something blows up, to

# avoids the "Premature end of HTTP headers" Web server confusion when errors are

# output headers
BEGIN {
    print qq{Content-type: text/html\n\n};
};
```

Perl 5 programmers should be doing use CGI::Carp 'fatalToBrowser' instead of this.

Perl 6 adds support for BEGIN blocks in the middle of expressions. BEGIN blocks can now compute values.

```
# Perl 6
# BEGIN blocks run only once at startup and can pre-compute expressions
# These two lines are equivalent:
my $seconds_in_a_day = BEGIN { 60 * 60 * 24 };
my $seconds_in_a_day = 86400;
```

Applying Perl's constant expression-folding logic during the optimizing phase would prevent this value from being calculated more than once anyway. Wrapping a BEGIN block around a file test (or anything else that's nonconstant and would change over the course of the program run) would change the program's behavior. The value computed at startup is used every time the expression is encountered.

```
# Perl 6
# BEGIN blocks run only once at startup and can precompute expressions
my $filename = 'data.txt';
my $f = open '>>', $filename or die $!;
for 1..100 {
    $f.print rand(), "\n";
    print "$filename is ", -s $filename, "bytes long right now.\n";
    print "It was ", BEGIN { -s 'data.txt' }, " bytes when we started.\n";
}
```

BEGIN blocks are closely related to macro declarations, briefly mentioned in PerlSubroutines. BEGIN blocks shouldn't use lexical variables initialized outside the BEGIN block, as the initialization logic wouldn't have yet run when the BEGIN block runs. In this example, $filename and $f are both undef when the BEGIN block runs.

Inline BEGIN blocks are useful for autonumbering things. Perl 6 has a special syntax for creating enumerations, but if you were to build your own enumeration, it could look like this:

```
my $field; BEGIN { $field  = 0; };
sub up    () { BEGIN { $field++ } }
sub down  () { BEGIN { $field++ } }
sub left  () { BEGIN { $field++ } }
sub right () { BEGIN { $field++ } }
```

When autonumbering is what you want, it's nice not to have to renumber things manually as items are added to the list and removed from it.

END Blocks

END { } is the opposite of BEGIN { }. Unless something truly foul happens, the END { } blocks run before the program exits. They're useful for cleanup, but perl will free any memory and close any open files when the interpreter exits. (And if it doesn't, a reasonable operating system will.)

if Blocks

if blocks conditionally execute a block.

```
# If statement - Perl 6 only
if $num {
    print "$num is a true value\n";
}
# If statement - Perl 5 and 6
if($num) {
    print "$num is a true value\n";
}
```

You can also chain if blocks together with elsif statements. One, at most, will be run.

```
# if statement with elsif blocks - Perl 5 and 6
if(! defined $num) {
    print "Not even defined.\n";
} elsif($num == 0) {
    print "Zero.\n";
} elsif($num == 1) {
    print "One.\n";
} else {
    print "I don't know what it is.\n";
}
```

You can use if as a clause on the end of a statement.

```
print "Zero\n" if ! $num;
```

unless is a variant of if with inverted logic.

```
print "Zero" unless $num;
```

unless makes otherwise awkward expressions read logically.

given Blocks

given statements know how to test values in an intelligent, type-dependent way. when blocks save chaining if and elsif blocks. See Chapter 9 for more information.

sub, macro, method, rule

sub defines a subroutine.

```
# Simple subroutine definition - Perl 5 or Perl 6
sub guess {
    rand > 0.5 ? "Yes" : "No";
}
# Simple anonymous subroutine (reference) construction - Perl 5 or Perl 6
sub { rand > 0.5 ? "Yes" : "No"; };
```

Like other blocks, the last statement of the block to execute is the value of the block. When called, the guess() function will return either Yes or No. return exits the currently executing function and transfers control to from wherever it was called.

macro blocks are very much like normal sub subroutines, but their code is spliced into wherever they're used and optimized in that context.

method is a specialized form of sub for creating methods in objects.

rule compiles a named pattern matching rule. Rules can call other rules or subroutines, and subroutines can call rules. The grammar is similar to Perl 5's extended regular expressions (regular expressions with the x flag). Chapter 11 covers subroutines.

for and loop Blocks

Perl 5's for statement will iterate over a list or emulate C's for statement when given three arguments delimited by semicolons. The three-argument version of Perl 5's for statement is modeled after the C language's for statement. Perl 5's three-argument for is Perl 6's loop. The for statement in Perl 6 always takes a list of values to iterate over, which is how for in Perl 5 is most often used.

```
# Perl 5 or Perl 6 - loop
for my $thing (@things) {
    process($thing);
}
```

$_ is topicalized to each element of the list or array if no other scalar is provided.

```
# Perl 5 or Perl 6 - loop
for (@children) {
    process($_);
}
```

Like if, unless, while, and loop in Perl 6, for can be used as a modifier on a statement.

```
# Perl 5 or Perl 6 - loop
process $_ for @children;
```

Statement modifiers such as this can be written without parentheses in Perl 5 even though the block forms require them.

loop() initializes, tests, and increments, using three expressions.

```
# Perl 6 - simple loop() example
loop(my $index = 0; $index < 100; $index++) {
    print $index, "\n";
}
```

This will loop from 0 to 99. To loop to 100, use <= rather than <. Perl 5's for() is overloaded to also do this.

loop by itself is the preferred Perl 6 idiom for creating endless loops.

```
# Perl 6 - infinite loops with loop { }
loop {
    all(@cows).location == $home;
}
```

last and redo control looping.

gather

Perl 6 introduces gather { } and take. gather { } works with loop constructs such as for. Every argument to take inside the gather { } block becomes another return value in the list of return values of gather { }.

```
# Perl 5 - build one list from another list
my @processed_values;
for my $value (@values) {
    # process $value
    push @processed_values, $value;
}
# Perl 5 with Perl6::Gather - build one list from another
use Perl6::Gather;
my @processed_values = gather {
    for my $value (@values) {
        # process $value
        take $value;
    }
};
```

Unlike map { }, a for loop contained in a gather { } may redo, next, and use other loop control devices. for doesn't need to contain a loop at all, it may contain several, or in Perl 6 it may use zip and a loop block prototyped to accept several values in each iteration.

```
# Perl 6 - gathering from a loop that eats several arguments each iteration
my @sore_feet = gather {
    for zip @pins, @needles -> $pin, $needle {
        take walk_on($pin, $needle);
    }
}
```

The gathered function returns undef if nothing has been gathered in the current gather block. If anything has been gathered, it returns an array reference to an array holding the items taken.

Perl6::Gather is a source filter and is thus not recommended for serious implementation work.

hash Blocks

hash blocks aren't really code blocks. hash is a type identifier that serves as a sort of typecast to force a context. Braces used to construct hashes aren't code blocks exactly, but they can contain code. With the hash keyword in front of them, code in the braces will be executed with the expectation that it will evaluate to a list of pair objects. Chapter 8 explains hash construction and initialization.

POST Blocks

POST { } blocks always run after the block they're in runs. This gives routines a chance to clean up. It simplifies writing blocks that may exit in numerous successful and unsuccessful scenarios. Other languages have hung finally blocks after the block they modify. Perl doesn't. Instead, POST { } goes inside the block it cleans up after.

Hook::Scope by Arthur Bergman gives Perl 5 a knock-off version.

```
# Cleanup regardless of whether we left by error, return, or fall through
# Perl 5
use Hook::Scope 'POST';
use IO::Handle;
sub perform_transaction {
    open my $f, '>', 'transaction.log' or die $!;
    while(<STDIN>) {
        die unless $_;
        $f->print($_);
    }
    POST {
        $f->print("--------------------------\n");
        $f->print("end of log ", scalar localtime, "\n");
        $f->print("--------------------------\n");
        $f->close;
    };
}
```

Here's the same example again, this time written in Perl 6:

```
# Cleanup regardless of whether we left by error, return, or fall through
# Perl 6
sub perform_transaction {
    my $f = open '>', 'transaction.log' or die $!;
    while(<STDIN>) {
        die unless $_;
        $f->print $_;
    }
    POST {
        print $f "--------------------------\n";
        print $f "end of log ", scalar localtime, "\n";
        print $f "--------------------------\n";
        close $f;
    }
}
```

Whether these routines exit by falling through to the end, throwing an exception, or returning at some point, the POST { } block runs regardless. An is post trait is available in Perl 6 to attach POST-time behavior to a lexical variable created in that scope. See the example in "UNDO Blocks".

Should multiple POST { } blocks be put in a block, all of them run on the exit of that block, and they run in the order they were declared.

Hook::LexScope also accepts a 'PRE' option that provides PRE { } blocks.

CATCH Blocks

CATCH { } blocks intercept death when die is invoked. Only one CATCH { } can be specified in a block. When die is called, perl goes into a loop where it looks for a CATCH handler, and if it can't find one, it exits from the current block or returns from the current subroutine. Eventually it will find itself back in a block that defined a CATCH handler, or it will exit completely from the program. If it exits completely from the program, the default error handler is said to run, and you see the message from die and Perl's usual diagnostics. Like POST { }, CATCH { } goes inside the block it guards, not around it or attached to the end of it. This is different from the arrangement that Perl 5 has with eval { }, which wraps around the outside of the block being guarded. See Chapter 15 for details on error handling.

KEEP Blocks

Should a block exit successfully, it may be desirable to update internal state, committing any changes.

Perl 6 defines a KEEP { } block that runs when the enclosing block exits successfully. An is keep trait is available on lexical variables and runs when the KEEP { } logic for that blocks runs, if it runs. Perl 5 has no direct equivalent.

UNDO Blocks

Should CATCH { } fail to successfully deal with the error, any UNDO { } blocks in the current scope will run. They're tasked with rolling back any changes and doing any cleanup needed.

You can attach UNDO-like logic to variables using traits.

```
my $dire_predirection is undo { $dire_prediction = "Told ya so!" } =
    "Something bad is going to happen!";
```

Perl 5 has no direct equivalent.

Loop and Block Control Keywords

I mentioned last as a way of exiting from a block. It works something like return, but it provides no value to return, and it ends iteration in a loop rather than exiting a subroutine.

last

last gets you out of a for loop, a loop loop, a while loop, or an if statement. In the case of a loop, the loop stops looping. You can immediately embed one kind of block in another.

```
# Perl 5 - example usage of last keyword
for my $thing (@things) {
    $thing->process();
    last if $quitting_time;
}
```

You shouldn't use last to exit a grep or map in Perl 5. It can't exit any block type that allows a return value. Specifically, you can't last from subroutines and do blocks.

next and NEXT Blocks

The next keyword is used in while statements, for loops, and loop loops to skip the rest of the loop. In a loop, the iterator is executed again. In all cases, the loop test is run again. If the loop test permits, the loop is run again.

```
# Perl 5 - example usage of next keyword
for my $thing (@things) {
    next unless $thing->processable();
    $thing->process();
}
```

next doesn't work in do { } blocks, as do blocks may generate a value and something else may depend on getting this value.

```
# next may not be used in a block that is expected to result in a value
perl -e 'do { next; };'
Can't "next" outside a loop block at -e line 1.
# bare blocks in void context in Perl 5 are not expected to produce a
value
perl -e '{ next; };'
```

In Perl 6, after the body of the loop executes and before the next iterations, any NEXT blocks inside it execute. Executing a next instruction just speeds this along: the NEXT block runs immediately rather than waiting for the end of the block to be reached.

Perl 5 has a continue block that can be attached to the end of a block. Between each iteration, it runs. (Actually, Perl has had a continue block since Perl 1.0, which was long before my time.)

```
# Perl 5 - print numbers, randomly skipping some, but always printing a
# message between them - demonstrates next and continue { }

for my $num (1 .. 10) {
    next if rand 1 > 0.5;
    print $num, "\n";
} continue {
    print "continuing\n";
}
```

This is useful for structuring code to have obvious intentions.

redo

redo is similar to next, but the iterator isn't run in a loop loop and doesn't step to the next list item in a for loop. redo sends control back to the top of the loop to have it run again. Control transfers directly to the body of the for, loop, while, do while, or do block.

```
# Redo - Perl 5
my $num = 3;
{
    print "hi\n"; $num--; redo if $num;
};
```

You can use redo to create lightweight loop structures.

```
{
    try_to_start_engine();
```

```
    last if $temp > 200;
    redo if $temp < 30;
}
```

A certain technical reviewer considers this an excellent alternative to do { ... } while structures in cases where redo is needed, as redo and last aren't available in do { } blocks.

skip

skip continues examining alternatives in a given block, going to the next when { } block, rather than exiting the given { } block. Otherwise, the given { } would exit successfully after the first matching when block and consider no more when { } cases. skip exists in Perl 6 but not in Perl 5. See Chapter 9 for details on the given and when statements.

Variable, Scope, and Blocks

Variables created in a block are visible until the end of that block. The code block is the scope of a lexical variable. Blocks accept input as arguments and return the results by using return or by letting the values fall off the end. In this way, data moves into and out of the scope.

Blocks May Return Lists

Blocks in Perl can generate lists of data. This applies to do blocks and to subroutine definitions alike.

```
# Blocks that can be used in expressions may evaluate to lists of
# values, not just one single result value - Perl 5
my @two_uniqe_numbers = do {
    my $rand1 = int rand 100;
    my $rand2;
    try_again:
    $rand2 = int rand 100;
    goto try_again if $rand2 == $rand1;
    $rand1, $rand2;
};
```

This initializes @two_uniqe_numbers without cluttering the main block with a lot of variables (or code). No parentheses are needed around $rand1, $rand2, as the precedence has no ambiguity.

Stricture, Variable, Scope, and Blocks

Variables used in functions should be declared in that function. If a variable is used only inside a loop, declare it in that loop. If the whole file needs access to it, turn the file into an object and make the variable an instance variable.

When variables go out of scope, they drop their reference. Things without references to them are collected by the garbage collector in Perl 6 or dereferenced and freed immediately in Perl 5. Objects that lose their reference have DESTROY() invoked on them. File handles are closed. Blocks can be used to automatically close files, throw away data structures, and destroy temporary objects.

```
my $data = do {
    open my $file, '<', 'file.txt' or die $!;
    read $file, my $buffer, -s $file;
};
```

At the end of the block, or soon after, $file loses its last and only reference and is freed. Freeing a file handle flushes and closes it.

REFERENCES AND THANKS

Apocalypse 4, at http://dev.perl.org, deals with syntax, including the block structure of programs.

Arthur Bergman wrote Hook::Scope. Damian Conway wrote Perl6::Gather.

Summary

This chapter doesn't contain anything fundamentally new. Each change is something that people often try to do and fail and then settle for something less elegant. For instance, Perl 6's propensity for generating closures at the drop of a hat allows user-defined code to replicate anything done in the core language. Consistent rules for semicolons on the end of blocks and for creating code blocks in the first place are both essential to letting users concoct their own loop structures, iterators, and other language extensions. map and sort don't require the keyword sub stuffed before the code block, and neither should filters and sorters written in Perl.

Along with Perl 6's pushes for object orientation and extensibility, there's a push for better error processing, and UNDO and KEEP blocks help support this. The is undo and is keep traits on lexical variables make package global variables less important by generalizing the concept of the local keyword and applying it to lexicals. Should a variable need its value restored under certain conditions, it can be expressed clearly and explicitly in Perl. And the continue { } block that's as old as Perl looks like it's finally done for, but the semantics of placing control blocks in the blocks they control has allowed other blocks such as continue to be created. Specialty blocks such as NEXT { }, the successor to continue { }, now have the full advantage of access to lexical variables created in the block they modify. They can be mingled with the code in an order that reads well, such as near what they're actually undoing or catching.

CHAPTER 11

■■■

Subroutines

Each problem that I solved became a rule which served afterwards to solve other problems.

—Rene Descartes

Subroutines are code reuse at the most basic level, and code reuse is a good thing. Other control structures will execute one of several bits of code, will execute code conditionally, or will execute code repeatedly, but only by using subroutines in their various forms can you reuse code between different parts of a program. Macros, methods, closures, and multimethods are all forms of subroutines, and all serve essentially this purpose.

Tom Christiansen's 1996 article, "Seven Deadly Sins of Perl", listed implicit behaviors and hidden context dependencies as the first sin. In Perl, one subroutine name has many behaviors, and the selected behavior depends on the return type expected, or the *context*. Unlike the types of variables passed in as arguments, the expected return type isn't readily obvious, and programmers don't expect a programming language to go through the trouble to infer the expected return type as Perl does. Overloading on return type is the magic that lets functions, especially built-in functions, do something useful in any reasonable situation. In Perl 6, references are readily useful as whatever they reference (such as an array or hash), so it's OK for a function to always return a reference rather than returning a reference conditionally when a single return value is expected and returning a list of values where multiple values are expected. This avoids surprises by making the behavior of functions nearly identical regardless of whether a single value or multiple values are expected of it. Perl 6 introduces an object context that further allows a single returned value to behave in the many different ways a programmer may be using it; therefore, there's no longer a wrong way to use built-in functions, at least with regard to context.

The second sin in Christiansen's "Seven Deadly Sins of Perl" article was that parentheses alter the semantics of a program, changing its behavior. Parentheses are largely optional in Perl, so the fact that function calls behave the same way with and without parentheses around arguments is consistent with parentheses around the function call itself (causing the function to behave differently). Subtle changes to context often harm programmers. In Perl 6, *list context* and *list construction* are no longer necessarily the same. Whether or not an expression is parenthesized, it will behave identically. Each function call is still expected to return a single item (possibly a reference), just like when the function is called outside an expression that builds a list. This is important, as the results of one function call are often used as an item in the argument list in another function call. List context is now explicitly provided by certain operators, such as *, which is the list-flattening operator. The new `list` keyword also requests list context. Finally, subroutines may be *prototyped* (have meta-information about the arguments attached to them) to provide list context to some or all of their arguments. This gives programmers more control, allowing them to mix and match list building and list context generation.

Adjusting list building to not provide list context requires changes to how arrays, hashes, and subroutines behave in scalar context. An *object context* is recognized, where the result of a built-in function contains named methods that are useful for extracting whatever details are desired. As you'll see, Perl 6 built-ins like to return objects that encapsulate information in most places that Perl 5 built-ins return lists. Arrays and hashes in scalar context are usually in *reference context*, where a reference to the array or hash is produced. This allows parameter lists full of array and hash references to easily be built. A special case of scalar context named *numeric context* takes the length of an array rather than a reference to the array. With regard to using @array to mean the length of the array, most Perl 5 idioms will work unchanged.

This chapter talks about `Perl6::Contexts` as far as it relates to subroutine call conventions. `Perl6::Contexts` prevents the default of flattening hashes and arrays, and it introduces boolean, string, numeric, and reference contexts.

I document `Class::Multimethods` in the "Formal Parameter Lists" section. This module allows declarations of multiple methods of the same name, where each handles different combinations of types or numbers of arguments.

`Sub::Lexical` gives Perl 5 lexically scoped subroutines, a feature slated for Perl 6. Perl 6 subroutines may have package (class) scope or be scoped to a block such as `my` variables.

`Want` lets you accomplish semi-lazy list generation and provides detailed context information comparable to what Perl 6 offers.

Type-only prototypes and list flattening are concepts unique to Perl. Parameter prototypes and explicit list flattening are new to Perl as of Perl 6 but are standard fare in other languages.

Changes for Perl 6

Parentheses no longer provide list context to the items inside them. List flattening is off by default in Perl 6 but is available upon request with the new list-flattening operator, *. `list` or `@( )` provides list context in Perl 6 as well, though creating list context inside an expression that wants scalar context isn't very useful without list flattening.

Perl 5 parameters are read/write by default when referred to as `$_[0]` through the last argument. This feature lets user code `tie`, `bless`, or assign to variables passed in as arguments and have the change affect the original variable. `open` in Perl 5, for example, uses this to modify its first argument to contain an `IO::Handle` object. Perl 6 makes parameters read-only by default, though the `is copy` trait creates a local copy that can be used as a variable, and the `is rw` trait causes changes to the parameter to be synonymous with the variable or `lvalue` passed in. This replaces direct access to `@_` in Perl 5, making the feature less esoteric.

```
# Modify argument - Perl 6
sub tweak_args (int $num is rw) {
    $num++;
}
my $foo = 0;
tweak_args($foo);
print $foo, "\n";
```

This would print 1.

```
# Modify arguments - Perl 5
sub tweak_args {
    $_[0]++;
}
my $foo = 0;
tweak_args($foo);
print $foo, "\n";
```

Perl 5 copies values when the arguments are read from the argument array, @_, using assignment, shift, or other constructs that copy values, but the argument array can be directly manipulated to change the originals. Perl 6 allows the originals to be modified only if they're prototyped with the is rw trait. When arguments are passed as scalars containing references, you won't want the is rw and is copy traits, as they apply to the reference, not the data structure to which the reference points. The data structure being pointed to is implicitly read/write unless some other mechanism prevents it.

The * operator has been liberated from the tyranny of globs, where it was used to access the package symbol table. Perl 6 reassigned * to list flattening, and it's now known as the *slurpy* operator, so called because it "slurps up" all available values. Argument lists in function calls in Perl 5 flatten by default, and prototypes or the reference operator, \, is needed to pass an array or hash by reference. Perl 6 changes the default. Arrays and hashes turn into references of themselves. Arrays and hashes don't flatten at all in list context unless explicitly flattened with the flattening operator, *. To get Perl 5 list semantics for arrays, use the list-flattening operator, *, anywhere a reference operator, \, wouldn't be used.

New in Perl 6

Perl 6 adds optional formal parameter lists. Perl checks named parameters to verify that required parameters are present and no unknown parameters have been passed. One routine may be called using a mix of named parameters and positional arguments. The formal parameter lists in a function prototype also impose contexts on arguments in calls to that function, as do Perl 5 prototypes.

Perl 6 reforms the relationship between references and subroutines. The programmer performs list flattening explicitly using the list-flattening operator, *. References, on the other hand, are automatically taken and dereferenced, lessening the consequences of arrays and hashes arriving in subroutines as references. Arrays and hashes turn into references to themselves in the default scalar context. In contrast, Perl 5 places function arguments in list context and then applies the list-flattening rules, which made passing multiple independent hashes or arrays difficult compared to explicit list flattening.

Perl 6 has various new subroutine constructors: Object methods behave more like other object-oriented languages. Macros remove redundant code without the performance penalty of subroutine calls. Prototypes declare parameters, and they have more access to the information about what's going on in the program. Types can be checked as in other languages. Arguments can be passed by name while retaining all the features of prototypes. I'll discuss each of these along with their Perl 5 counterparts in this chapter.

Subroutines declared using method add logic to track the current object. This object reference is automatically read, maintained, and made available to the programmer. Routines created with the method keyword are subject to the rules of inheritance, making them reusable not only in the current program but from objects that subclass it.

You can place the multi keyword before a method declaration, subroutine declaration, and anything else that may be called with different configurations of arguments. Declared as multi, routines add prototype signature matching to facilitate overloading on argument types. This allows multiple routines with the same name to be declared, and the one used for any given call is the one most closely matching the actual number and types of the arguments passed.

Perl 6 lets you define operators as if they were subroutines.

```
# Declaring a +++ operator in Perl 6
sub infix:+++ {
    $^a++ + $^b;
}
```

Operators in Perl 6 are just funny-looking subroutine calls that take one or two arguments.

You can define macros in a similar way, but they have access to information about the current status of source code parsing. Macros, created with macro, remove redundant code without the performance penalty of subroutine calls. Macros are routines that contain mostly constant logic or compute constant values. Their code is spliced into wherever they're used. This makes maintaining code easier, allowing frequently occurring expressions to be factored out, all without the overhead of a subroutine call. They also make it easier for the optimizer to do its job. Constant expressions and values are folded in the context of the call, so most of the macro may be optimized away.

{ } creates anonymous hashes as it did in Perl 5 but only if it doesn't immediately appear to contain pairs, created by =>. Otherwise, it's a sub { } that may build a hash and evaluate to it.

Parameters, Arguments, Traits, Properties, and Attributes

Listing 11-1 shows the taxonomy of subroutine parts. It's a quick reference chart of what I'll carefully introduce in this chapter. Don't worry if it doesn't make sense now.

Listing 11-1. *Subroutine Part Nomenclature*

```
# Perl 5 nomenclature:
sub foo
    ($foo, $bar, $baz)  # <-- parameters
{ ... }
foo(
    1, 2, 3             # <-- arguments
);
```

Note that Perl 5 lacks native parameters.

```
# Perl 6 nomenclature:
my $foo
    is constant  # <-- trait
;
return 1
    but false    # <-- property
;
class Foo::Bar {
    has $.quux;  # <-- attribute
}
# Note that attribute/property is exactly the other way around in Perl 5
# documentation:
my $foo
    : shared     # <-- attribute
;
$foo->
    bar          # <-- property
;
```

Procedure, *routine*, *subroutine*, and *function* are all terms for named blocks of code.

Methods are named blocks of code, too, but they're used through the method call syntax that looks like $object->method() in Perl 5 and $object.method() in Perl 6.

A rule of thumb is that subroutines that *calculate* are called *functions*, and subroutines that *act* are called *procedures*. Subroutines called inside objects using object references are *methods*.

I'll use the term *subroutine* when I want to be intentionally generic.

Perl 5 uses the keyword sub to create methods in classes and subroutines for procedural use. Perl 6 introduces four new keywords.

- sub declares a subroutine, much like it does in Perl 5.

- macro declares a block of code that's spliced into the program where calls to it appear.

- rule declares part of a grammar.

- method declares a subroutine that's callable with the object call syntax and is inheritable in object subclasses.

- submethod declares a method that doesn't participate in inheritance.

Calling Subroutines

Given a subroutine named process_stuff, you'd call it with the following expression:

```
process_stuff();
```

To pass it the numeric value 1, you'd do the following:

```
process_stuff(1);
```

Values you pass are called *arguments*. Besides accepting values, subroutines evaluate to and return values. To save the value the function computes, write this:

```
 my $result = process_stuff(1);
```

Lists of values can be returned from and passed to subroutines, like so:

```
my @output_array = process_stuff(1, 2, 3, @input_array);
```

The return value of one function call may be used as a value to pass to another, like so:

```
process_stuff(process_stuff(1));
```

For Perl 5, you may need to instead write this:

```
process_stuff(scalar process_stuff(1));
```

The scalar keyword asks the expression after it to produce a single value. Perl 6 provides scalar context in argument lists by default.

In Perl 6, you may need to instead write the following:

```
process_stuff(* process_stuff(1));
```

This is required when the results of process_stuff(1) are multiple and should be used as the individual arguments to the other call to process_stuff(). Perl 5 does this by default.

Optional Parentheses

Functions already defined or built into perl may be called without parentheses around their arguments.

```
process_stuff 1, 2, 3;
```

Foregoing optional parentheses helps make pathological cases such as the following easier to read and type:

```
print(reverse(sort(keys(%hash))));      # Perl 5 - pathologically parenthetic
print reverse sort keys %hash;          # Perl 5 - no unneeded parentheses
print(reverse(sort(%hash.keys)));       # Perl 6 - pathological
print reverse sort %hash.keys;          # Perl 6 - no unneeded parentheses
```

The following are some alternate idioms for grouping expressions:

```
%hash.keys ==> sort ==> reverse ==> print;  # Perl 6 - pipeline operator
%hash.keys.sort.reverse.print;              # Perl 6 - autobox
%hash->keys->sort->reverse->print;          # Perl 5 - autobox
```

The Perl 5 autoboxing example requires the autobox, autobox::Core, and Perl6::Contexts modules.

In each example, %hash evaluates first, then keys, then sort, and then reverse, and finally print prints the result of that. Perl evaluates expressions inside parentheses first, since their values are needed to perform the other function calls. Likewise, it evaluates expressions on the right first when the expression isn't explicitly grouped with parentheses.

The Perl 6 pipeline operator, ==>, and its twin, <==, move data from expression to expression. This solves cases where parentheses would otherwise be required to clear up ambiguity. Data moves from right to left in the first example—the pipeline can do the same but without parentheses to associate arguments with their respective function. Or it can move data the other way if that helps you wrap your mind around the problem.

To find out where parentheses are assumed, use B::Deparse, -p at the command prompt for your operating system.

```
$ perl -MO=Deparse,-p -e 'print reverse sort keys %hash;'
# outputs:
# print(reverse(sort(keys(%hash))));
```

Functions also tend to take as their last argument any variable-sized list, so parentheses are often not needed. Function calls will look like function $something, $something, @stuff, where @stuff is a whole bunch of stuff to process that could come from another function. sort, for instance, takes an (optional but recommended) code block and then any number of data items to sort. These data items may come from an array or another function.

```
# Many functions (such as sort) take a list of things to be
# processed as the last argument
sort { $a <=> $b }    @stuff;    # Perl 5
sort { $^a <=> $^b }, @stuff;    # Perl 6
sort { $a <=> $b } grep { $_ % 2 } @stuff;        # Perl 5
sort { $^a <=> $^b },  grep { $_ % 2 }, @stuff; # Perl 6
```

<== in Perl 6 supplies the variable-sized list of arguments, with any positional or fixed arguments still attached to the function call.

```
sort { $^a <=> $^b } <== grep { $_ % 2 } <== @stuff;  # Perl 6
```

Built-in functions are always prototyped, so parentheses are optional when the rest of the things in the expression are arguments to the function call. Omitting parentheses also works when a small, fixed number of arguments is prototyped. scalar will never gobble up more than one thing, for example. Arguments don't need to be grouped when the rest of the comma-separated values on the line belong to that last function call. You'll need parentheses to explicitly separate which arguments go to which function call.

```
process_stuff(1, 2, process_stuff(50, 51), 3, 4);
```

Use or to test for the failure of built-in functions that perform input.

```
open my $fh, '<', 'file.txt' or die $!;      # perl 5
my $fh = open '<', 'file.txt' or die $!;     # perl 6
```

open will return the special undef value should it fail. $! will contain the text of the error message. or, and, err, and xor operate at very low precedence. They will always run after everything before them. The second line is equivalent to my $fh = open('<', 'file.txt') or die($!).

■No ampersand in function calls Don't place ampersands, &, in front of function names when making function calls. Ampersands disable prototypes in Perl 5, which probably isn't what you want. It was useful in Perl 4, but it has other purposes entirely in Perl 5 and yet another completely different purpose in Perl 6. The list-flattening operator, *, serves the purpose of disabling prototypes in Perl 6, replacing the Perl 5 meaning of &func.

Subroutine Style: No Globals

You may be thinking to yourself, "Why bother to pass and return data when I can just leave it in global variables?" Here's why: A human searching through the program can't easily trace the flow of data. You can't look at a subroutine call and easily decide whether it or another subroutine it calls disturbs any given variable. You have to trace through all the code. Subroutine reuse is almost impossible. You don't know when any of the potentially thousands of global values may have been already set, waiting to be operated on by a function, so before you can try to use that subroutine or any subroutine it uses, you must back up all the values that may be overwritten and then restore them when you're done. Subtle bugs are hard to find and easy to introduce. All in all, it quickly becomes more work than passing the variables as arguments. Passing arguments allows private data, private data keeps things separate, and separation is the cornerstone of organization.

Contexts

Many built-in functions behave differently depending on how you're trying to use them—or the *context* in which they're used. User-defined functions may be written to return different values in different contexts as well.

The section "Creating Subroutines" explains how a function is able to learn the context it's being called in and how it's able to adjust its behavior accordingly. Right now, I'm still concerned with calling functions, and that means dealing with contexts from the caller's perspective.

Useful Context

If you're using the result of localtime as a single value, you'd probably like a nicely formatted, human-readable rendering of the time. But if it always returned the rendered time, then it'd be difficult to obtain the current year, month, day, minute, hour, or second. When you use localtime as if it were a list of values, you get just that—the individual numbers that make up the time and date. This behavior has the technical name of *function overloading on return type*. Contexts control this overloading by specifying the desired return type.

```
# List and scalar context behaviors - Perl 5

print join ", ", localtime(), "\n";
# outputs: 36, 6, 0, 3, 8, 114, 3, 245, 0,

print localtime() . "\n";
# outputs: Wed Sep  3 00:06:36 2014
```

Perl 5 has three possible contexts: scalar, list, and void. Concatenation in Perl 5, ., enforces scalar context on its operands, asking for a single string value. Function calls provide list context in Perl 5, asking for as many values as an expression cares to provide. These rules make code sequences like this work:

```
# Perl 5 - list context and multiple return values allows easy
# gluing together of functions
use POSIX;
print strftime "%Y-%m-%d %H:%M\n", localtime;
```

The list generated by `localtime` is exactly what was expected by `strftime`. (Perl's built-ins generally follow POSIX, and the `POSIX` module generally does, too.)

Perl 6 changes this behavior. Subroutine calls used as arguments to other subroutine calls, such as with the `print "..."`, `localtime` arrangement previously, don't provide list context to subroutines used in the argument list (`localtime` in this example). Instead, `localtime` would return an object encapsulating information about the current time and date, which another function, such as `strftime`, would know how to use.

Object Context

Object context makes possible such tasks as `srtftime.wday` in addition to neatly communicating sets of values between functions. Object context is generated both by attempting a method call on the return value of a function, as with the `$subref.assuming` example later in this chapter, and also when a scalar result is expected from a built-in. User-defined functions can do this, too, of course.

List flattening in argument lists, using the * Perl 6 operator, will seldom be needed when connecting built-in functions. (User-defined functions can and should also take advantage of object context.) The return value of one is immediately useful in a call to another.

Void Context

Void context is provided to plain statements not at the end of any function or block.

```
# Warning about void context - Perl 5
use strict;
use warnings;
my $arbitrary_variable;
$arbitrary_variable;
```

This produces the diagnostic warning `Useless use of private variable in void context.` A for statement is valid only in void context because it produces no value. Other things with side effects, such as function calls or assignments, are valid in void context and other contexts as well.

List Context

List context is attained in different ways in Perl 5 than in Perl 6. Providing list context to an expression isn't the same as building a list. It's possible to build a list from expressions where each expression is evaluated in scalar context. (Indeed, this is the default in Perl 6.)

You have several ways to create lists (which isn't the same as list context) in Perl, and these haven't changed between Perl 5 and Perl 6. Function and method call arguments are part of a list unless the function was prototyped to accept no arguments or a single argument. Lists are built in list context with the comma operator, `,`, but parentheses are needed to group together the terms to be assigned, such as `my @arr = (1, 2, 3);`. `{ }` builds lists of pair objects in Perl 6 and a list of interspersed keys and values in Perl 5. `[ ]` builds a list of values to create an anonymous array. Hyper operators and the pipeline operators in Perl 6 also build lists.

Creating lists of values is inarguably valuable, but providing list context to expressions is far less important in Perl 6 than in Perl 5; this is because object context is available to communicate collections of related values. When list context is provided to an expression in Perl 6, the result doesn't necessarily flatten but may instead turn into a reference to an array, a stringification of the list, or present itself in other ways. You should use list flattening when traditional Perl 5 list context is desired.

In Perl 5, merely placing an expression inside parentheses provides list context to the items inside the parentheses. Perl 6 lists don't provide list context to the items inside them. To provide list context to an expression using Perl 5, do this:

```
# These two lines both force process_something() into list context - Perl 5
( process_something() );
some_function( process_something() );
```

Building a list in Perl 6 looks like any of these:

```
# These lines all force process_something() into list context - Perl 6
* process_something();

sort { $^a cmp $^b } <== process_something();
list process_something();
@things >>=<< process_something();
```

Each of these statements do very different things, but they all provide list context to process_something(). Only the list-flattening operator, *, and the pipeline operators, <== and ==>, emulate Perl 5 in that expression results are flattened as well as evaluated in list context. You can use the flattened list to initialize the elements of an array or provide multiple positional arguments in a subroutine call.

Perl 5 functions and list constructors provide list context to their arguments by default, but they don't have to do so. A prototype can override this, providing scalar context to a number of arguments and list context to the last. Perl6::Contexts also changes this default.

Perl 6 functions provide scalar context to their arguments by default, but they don't have to do so. A prototype can override this, giving list context to any or all of them. A Perl 6 prototype may also request list flattening, which implies list context, for a single trailing array or hash parameter.

Perl 6's * goes a step further than providing list context by also expanding the elements of the list into parameters. Writing some_function(* @arr) is the same as writing some_function(@arr[0], @arr[1], @arr[2]) for an array with three elements. Each element of @arr is passed as a separate argument when flattened with *. Perl 5 does this by default.

```
# Sometimes several array elements need to be passed as separate arguments

somefunc(@array[0], @array[1], @array[2], @array[3]); # yuck!
somefunc(@array);                                      # Perl 5 - much better!
somefunc(*@array);                                     # Perl 6 - much better!
```

Perl 5 code frequently uses slices to pick out array elements to serve as arguments.

```
# Array slice to reorder array elements passing each element
# as a separate argument

somefunc(@array[5, 3, 4, 1, 2]);      # Perl 5
somefunc(*@array[5, 3, 4, 1, 2]);     # Perl 6
```

Chapter 5 covered array slices. In Perl 5, running all the members of an array through a map { } is another common case.

```
# Arguments to functions may be computed using another function.
# Each item returned from map is a separate argument to somefunc.

somefunc(map { CGI::param($_) } qw/name address city state cc zip/);     # Perl 5

somefunc(* map { CGI::param($_) }, <<name address city state cc zip>>); # Perl 6
```

You should use [ ] around the map instead if a single argument is expected rather than a variable-sized list of parameters, each parameter being a value to process. A function that flattens its argument list, which is the default in Perl 6, sees them as the same.

Assigning to an array variable provides list context.

```
# Force process_something() into list context - Perl 5 and Perl 6
my @array = process_something();

# Force process_something() into list context but flatten it too - Perl 6
my @array = * process_something();
my @array >>=<< process_something();
```

Writing @array = (process_something()) would be redundant. Forcing list context is useful only when the context isn't currently list context and the list context behavior is needed for some reason. In practice, list context rarely needs to be forced, but scalar context often does. (* ...) should be seldom needed, but [ ] will often be needed; however, it may be useful to build an array reference while providing list context to the things being used to build it, which would require [* ...].

No such thing as an "array context" exists, though functions may be prototyped to expect an array, and an array reference context exists, which is a special case of reference context.

Scalar Context

Use context generation keywords to explicitly create scalar context. That's scalar in Perl 5 and any ref, int, bool, num, and int (or their uppercase counterparts) in Perl 6. Perl 6 defines scalar context creation operators, +, ~, and ?, for numeric, string, and boolean context, respectively. In Perl 6, arrays and hashes in reference context turn into references to themselves, as mentioned. Reference context applies when in scalar context, but not in numeric, boolean, or string scalar contexts. Reference context is the default for function and method argument lists.

You can pass scalar references manually, and this section shows how to do that. It's an alternative to prototypes and part of the mechanism of prototypes.

Scalar context is the default in Perl 6.

```
# Passing two arrays - Perl 6
do_something(@array1, @array2);
sub do_something (@array1, @array2) {
    # ...
}
```

You can pass arrays by reference (as scalars) manually with the reference operator, \, in Perl 5.

```
# Passing two arrays - Perl 5, naive case

use autobox;
use autobox::Core;

do_something(\@array1, \@array2);

sub do_something {
    my @array1 = shift->flatten;
    my @array2 = shift->flatten;
    # ...
}
```

Rather than explicitly taking references to arguments, the function itself may be prototyped to do it for you.

```
# Passing two arrays - Perl 5, with prototypes
# function definition must come before call to it

use autobox;
use autobox::Core;

sub do_something (\@\@) {
  my @array1 = shift->flatten;
  my @array2 = shift->flatten;
  # ...
}

do_something(@array1, @array2);
```

The second Perl 5 do_something() call lacks the \ operators before the arguments. It doesn't need them thanks to the prototype. The prototype creates scalar contexts for two positional arguments. In this particular scalar context, arrays turn into references to themselves.

Prototypes save the caller from having to use the reference operator to pass references to the arrays instead of the flattened contents of the arrays. This saves syntax when calling functions, moving it to the function definition where it's needed only once.

The Perl 6 example more closely tracks other languages, where parameters are declared, read, and typed, all in one shot. Perl6::Contexts does the same.

```
# Receiving two arrays and passing two arrays - Perl 5

use Perl6::Contexts;

sub do_something {
  my $array1_ref = shift;
  my $array2_ref = shift;
  # ...
}
do_something(@array1, @array2);
```

Without explicitly taking references with the \ Perl 5 operator, and without prototyping the subroutine, array and hash arguments are forced into scalar context. This doesn't work for lists returned from other functions, which do get flattened still, as you'll see in a moment.

Each of these examples passes the arrays by reference rather than flattening them. The Perl 6 example receives a view of the original array that can't be modified but isn't copied. This behavior can be changed in the prototype. The last one read the arguments as references and placed them in a scalar rather than flattening them. Working by reference is necessary for larger arrays (for efficiency) or for sharing data structures. The last example could also have used autobox and autobox::Core, in which case it would read my @array1 = shift->flatten; rather than my @array1_ref = shift; to match the previous examples and work on a copy rather than a reference.

Here's a test case for the previous example:

```
# Receiving two arrays and passing two arrays - Perl 5

use Perl6::Contexts;

sub do_something {
    my $array1_ref = shift;
    my $array2_ref = shift;
    print $array1_ref->[0], "\n";
    print $array2_ref->[0], "\n";
}
my @array1 = map int rand 100, 1 .. 10;
my @array2 = map int rand 100, 1 .. 10;
do_something(@array1, @array2);
```

This creates two arrays of random numbers, each having 100 elements, each element between 0 and 99. do_something() prints the first element of each array.

Hashes and scalars work as parameters, too. These examples use arrays as a simple case.

Scalar and List Context Confusion

Context can bite you if you're not careful. Consider the following:

```
# Subtle bugs with list versus scalar context - Perl 5
print reverse "Hi there kids";
print "\n";
```

This behaves as if the reverse isn't even there. Talk about confounding (for a novice, I mean)!

Perl 5's reverse reverses both strings and lists. A single string is just a list with one item in it. reverse takes its clues from the context. When a list is wanted *from* reverse, it assumes a list has been provided to it and reverses the list. When a single value is expected *from* reverse, it reverses a single value. The previous print example gives reverse a list context, so reverse provides a reversed list. A list with one item in it, when reversed, is the *same* list.

```
# Forcing scalar context example with reverse - Perl 5
print scalar reverse "Hi there kids";
print "\n";
```

This outputs sdik ereht iH. The following is a slightly more complicated example of getting a list where a single value is expected:

```
# Subtle bugs with list vs. scalar context - Perl 5

use Socket;

my $sockaddr = sockaddr_in($port, inet_aton($host));          # correct
connect($sh, $sockaddr) or die $!;

connect($sh, sockaddr_in($port, inet_aton($host))) or die $!; # wrong!
```

It looks like you should be able to just take the expression sockaddr_in($port, inet_aton($host)) and move it directly into the connect call's argument list, but if you do, it will change from evaluating in scalar context to evaluating in list context, and sockaddr_in behaves differently in each context. In scalar context, it builds the SOCKADDR_IN data structure required by connect. In list context, it takes the data structure apart. The scalar keyword explicitly forces scalar context.

```
connect($sh, scalar sockaddr_in($port, inet_aton($host))) or die $!; # fixed
```

You can also avoid this problem with a prototype that specifies that the function takes two scalar values. It just so happens that connect is prototyped, so perl does this for connect. The "wrong" example works even though I said it shouldn't according to this discussion. I'll cover prototypes in the "Prototypes" section.

■**Nonsense context cases** There's no logical, obvious behavior for humans to expect of reverse when used in a scalar context with a list of arguments: print scalar reverse "hi", "there", "kids", "\n";. What happens when you run it? There's *no single rule* describing what built-ins do in scalar context when they're fed a list. Each function and built-in function responds to combinations of context and argument types differently. It may decide how to behave based on the length of the argument list, or it may decide from what context it is in, or both.

Creating Subroutines

The flip side of the coin from the subroutine call is the subroutine definition. They mirror each other. For each argument passed, a parameter is read. For each result value used from the function call, a value is returned inside the function. To create a subroutine, you must read the arguments and compute the return values.

The following sections introduce some basics on which to build. From then, this chapter is about tricks, features, and idioms related to defining subroutines.

Creating Subroutines in Perl 5

To start, name the subroutine. The best names explain what the subroutine does, not how it does it. (The best comments explain why something does what it does, not how it does it. Save the how for code, I guess.)

Got a name? Good. In its basic form, a subroutine looks like this:

```
# Simplest possible subroutine - Perl 5 or Perl 6
sub your_name_here {
}
```

That subroutine reads no arguments and returns no value. (But if one is read, undef will be provided.) The following one does return a value:

```
# A useless subroutine that reads arguments and returns something
# Perl 5

sub your_name_here {
    my $output;
    for(@_) {
        $output .= "Why did you pass me '$_'?\n";
    }
    return $output;
}
```

Remember that return is optional at the end of the block. return $output; could have been written as $output; instead in this example. The return keyword is required to force a subroutine to return before it reaches the end of the block.

Reading Context in Subroutines

Subroutines can determine what context they're executing in using the wantarray built-in function in Perl 5. Remember that *context* just means how the return value is being used and whether the result is used at all.

wantarray returns undef for void context, returns 0 for scalar context, and returns 1 for list context. wantarray is kind of a misnomer—it should have been called wantlist.

```
# Three basic possible context scenarios - Perl 5
sub return_garbage {
    return unless defined wantarray;
    return 1 if ! wantarray;
    return (1, 2, 3) if wantarray;   # or just return (1, 2, 3)
}
```

Subroutines can sense context to do the right thing when returning an array. Return the elements of an array when a list is expected and a reference to the array when a scalar is expected. The following is a common idiom in Perl 5:

```
# If they use us as a reference, be a reference, if they use us as a
# list, return a list - Perl 5
sub get_field_names { return wantarray ? @field_names : \@field_names; }
```

Want, a CPAN module by Robin Houston, gives Perl 5 a want function that's open and extensible, like Perl 6's. The want function takes the name of a context and returns a true or false value to indicate whether the subroutine is executing in that context. It understands VOID, SCALAR, LIST, RVALUE, LVALUE, CODE, HASH, ARRAY, GLOB, and OBJECT. want('OBJECT') returns true if the caller is expecting you to return an object reference. These names are consistent with the return values of the ref built-in where they overlap. See perldoc -f ref for more information on these names.

want does more than tell how the return values are being used. It tells you how many arguments are expected. Passing it a number, it indicates true or false to indicate whether at least that many return values are expected. If the result of the function is being assigned to an array variable or is used in a for loop (or other similar situations), then the subroutine is effectively being asked for an infinite number of values. See Listing 11-2.

Listing 11-2. *Generating Finite Lists for Function Results*

```perl
#!/usr/bin/perl
# Compute prime numbers, but only as many as actually needed
# Perl 5

use strict;
use warnings;
use Want;

sub prime_numbers {
    my $i = 0;
    my @results;
    if(want('Infinity')) {
        die "Infinite list of primes requested - almost certainly an error";
    }
    while(want(scalar @results)) {
        # print "debug: i: $i\n";
        # print "debug: results: ", scalar @results, "\n";
        my $divisible_by = $i - 1;
        while($divisible_by > 1) {
            if($i % $divisible_by == 0) {
                # print "debug: $i is divisible by $divisible_by\n";
                last;
            }
            $divisible_by--;
        }
        push @results, $i if $divisible_by == 1;
        $i++;
    }
    @results;
}

# A test case and example usage of our function:
my ($first_prime, $second_prime, $third_prime) = prime_numbers();
print join ", ", $first_prime, $second_prime, $third_prime; print "\n";

# Another test case and example usage of our function:
my @primes;
($primes[0], $primes[1], $primes[2], $primes[3], $primes[4]) =
    prime_numbers();
print join ", ", @primes; print "\n";
```

Before the result-generating loop starts, this program makes sure an infinite number of results haven't been requested. *Arbitrary number* may be a better expression—they aren't explicitly requesting an infinite number, merely as many as you care to produce, but this subroutine delegates that decision to its caller by rejecting this case. Another program may default to a reasonable value, such as 100.

`while(want(scalar @results))` is the heart of this routine. In English, it says, "As long as I don't have as many results as wanted, keep computing more results". The contents of the `@results` array are returned at the end of the function.

As long as there aren't enough result values, it tries to factor `$i` in another `while` loop. After that, regardless of whether it was able to factor `$i`, it increments `$i` using `$i++`.

The number of items in `@results` grows by one every time it's able to find something it can't factor. If you set `$divisible_by` at one less than the number you're trying to factor, and then count down to one without finding something you can evenly divide `$i` by, then you've found something divisible only by itself and one. That's what a prime number is. (By the way, you can do this in more efficient ways.) The inner loop stops, using the `last` keyword, as soon it finds a factor. Stopping saves CPU—it doesn't matter how many factors each number has, only whether it has a factor. At the end of the inner loop, you know whether you've found a factor by whether the `$divisible_by` counter made it all the way down to one or whether it stopped first. This is tested for by doing if `$divisible_by == 1`. If that's the case, it does a `push @results, $i` and adds `$i` to the list of results.

The Want manual page is good reading. I highly recommend it. Also, `http://www.perl.com/pub/a/2001/10/23/damians.html` has an example of generating *lazy lists* in Perl 6, where data from an infinite series is generated as it's needed.

Reading Context in Perl 6 Subroutines

Perl 6 has a built-in want function that provides the same information as the Want module does in Perl 5. Perl 6's want returns a junction of strings containing names of valid contexts for the current subroutine. `'String' eq want` and `'Int' eq want` may both be true. In a list context, it coughs up the expected type of the first return value, then the number of return values expected, and then the expected return type for each additional return type after the first.

```
# want() in Perl 6 returns the desired type of various return values by
# position
my ($primary, $count, * @secondary) = want;
```

Methods in a proxy object returned by want provide access to the same data. `want.rw` indicates that an lvalue is wanted. An lvalue is a variable or a function that returns something usable as a variable, such as `substr` does. `want.count` indicates how many return values are expected, possibly Inf. want responds to numeric context by returning `want.count`. In Perl 6, `want >= 2` is equivalent to the Perl 5 expression `want(2)`.

Prototypes

A *prototype* is an optional part of a Perl subroutine or method definition. It's the part that appears in parentheses after the name of the subroutine.

```
# Sample declaration with prototype - Perl 5
sub do_more_for_less ($) {
}
```

($) is the prototype in this example. Prototypes tell perl how to interpret the arguments in calls to that function. Prototypes can, among other things, force scalar context on an argument in a call to that subroutine, so it does the right thing even if you neglect to put the scalar keyword in the call.

```
# Subroutine prototypes provide context to arguments in function calls
# removing the requirement to put "scalar" before things that generate
# lists - Perl 5
sub foo ($) {
    print $_[0], "\n";
}
foo(localtime);
```

Try this again without the ($) in the definition for foo(), and compare what's printed.

Prototypes are sometimes called a *pill* in slang, as it looks sort of like a pill when a few sigils are in it: ($$;$@).

Prototypes don't just force contexts; they also give perl clues about how to interpret the argument list. Providing these clues is the topic of the next section.

Prototype can be a verb, too; if you declare a subroutine and give it a prototype, you've *prototyped* it.

Forward Declarations

A declaration of a subroutine that includes a prototype pill but no function body registers information as perl compiles. This associates the subroutine name with type information, argument names, whether those arguments are optional, and information about argument's traits. With or without a pill, a subroutine definition without a body is a *forward declaration* or *stub*.

Forward declarations look like subroutine definitions but lack the body that contains the code.

```
sub do_more_for_less ($);        # <-- forward declaration - Perl 5
sub do_more_for_less ($) { ... }; # <-- forward declaration - Perl 6
do_more_for_less(15.95);         # <-- subroutine call
sub do_more_for_less ($) {       # <-- actual subroutine definition
    print "You always get mojo for $_[0]!\n";
}
```

The prototype pill must agree with how the function is actually called, or you'll see an error such as one of the following:

```
Not enough arguments for main::do_more_for_less at - line 3, near "()"
Prototype mismatch: sub main::do_more_for_less ($) vs none at - line 6.
```

The prototype declaration construct serves humans and computers alike. It allows humans to move the code portion of the subroutine to the bottom of the file to make the flow of code more natural. When nothing special is being done in the way of argument handling or definition, then no prototype is needed; prototypes also serve to warn humans and computers alike that a subroutine has interesting or useful semantics.

A prototype is an example, of sorts, of how a subroutine is to be used. Prototypes are never arbitrary expressions. The sigils have approximately the same meanings as when you use them on ordinary variables. In the "Formal Parameter Lists" section, I'll show you some more complex prototypes, but I'll stick to simple parameter lists that include only these characters: $, @, \, *, %, and ;. Prototypes using only these characters are *context-only prototypes*.

Prototypes Generate Signatures from Subroutine Names and Usages

A prototype declaration—the subroutine and the prototype pill—specify a *signature*. Subroutines are recognized by their name and by their signature.

A subroutine may be defined once, with one name and one signature, but no call matches it because the signature in the declaration doesn't match the call. Perl is able to detect an error at compile time in this case.

It may also happen that several subroutines have the same name but different signatures, and which one is called depends on which, if any, match the number and types of arguments in the subroutine call. This is called *function* (or *method*) *overloading on signature*.

It never happened in Perl 5 that a decision was made by perl on which subroutine to call between several subroutines with the same name. Multiple subroutines with the same name aren't allowed in the same package. In Perl 6, multiple subroutines of the same name may be distinguished by their usage. The usage will be consistent with only one of the signatures, or else the compiler wouldn't have allowed the duplicate subroutine to be defined in the first place.

Chapter 14 gives examples of multiple methods with the same name and different signatures. For now, this chapter covers the ideas that prototypes can come before disembodied subroutine definitions and that the defined usage must match the actual usage.

Context-Only Prototypes

Perl 5 prototypes create contexts for arguments in calls to that function. These contexts aren't too different from the familiar scalar and list contexts. They don't give names to the arguments to use as an alternative to passing by position, and they don't specify traits. Still, they're useful for writing clear, concise code.

Context-only prototypes are called *siglets* in Perl 6 lingo, and they're still available in Perl 6 with a few changes. Variable names, type information, and trait information may all be omitted, but the commas may not be. In it's simplest context-only form, Perl 6 prototypes are sigils separated by commas. The semicolon doesn't delimit required parameters from optional ones as in Perl 5. Instead, you must prefix the optional parameter's sigils with ?. A few scenarios stand out where Perl 5–style, context-only prototypes are useful, described next.

Zero Arguments

Zero-argument subroutines are useful in Perl 5 as constants. The POSIX module defines many constants, such as O_CREAT, which is used as a bitmask by the sysopen function. When they appear in code, they don't need parentheses.

```
# Functions prototyped to zero arguments may be used without parentheses
# and without trigging warnings - Perl 5
sysopen my $fd, $path, O_CREAT, 0644;
```

The constants module creates constants using this technique.

Zero-argument prototyped functions won't steal (unexpectedly take) arguments from other functions.

```
# cr() binds to no argument, Perl 5
sub cr () { "\n"; }
print 'We have no use for your kind', cr, 'He monotoned', cr; # good
print 'We have no use for your kind', cr 'He monotoned', cr;  # syntax error
```

The expression cr 'He monotoned' results in the following syntax error:

```
String found where operator expected at - line 3, near "cr 'He monotoned'"
```

Chapter 4 mentioned that the perl grammar expects one of two things at any given moment: an operator or an expression. You can use cr with an operator but not an expression.

```
print cr x 10; # good - cr used with an operator - Perl 5
```

Constant items and the result of operators operating on arguments and arguments of every sort are all expressions.

One Argument

Single-argument prototyped functions won't steal (unexpectedly take) arguments from other functions.

```
# foo() only binds to one argument, Perl 5:
sub plus_one ($) { $_[0] + 1; }
print join ", ", 10, 20, 30, plus_one 40, 50;
print "\n";
# prints: 10, 20, 30, 41, 50
```

plus_one took as an argument only 40—it didn't accidentally also gobble up 50.

First Argument Is a Code Block or Code Reference

The following allows emulation of the built-ins sort, map, and grep when used with a code block:

```
sub first (&@) {
    my $coderef = shift;
    while(@_) {
        return $_[0] if $coderef->($_[0]);
        shift;
    }
    return undef;
}
print(first { $_[0] % 3 == 0 } (10 .. 40)), "\n";
```

first returns the first argument for which the code block returns true. The code block provided first here looks for something that's cleanly divisible by three.

The case presented here is grep BLOCK LIST and map BLOCK LIST. It isn't possible to emulate grep EXPR, LIST and map EXPR, LIST in Perl 5, though Perl 6 macros may do this.

Context-Only Prototype Symbols (Perl 5)

Those were the most useful applications for Perl 5 prototypes. Other symbols exist (see Table 11-1).

Table 11-1. *Perl 5 Function Prototype Sigils and Symbols*

Symbol	Description
@	Array.
%	Hash.
&	Code reference or block.
*	Glob—anything may be coerced to glob.
$	Scalar—forces scalar context for the caller.
\	Metasymbol—the next type expected will be taken by reference. Useful for accepting arrays and hashes.
;	Separates optional arguments from required arguments. Arguments prototyped after the semicolon aren't required. If they aren't passed, no compile time warning will be issued.

% makes sure that the list passed in has an even number of things, which is consistent with a list of intermixed keys and values in Perl 5.

Formal Parameter Lists

Prototypes in Perl 6 specify not only the parameters types, as do prototypes in Perl 5, but also name the parameters, attach traits, and specify default values.

Naming the parameters allows parameters to be passed by name rather than by position. It consolidates the steps of declaring a variable and reading arguments into it.

Prototypes that include both type information and variable names for the parameters are *formal parameter lists*. They're formal because the compiler can and will verify your declaration, checking the declared types against what's actually passed in.

Think of arguments as party guests and parameters as party invitations. If a guest doesn't show up (an argument isn't passed), this is usually OK; but if they said they were going to be there (prototyped as a required argument), then it isn't OK. Should a guest (argument) show up who isn't on the invitation list (parameter list), it would be completely unacceptable. Such manners will not be tolerated. Also, some parties have open invitations or wind up being open after a few hours. Such is the case with the slurpy operator when used in function prototypes.

The Perl6::Parameters module for Perl 5 makes named parameters available to Perl 5. This module isn't recommended for serious production work as it is a source filter. See the comments about source filters in the "Cons of Switch in Perl 5" section of Chapter 9.

Formal Parameter Lists (Perl 6)

The primary source of type information in a parameter list comes from good old-fashioned sigils, just like you're using already and like Perl 5 prototypes use. Since we're declaring the variables at the same time, lexically scoped to the function, perl needs to know the variables names.

```
# Parameters, Perl 6
sub do_something ($foo, $bar, $baz) {
    print $foo, $bar.get($baz), "\n";
}
```

Variables defined this way are defined lexically scoped. Here, $foo, $bar, and $baz are plain old scalars. They could have just as easily been introduced as hashes and arrays.

```
sub dosomething (@foo, $bar, %baz) {
   print @foo, $bar.get(%baz), "\n";
}
```

Object types modify scalars.

```
# Parameter object types, Perl 6
sub dosomething (Gronkulator $foo, Burgler $bar, BoatAnchor $baz) {
}
```

Arrays may be typed to contain objects of a given type in Perl 6.

```
# Arrays of types - Perl 6 only:
sub dosomething (@foo is Array of Gronkulator) {
}
# or, alternatively:
sub dosomething (Array of Gronkulator @foo) {
}
```

Perl 6 subroutines and methods can specify the return type.

```
sub dosomething (Array of Gronkulator @foo) returns BoatAnchor {
}
```

Types are specified for variables using traits. Consistent with Listing 11-1 near the start of this chapter, is introduces traits. returns is just another way to introduce traits.

Overloading on Type with Prototypes

Subroutines declared multi are overloaded on argument type and return type. This is traditionally used with method calls, as documented in Chapter 14, but subs may be multi, too.

Overloading implies that something does double duty—and that thing is the function's name. One name is used multiple times. I'm overloading on type, which means that the prototype of the function is considered along with the name to decide which should be called.

The built-in for in Perl 6 may accept either a subroutine reference and then a list or else a list and then a subroutine reference.

```
# Example prototypes for for(), Perl 6:

multi sub for (@arr, &code) { ... };
multi sub for (&code, @arr) { ... };

# example usage of for(), Perl 6:
```

```
for @things { .depackage() and .play_with() and .shelve(); };
for -> $thing, $receipt { $receipt.lose(); $thing.break(); },
    zip @things, @receipts;
```

Changing the order of arguments is pretty useless except for routines that are used often and must cater to idiomatic uses. Different versions of the same routine will more commonly take some arguments that are completely different, take the same information in different formats, or take more or less information.

Class::Multimethods gives Perl 5 this feature, minus some polish in syntax (see Listing 11-3).

Listing 11-3. *Multimethods Example for Perl 5*

```
use Class::Multimethods;

multimethod toy_for => ('CODE', 'ARRAY')
                    => sub {
    my $code = shift;
    my $arr = shift;
    my @arr = @$arr;
    $code->($_) for @arr;
};

multimethod toy_for => ('ARRAY', 'CODE')
                    => sub {
    my $arr = shift;
    my $code = shift;
    my @arr = @$arr;
    $code->($_) for @arr;
};

my $numbers = [ 1 .. 20 ];
toy_for(sub { print "$_\n" }, $numbers);
toy_for($numbers, sub { print "$_\n" });
```

Potential types for the parameter list are ARRAY, HASH, CODE, $, #, and any object type. $ is any scalar, and # is any scalar that happens to contain a number. Object types are objects you've created yourself or objects created by CPAN modules.

The documentation for Class::Multimethods is good reading, using pegs and holes of various shapes as examples.

Named Parameters

Naming arguments, rather than relying on their position to indicate purpose, makes functions more mnemonic and allows you to easily add future parameters, optional or otherwise, without breaking large amounts of existing code.

- Arguments passed as pairs

- Names of pairs matching parameters in the prototype

In Perl 5, it's tedious and verbose to write out all the checks that verify the following:

- No unwanted arguments are passed.

- No required arguments have been omitted.

- Passed items are the correct type.

Perl 6's compiler checks all this for you. Perl 5 currently has no way to process what may be position parameters, named parameters, or mixtures.

Passing arguments in the style of a hash is consistent with the Perl 5 tradition of faking named parameters and may look like this:

```
# Fake named parameters - Perl 5

use Perl6::Variables;

sub do_something {
    my %args = @_;      # hash is initialized from the argument list
    my $name  = %args{name};
    my $color = %args{color};
    # ...
}

do_something(name => 'Fred', color => 'red');

# True named parameters - Perl 6 or Perl 5 with Perl6::Parameters:

sub do_something ($name, $color, ?$shape) {
    # ...
}

# Call to a routine that uses either faked or true named parameters
# Perl 5 or Perl 6

do_something(name => 'Fred', color => 'red');
```

The call to do_something() is identical in Perl 5 and Perl 6, but the mechanism is different.

The question mark, ?, before a parameter list item indicates an optional parameter. All arguments after the optional parameter should also be optional to deal with calls where arguments are passed by position. The slurpy operator, *, discussed in the "List Context" section, is considered optional in that it will soak up zero or more remaining arguments. A parameter prefixed with a plus, +, is also considered optional and may come after optional parameters in the list. The + prefix indicates the parameter is available only by name, not by position.

The slurpy hash, *%, is special. It soaks up into a hash variable all named parameters that don't match any other parameter names. This lets people make up new parameters when they call the function, and it lets you provide a generic mechanism for dealing with this.

```
# Engineer new parameters on the fly - Perl 6

sub html_tag ($name, *%params) {
    print qq{<$name};
    for %params {
        my $name = $_.key;
        my $value = $_.value;
        print qq{ $name="$value"};
    }
    print qq{>};
}

html_tag(name => 'body', bgcolor => 'chartreuse');

# Outputs: <body bgcolor="chartreuse">
```

This function takes the name of an HTML tag (required) and then any number of additional optional named parameters. The call to the html_tag() function creates a body tag, and that body specifies chartreuse for the background color. No prior knowledge of the options to various HTML tags are required if the code just assumes that whatever is passed is correct. This is especially useful for writing object methods in subclasses that call the superclass. If the superclass adds a new parameter, it doesn't break subclasses. Chapter 14 has an example of this in the "Slurping Up Parameters for Inheritance" section.

The slurpy array, *@, soaks up all remaining arguments into an array. A function such as grep or sort would use this prototype symbol after taking a fixed, optional code reference.

Mixing Positional and Named Parameters (Perl 6)

Named parameters make code self-documenting and allow you to easily add and remove arguments. You don't have to remember in which order arguments are expected. Any combination of arguments may be optional without needing to pad the argument list with 0s or undefs.

Positional parameters aren't desirable for routines that require a large number of optional parameters, but named parameters aren't desirable for routines that expect exactly one parameter. Perl 6 lets you have it both ways. The same routine accepts both named and positional arguments. These two calls are equivalent:

```
# Perl 6 - named parameters may be passed by position:
html_tag(name => 'body');   # named parameter
html_tag('body');           # positional parameter
```

Positional parameters may be passed by name, even though they're positional. To the limited degree that it makes sense, both may be mixed, like so:

```
# Perl 6 - mixing named and positional parameters:
html_tag('body', bgcolor => 'chartreuse');
```

The pair slurp prototype symbol, *%, won't slurp up positional data. Use *@ for that. To satisfy *%, pairs must be passed, and that's what's done here for bgcolor.

Formal Parameter Lists (Perl 5)

Perl6::Parameters backports a version of this concept to Perl 5.

The various Perl 5 constants returned by ref() are supported as metatypes.

```
sub do_something (ARRAY @foo, HASH $bar, CODE $baz, REGEXP $qux) {
    # ...
}
```

ARRAY, HASH, CODE, SCALAR, GLOB, and REGEXP are supported. REF turns the variable into a reference to what was passed. Other things are ignored.

GLOB has no Perl 6 counterpart (and there's much rejoicing). Regular expressions are anything but regular. They're now called *rules*, or a *rule* in the singular.

These type names are consistent with what the built-in function ref returns and with what the optional extension want returns, at least where they overlap.

At the time of this writing, Perl6::Parameters doesn't agree with the Perl 6 specification. *% and *@ don't exist. ? isn't used to tag optional parameters, but instead ; separates the required from the optional as in Perl 5.

The typesafety module, documented in Chapter 16, and the Perl6::Parameters module, documented here, don't work together. Both use the prototype area of the function declaration for different purposes. The problem isn't expected to be resolved.

Lexically Scoped Subroutines

Perl 6 introduces to the core language the ability to declare subroutines visible only within the current block.

```
# Lexically scoped subroutines - Perl 6

my $factorial = do {
    my sub fac ($num) {
        return 1 if $num == 1;
        return $num * fac($num - 1);
    }
    fac(7);
}
```

Here, fac() is (normally) callable only from within the do block.

Perl 5's Sub::Lexical CPAN module adds this feature to Perl 5. It's implemented using a source filter.

```
# Lexically scoped subroutines - Perl 5

use Sub::Lexical;

my $factorial = do {
    my sub fac {
        my $num = shift;
        return 1 if $num == 1;
        return $num * fac($num - 1);
```

```
    }
    fac(7);
};
```

It's cleaner, when writing recursive code, to create a lexical context to put variables in than it is to pass those variables back to the function each call when the recursive function needs only a single copy of the variable. Lexically scoped subroutines allow this without pulling the outer lexical scope with variables that are of use only to a small stretch of code.

Pointy Subroutines

-> has a new purpose in Perl 6: binding arguments to code blocks. -> is approximately the same as an anonymous sub with parameters, except the parameters don't require parentheses around them.

```
# These two lines are equivalent, Perl 6
-> $foo, $bar, $baz { ... };
sub ($foo, $bar, $baz) { ... };
```

The following three lines are equivalent:

```
# Define a code block with arguments and then immediately invoke it
-> $foo, $bar, $baz { ... }.($arg1, $arg2, $arg3)      # Perl 6 pointy
sub ($foo, $bar, $baz) { ... }.($arg1, $arg2, $arg3);  # Perl 6 regular
sub { my($foo, $bar, $baz) = @_; ...; }->($arg1, $arg2, $arg3); # Perl 5
```

This leaves no place to specify the return type or apply traits to the subroutine itself. Pointy subroutines aren't considered subroutines at all as far as return is concerned, and return will return out of the enclosing subroutine. Normally one doesn't define a subroutine and immediately call it but rather provide it as an argument for map, grep, or for, all of which want code blocks.

```
# Map statements and blocks, Perl 6
# these lines are equivalent
map { $_.some_function() }, @things;                    # compatibility block
map sub ($thing) { $thing.some_function() }, @things; # normal block
map -> $thing { $thing.some_function() }, @things;    # pointy block
```

for in Perl 6 wants an array as its first argument and the code block as its second, so the arguments to the code block appear to move before the code block.

```
# Perl 6 - for statements and blocks - these lines are equivalent
for @things { print $_, "\n"; };                        # compatibility block
for @things sub ($thing) { print $thing, "\n"; };   # compatibility block
for @things -> $thing { print $thing, "\n"; };      # pointy block
```

This is the opposite order that map and grep take their arguments. It has nothing to do with -> itself. for, like other control structures, requires no comma between arguments because of some trick. The old block style isn't really called *compatibility*. It's still the shortest way to write a block that requires only one argument or processes a list of like things. I don't know of a module offering pointy subroutines to Perl 5.

Placeholders

Even terser than pointy subroutines, Perl 6 allows code blocks to declare their parameters from within by their mere mention. The variables may be given any name as long as that name starts with the caret, ^. The code block is presumed to have a parameter list of the placeholder variables in alphabetic order for the current locale.

```
# Implicitly declared parameters with placeholders

# use Perl6::Placeholders;      # uncomment for Perl 6

my $add = { $^a + $^b };        # Create a sub that adds its two args

print $add->(1, 2), "\n";       # Call it - Perl 5
print $add.(1, 2), "\n";        # Call it - Perl 6
```

See the Perl6::Placeholders module by Damian Conway to play with this syntax in Perl 5. 1 is assigned to $^a and 2 is assigned to $^b by virtue of the letter *a* coming before the letter *b*. In this book and other examples, you'll often find the code block using $^a, $^b, $^c, and so on, but $^aardvark, $^bison, and $^camel work just the same.

```
# Map example updated to include placeholders example
map { $_.some_function() }, @things;                   # comparability block
map sub ($thing) { $thing.some_function() }, @things; # normal block
map -> $thing { $thing.some_function() }, @things;    # pointy block
map { $^thing.some_function() }, @things;             # placeholder
```

Placeholders are preferred for small blocks that accept a few arguments.

Subroutine References

&foo is a subroutine reference in Perl 6. This is the same as \&foo in Perl 5. Use a subroutine reference when passing a reference of a subroutine to somewhere else (rather than passing something to the subroutine).

```
# Passing foo() to bar()

# Perl 5

sub foo { ... }
bar(\&foo);

# Perl 6

sub foo { ... };
bar(&foo);
```

This lets bar() call foo() later rather than calling foo() immediately and sending the result. This technique is important if bar() needs to call foo() repeatedly, conditionally, or with arguments that don't exist yet. The sole purpose of bar() may be to compute and collect the arguments to foo() or to interchangeable routines with foo() among them.

Use a subroutine reference when calling methods on the subroutine object itself.

```
# Calling a method on the subroutine object
\&foo->curry(1);      # Perl 5 assuming autobox and autobox::Core
&foo.curry(1);        # Perl 6
```

The next section shows some examples of currying.

Currying

assuming, when called on an object representing a subroutine, allows you to partially call a function. That is, you call it with some of the required arguments and get back a subroutine reference with a new prototype that wants only the arguments that haven't been provided yet. This is *currying*, and this section shows how currying is done in Perl.

```
# Incrementally specify arguments to customize functions - Perl 6

sub moon ($color, $phase) {
    print "The $color moon is $phase.\n";
}

my &waxing_moon = &moon.assuming(phase => 'waxing crescent');
&waxing_moon.(color => 'golden'); # "The golden moon is waxing crescent"

my &blue_waxing_moon = &waxing_moon.assuming(color => 'blue');
&blue_waxing_moon.(); # "The blue moon is waxing crescent"
```

Each returned object is independent of others. You can customize this same subroutine in several ways.

Here's the same example written for Perl 5:

```
# Simple currying example - Perl 5

use autobox;
use autobox::Core;
use Perl6::Parameters;

sub moon ($phase, $color) {
    print "The $color moon is $phase.\n";
}

my $moon = \&moon;          # take a reference to our moon routine
my $waxing_moon = $moon->curry('waxing crescent');
$waxing_moon->('golden'); # "The golden moon is waxing crescent"

my $blue_waxing_moon = $waxing_moon->curry('blue');
$blue_waxing_moon->();     # "The blue moon is waxing crescent"
```

This also works with Perl 5's fake named parameters. Like other subroutine styles in Perl 5, named parameters and positional arguments may not be mixed. Each function understands only one or the other.

```
# Currying example with named parameters - Perl 5

use autobox;
use autobox::Core;
use Perl6::Variables;

sub moon {
    my %ops = @_;
    my $color = %ops{color};
    my $phase = %ops{phase};
    print "The $color moon is $phase.\n";
}

my $moon = \&moon;          # take a reference to our moon routine
my $waxing_moon = $moon->curry(phase => 'waxing crescent');
$waxing_moon->(color => 'golden'); # "The golden moon is waxing crescent"

my $blue_waxing_moon = $waxing_moon->curry(color => 'blue');
$blue_waxing_moon->();      # "The blue moon is waxing crescent"
```

DBI, the Database Interface, attaches values to logic, too.

```
# DBI's prepare() and execute() statements kind of curry - Perl 5

use DBI;

my $dbh = DBI->connect('...'); # depends on your database
my $sth = $dbh->prepare('select * from foo where foo.id = ?');
$sth->execute(5);   # 5 is substituted in for the ?
while(my $row = $sth->fetchrow_hashref) {
    # process results
}
```

For the connect() statement for your database, see DBD::MySQL, DBD::Pg, or whichever applies to your database system. This prevents the need to escape data because data is sent in binary-clean, length-counted buffers. To properly curry, it wouldn't require all the values at once, and it would return a new object or code reference to an object instance or closure that contains the partially specified set of data.

Not Covered in This Chapter

Briefly, I'll now mention some features related to subroutines that aren't covered in this chapter either because they're beyond the scope of this book (Perl 6 concepts and Perl 6–like features on top of Perl 5) or because I cover them comprehensively in another chapter.

Anonymous Subroutines

Anonymous subroutines may appear anywhere a value is expected. They have multitudes of uses. Small bits of logic can be put right where they're needed, and logic can be passed around as arguments. Subroutines don't have to be named just so that they can be called or have a reference taken to them. You can avoid massive amounts of cutting and pasting and spaghetti code when writing routines so that only the common logic appears in the subroutine and the variable logic is passed in as a code reference. Chapter 9 used anonymous subroutines heavily in its examples.

```
# Example anonymous subroutine - Perl 5
sub { print @_, "\n" }->(1..10, rand);

# Example anonymous subroutine - Perl 6
{ print @_, "\n" }.(1..10, rand);
```

This topic is a chapter unto itself; see Chapter 19.

Macros

Perl 6 macros combine the best bits of C's inline and C's cpp. The code is parsed once but optimized for each location for which it's called. Constant expressions are optimized away at compile time. A macro may also temporarily take over the job of parsing input. The semantics are subject to change; this topic would require its own chapter, so it's sadly beyond the scope of this book.

Methods

To make the method magic happen, you need an object; to get an object, you need a class from which to construct objects. That class needs methods. Finally, you need a program to create an instance of that class and invoke the method on it. Method calls are function calls across objects. The first argument is the reference to the object in which the method was called. Perl 5 requires you to manually read this argument and track it as a variable. Perl 6, like most languages, has special glue to do this for you, which is exactly what the method keyword buys you. Perl 5 requires that you manually look up instance data in this variable, using it as a hash reference or array reference or other reference. This is required so that different object instances from the same class each have separate data even though they share the same code.

In Perl 6, it's no longer possible to write methods using the sub keyword. Plain subroutines aren't part of the public interface of an object.

Writing objects is beyond the scope of this chapter; see Chapter 14.

Rules

Perl 6's replacement for regular expressions may be used inline, as in Perl 5, and they may also be declared in blocks similar to subroutines. Flags come before rather than after the expression. The x modifier is assumed, meaning whitespace is used to separate parts of the pattern rather than match literal whitespace, and comments are treated as comments. Rules are modular and may reference each other, as well as subroutines, by name to construct a grammar. Subroutines likewise may invoke rules by name. Rules define advanced features such as variable-width look-behinds, backtrack control, assignment of matches directly to variables, and other features previously found only in the SNOBOL language. These are implemented for Perl 5 in the `Perl6::Rules` module. The `Perl6::Rules` module came out after the table of contents was fixed for this book, but I sincerely hope to cover it in a future edition.

RESOURCES

The article "Perl 6 Is Not Just for Damians," viewable on the Web at `http://www.perl.com/pub/a/2001/10/23/damians.html`, has a currying example, among other Perl 6 examples.

`perldoc perlsub` contains the Perl 5 standard documentation for subroutines.

Confused about context? Check out Mark Jason Dominus's excellent essay on context at `http://perl.plover.com/context.html`.

Apocalypse 6 covers subroutines in Perl 6; it's available at `http://dev.perl.org/perl6/apocalypse/AO6.html`. This chapter corresponds to that document.

Summary

Automatically taking references of arrays and hashes, and passing by reference, is part of a broader move to make references comfortable in Perl 6.

Another theme is making subroutines and objects easier to define. Perl 5's accomplishment was making them easy to use, which shifted work from the common case (each use of a subroutine or method) to the less common case (declaration of the subroutine or method).

Through traits, attributes, and explicit flattening, programmers are given more control, and more control means fewer surprises. This was accomplished at the same time Perl was made more helpful, so the required syntax is actually less verbose in Perl 6, even with the additional programmer control. Placeholders, as another example of easy but explicit syntaxes, offer the power of formal parameter lists without the programmer ever actually needing to declare the parameters. Subroutines using placeholders in place of a formal parameter list may have values passed by name, but the subroutine never needs to explicit read the variables or repeat the names of variables in a list. Perl, at compile time, is still able to check for correct usage of the subroutine.

Other features, such as references to subroutines and currying, are ideas that Perl 5 programmers already apply but aren't as elegant to implement as they could be, so the idioms fell short of becoming universally recognized as good style. Perl 6 irons out just a few obstacles to make these techniques cleaner.

## PART 3

Threads and Objects

CHAPTER 12

■ ■ ■

CPAN Modules

The whole intent of Perl 5's module system was to encourage the growth of Perl culture rather than the Perl core.

—Larry Wall in 199705101952.MAA00756@wall.org

CPAN is a repository for reusable software modules. Perl blurs the distinction between the language's core and optional modules, and Perl 6 lessens this distinction further. Early in the brainstorm process for Perl 6, it was decided that a shortcoming of Perl culture is the hesitation among novices to actually go to http://search.cpan.org, hunt down a module, and then install it. Too many people aren't using the greatest feature of Perl—CPAN. Worse, hosting services providing shared hosting seldom keep modules up-to-date, almost never add modules at users' requests, and often don't provide shell accounts so that their customers can do it on their own without breaking out a cross-compiler. Then there's the question of what should be bundled with Perl 6—one camp thinks the Perl 5 distribution comes with too many things and is thus too large (and they're right), and another camp (also correctly) asserts that Perl 5 doesn't come with numerous important modules. It's also nearly impossible to deprecate a module and ultimately remove it; modules must be supported for eternity, or else updating Perl would break existing programs. It was decided that Perl 6 should *automatically* fetch and install modules that aren't installed already.

Applications start up slowly when a large number of modules are used. CGI scripts bog down, compromising throughput. The short life of a script running in a CGI environment prompted technologies such as mod_perl and pperl (Persistent Perl) to get rid of compiling the code again each hit. These technologies are useful but aren't appropriate for casually writing large numbers of Web applications or for hosting companies to provide shared hosting. Perl 6 breaks apart the compile phase from the execute phase. (However, the compiler will turn around and immediately execute the compiled program if directed, making it a single-command affair.) This lets a program be compiled once and then run any number of times.

Modules also present problems with application distribution. Although most modules are licensed under terms favorable to redistribution and integration into other products, anyone the application is distributed to would need to go through the entire installation process for each module. Thankfully, PAR, the *Perl ARchive* format, allows for the distribution of bundled modules in a ready-to-run format. ActiveState's compiler for Microsoft Windows also builds .exe files bundled with everything they need. Perl 6 too compiles down to an executable and can link "statically," attaching most kinds of dependencies.

Blurred Distinction Between Core and CPAN

When core features are proposed, they're (usually) rejected for one of three reasons.

- CPAN already has an implementation.

- It should be implemented as a CPAN module.

- A more general facility should be conceived to allow the idea to be implemented as a module.

Besides avoiding bloat and warding off core complexity, this attitude has the advantage of making it extremely rewarding to write modules. You aren't confined to a box, technically or socially, in what you can do. Features such as attributes and lexically scoped warning bits are designed to make extensions possible.

Precompiling

If one program uses five modules, and each of those modules uses five more, perl has to parse twenty-five modules worth of source code to parse every time the program is run. For applications such as CGI where many requests need to be handled quickly, this quickly becomes unacceptable (or, rather, becomes unacceptably slow).

When to Compile

Good and bad reasons exist to precompile Perl to bytecode. The following are good reasons:

- To speed up CGI applications that take a while to parse because they're large

- To speed up applications that take a while to parse because they use source filters

- To avoid the complexity of using the `AutoSplit` module

Source filters (such as `Perl6::Variables`) dramatically increase a program's startup time. This is in part because of the sheer volume of code they must load to do their work, but the source filter itself may spend a significant amount of time trying to understand the code it's filtering. Precompiling source code to bytecode saves you from this.

`AutoSplit` delays the compilation of source code that isn't used each run. When a delayed load function is called, perl compiles it at that time. You get no savings for long-running programs that eventually call each routine; however, CGI applications, which are normally short-lived, can avoid compiling most subroutines in a typical run. It's too much work and too error prone to apply `AutoSplit` to CPAN modules, where the bulk of an application is likely to be. It's much easier to make your own bytecode-compiled stashes of them. Beware that many modules are spread across numerous files.

Also, you should avoid the following poor reasons of precompiling modules:

- To keep the source code secret

- To distribute code as a single package

Any attempt to encrypt code and have it still be runnable is doomed to failure. A locked door with the key sitting next to it is locked only in the technical sense. With just a little glue and the Perl debugger, B::Deparse can reconstruct something close to the original source code from the bytecode.

Use PAR instead of B::Bytecode to distribute code together with module decencies, or see Inline::File for a simple way to stuff a few dependent files onto the end of a script. See the later "Distributing Perl Programs" section.

The Perl 5 Bytecode Compiler Chain

B::Bytecode is the workhorse of Perl 5 bytecode compilation. It stores bytecode for a program using a format understood by ByteLoader (among other things—see perldoc B::Bytecode). Most modules may be dumped in this fashion, and many of those will still work in bytecode form, too.

ByteLoader, when used, interprets the rest of the file as Perl 5 bytecode. To make this work, you must create the beginnings of a module that uses ByteLoader and prepend the bytecode to that beginning.

```
# Compiling the CGI module at the shell:
perl -MO=Bytecode,-H /usr/local/lib/perl5/5.9.2/CGI.pm >CGI.pmc
```

The -H option automates writing a suitable call to ByteLoader, making this a single-step operation. Replace /usr/local/lib/perl5/5.9.2/CGI.pm with the correct path to a module. (Your factory-original CGI.pm is likely to be in another place.) The following version is equivalent to the previous one:

```
# Compiling the CGI module at the shell in two steps:
$ echo 'use ByteLoader;' > CGI.pmc
$ perl -MO=Bytecode /usr/local/lib/perl5/5.9.2/CGI.pm >> CGI.pmc
```

The first command creates the CGI.pmc file and writes a single line to invoke ByteLoader to handle loading the bytecode to follow. The .pmc extension implies bytecode-compiled Perl and is recognized by use just as .pm is. perl by itself has no idea what to do with the bytecode and will just report a syntax error as it looks nothing like Perl source. When using modules, perl looks for .pmc files first and then looks for .pm files. Should it find both, the .pmc is used if it's newer.

The second line parses a Perl program. The -M flag tells perl to use a module, in this case, O. O is told, via its argument mechanism, to load Bytecode. Other than the -M argument, this is exactly like any other invocation of perl on Perl source. The output is redirected and appended to the end of CGI.pmc.

■The O Module   O is a sort of gateway to modules that run before, or instead of, another program. This includes optimizers, compilers, decompilers, and code analysis tools. See perldoc perlmodlib's list of B:: modules.

This example assumes the compiled bytecode files are being grouped into a special library directory and you're using use lib at the top of your program to give this special directory priority over the existing entries in your @INC path. Moving between bytecode-compiled versions of modules and the source versions is then as easy as commenting out the use lib line.

You can verify the pmc version is being used by naming it something other than CGI.pmc, but don't do this other than as a test, because the module won't correctly initialize itself when it declares a package differing from the name of the module used. For example, if it were called fred.pmc, it would still declare the package CGI, and the CGI package would be populated with methods.

It's safe to mix bytecode-compiled and source versions of modules. Many modules are composed of a main module and several helper modules, and it's okay to compile the main module and not the helper modules, or only some of the helper modules.

Automatically Compiling and Caching Modules

The ByteCache module compiles modules on demand and stores precompiled bytecode to disk for later use. Place use ByteCache; before any other use statements for modules that should be byte cached and after any modules that shouldn't be byte cached.

```
# Automatic precompilation on demand:
use ShouldNotBeCompiled;
use ByteCache;
use ShouldBeCompiled;
```

ShouldNotBeCompiled won't be precompiled, but ShouldBeCompiled will be. ByteCache doesn't automatically recompile stale caches of bytecode-compiled modules when the source version is updated.

Compiled Bytecode Style

Consider only compiling modules you got from CPAN and aren't likely to edit as part of developing and maintaining your project. Also consider sticking to modules not likely to be updated often. Consider which modules should be compiled rather than using ByteCache unless you're willing to deal with the increased potential of problems stemming from incompatible modules and stale caches.

Put the bulk of your code into modules and compile those, but keep the main program a regular, noncompiled .pl file. Put any configuration values that aren't in configuration values in the main program and pass those values to the constructors of the compiled modules. This reduces the chance of having to recompile a module to change a simple value and makes the values easier to find. It also lets you easily make test versions of the program that use new versions of modules. Hard-coded path information, such as paths to config files, definitely belongs in the main .pl, never in the modules. You'll want to run two copies of the program sooner or later, and this lets you easily copy the main program, make a few trivial changes, and reuse the bulk of the code.

Place a use lib line at the top of the main program that points to the cache of compiled modules. Should you need to stop using the bytecode-compiled modules temporarily while testing, this line would need only be commented out.

Perl *can* compile code, but don't let it get in the way of developing or maintaining your code. If it becomes more trouble than it's worth, stop doing it.

Modules on Demand

Perl 6 eliminates the drudgery of installing modules. Code may be distributed without any of its dependencies, and, assuming the dependencies are available via CPAN, they'll be fetched automatically. Perl 5 can do something such as this with the Acme::Intraweb module.

```perl
#!/usr/bin/perl
# Perl 5 - automatically installs Event and Coro as needed

use strict;
use warnings;
use Acme::Intraweb;
use Event;
use Coro;


async { ... }; # do something with Coro
```

Acme::Intraweb was created for amusement value. People trying to refer to the Web as it exists on the Internet *and* an intranet will sometimes blend the names, resulting in *intraweb*. This is apparently a module for people who want things to *just work*. I'm not sure how serious Jos Boumans was when he created this module, but I doubt he expected the idea of automatic module fetching and installation to be taken as seriously as it was. It requires CPANPLUS to be installed and configured. The work done in the previous example could also be done with these shell commands:

```
$ cpanp i Event
$ cpanp i Coro
```

Since Acme::Intraweb isn't core in Perl 5, the dream of truly automatic dependency fetching hasn't yet been realized. Perhaps you should paste the (extremely short) code behind Acme::Intraweb into your programs and hope that your users have CPANPLUS installed and configured. No, you'd probably better just use PAR, but Acme::Intraweb is a great demonstration of this gossip-worthy new feature.

ByteCache uses the same trick as Acme::Intraweb—both store a code reference in @INC that perl runs when it gets to that point in @INC while looking for a module.

Distributing Perl Programs

As the "Modules on Demand" section said, Perl 6's habit of fetching CPAN modules and installing them automatically greatly simplifies distributing programs. There's no need to bundle half of CPAN with the program, especially when new versions of modules appear every day. However, Perl 5 programs that use CPAN modules must be bundled with something, even if it's just a means of fetching them, and bundling modules is still the preferred mechanism.

Perl Archive

PAR is recommended for serious use. PAR is the preferred way to bundle a program and the modules on which it depends. One PAR file may contain numerous modules. The name PAR is a take-off on JAR, the *Java Archive Format*, which accomplishes something similar. Like `.jar` files, `.par` files are in the `.zip` format.

PAR archives can be fetched over the network.

```
# Perl 5 - using a .par file transparently over the network
use PAR;
use lib 'http://perl6now/various_modules.par';


# Which might give you these modules, ready for immediate use:
use Perl6::Variables;
use Quantum::Superpositions;
```

This depends on LWP being installed already. Modules with binary parts (XS modules) are tied to the platform on which they were built. Both the processor and operating system (kernel version or operating system release number) must match closely. Using a `.par` file on the local machine is the normal case. It may be provided to use `lib`.

```
# Perl 5 - using a .par file
use lib 'various_modules.par';
```

This uses the `various_modules.par` file in the current directory as a source of modules.

`.par` files are created with the pp utility, which is included in the PAR distribution on CPAN.

```
$ pp -p -o stuff.par directory/
```

The `-o` option specifies the file to which to write. `directory/` could be a file instead of a directory, but I'm not sure why you'd do this. The `-p` option tells pp to create a `.par` file. Other options will cause it to generate a binary executable for the current platform (that's the default) or into a `.pl` file (that's the `-P` option). Executables are entirely stand-alone and include perl, its libraries, the core modules, the application, and its libraries. This format is suitable for distributing programs with the one platform dependency caveat that will affect users of Unix-like systems. Bytecode compilation, as discussed previously, has experimental support in pp with the `-f Bytecode` option.

REFERENCES AND THANKS

The Larry Wall quote is care of `http://history.perl.org/PerlTimeline.html`.

Malcolm Beattie and Benjamin Stuhl wrote `B::Bytecode`. `B::Bytecode` has an especially experimental mode where it generates C code to be compiled into an executable. This executable still links to the Perl run time and still executes Perl interpretively, but it's an interesting hack with a lot of potential.

Autrijus Tang wrote PAR. For more information on PAR, visit `http://aut.dyndns.org/par-tutorial/` and `http://par.perl.org`.

Tom Hughes and Simon Cozens wrote `ByteLoader`. Jos Boumans wrote `Acme::Intraweb`.

`Acme::SoftwareUpdate` demonstrates a similar idea to `Acme::Intraweb` with Perl 5. It doesn't download and install modules for you when the module isn't found at all, but it does look for updated versions of modules you do already have installed.

Despite efforts to convince folks of the inherent futility, people still try to hide secrets in binary executables. If you're one of these people, you may have some small measure of success writing truly obscure Perl, but you're probably better off writing C. *Secure Programming Cookbook* (O'Reilly, 2003) by John Viega, et. al., has examples of allocating secure memory, detecting debuggers, encoding data in memory, writing self-modifying executables, and performing other such tasks. C is inherently less interesting to decompile than Perl (or Java or Python for that matter).

Summary

Remember that (like so many modules documented in this book), B::Bytecode *isn't* stable but is considered a working prototype. Generally, when it fails, it fails completely rather than subtlety. The status of other modules mentioned in this section varies between experimental, proof of concept, and production. This doesn't mean that bug reports aren't welcome, but reported bugs may not necessarily be fixed in a timely fashion.

This chapter has run quite a gauntlet, touching on the topics of fetching and installing modules, compiling frequently run code, and bundling code in a format suitable for distribution as an application.

Perl 5 has come a long way as an applications programming language, and that necessarily entails bundling dependent modules, at least for any sort of serious applications programming. An applications programming language that didn't let you use libraries wouldn't be much of an applications programming language. This started when Web applications become popular as applications and large numbers of nontechnical users wanted to run them, and it naturally continues with desktop-based, graphical applications. This is all part of Perl's expansion into new niches that have spurned so much of its past development.

B::Bytecode overcomes one traditional problem of interpreted languages—slow startups. PAR solves how to distribute a single file rather than a mess of source code files or even multiple bytecode files.

Without Perl 6, there are still barriers to distributing Perl applications. For example, there's no good way to distribute cross-platform Perl applications that depend on noncore XS modules, but the equivalent isn't possible in other languages either. Binary plug-ins are hard. A programmer or company distributing applications to Windows, Linux, and Mac OS X users should have no reservations about building three executables, one for each, as long as they aren't concerned with trying to hide secrets in the source code. An IT department should have no qualms with the idea of creating applications and utilities for internal use and deploying them to company workstations for users.

All in all, today's Perl 5 is far more useful than the Perl 5 of just a few years ago, and Perl 6 plots key features to make Perl more useful still.

CHAPTER 14

■■■

Objects

The basic change here is that, rather than just supporting scalars, arrays, and hashes, Perl 6 supports opaque objects as a fourth fundamental datatype.

—Larry Wall, Apocalypse 2

Objects are instances of classes. Classes are reusable logic. The logic may be reused not only in different programs but multiple times in the same program. Each instance of reuse has its own private data, cleverly named *instance data*.

This chapter is about the Perl6::Classes module, the Attribute::Property module, and Apocalypse 12, the object specification for Perl 6.

Perl6::Classes gets the basics of Perl 6's class creation syntax down, but it changes Perl 5 more radically than other modules mentioned in this book and is more easily thrown because of that. Like most other modules in the Perl6 namespace on CPAN, it's a demonstration, not intended for production code or serious applications.

Attribute::Property adds proper attributes to Perl 5. As it so happens, *attribute* is another word for *instance data* (though methods are also considered to be attributes of a class). The addition of proper instance data to Perl is the most significant new feature, and Attribute::Property is production quality, so this chapter favors it.

I give a brief initial example of object creation and use without much explanation. This makes a case for using objects as tools in writing code. This chapter first covers objects from the perspective of code using them. Next, this chapter covers how to create objects.

I also illustrate how to navigate interfaces, deal with return values, and call methods. If you've managed to call a method, you've probably used the . operator, the -> operator, indirect object syntax, or autoboxing.

Method calls may be made to methods defined by the object as well as the default constructor, inherited from object Object, and accessors, automatically generated for instance data fields.

The "Constructors" section shows how you don't have to construct objects and explains that Perl is high enough level that initialization, now a separate concept, is the only essential part of implementing an object.

The "Initialization" section shows how to set up the initial state of an object. Data is pumped directly into instance variables, except when there's no corresponding instance variable, and then you may do whatever you like with it (but you should do *something* with it).

The "Inheritance" section shows how to redispatch to parent methods, preserving parameters meant for them while extracting the ones meant for you. I show the ups and downs of extending classes, at least as far as who can see whose data and methods.

The "Object Contexts" section covers how to use objects in contexts other than object context, which results in method calls asking the object to present itself for that context. This is another way that methods may be called.

Methods may be invoked when values are assigned to method calls. Methods, when properly created, are lvalues, and are valid on the left-hand side of an assignment or other mutating operator or function. The "Assigning to Method Calls" section has examples.

Changes for Perl 6

Sometimes we identify the words with the object—though by courtesy of idiom rather than in strict propriety of language.

—Samuel Taylor Coleridge

Paraphrasing perldoc perlobj, a Perl 5 object is just a reference, a class is just a package, and a method is just a subroutine.

Put more verbosely, an object is a reference to a data structure that has been associated (using bless) with a package. A class is just a package, which is nothing more than a collection of subroutines defined after a package statement. A method is just a subroutine written to expect the data structure as its first argument.

This means that you, the programmer, had to do most of the work of creating the presentation of an object by adapting existing constructs. Perl 6 eases the job of creating objects just as it eases the job of writing subroutines.

package is now written as class. (And this is one of the cosmetic differences by which a Perl 6 program is recognized.) strict and warnings are turned on automatically when a class declaration is seen. sub is now spelled as method when you're writing a method. And an object is more like a closure than a hash or array. Instance data has all the benefits of strict. Now there's have no danger of accidentally autovivifying a new instance field by mistyping a variable name and then having it go undiagnosed. Instance variables are declared with has $.foo inside the class body. Instance data has a *secondary sigil*, either a dot or a colon. A dot makes something *public*— that is, visible from outside of the class. A colon makes it *private*.

```
# Perl 6 class definitions, and public and private instance variable
# definitions

class foo {
    has $.bar; # public instance variable
    has $:baz; # private instance variable
    method quux { ... }
}
```

Construction and initialization are separate but related concepts. A default constructor creates the object and does the initialization.

```
# Perl 6 objects automatically initialize themselves

class foo {
    has $.bar;
    method print_bar { print $.bar, "\n"; };
}

my $foo = foo.new(bar => 30);
$foo.print_bar();  # prints 30
```

Programmers will often need to take over the object's initialization, but they don't need to ever touch the bless built-in function if they don't want to do so. Instance variables may be initialized from expressions. BUILD routines are called to do any further initialization.

Should you need to construct an object manually, bless is a method of objects (inherited by all objects from the base object), creating an interesting bootstrapping scenario. bless associates storage for instance variables (or whatever the class uses for data) with a package that defines the methods that operate on the data. In Perl 6, most objects don't care how the data is stored, only that certain features are available.

The current object's reference is automatically read and placed into $_ when a method is called.

```
# $_ contains a reference to the current object during method calls
# Perl 6

class foo {
    method bar { $_.baz() };
}
```

Perl 5 programmers are used to reading the current object as $self or $this. All the stuff about named parameters outlined in Chapter 11 still applies. SUPER is gone. Instead, next METHOD redispatches to the next closest match, quite probably in a superclass.

The method call and dereference operator, ., renamed from -> in Perl 5, may be invoked on nothing. That is, it works as a unary operator, defaulting to $_. Hence, .method is a method call on the current object.

Perl 6 has gained, among other contexts, an *object context*. When the return value of a built-in or generously equipped user code is used as an object, an object is provided. User-defined routines use the want built-in to test which context they're running in and behave accordingly.

Everything is an object. This is related to the previous point. An object may never be actually created if a number is only ever used as a number. When a built-in's result or a primitive datatype is used as an object, an object is provided. For all intents and purposes, all built-ins return objects and all primitive types are objects. This covers built-in functions, numbers, strings, arrays, and everything else. Perl gives as much or as little information as is required at any point. A built-in function may generate a single value or provide detailed information. A number can be just a number or a gateway to trigonometric operations.

Perl 6 and Perl6::Classes both support anonymous *inner classes*—classes defined inside other classes and used as unnamed return values where an object is expected. Inner classes are similar to anonymous subroutines in concept and syntax.

Perl 6 classes may export their methods into another class where they may be used as functions. This is often done to extend the language with new or replacement keywords. It's a Perl idiom that frequently used parts of an API (that don't require more than one object instance) be available for export. Perl 5 traditionally uses the bundled `Exporter` module to accomplish this. Perl 6 uses the `is export` trait, applied to methods. `Perl6::Export` makes a source filter version of this available to Perl 5. Aside from this brief mention, this feature isn't documented in this chapter. It's another source filter by Damian Conway.

Perl 6 methods may be declared `multi`, in which case multiple methods with the same name may exist, and the one that most closely matches the types of the arguments of any given call gets to handle that call. Multiple dispatch semantics are based on type semantics, and Chapter 16 deals in depth with the concept of types.

Terminology

I use the terms *class* and *package* interchangeably even though they aren't interchangeable. A class is built on top of a package in Perl 5, but discussion after a block of code benefits from using the same keyword as is used in the code. Examples in this chapter never use a package other than `main` without defining a class in it. In other words, this chapter doesn't declare packages and then not build objects out of them.

The terms *attribute* and *property* don't have intuitively obvious meanings, and Perl 5 and Perl 6 disagree on what they do mean. I'm skirting the whole issue by referring to variables specific to instances of an object as *instance data*. Attributes are some visible facet of a class and represent the public interface presented by that class to other code in the program. Properties and traits are facets of variables, subroutines, and objects, and they correspond to Perl's implementation of the item. For an illustrated guide to the names, check out the section "Parameters, Arguments, Traits, Properties, and Attributes" in Chapter 11.

About Objects

Objects make complex data structures easier to handle. They support error checking and centralize the work of dereferencing a data structure. Changes to the structure require changes in one place rather than everywhere the structure is accessed. Objects make networks of structures easier to swallow. Specifically, rather than littering your code with explicit paths through the network of structures, each node is smart enough to find the next hop on its own. Code needs to ask only the first node, and the first node can propagate the request or return as needed.

Chapter 9 had a brief example of building objects to replace cases from switch statements. Listing 14-1 shows the example, updated for `Perl6::Classes`.

Listing 14-1. *Objects May Be Built As Collections of Cases from Switch Statements*

```
# Dispatch to object methods - Perl 5 with Perl6::Classes and subclasses
# overriding methods

# in file SiteCom/HTML/Color.pm:

use Perl6::Classes;

class SiteCom::HTML::Color {
```

```
    submethod BUILD { } # not required
    # people shouldn't use the base class directly so these are
    # place holders:
    method print_tag { die "subclass responsibility" }
    method get_hex   { die "subclass responsibility" }

}

# SiteCom/HTML/Color/Red.pm:

class SiteCom::HTML::Color::Red is SiteCom::HTML::Color {
    method print_tag { print qq{<font color="red">}; }
    method get_hex   { '0xff0000'; }
}

# SiteCom/HTML/Color/Green.pm:

class SiteCom::HTML::Color::Green is SiteCom::HTML::Color {
    method print_tag { print qq{<font color="green">}; }
    method get_hex   { '0x00ff00'; }
}
# SiteCom/HTML/Color/Blue.pm:

class SiteCom::HTML::Color::Blue is SiteCom::HTML::Color {

    method print_tag { print qq{<font color="blue">}; }
    method get_hex   { '0x0000ff'; }
}

# colors.pl:

package main;

use SiteCom::HTML::Color;
use SiteCom::HTML::Color::Red;
use SiteCom::HTML::Color::Green;
use SiteCom::HTML::Color::Blue;

my $red = SiteCom::HTML::Color::Red->new();
my $green = SiteCom::HTML::Color::Green->new();
my $blue = SiteCom::HTML::Color::Blue->new();
$red->print_tag();
```

Each class declaration and the main program must be a separate file. This isn't a restriction of Perl 6 but of Perl6::Classes, which can't handle a second class block after the first ends.

You can use compatible classes (subclasses of a common type) in place of each other where each behaves in a slightly (or significantly) different way while still providing all the utility expected of the base class. In this example, SiteCom::HTML::Color is the base class.

Not only are different classes different, but individual instances of a single class are also different from one another, thanks to the magic of instance data. Listing 14-2 shows a rewrite that makes instances of the same class configured for the colors red, green, and blue. When objects vary only in specific data and not in behavior, it makes more sense to accept the configuration data as arguments to the constructor in order to customize the object instance.

Listing 14-2. *Objects with Instance Data Have Configurable Personalities*

```
# Dispatch to object methods - Perl 5 with Attribute::Property and
# instance data

package SiteCom::HTML::Color;

use Perl6::Variables;
use Attribute::Property;

sub tag :Property; # instead of Perl 6's "has $.tag;"
sub hex :Property;

sub new :New;

sub print_tag { my $_ = shift; print $_->tag; }
sub get_hex   { my $_ = shift; $_->hex; }

# colors.pl:

package main;
use SiteCom::HTML::Color;

my $red = SiteCom::HTML::Color->new(
    tag => '<font color="red">',
    hex => '0xff0000',
);
my $green = SiteCom::HTML::Color->new(
    tag => '<font color="green">',
    hex => '0x00ff00',
);
my $blue = SiteCom::HTML::Color->new(
    tag => '<font color="blue">',
    hex => '0x0000ff',
);

$red->print_tag();
```

Comment out use SiteCom::HTML::Color to make this work as a single file. Otherwise, split it into color.pl and Site/HTML/Color.pm.

The arguments to the constructor configure the class to take on the desired personalities, where each configured class is an individual object. Of course, you can mix subclassing and configuration. Subclasses can use configuration data in superclasses, and subclasses can reimplement methods defined by superclasses.

Calling Methods

Perl 5 uses -> between the object and method name to perform a method call. It looks a lot like a subroutine call otherwise.

```
# Perl 5, function call and method call syntax

some_function('some', 'arguments');            # functional call
$some_object->some_method('some', 'arguments'); # method call
```

Perl 6 uses . between the object and method name to perform a method call.

```
# Perl 6, function call and method call syntax

some_function('some', 'arguments');            # function call
$some_object.some_method('some', 'arguments'); # method call
```

See the Acme::Dot module for a toy implementation of . as the dereference operator in Perl 5.

Objects That Hold Methods That Return Objects

Objects contain methods and data. Methods perform tasks, such as return data. Sometimes methods return other objects. Sometimes they accept other objects as arguments. Using complex software, such as the LWP module or the Tk module, it's critical to learn to navigate documentation for the various objects in the system.

```
# Perl 5 - fetch a document using LWP:

use LWP::UserAgent;

my $user_agent = LWP::UserAgent->new();
my $response = $user_agent->get('http://perl6now.com/');
my $html = $response->content;
print $html;
```

Before this finishes, it has called methods in two different kinds of objects. $response is an instance of HTTP::Response, but looking at this code, you have no way to know that.

It'll often happen that you'll get an object back from a method and you won't have any idea what to do with it. Use the ref built-in to discover what kind of object it is.

```
print ref $response, "\n"; # prints "HTTP::Response"
```

Now you know which package contains the documentation for the object $response holds. A trip to perldoc HTTP::Response tells you about content(), is_success(), content_type(), and several other methods.

ref tells you what kind of a reference any given reference is. For an array reference, the string 'ARRAY' is returned. Hash references give 'HASH'. For objects, the package (or class) defining the object is given. Respectable modules include documentation, and perldoc extracts this documentation from the module for display to you. (See also the examples for Want in Chapter 11 for more examples of reference types.)

Perl subroutine calls often omit the parentheses around their arguments. Perl method calls likewise omit the parentheses when they have no arguments. They do require the parentheses when a method call has arguments.

```
# These two lines are the same - Perl 5:

$foo->bar()->baz()->qux();
$foo->bar->baz->qux;

# these two lines are the same - Perl 5:

$foo->bar()->baz()->qux(10);
$foo->bar->baz->qux(10);
```

This condenses chains of calls to accessors. Currently, Perl 6 allows this only for methods that require no arguments.

▪Method calls are space sensitive The parentheses after a method name must not have a space before them. $obj.foo() is correct. Otherwise, the parentheses will group an expression into being a single argument rather than create an argument list.

Autoboxing

A *box* is an object that contains a primitive variable type. Boxes endow primitive types with the capabilities of objects. This is essential in strongly typed languages but never strictly required in Perl. Programmers may write something such as my $number = Int->new(5). This is manual boxing. To *autobox* is to convert a simple type into an object type automatically, or only conceptually. The language does this. It makes a language look to programmers as if everything is an object; the interpreter is free to implement data storage however it pleases. Autoboxing is really making simple types such as numbers, strings, and arrays appear to be objects.

int, num, bit, str, and other types with lowercase names are primitives. They're fast to operate on, and they require no more memory to store than the data held strictly requires. Int, Num, Bit, Str, and other types with an initial capital letter are objects. These may be subclassed (inherited from) and accept traits, among other things. These objects are provided by the system for the sole purpose of representing primitive types as objects, though this has many ancillary benefits such as making is and has work. Perl provides Int to encapsulate an int, Num to encapsulate a num, Bit to encapsulate a bit, and so on. Because Perl's implementations of hashes and dynamically expandable arrays store any type, not just objects, Perl programmers almost never are required to box primitive types in objects. Perl's power makes this feature less essential than it is in other languages.

Autoboxing makes primitive objects and their boxed versions equivalent. An int may be used as an Int with no constructor call, no passing...nothing. This also applies to constants, not just variables.

```
# Perl 6 - autoboxing associates classes with primitive types:
```

```
print 4.sqrt, "\n";
```

This is perfectly valid Perl 6.

All this applies to hashes and arrays, as well.

```
# Perl 6 - autoboxing associates classes with primitive types:
```

```
print [ 1 .. 20 ].elems, "\n";
```

The language is free to implement data storage however it wants, but the programmer sees the variables as objects.

Expressions using autoboxing read somewhat like Latin suffixes. In the autoboxing mind-set, you may not say that something is "made more mnemonic" but has been "mnemonicified".

Autoboxing may be mixed with normal function calls. In the case where the methods are available as functions and the functions are available as methods, it's only a matter of personal taste how the expression should be written.

```
# Calling methods on numbers and strings, these three lines are equivalent
# Perl 6
```

```
print sqrt 4;
print 4.sqrt;
4.sqrt.print;
```

The first of these three equivalents assumes that a global sqrt function exists. This first example fails to operate if this global function was removed and only a method in the Num package was left.

Perl 5 had the beginnings of autoboxing with file handles.

```
use IO::Handle;
open my $file, '<', 'file.txt' or die $!;
$file->read(my $data, -s $file);
```

Here, read is a method on a file handle and was opened but never *blessed*. This lets you write something such as $file->print(...) rather than the often ambiguous print $file .... To many people, much of the time, this also makes more conceptual sense.

Reasons to Box Primitive Types

What good is all this?

- It makes conceptual sense to programmers familiar with using object interfaces as *the* way to perform options.

- It's an alternative idiom. It doesn't require the programmer to write or read expressions with complex precedence rules or strange operators.

- Many times those parentheses would otherwise have to span a large expression; the expression can be rewritten such that the parentheses span only a few primitive types.

- Code can often be written with fewer temporary variables.

- Autoboxing provides the benefits of boxed types without the memory bloat of actually using objects to represent primitives. In other words, autoboxing "fakes it".

- Strings, numbers, arrays, hashes, and so on, have their own APIs. Documentation for an exists method for arrays doesn't have to explain how hashes are handled, and vice versa.

- Perl tries to accommodate the notion that the "subject" of a statement should be the first thing on the line, and autoboxing furthers this agenda.

Perl is an idiomatic language, and this is an important idiom.

Subject First: An Aside

Perl's design philosophy promotes the idea that the language should be flexible enough to allow programmers to place the *subject* of a statement first. For example, die $! unless read $file, 60 looks like the primary purpose of the statement is to die. Although that may be the programmer's primary goal, when it isn't then goal, the programmer can communicate his real primary intention to programmers by reversing the order of clauses while keeping the same logic: read $file, 60 or die $!. Autoboxing is another way of putting the subject first. Nouns make good subjects, and in programming, variables, constants, and object names are the nouns. Function and method names are the verbs. $noun->verb() focuses the reader's attention on the item being acted on rather than the action being performed. Compare this to $verb($noun).

Autoboxing and Method Results

In Chapter 11, you saw examples how to write an expression. Here are the examples again:

```
# Various ways to do the same thing:

print(reverse(sort(keys(%hash))));          # Perl 5 - pathological parenthetic
print reverse sort keys %hash;              # Perl 5 - no unneeded parenthesis

print(reverse(sort(%hash.keys)));           # Perl 6 - pathological
print reverse sort %hash.keys;              # Perl 6 - no unneeded parenthesis

%hash.keys ==> sort ==> reverse ==> print;  # Perl 6 - pipeline operator

%hash.keys.sort.reverse.print;              # Perl 6 - autobox

%hash->keys->sort->reverse->print;          # Perl 5 - autobox
```

This section deals with the last two of these equivalents. These are method calls:

```
use autobox;
use autobox::Core;
use Perl6::Contexts;
```

```
my %hash = (foo => 'bar', baz => 'quux');

%hash->keys->sort->reverse->print;          # Perl 5 - autobox

# prints "foo baz"
```

Each method call returns an array reference in this example. Another method call is immediately performed on this value. Feeding the next method call with the result of the previous call is the common mode of using autoboxing. Providing no other arguments to the method calls, however, isn't common.

Perl6::Contexts recognizes object context as provided by -> and coerces %hash into a reference, suitable for use with autobox. autobox associates primitive types, such as references of various sorts, with classes. autobox::Core throws into those classes methods that wrap Perl's built-in functions. In the interest of full disclosure, Perl6::Contexts and autobox::Core are my creations.

Autobox to Simplify Expressions

One of my pet peeves in programming is a pair of parentheses that span a large expression. It seems like just about the time I'm getting ready to close the parentheses I opened on the other side of the line, I realize that I've forgotten something, and I have to arrow back over or grab the mouse. When the expression is too long to fit on a single line, it gets broken up, and then I must decide how to indent it if it grows to three or more lines.

```
# Perl 5 - a somewhat complex expression

print join("\n", map { CGI::param($_) } @cgi_vars), "\n";

# Perl 5 - again, using autobox:

@cgi_vars->map(sub { CGI::param($_[0]) })->join("\n")->concat("\n")->print;
```

The autoboxed version isn't shorter, but it reads from left to right, and the parentheses from the join don't span nearly as many characters. The complex expression serving as the value being joined in the nonautoboxed version becomes, in the autoboxed version, a value on which to call the join() method.

This print statement takes a list of CGI parameter names, reads the values for each parameter, joins them together with newlines, and prints them with a newline after the last one.

Pretending that this expression is much larger and it has to be broken to span several lines, or pretending that comments are to be placed after each part of the expression, you can reformat it as such:

```
@cgi_vars->map(sub { CGI::param($_[0]) })  # turn CGI arg names into values
        ->join("\n")                       # join with newlines
        ->concat("\n")                     # give it a trailing newline
        ->print;                           # print them all out
```

You could also write it as follows:

```
sub { CGI::param($_[0]) }->map(@cgi_vars)    # turn CGI arg names into values
        ->join("\n")                          # join with newlines
        ->concat("\n")                        # give it a trailing newline
        ->print;                              # print them all out
```

map() is *polymorphic*. The map() method defined in the CODE package takes for its arguments the things to map. The map() method defined in the ARRAY package takes for its argument a code reference to apply to each element of the array.

Methods on Code References

Perl 6 presents built-in operators as functions. + is &binary:+, for instance. Function references autobox. Methods from the Code class may be called in code references. This combination of features unleashes extreme (but not ultimate) power. For example, built-in operators may be curried: &binary:+ .curry(5) creates a code reference that takes an argument and adds 5 to it. Wielding this power will take some imagination.

Chapter 11 has some examples of calling methods on code references (and functions) to learn about the arguments they take, curry them, and perform other subroutine-related tasks.

Constructors

It's tempting to completely omit this section and pretend like there's no such thing as a constructor, but then I couldn't share the news that you don't need to write one. Perl gives you a generic constructor.

```
# Perl 6's default constructor initializes instance data from
# named argument pairs

class Some::Class {
    my $.foo;
    my $.bar;
}

class main;

my $some_object = Some::Class.new(foo => 10, bar => 20);
```

This automagically loads 10 into $.foo and 20 into $.bar.

new is defined by the object Object, which is inherited by all objects. (Hence, any object will respond true to $ob is Object.)

Attribute::Property has a generic constructor with like semantics. It's available upon request.

```
package Some::Class;

use Attribute::Property;

sub new :New;
```

```
sub foo :Property;
sub bar :Property;

package main;

my $some_object = Some::Class->new(foo => 10, bar => 20);
```

This loads 10 into $_->foo and 20 into $_->bar.

For Perl 5 with Attribute::Property in effect, new may be given a code block. The first argument is the already constructed object.

```
sub new :New {
    my $_ = shift;
    $_->order_pizza();
    $_->eat_bonbons ();
    $_->walk_around_in_bunny_slippers();
    return $_;
}
```

This assumes that pizza delivery, bonbons, and bunny slippers are available and, specifically, that these methods exist to access them. As I'll talk about in the "Custom Constructors" section, actually constructing a class isn't that interesting in a high-level language. The initialization of instance data and data structures better fits our level of abstraction. Let Perl worry about setup and teardown. $_ is returned back out of the constructor. This logic could have reblessed $_ into a subclass and returned that instead if it liked, but in almost every case you just want to return the $_ you're given.

Custom Constructors

You may override the constructor, but you have a better alternative, which I'll cover in a moment. Additionally, Perl6::Classes doesn't support custom constructors. To bless a hash reference, array reference, or other reference in Perl 5, write an old-style object instead. Attribute::Property requires that you use a blessed hash for the object implementation.

The following are reasons to create a custom constructor when writing Perl 6:

- You can create custom signatures for often-used constructors that require an idiomatic interface.

- You can specify versions of the same constructor, one requiring a more-specific type for an argument, another requiring a less-specific type.

- You can specify an alternate implementation for the object than the default P6opaque.

Perl 6 classes are, by default, built on top of P6opaque objects that may present themselves as hashes even though they aren't exactly hashes internally, though they may be close for all you know. This implementation detail is hidden from you, and it's something you shouldn't need to think about—it just does what you need. Likewise, Attribute::Property hides the implementation details of the class (but you happen to know that it is in fact still a blessed hash reference).

You can achieve specialized type constructor signatures beyond the standard list of named parameters with prototypes on the constructors.

```
# Manually initializing instance variables from a custom method signature,
# Perl 6

class MyType {
    has $.foo;
    has $.bar;
    has $.baz;
    method new (MyType $_; Foo $foo, Bar $bar, Baz $baz) {
        $.foo = $foo;
        $.bar = $bar;
        $.baz = $baz;
        .bless();
    }
}
```

This invokes bless on $_, which is the object on which new was invoked. As bless is a method invoked on a class, there's no blessing apart from class construction. Specifically, new isn't invoked on a string. Class names are objects that represent a null instance of themselves. MyType occurring in code after MyType had been defined is an undef blessed into the MyType class.

This example becomes redundant because it loses the magic of the default constructor. Besides declaring the parameters, the parameters must be copied into instance variables.

Should you desire multiple different constructors for a class, declare each with the multi keyword and make it a multi method. Each must have different type requirements. One of the types for one of the constructors may be more specific, and the other may be more general. Or two different constructors may require two entirely different types. Different constructors may require different numbers of arguments. Apocalypse 12 outlines the best match runs, where the best match is decided by a complex set of rules.

Initialization

Instance fields, or attributes, usually need to be set to some initial value. This initial value may be provided by arguments passed to the constructor, or it may be the result of a computation performed when a new instance of the class is created.

Data initializing, such as creating instances of other objects to delegate to, is usually done in the constructor. Perl 6 breaks apart the concepts of *class construction* and *class initialization*. Most classes will need to initialize themselves. Few will need to construct themselves.

Initialization from Constructor Arguments

Anything passed into new when the class is created is latched onto and remembered by the class, assuming there's an instance data field of the same name. The instance data of a class is initialized in much the same way that parameters are initialized on a call to a subroutine. When the logic runs, variables have values provided by the caller.

```
# Dog is dependent on the logic calling its constructor to provide a tail, or else
# the chase_bunnies() method won't have a tail to delegate to - Perl 6:
```

```
class Dog {
    has $.tail;
    method chase_bunnies { $.tail.chase_bunnies }
}
```

Here's that example again, this time written for Perl 5 using Attribute::Property:

```
# Dog is dependent on the logic calling its constructor to provide
# a tail, or else chase_bunnies() method won't have a tail to
# delegate to - Perl 5

package Dog;

use Attribute::Property;

sub tail :Property;
sub new  :New;
sub chase_bunnies {
    my $_ = shift;
    $_->tail->chase_bunnies;
}
```

This has the same caveat—the constructor must provide a tail, or else calls to chase_bunnies() won't have a tail to which to delegate. You can test for this with the following:

```
# Dog is dependent on logic calling its constructor to provide a tail, and
# the lack of a tail is tested for - Perl 5

package Dog;

use Attribute::Property;
use Carp 'confess';

sub tail :Property;
sub new  :New {
    my $_ = shift;
    print "debug: @_\n";
    confess "tail is required" unless defined $_->tail;
    $_;
};
sub chase_bunnies {
    my $_ = shift;
    $_->tail->chase_bunnies;
}
```

Here's the rest of the logic to demonstrate:

```
package Tail;

use Attribute::Property;
```

```
sub new :New;

package main;

my $tail = Tail->new;
my $dog = Dog->new(tail => $tail);
```

Had tail => $tail been omitted from the constructor call, the fatal error tail is required, along with a stack backtrace, would have been printed.

There's a flip scenario, too. It's an error if unexpected parameters are passed. This prevents programmers who are using the class from mistyping names of optional parameters and having the error go undetected. Keeping the Dog and Tail classes defined previously but mistyping the constructor call demonstrates this.

```
package main;

my $tail = Tail->new;
my $dog = Dog->new(tali => $tail);
```

This dies with the fatal error No such property "tali" in Dog->new. It's nice to know Perl is watching out for you.

Self-initialization

Not everything will be provided by the object's creator, though, and you must often look to the outside world.

A Dog object may want to instantly, upon creation, generate a Tail to use. Perhaps one isn't provided to the constructor, so it must be grown. (Dogs have tails—they aren't specialized cases of tails—so you delegate rather than subclass.) In Perl 6, and with Perl6::Classes, you do this with the BUILD submethod, as shown in Listing 14-3.

Listing 14-3. *Initializing Instance Data at Construction Time*

```
# Initializing instance data, Perl 6

class Dog {
    has $.fleas;
    has $.tail;
    has $.location;
    method tail { $.tail }
    submethod BUILD {
        $.location = 'couch';
        $.fleas = 0;
        $.tail = Dog::Tail->new;
    }
    method chase_bunnies { $.tail.chase_bunnies }
}
```

```
class Dog::Tail {
    has $.cockleburs;
    method wag { ... }
    method clear_coffee_table { ... }
    method chase_bunnies { $.cockleburs += int rand 40 }
}
```

Creating objects to delegate to is one form of initialization. When the Dog's chase_bunnies()
method is called, it's delegated to the tail, which gains $.cockleburs.

More generally, resources needed by the class are allocated, including exclusive locks,
connections, storage, system resources, and graphical resources. Data structures are also
allocated—but languages such as Perl make it more a matter of construction than allocation.
A corresponding DESTROY submethod returns resources to the system that aren't automatically
collected by perl. Memory is automatically collected, as are file handles and sockets.

I created this Perl 6 example in a style to match the Perl 5 example. Good Perl 6 style
would place the initialization logic for $.tail and $.location on the same lines as these
attributes are created.

```
# Perl 6 - Instance variables initialized at the point of declaration

has $.tail = Dog::Tail.new;
has $.location = 'couch';
has $.fleas = 0;
```

These initializations are run for each newly created object at the time that the new object
instance is created. This is the same time that the BUILD method runs, if BUILD is provided.
Complex and order dependent initialization logic should be placed in BUILD.

Listing 14-4 shows the example again for Perl 5 with Attribute::Property.

Listing 14-4. *Object Initialization with* Attribute::Property

```
# Initializing instance data, Perl 5 with Attribute::Property

package Dog;

use Attribute::Property;

sub fleas    :Property;
sub tail     :Property;
sub location :Property;

sub new :New {
    my $_ = shift;
    $_->tail = Dog::Tail->new;
    $_->fleas = 0;
    $_->location = 'couch';
    return $_;
}
```

```
sub chase_bunnies {
    my $_ = shift;
    $_->tail->chase_bunnies;
}

package Dog::Tail;

use Attribute::Property;

has cockleburs :Property;

sub wag {  }
sub clear_coffee_table {  }
sub chase_bunnies {
    my $_ = shift;
    $_->cockleburs += int rand 40;
}
```

You can mix both approaches. If a prerequisite object wasn't passed to the constructor, you could create one yourself, using default values. Alternatively, some data may be required as an argument to the constructor, and other resources may be created internally.

Publicly Visible Instance Data

Instance variables generated by Attribute::Property are both readable and writable from outside the object. Obviously they're also readable and writable from within the object. Perl 6 instance variables by default aren't *writable* from outside of the object; private attributes aren't *readable* from outside the object.

```
# Attribute::Property attributes are readable and writable
# even outside the class - Perl 5

package Foo;

use Attribute::Property;

sub new :New;
sub foo :Property;

package main;

my $foo = Foo->new(foo => 10);
$foo->foo = 20;
print $foo->foo, "\n";
```

This prints 20. The value of the foo attribute was altered from outside the Foo package, breaking encapsulation. Often this is exactly what you meant. It's trivially easy to create objects to serve as records or structures.

Perl 6 attributes don't allow this, by default, but they can provide it. The is rw property asks for it. The following example is equivalent to the previous one:

```
# Attributes are readable outside the class by default and
# writable by request - Perl 6

class Foo;

has $.foo is rw;

class main;

my $foo = Foo.new(foo => 100);
$foo.foo = 20;
print $foo.foo, "\n";
```

This also prints 20. To make $.foo readable but not writable by code outside the class definition, remove is rw. For a Perl 6 instance variable that's neither readable nor writable from outside the class definition, use a colon instead of a dot in the name and call it $:foo.

Writing Methods

The publicly visible interface of a class is composed of methods, which code outside the object may call, and instance variables, which automatically generate accessor methods. This applies to both Perl 6 and Attribute::Property in Perl 5.

Simple classes serving as data structures are useful and easy to create, but one of the points of object orientation is that logic is bundled with data. This logic is methods, and they must be written to make a class that does interesting things beyond passively storing data.

Methods are closely related to subroutines. In Perl 5, methods are subroutines. Methods have persistent storage—data that retains its values from one call to the next—called *instance data*. Each object has its own instance data.

Current Object

For Perl 5, the object reference of the current object arrives as the first argument to the method. This object reference is needed to retrieve instance data; it's also needed to redispatch calls (call other methods in the current object) and, of course, to pass a reference to the current object to other objects.

Perl 6 methods are *topicalizers*. Perl 6 automatically reads the reference to the current object into $_ , the *current topic*, or default variable. The method call and dereference operator, ., defaults to $_ . This is handy for writing small methods.

```
# Perl 6 - $_ is the current object and . defaults to it

method foo {
    .bar;
    .baz;
}
```

Because of this definition, calling foo() on an object is the same as calling both bar() and baz() on the same object.

Here's the same example for Perl 5:

```
# Perl 5 - read the current object reference and redispatch to it

use Attribute::Property;

sub foo {
    my $_ = shift;
    $_->bar;
    $_->baz;
}
```

Both of these should exist within some kind of a class, like the initialization examples.

Named Parameters

Code calling a method provides values for that method to work on, and it does so using the parameter names themselves.

```
# Perl 6 - named parameters - baz => 10 provides 10 to $baz

class Foo {
    method bar ($baz, $quux) {
        ...
    }
}

class main;

my $foo = Foo->new;
$foo->(baz => 10, quux => 20);
```

Constructors did something close to this, except the names given in the call to the method were names of instance variables, created with has $.var or created with sub var :Property in Perl 5 with Attribute::Property. Here, the names of the named parameters correspond only to my variables, not to instance variables.

The following is that simple example again in Perl 5:

```
# Perl 5 - fake named parameters - baz => provides to 10 to %opts{baz}

package Foo;

use Perl6::Variables;

sub baz {
    my $self = shift;
    my %opts = @_;
    # ...
}
```

```
package main;

my $foo = Foo->new;
$foo->(baz => 10, quux => 20);
```

This fakes the Perl 6 behavior using the old make-a-hash-from-the-parameters trick.

Binding Lexicals to Instance Data

This chapter uses primarily Attribute::Property to access object instance data. Without Attribute::Property, Perl 5 programmers take advantage of the object being a blessed hash (when it's a blessed hash, at least) and use it as a hash to get at the instance data. This works, but it's disadvantageous to type $_->{foo} rather than merely $_->foo or $.foo. Using the object as a hash reference makes it cumbersome to access arrays and other data structures stored in instance data, as the programmer is forced to work by reference. Methods in Perl 5 programs will often copy instance data out of the blessed reference.

```
# Perl 5 - object method that copies data out of the object reference

use Perl6::Variables;

sub paint {
    my $self = shift;
    my ($what, $color) = %self{'what', 'color'};
    # do stuff with $what, $color
}
```

Binding lets you alias the lexicals to instance data fields.

```
# Perl 5 - object method that aliases lexicals to data in the object reference

use Data::Alias;
use Perl6::Variables;

sub paint {
    my $self = shift;
    alias my ($what, $color) = %self{'what', 'color'};
    # do stuff with $what, $color
}
```

alias provides scalar aliases to hash subscripts in this example. Modifications made to $what directly affect %self{'what'}. alias also lets you avoid having to work by reference.

```
# Perl 5 - hashes and arrays may be bound to references

use Data::Alias;
use Perl6::Variables;

%self{'colors'} = [];
alias my @colors = @{ %self{'colors'} };
push @colors, 'red'; # same as %self{'colors'}->push('red');

print %self{'colors'}[0], "\n";
```

@{ ... } extracts an array from an array reference in Perl 5. I've been using autobox in this book and writing $arrayref->flatten, but this example needs a real @{ ... } to which to bind. Using Data::Alias to bind lexicals to instance data avoids the speed penalty of a method call present when accessing instance data using Attribute::Property.

Block Scope and File Scope Classes

Perl 6 accepts two styles of class declaration to suit your mood and needs.

```
# class used with a block - Perl 6

class SomeClass {
    method some_method { ... }
}

# class statement used with file scope - Perl 6

class SomeClass;

method some_method { ... }
```

The *file-scoped* personality of class places all the code until the end of the file or the next class declaration in the specified class. This is preferable for large classes that occupy a file exclusive of other classes.

Perl 5 has an idiom to do the same thing as Perl 6's block scoped classes.

```
package SomeClass;

{

    sub some_method { }

}
```

The { } just create a code block. This simulates the class SomeClass { } syntax of Perl 6. It prevents lexicals from spilling over from one class definition to the next when more than one is in the same file.

Inheritance

I intentionally mentioned delegation before inheritance. *Delegation*, simply put, is the act of objects holding references to each other and using those references to call methods in each other to get work done. Delegation allows objects to be arranged into useful structures. The opposite is one big amalgamation of data and logic, and that's what *inheritance* gets you. Inheritance isn't all bad. Just remember two simple rules.

- When something *is* a special case of something else, it inherits from that other thing. This is an "is a" relationship.

- When something *has* something else, it delegates to that other thing.

A car has a tire, but it isn't a tire. A bird has a beak, but a bird isn't a beak. A car is a specialized case of a carriage. A parrot is a specialized case of a bird.

Inheritance Syntax

Perl 5 classes inherit with the base pragmatic module.

```
# Inheritance, Perl 5

package Mutt;
use base 'Dog';
```

Perl 6 classes inherit by stating their is relationship in the class definition:

```
# Inheritance, Perl 6

class Mutt is Dog {
}
```

You can also use is inside the class block just like has.

```
# Inheritance, another syntax, Perl 6

class Mutt {
    is Dog;
}
```

This is useful for subclassing several classes, and, yes, multiple inheritance works in both Perl 5 and Perl 6. Should class be used in its file-scope form, is still works.

```
# Perl 6 - file-scoped class with inheritance:

class Mutt is Dog;

# or:
class Mutt;
is Dog;
```

has is subject to the same rules as is, but you'll seldom want to take advantage of this.

```
# Perl 6 - concise class definition

class Mutt is Dog has $.tail;
```

This is handy for creating numerous objects in a row, each serving as a simple structure, possibly extending other structures.

```
# Perl 6 - concise class definitions

class Dog has $.tail has $.name has $.breed;
class Mutt is Dog has $.breed = 'unknown';
class Mix is Dog has $.mothers_breed has $.fathers_breed;
```

A Dog has only a `$.tail`, a `$.name`, and a `$.breed`. A Mutt has everything that a Dog has, but its `$.breed` is initialized to `'unknown'`. A Mix has everything that a Dog has but also has a `$.mothers_breed` and `$.fathers_breed`.

Subclass Instance Variables Hide Superclass Instance Variables

Parent classes instance variables don't conflict with subclass instance variables of the same name. For a Mutt, the Dog logic that uses `$.breed` doesn't see the `$.breed` variable created in Mutt. Each class can see the nonprivate instance variables of its parent, but its parent can't see its child's instance variables.

This behavior is similar to the scoping rules of lexical variables.

```
# Instance variables in subclasses mask instance variables of the same name in
# parent classes, much like lexical variables in nested blocks
# Perl 5 or Perl 6

my $Dog;
my $Mutt;

$Dog = sub {
    my $tail;
    my $name;
    my $breed = 'generic dog';
    $Mutt = sub {
        my $breed = 'unknown'; # masks $breed variable in enclosing block
        return $breed;
    };
    return $breed;
};

print $Dog->(), "\n";
print $Mutt->(), "\n";
```

This prints generic dog and then unknown. Perl 6 classes may or may not be implemented in terms of lexical scopes, but the effect is the same.

Just like lexical scopes, parent classes can't see the instance variables of their child classes.

Subclass Methods Hide Parents Methods

When a method is called in a class, similar rules apply. Subclass methods with the name and a matching type signature take priority.

This makes sense conceptually as well. Subclasses are allowed to know things about their parent classes, but parent classes shouldn't know anything about their child classes. Different classes will subclass them in the future, and they shouldn't break when this happens. When parent classes do expect something of a child class, the class is unfinished, or *abstract*, and it should document exactly what the subclass is required to provide. Should a parent class actually need an instance variable in a child class, it may attempt to call the public accessor for it, just as any other code would do.

```
# Superclasses must use the public interface to get instance data
# from child classes - Perl 6

class Dog {
    has $.tail;
    has $.name;
    has $.breed = 'generic dog';
    method describe_dog {
        if(is Mix) {
            return sprintf "A mix between a %s and a %s",
                .mothers_breed(), .fathers_breed();
        }
        return $.breed;
    }
}

class Mix is Dog {
    has $.mothers_breed;
    has $.fathers_breed;
}
```

Here, is is tested against the current object, stored in $_, and mothers_breed() and fathers_breed() are called on the current object. If this current object happens to be a Mix that subclasses another class and inherits its methods, then the current object exhibits special behavior. However, this logic inside that if statement really should be moved into a describe_dog() method in the Mix class. If this logic were moved into Mix, it would override the describe_dog() method in Dog when describe_dog() is called on an object that happens to be a Mix. Again, superclasses shouldn't know anything about their subclasses.

```
# Subclass methods override parent class methods, Perl 6

class Dog {
    has $.tail;
    has $.name;
    has $.breed = 'generic dog';
    method describe_dog {
        return $.breed;
    }
}

class Mix is Dog {
    has $.mothers_breed;
    has $.fathers_breed;
    method describe_dog {
        return sprintf "A mix between a %s and a %s",
            $.mothers_breed, $.fathers_breed;
    }
}
```

This slight adjustment to the previous example takes advantage of method inheritance to let Mixes behave differently than generic Dogs. Since the logic is now in the package with the data it uses, as it should be, it no longer must use the public interface of a child class but can instead access the instance variables directly. $_.mothers_breed, a method call, becomes $.mothers_breed, an instance variable access.

The following is the same example in Perl 5:

```
# subclass methods override parent class methods, Perl 6:

package Dog;

use Attribute::Property;

sub tail :Property;
sub name :Property;
sub breed :Property;

sub new :New {
    my $_ = shift;
    $_->breed = 'generic dog';
}

sub describe_dog {
    my $_ = shift;
    return $_->breed;
}

package Mix;

use base 'Dog';
use Attribute::Property;

sub mothers_breed :Property;
sub fathers_breed :Property;

sub describe_dog {
    my $_ = shift;
    return sprintf "A mix between a %s and a %s",
        $_->mothers_breed, $_->fathers_breed;
}
```

Perl 5 implements method inheritance but not instance variable inheritance. Perl 5 class implementations based on a blessed hash reference lump all the instance variables together, introducing the possibility that a child class will accidentally reuse the same instance variable name as a parent class and clobber it.

Slurping Up Parameters for Inheritance

The Perl 6 parameter lists explicitly name parameters they're expecting, but they can also accept parameters that haven't explicitly been named. The Perl 6 parameter slurp syntax does this, with *%var for slurping up named pairs and *@var for slurping up positional items. Named parameters are populated as expected, with the leftovers going into whatever slurped them up.

```
# Perl 6 - slurping up parameters beyond what's explicitly named

class Foo;

has $.bar;

method foo ($foo, $bar, *%everything_else) {
    $.bar = $bar;
    print "baz: %everything_else{baz}\n";
    # next METHOD;
}

class main;

my $foo = Foo->new;
$foo->foo(foo => 10, bar => 20, baz => 25);
```

This mixes named parameters, unnamed parameters (dumped into %everything_else), and method redispatch, if you were to uncomment next METHOD. Should this redispatch, the parent will see all the arguments you've gotten.

```
# Perl 5 - slurping up named parameters beyond what's explicitly named

package Foo;

use Perl6::Variables;
use Attribute::Property;
# use NEXT;

sub new :New;
sub bar :Property;

sub foo {
    my $_ = shift;
    my %args = @_;
    $_->bar = delete %args{bar};
    print "baz: %args{baz}\n";
    # $_->NEXT::foo(%args);
}
```

```
package main;

my $foo = Foo->new;
$foo->foo(foo => 10, bar => 20, baz => 25);
```

Everything goes into %args, whether it's expected it or not, and foo() must pick out what's needed. Unlike the Perl 6 example, this assumes that the superclass won't ignore arguments it doesn't recognize, which may be the case if it's a constructor using Attribute::Parameter. delete returns the argument it deleted, so you're able to remove items from the %args and use them at the same time. Should the $_->NEXT::foo(%args) and use NEXT lines be uncommented, the search for a method of the same name, foo, would resume, looking through the parent classes.

Accepting named parameters without typing the name of each, or even knowing which parameters may be passed, is a huge feature. This convenience of named parameters blended with the power of programmatically processing the arguments is the only level of extraction extreme enough to be suitable for Perl 6.

Perl 6 can slurp up both remaining position arguments and parameters alike. Perl 5 takes its cues from the programmer, not the data, about which parameters are pairs and which aren't.

Attribute::Property, like Perl 6, can pick out named parameters that are explicitly expected while passing through those that aren't. When requested, this feature replaces the default behavior of dying on unknown parameters.

```
package Poodle::Standard;
use base 'Dog';

use Attribute::Property;
use Perl6::Variables;
use NEXT;

sub new :New(passthrough) {
    my $_ = shift;
    my %attributes = @_;   # corresponds to *%_ in Perl 6
    delete %attributes{haircut};
    $_->NEXT::new(%attributes, breed => 'standard poodle');
    $_;
}

package main;

my $poodle = Poodle::Standard->new(
    haircut => 'orbs',
    name    => 'Lily',
);
```

Subclasses often redefine methods. The parent class has the original method, but the subclass definition of the same name trumps it. When this is done, it's common to add new parameters and handle them but also call the original definition to do what it does.

The constructor of an Attribute::Property class picks out parameters that are instance variables. With the passthrough argument to the :New traitlike thing, it slurps up the rest and provides them to the initialization block for processing.

This new() constructor adds a parameter, breed, and removes one, haircut. It accepts unknown parameters, thanks to passthrough, but the parent may not specify passthrough, so you should remove unknown parameters.

This constructor, new(), can deal with parameters other than those that correlate to instance variables. These are read into %attributes.

Slurping up unrecognized variables and passing them along to other methods or superclass methods saves you from typing a list of each expected variable. It also saves having to introduce a new multi method every time a new parameter is introduced. A single existing superclass method can gain parameters without breaking the interface for subclasses. This radically reduces the "cruft" of a large object-oriented program.

You have no need to redispatch to the superclass to populate instance variables from parameters. Only parameters relating to noninstance data should concern you and warrant redispatch.

See the documentation for the NEXT core module. Chapter 11 explains manual argument processing.

Classes As Hashes

Perl 5 objects are usually implemented as blessed hash references, though any reference will work. When blessed, the hash references associate with a package, but they don't stop being hash references. A daring programmer could peek under the hood and look at the instance data contained in the object. This is known as *breaking encapsulation* and isn't recommended.

```
# Breaking encapsulation - Perl 5

package Dog;

use Attribute::Property;
use autobox;
use autobox::Core;

sub new :New;

sub breed :Property;
sub name :Property;

package main;

my $dog = Dog->new(name => 'fido', breed => 'mutt');

print 'name is ', $dog->{name}, "\n";   # also known as $dog->name
print 'breed is ', $dog->{breed}, "\n"; # also known as $dog->breed

for my $key ($dog->keys()) {
    print $key, ' is ', $dog->{$key}, "\n";
}
```

The accessor $dog->name was generated by Attribute::Property in Perl 5 or by Perl 6. $dog->{name} uses the object directly as a hash, which works if the object is based on a hash, but you shouldn't count on the implementation staying a hash, so $dog->name is preferable. If you're willing to depend on the object being implemented as a hash, though, you can iterate over all the instance data and do other hash operations on it. To test if an object is based on a hash, write the following:

```
# Perl 5 - is $dog based on a hash?

if($dog->isa('HASH')) {
    ...
}
```

Perl 6 takes the basic idea of using an object as a hash but cleans up the semantics. An object doesn't need to be implemented on top of a hash to be used as a hash. Subscripting the object reference as if it were a hash gets the instance variable of that name, just like in the Perl 5 example.

```
# Using an object reference as if it were a hash reference - Perl 6

class Dog {
    has $.breed;
    has $.name;
}

class main;

my $dog = Dog->new(name => 'fido', breed => 'mutt');

print 'name is ', $dog.{name}, "\n";    # also known as $dog.name
print 'breed is ', $dog.{breed}, "\n";  # also known as $dog.breed

for my $key ($dog.keys) {
    print $key, ' is ', $dog.{$key}, "\n";
}
```

$dog.{name} is identical to the hash reference syntax because it's the hash reference syntax. By subclassing the Hash package, Perl 5's tie can be simulated in Perl 6. Methods handle requests to get values, set values, list keys, and so on. No instance variable with a given name needs to exist to use that name in a hash subscript.

Callbacks

Registering logic to run in a given event is a common enough practice in object-oriented programming that languages give it special consideration.

```
# Perl 6 - a class to register event listeners (the first method)
# invoke a method to the registered listeners (the second method)
```

```
class EventGenerator {
    my @.events;
    method add_event_listener { push @.events, $^event }
    method invoke_event_listeners { @.events>>.receive_event }
}
```

add_event_listener() takes an object reference and pushes it onto the @.events array. Objects registering as a *listener* must define a receive_event() method. One listener may even need to define several methods if one subscription requires so, but invoke_event_listeners() in this example merely invokes receive_event() on each object stored in @.events.

>>. is the hyper version of ., the dereference and method call operator. These two lines are equivalent:

```
# >>. calls a method on each element of a list or array, Perl 6:

method invoke_event_listeners { @.events>>.receive_event }
method invoke_event_listeners { .receive_event for @.events }
```

The following is the same example using Attribute::Property and without the hyper operator:

```
# Perl 5 - a class to register event listeners and invoke a method on
# them

package EventGenerator;
use Attribute::Property;
use autobox;
use autobox::Core;

sub events :Property;

sub new :New {
    my $_ = shift;
    $_->events = { };
}

sub add_event_listener {
    my $_ = shift;
    my $callback = shift;
    $_->events->push($callback);
}

sub invoke_event_listeners {
    $_->events->foreach(sub { $_[0]->receive_event() });
    for($_->events->flatten) {
        $_->receive_event();
    }
}
```

Properties created with `Attribute::Property` are scalars, so arrays and hashes are used by reference.

Objects and Contexts

Context requires hooks into every aspect of Perl, and objects are no exception. Object methods know what context they've been called in, thanks to want. One possible context is object context, tested for with want('OBJECT'). Object references themselves obviously satisfy the requirements of object context, but they may also morph into numbers, strings, and boolean values.

Object Context

Built-in functions return objects when their results are used as objects. That is to say, they have an object context behavior. User-defined functions and methods may respond to object context as well.

```
# Method calls work in a context, and this context is propagated to
# the method being called - Perl 5

package ContextTest;

use Want;
use Attribute::Property;

sub new :New;

sub context {
    my $_ = shift;
    return if want 'VOID';
    return 0 if want 'SCALAR';
    return { } if want 'HASH';
    return [ ] if want 'ARRAY';
    return $_ if want 'OBJECT';
}

package main;

my $context_test = ContextTest->new();

$context_test->context->{foo};    # provide hash context to context()
$context_test->context->[0];      # provide array context to context()
$context_test->context->context;  # provide object context to context()
```

An object may return itself, as this example does. This is handy for mutators that change the internal state of the object but don't have anything else to return, because the result can be immediately used to make another method call on the object. Many objects will return an instance of another class.

As an amusement, as long as context() keeps returning $_, you can keep calling context() in it again.

```
$context_test->context->context->context->context;
```

Inner classes, iterator objects, and references to delegate objects are good picks for things to return in object context.

Default Stringification, Numification, and Booleanification

The examples so far in this chapter have shown how to do useful things with objects by calling methods in them. That's all well and good, but objects could be more immediately useful.

Strings turn into numbers automatically when they're used as numbers. Numbers likewise turn into strings. Both numbers and strings can be tested for truth, such as in an if() statement. Well, objects can do all these things as well. By default, objects are always true unless they fail to instantiate. Numerically, in Perl 5, objects contain the address in memory at which that data is stored. As strings, they become unique identifiers that are useful for distinguishing one instance of a class from another. These are just defaults.

```
# Default booleanification, numification, and stringification, Perl 5

use CGI;

# Default booleanification

my $cgi = CGI->new or die "failed to create CGI object";

# Default numification

printf "%x\n", $cgi + 0;

# Default stringification

print $cgi, "\n";
```

For me, this prints 8138170, CGI=HASH(0x8138170) and doesn't die when it tests the truth of the object.

Under the default stringification logic, objects stringify to a string that's guaranteed to be unique and distinct from what all other instances of other objects stringify to.

The memory address holding the instance data for the object, the storage implementation, and the name of the package are combined. This unique name can compare two objects to see if they're the same instance.

The numeric value of a class is also useful for comparing two object references to see if they refer to the same object instance.

```
# Different object instances have different instance data and different
# numeric values - Perl 5

use CGI;
```

```
my $cgi_one = CGI->new;
my $cgi_two = CGI->new;

die if $cgi_one == $cgi_two;
```

This doesn't die. The =:= operator in Perl 6 does the same, even if other comparative behaviors of classes are changed, as we'll do in a moment here.

Custom Stringification, Numification, and Booleanification

The defaults are good, but they aren't always what you need at any given moment.

Objects may present themselves as numbers and decide their own truth or falsehood when used as boolean values.

Generic Example

Listing 14-5 demonstrates the various operations that can be overloaded.

Listing 14-5. *Overloading for Custom Presentation*

```
# Perl 5 - overloading stringification, numification, and booleanification
# to make object references behave as intelligent variables

package Pet;

use Attribute::Property;

sub species :Property;
sub age     :Property;
sub dead    :Property;

use overload '""' => sub {
    my $_ = shift;
    for($_->species) {
        return 'Fido'       if $_ eq 'dog';
        return 'Miss Priss' if $_ eq 'cat';
        return 'Poly'       if $_ eq 'bird';
        return 'Bill';      # default
    }
};

use overload 'bool' => sub {
    my $_ = shift;
    return not $_->dead;
};
```

```
use overload '0+' => sub {
    my $_ = shift;
    return $_->age;
};

sub new :New;

package main;

my $pet = Pet->new(species => 'dog', age => 4);
print $pet, ' ';                  # prints Fido
mourn() unless $pet;  ·           # is it alive?
print "is in great shape for ", int $pet, " years old!\n";
```

This uses only a tiny portion of the overload interface but demonstrates how objects and contexts mesh. An object completely using the overload interface implements custom behavior when used with each possible operator. That is, the meaning of each operator is overloaded to mean different things depending on which class of objects it's used on when it's used on objects.

The following is the class definition again, this time for Perl 6:

```
class Pet is String is Num is Bool {
    has $.species;
    has $.age;
    has $.dead = 0;
    method prefix:~ () {
        # string context
        return 'Fido' if $.species eq 'dog';
        return 'Miss Priss' if $.species eq 'cat';
        return 'Poly' if $.species eq 'bird';
        return 'Bill'; # default
    }
    method prefix:? () { return not $.dead; }   # boolean context
    method prefix:+ () { return $.age; }         # numeric context
}
```

For the Perl 6 example, the names of the methods to present the object in various contexts are likely to be wrong, as no official judgment has been made on them at the time of this writing. A lot of the Perl 5 boilerplate is conspicuously absent—it isn't needed. The default constructor initializes the instance variables from named parameters of the same name. $_ isn't shifted off the argument stack, but instead $_ is topicalized to be the current object, and instance variables such as $.age are read from the current object automatically.

This doesn't use Perl 6's operator overloading interface, merely the numification, stringification, and booleanification interface. In a sense, I'm comparing two dissimilar things, but the end result is the same, at least for this example.

Sorting and Equality Comparisons

Comparing two objects' references to see if they refer to the same object instance is useful, but perhaps doing this for the purposes of sorting other logic is often more useful. You can overload the comparison operators, <=> and cmp, to allow objects to be sorted, perhaps even according to complex internal state, as shown in Listing 14-6.

Listing 14-6. *Overloading Comparison Operators to Allow Sorting*

```perl
# Custom numification and comparison, Perl 5

package Dice;

use strict;
use warnings;

use Attribute::Property;

sub new :New;

sub number :Property;

my $get_number = sub {
    my $_ = shift;
    return $_->number;
};

use overload '0+' => sub { $get_number->(@_) };
use overload '""' => sub { $get_number->(@_) };

use overload '<=>' => sub {
    my $_ = shift;
    my $other = shift;
    my $self_number = $_->number;
    my $other_number = ref $other ? $other->number : $other;
    ($self_number, $other_number) = ($other_number, $self_number) if shift;
    return $self_number <=> $other_number;
};

sub roll {
    my $_ = shift;
    $_->number = 1 + int rand 6;
}

package main;

my $die1 = Dice->new;
my $die2 = Dice->new;

$die1->roll;
$die2->roll;
```

```
print "Rolled: $die1 $die2\n";
print "At least it isn't snake eyes\n" unless $die1 == $die2 and $die1 == 1;
printf "Sorted: %s\n", join ' ', sort { $a <=> $b } $die1, $die2;
```

This sample Dice class is sortable. When sorted, dice created from this class are ordered by the value rolled. This may be useful if other information were contained in the object. Perhaps you're sorting racehorses by time to the finish line and then generating a report on the riders, past wins, and horse names.

You can compare two instances of the Dice class for equality. Rather than testing that the two instances are the same die, the values rolled are compared. I've redefined "sameness"—having the same roll is adequate for these purposes.

To sort lexigraphically, you'd need to define cmp as well. It isn't enough to define logic for 0+, numification, and "", stringification. perl wants you to perform the actual comparison as well.

<=>'s implementation is more involved than the overload definitions for previous examples. overload requires this of binary operators (operators that take two arguments). Methods in Perl 5, by convention, require that the object arrive as the first argument, and the -> operator in Perl 5 provides this object as the first argument. When an overloaded object is used with a raw string or number, and that string or number comes first, the arguments must be swapped so that the object reference comes first. Some binary operators, such as +, don't care about the order of their arguments, but others, such as <=>, do. If the third argument to the overload logic for a binary operator is true, then you know the arguments have been swapped to place the object first. This example unswaps the values after numeric representations have been obtained.

Unique Data Signatures

I'll present one last comparison example (see Listing 14-7). Perhaps you want to remove duplicate records from a little flat-file database. For the purposes of defining what is and isn't a duplicate, some fields are relevant and some aren't.

Listing 14-7. *Considering Multiple Fields in Comparisons with Signatures*

```
package Pet::Hash;

use strict;
use warnings;

use Attribute::Property;
use Digest::MD5;

sub new :New;

sub name :Property;
sub species :Property;
sub age :Property;
sub dead :Property;

sub get_hash {
    my $_ = shift;
    return Digest::MD5::md5_hex join '|', $_->name, $_->species;
}
```

```perl
use overload '0+' => sub { my $_ = shift; return hex $_->get_hash; };
use overload '""' => sub { my $_ = shift; return $_->get_hash; };
use overload '<=>' => sub {
    my $_ = shift;
    my $other = shift;
    my $self_number = $_->get_hash;
    my $other_number = ref $other ? $other->get_hash : $other;
    ($self_number, $other_number) = ($other_number, $self_number) if shift;
    return $self_number <=> $other_number;
};

package main;

use Perl6::Variables;

my @pets = (
    Pet->new(species => 'dog',  age => 4, name => 'Sherry'),
    Pet->new(species => 'cat',  age => 3, name => 'Fluffy'),
    Pet->new(species => 'dog',  age => 4, name => 'Sherry'),
    Pet->new(species => 'bird', age => 2, name => 'Chirpy'),
);

my %pets;

for my $pet (@pets) {
    %pets{$pet} = $pet;
}

@pets = values %pets;
```

After this is done, `@pets` will contain a unique list of pets, using this definition of "unique" created in the get_hash() method. get_hash() creates a digest, using MD5::Digest, of the significant fields. A digest is also referred to as a *signature*. The chances of two different sets of data accidentally hashing to the same value are almost none. Pets age with time, so $_->age isn't useful for deciding if two different records refer to the same pet. $_->name and $_->species are useful, though. The string and numeric representations of each instance come from this. Even though Perl's default stringification logic always distinguishes one instance of an object from another instance, you're able to change these rules and define objects to be identical when they're similar in prescribed ways.

Assignments to Methods Calls

Anything that can be assigned a value is an lvalue. Obviously this includes variables, hash subscripts, and array subscripts, but it also includes certain built-in functions and specially written user-defined functions and methods. The Perl 5 lvalue system, where a variable or built-in lvalue function had to fall through, has been swapped out for another system in Perl 6.

The new system works more like Perl 5's tie did, where a specially named method is invoked to process the assignment (or other mutating operator). (The tie built-in functions and encapsulating classes for Perl 5 are documented in perldoc perltie.) Assignment to a method call triggers a special code block attached to a trait attached to the method.

```
# Perl 6 - lvalue methods may be assigned to

class Dog {
    has $.laziness;
    method age will STORE { $.laziness += $_; } {
        $.laziness++;
        return $.laziness;
    }
}

class main;

my $dog = Dog->new;
# these two lines are equivalent:
$dog.age = 12;      # uses the will STORE { } block
$dog.age(12);       # uses the normal method body block
```

The first block in the method age declaration goes to will STORE, and the second is the actual body to age().

```
# Perl 5 - lvalue methods may be assigned to

package Dog;

use Attribute::Property;
use Want;

sub new       :New;
sub laziness :Property;

sub age :lvalue {
    my $_ = shift;
    if (want qw<LVALUE ASSIGN>) {
        (my $arg) = want('ASSIGN');
        $_->laziness += $arg;
        lnoreturn;
    } else {
        $_->laziness += shift;
        rreturn $_->laziness;
    }
    return;
}
```

```
package main;

my $dog = Dog->new;
# these two lines are equivalent:
$dog->age = 12;
$dog->age(12);

print $dog->age, "\n";
```

The age() method has the :lvalue traitlike thing on it. This tells perl that calls to this method (or subroutine) may be the target of assignments, just like a variable.

The if(want qw<LVALUE ASSIGN>) { } block handles the case to which the method, $dog->age, is assigned. The list of values being assigned is available as want('ASSIGN'). This must be read as a list. lnoreturn ends the condition where a value is being assigned in. This special form of return provided by Want must be used. Otherwise, the else executes, and the normal rules apply except that rreturn is used. A regular old return must end the block and be the default case. This is a special limitation and is needed to placate perl.

Attribute::Parameter works by using a combination of tie and lvalue methods. The lvalue methods return tied scalars that trigger code blocks when assigned to. This effectively emulates Perl 6's behavior, where assignment to a method may trigger active logic rather than merely leaving the result of the assignment in a scalar or hash. This is an advanced trick.

Roles

Roles cross mix-ins with a system of interfaces parallel to traditional "is a" semantics. Objects are tested for roles with the does keyword. Add to this has for testing whether an object defines a method, which works on methods introduced through both traditional subclassing and the methods introduced with roles. As roles are parallel to inheritance, they're parallel to the language's type system. Otherwise, strongly typed code can't be assured of receiving an object that does a given role, so a form of explicit type case analysis must always be performed before methods associated with an object's role may be used.

Roles are introduced in Perl 6 with the does keyword.

```
# Perl 6 - some critters using the CrossRoads role:

class Armadillo {
    does CrossRoads;
}

class Chicken {
    does CrossRoads;
}
```

Presumably, the CrossRoads role will offer something such as a cross_road() method and perhaps others. Let's assume this role also defines an abort_road_crossing() method.

```
# Perl 6 - a method that works on objects that may or may not have
# the CrossRoads role

method swerve_to_avoid (Object $critter) {
    if($critter does CrossRoads) {
        $critter.abort_road_crossing;
    } else {
        # what are we doing off road?
    }
}
```

Perl 5 programmers can get at this logic, too, if they want.

```
# Perl 5 - simple roles example

# Implementation of the role:

package CrossRoads;
use Class::Role;       # with no argument, we are a role
use Attribute::Property;

sub currently_crossing_road :Property;

sub abort_road_crossing {
    my $_ = shift;
    $_->current_crossing_road = 0;
}

sub cross_road {
    my $_ = shift;
    $_->current_crossing_road = 1;
}

# Some critters using the Cross Roads role:

package Armadillo;
use Class::Role 'CrossRoads';

package Chicken;
use Class::Role 'CrossRoads';

# Some other class that gets a critter as an argument

package main;

sub swerve_to_avoid {
    my $_ = shift;
    my $critter = shift;
```

```
    if($critter->isa('CrossRoads')) {
        $critter->abort_road_crossing;
    } else {
        $_->get_back_on_the_road;
    }
}
```

Perl 5 doesn't distinguish between inheritance, tested with isa, and roles. The Perl 5 implementation of roles doesn't have a does keyword.

> ## RESOURCES
>
> Apocalypse 12, at http://dev.perl.org, explains how objects in Perl 6 are implemented. This discussion was based primarily on this documentation.
>
> For a tutorial and detailed explanations of operator overloading, blessing, and other Perl 5 object trickery, read Damian Conway's excellent *Object-Oriented Perl* (Manning Press, 1999).
>
> Luke Palmer wrote the Class::Role and Perl6::Classes modules. chromatic, the primary champion of roles in Perl 6, wrote Class::Roles, which is heavier on syntax. Class::Roles wasn't documented in this chapter, but it's noteworthy for offering a more authoritative look at the idea of roles. Juerd Waalboer and Matthijs van Duin wrote the Attribute::Property module used heavily in this chapter. NEXT is another Damian Conway module.

Summary

Writing objects can be as simple as defining some instance variables, or you can take control for tight integration of objects into the language. Features exist to make things mindlessly easy, and features exist to perform tasks that aren't normally possible.

Named parameters are easy to fake badly in Perl 5 but hard to do well. Perl 6 gets it right. Automatically initializing instance data from arguments to the constructor is a neat trick that makes programming easier.

Perl 6 follows the lead of other languages, putting a workable implementation of data inheritance in the core. This certainly makes things much easier if for no other reason than getting all the Perl programmers to speak a common language (so to speak).

Autoboxing has proven a popular feature for new languages. Ruby uses it to good effect, C# has it, and Java just hopped on the bandwagon. It's useful for keeping your brain in an object mode while you write code that doesn't make the computer burst at the seams with object instance data overhead. You can have your primitive types and call methods on them, too.

Stringification, numification, and booleanification have existed in other languages for years, and they make things possible that wouldn't otherwise be. Perl 5 does this, but Perl 6 lets you do it without overloading operators, and that really makes things easier—and more inviting.

I haven't seen assignment to method calls in other languages, and this serves to make code impossibly expressive.

All in all, code gets written faster (or doesn't have to be written at all), objects blend in better, and you have more fun things to try.

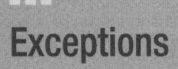

## CHAPTER 15

Exceptions

Perl 6 introduces syntax to ease recovering from error conditions. It represents errors with objects rich in meta-information. Building robust error checking into a program is easier and more visually appealing than ever. Programs that don't expect errors are sure to do the wrong thing when they do occur, frustrating both the user and the programmer. The best a program can do is attempt to recover to a usable state by restoring state to what it was before the failing logic, prompting the user and then trying again. Essentially, Perl 6 eases the task of writing good code.

The syntactical sugar and utilities offered by the Error module let you write code using the "standard" try, catch, and finally clauses. These are useful for getting into the mind-set of catching errors and placing cleaned-up code in shared places outside the normal code and exception-handling code. I also use Hook::Scope, first introduced in Chapter 10. Although it doesn't exactly perform error handling, it mirrors Perl 6's block placement and general style.

A "haphazard exception model" is the seventh deadly sin according to Tom Christiansen's 1996 article "Deadly Sins of Perl".

Changes for Perl 6

Perl 6 moves error handling into the block. It isn't something that's placed around the block. try { } replaces eval { } for trapping errors, but placing a CATCH { } block inside another block turns that block into a try { } block regardless.

$@ and $? are obsolete. $! now serves double (triple?) duty. This makes it easy to rethrow errors. Merging these error indication variables makes it easy for try { } blocks to fail with both user-defined and operating system–defined errors while retaining information specific to the actual error type.

New for Perl 6

Objects that subclass the base exception object, X, represent different varieties of error. Error object instances encapsulate the specifics of actual errors. They're created when the error happens. Using subclasses to categorically group different kinds of errors lets the errors be handled categorically. This takes place with the smart-matching logic provided by ~~ and when.

$! contains the current error object—at least in object context it does. In string context, it's a string, and in numeric context, it's an errno error number, just like in Perl 5.

Exceptions

Not every error is an exception. Perl won't abort because of just any flaw in program logic. (However, flawed logic may cause problems such as deep recursion, which does trigger an exception.) An exception is a situation that Perl isn't prepared to deal with—an exceptional situation. Normal processing beyond the exception isn't possible. Perl documentation doesn't often use the word *exception*; it uses *fatal error* instead. However, I'll use *exception*, because these errors aren't fatal if caught, because the meaning of *exception* is clearer, and because other languages use the word *exception*.

A language defines what constitutes an exception. It also defines what happens when an exception is encountered. A language should help programmers gracefully deal with exceptions.

What Constitutes an Exception

The language defines certain things as illegal, and when these actions are attempted, an exception is generated, or *thrown.*

An error happens when a method call is attempted on a variable holding undef. This is part of a larger class of errors where a nonreference type is used as a reference. In Perl, runtime language errors such as these are common.

Something illegal according to the laws of mathematics, such as dividing by zero or asking for the square root of a negative number, will trigger an exception. perldoc perllexwarn and perldoc perldiag list the actions considered by Perl to be errors.

Usually, though, fatal errors happen in Perl when programmers *ask* for them to be thrown by calling the die built-in function. This takes place when assertions in the code have detected an impasse and when the present routine can no longer continue operating in any useful way. The sooner an error is detected, the easier it is for the program to recover from it.

Chapter 6 introduced the notion of using or die $! chained to I/O operations to signal errors, as I/O operations by themselves don't throw fatal errors (except for unhandled PIPE signals, which are another matter—see perldoc perlipc for information on signal handlers). It's also useful to test the return values of functions that may fail using or or err. Chapter 5 talks about using undef as slightly out-of-band data to signal failure. Should a routine return undef to signal failure, this isn't the same as throwing an exception, but it's easily promoted to an exception with an or die clause.

```
# Promoting failed return codes to exceptions - Perl 5 and Perl 6
my $something = some_function() err die;
```

How a routine signals failure, and whether it signals failure at all, depends on that routine, but undef is often used as a return value to signal failure. err detects undef but ignores 0. $! is only usefully set after I/O operations, so there's no point in including it in this case. However, you may want to provide a textual explanation of why the error is an error.

```
# Promoting failed return codes to exceptions - Perl 5 and Perl 6
my $something = some_function() err die 'I really need something to go on';
```

err, or, and and, as explained in Chapter 6, are very low precedence, so they run only after everything else in the statement has run. Here, err doesn't run until after the assignment.

Even if errors aren't caught in the program, dying when an impasse is reached is useful for debugging. The programmer may immediately see that foo.txt couldn't be opened, rather than wondering why there's no output and seeing a "successful" exit code.

For an uncaught error, the name of the file containing the code and the line number of the statement are printed, along with the name of the error and any details specific to that error.

When an Exception Is Thrown

die, or an internally generated error, exits blocks, exits subroutines, and ultimately exits the program, unless a Perl 6 CATCH { } block is found on the way. In Perl 6, try { } and CATCH { } stop the avalanche. In Perl 5, that's eval { }.

```
# Catching an error - Perl 5

eval {
    open my $fh, '<', 'foo.txt' or die $!;
    # ...
};
```

```
# $@ contains the text of any error message
```

Not using any of the new semantics, the Perl 6 version is similar.

```
# Catching an error - Perl 6

try {
    my $fh = open '<', 'foo.txt' or die $!;
    # ...
};
```

```
# The $! object contains the text of any error message if used as a string
```

Perl 5 code using eval { } either ignores the error completely or explicitly tests $@ immediately after the eval { }.

```
# Catching an error and then testing for the occurrence of an error - Perl 5

while(1) {
    eval {
        open my $fh, '<', 'foo.txt' or die $!;
        # ...
    };
    if($@) {
        print "Failed to open 'foo.txt': $@\n",
              "Please fix this problem and then mash the ",
              "[ENTER] key to try again.\n";
        <STDIN>;
    } else {
        last;
    }
}
```

It'd be nice if the eval { } block and the if statement were friendlier with each other so their relationship would be obvious. CATCH { } in Perl 6 makes the error handling for a block part of that block.

```
# Catching an error - Perl 6
loop {
    my $fh = open '<', 'foo.txt' or die $!;
    CATCH {
        print "Failed to open 'foo.txt': $!\n",
              "Please fix this problem and then mash the ",
              "[ENTER] key to try again.\n";
    };
    KEEP { last; };
};
```

Placing CATCH { } in the block it handles makes it easier for subroutines to catch their own errors. It satisfies the ideal that exceptions are indented and the default case (the body of the block that may throw an error) isn't. Most interestingly, lexical variables for the block being error handled are in scope. This happens naturally without any messy spillage rules. Perl 5's $@ doesn't retain all the properties of $!, but I'll talk about that in the later "The Error Object" section. This simple example of CATCH { } in Perl 6 doesn't take advantage of the CATCH { } being a specialized given { } block, which I'll demonstrate later.

Throwing Objects in Perl 5

Perl 5 started down the path of object-oriented errors. die accepts references and propagates those to be $@ outside the eval { } block.

```
# Perl 5 - throw objects as exceptions
eval {
    -f $file or die Error::MissingFile->new(-text => "$file missing");
    open my $fh, '<', $file or
        die Error::UnreadableFile->new(-text => "$file: $!");
    # ...
};
if($@) {
    if($@->isa('Error::MissingFile')) { ... }
    if($@->isa('Error::UnreadableFile')) { ... }
}
```

This example only successfully throws an object as the error for user-generated exceptions. Division by zero, null value dereferences, and other language-specified exceptions don't generate objects.

Perl 6's $! already contains a premade object, ready to be thrown—you have no need to call new() on a package to construct it.

The Error module builds on this, adding syntactical sugar and better semantics. The following is the same example, written to use Error:

```
# Throwing and then catching an error using Error.pm - Perl 5
use Error ':try';
try {
    -f $file or throw Error::MissingFile -text => "$file missing";
    open my $fh, '<', $file or throw Error::UnreadableFile -text => "file: $!";
    # ...
}
catch Error::MissingFile with {
    # ...
}
catch Error::UnreadableFile with {
    # ...
}
```

die is changed to throw to get at the semantics where an object encapsulates the error. You'll have no need to construct the actual object, as throw does this, but you must still specify the class of the error. This use of throw is equivalent to die Error::Simple->new($!). Error is provided for you as a base class that can be extended to create categories of errors using isa to perform the category test. It's assumed in this example that Error has already been subclassed into Error::MissingFile and Error::UnreadableFile. An empty inheritance from Error will create package Error::MissingFile; use base 'Error';. Alternatively, let the package auto-vivicate: @Error::MissingFile::ISA = qw(Error);. Error::Simple is a subclass of Error that's directly useful as an error to be thrown. Customize it by passing a string argument or by passing a recognized pair. Error doesn't solve the problem of built-in exceptions not generating objects. Perl 6 combines all the type comparisons into one large CATCH { } block; Error uses one catch { } block for each type comparison.

The Error Object

Perl 6's $! is an object that renders itself as a string or number when used as a string or number. Using it as a string generates a textual description of the error message. Using it as a number returns the system error number, if the error was generated from a call to the operating system.

Perl 5's $!, when used as a string, is a textual description of the error message and, when used as a number, is always the system error number. $@ contains any error text generated by user-defined errors created by explicit calls to die. $@ may or may not be an object, depending on whether the argument to die was an object. $@ may or may not know how to present itself as a string or number if it's an object.

User and System Errors

Error codes from operating system calls are better known as errno numbers, taken from the name of the C variable of the same purpose. On Unix-like systems, these are defined in /usr/include/sys/errno.h, along with symbolic constants. The string rendering of $! comes from the C function perror(). The POSIX module included with Perl makes the symbolic names defined in that file available as Perl constants. Use it like this: use POSIX ':errno_h';. Symbols such as E2BIG are then defined to be the error number of their numeric equivalents. Code wanting to know why it failed uses this.

```
# Perl 5 - handle different errors differently
use POSIX ':errno_h';
open my $f, '<', 'foo.txt' or do {
    print "Call tech support and ask for a new foo.txt\n" if $! == ENOENT;
    print "You aren't logged in as an authorized user\n"  if $! == EACCESS;
    # ...
};
```

Perl 5's $@ is set by eval { } blocks (though user code may assign to it). Unlike $!, $@ may contain any text or error, not just errors defined by the operating system. However, $@ doesn't retain any operating system–specific error code information, even when set from a die $! operation.

```
# Perl 5 - $@ does not remember $!'s errno value when set from $!
eval { open my $f, '<', 'foo.txt' or die $!; };
print $@ + 0, "\n";
```

In Perl 6, $! replaces $@ entirely. User-defined error messages, such as die "planets out of alignment", may be contained in $!, just like system-defined errors.

Distinguishing Error Classes

Using subclasses to categorically group different kinds of errors lets them be handled categorically as well. CATCH { } is approximately the same as given $! { }, but $_ is still available. In object methods, $_ is the usually the current object, so it's important that this value be available. Unlike a normal given block, CATCH { } is of course automatically invoked for exceptions thrown in the block (and blocks inside the current block). All the operations outlined in Chapter 9 apply. when, when provided a type name, performs a class membership test. This is the isa test in Perl 5. This class membership test, rather than numeric value comparison, is the encouraged idiom, but there's no reason that the numeric or string form of $_ couldn't be tested. The following is the Perl 5 running example rewritten for Perl 6:

```
# Perl 6 - handle different errors differently
{
    my $f = open <', 'foo.txt' or die;
    CATCH {
        when X::ENOENT  {
            print "Call tech support and ask for a new foo.txt\n"
        }
        when X::EACCESS {
            print "You aren't logged in as an authorized user\n"
        }
    }
};
```

Compare this to the sample use of Perl 5's Error module.

Unthrown Errors

A function that triggers a system call, as does any I/O function, may fail, but failure doesn't automatically throw an exception. The proto-exception, ready to be thrown, sits in $!.

```
# Perl 6 - unthrown proto exceptions:
my $fh = open '<', 'doesnt_exist.txt';
die $! unless $fh;
```

This is the same as saying my $fh = open '<', 'doesnt_exist.txt' or die $!;. Perl 6's die() defaults to $!, but I've left the $!s in these examples for clarity.

The Perl 5 Fatal module saves having to test for failure and explicitly raise an exception. The previous example could be written as follows:

```
# Perl 5 - automatically thrown exceptions:
use Fatal 'open';
open my $fh, '<', 'doesnt_exist.txt';
# die $! unless $fh; # not needed thanks to Fatal.pm
```

Pass as arguments to use Fatal any functions that should automatically raise an exception on failure. They can be user-defined functions (in the current package) or built-in functions. See perldoc Fatal for more information.

A when { } statement in a CATCH { } block marks $! as being handled. After the CATCH { } block, it's considered to no longer be an error. KEEP { } blocks are run instead of UNDO { } blocks in the present scope. A when { } statement doesn't need to be used—$! may also be marked as handled using the error object method $!.markclean(). Likewise, if no when { } block matches, the implied default case in a CATCH { } is to rethrow the error doing something such as die $!. This marks the error as active again, and UNDO { } blocks will run instead of KEEP { } blocks if the CATCH { } exits with the error still active. Test $! for truth to decide if it has been handled.

Unconditionally Executed Code

A block may exit normally by falling off the end or by executing a return statement. It's also possible for execution in the code block to stop prematurely, execute an error handler, and then fall through or return from there. Of course, it may stop prematurely but not have an error handler to invoke. It's nice to have a way to specify code to execute unconditionally, and that's what POST { } buys you. A POST { } block runs when the block it's inside of exits, no matter what the reason for the exit is. This is important in error handling, where cleanup may be required. Hook::Scope provides a POST { } block to Perl 5. The finally { } block provided by Error serves the same purpose.

Blocks Executed on Success

Should a block exit successfully, it may be desirable to update internal state, committing any changes.

Perl 6 defines a KEEP { } block that runs when the enclosing block exits successfully. An is keep trait is available on lexical variables and runs when the KEEP { } logic for that blocks runs, if it runs. The is keep trait attaches commit logic to variables to commit their values (or otherwise do something) when the block they're scoped to exits successfully.

Blocks Executed on Failure

Should CATCH { } fail to successfully deal with the error, any UNDO { } blocks in the current scope will run. They're tasked with rolling back any changes and doing any cleanup needed.

UNDO-like logic may be attached to variables using traits.

```
my $dire_predirection is undo { $dire_prediction = "Told ya so!" } =
    "Something bad is going to happen!";
```

When using Error, rollback logic such as this would be part of the otherwise { } clause (see the perldoc Error documentation).

REFERENCES AND THANKS

Apocalypse 4 defined the error-handling behavior for Perl 6 described in this chapter. Apocalypse 4 is about "syntax in the large", including anything relating to blocks. See "Error Indicators" in perldoc perlvar for more information about Perl 5's $!, $@, and $?. perldoc Error was a source for this chapter. Graham Barr and other folks wrote Fatal. perldoc -f die is, of course, required reading. warn, documented in perldoc -f warn, is closely related to die.

Chapter 9 explains the where syntax used in the Perl 6 CATCH { } blocks. The Carp module provides alternatives to die that generate more information, including stack backtraces.

Testing is another important topic and one that's closely related. See Inline::Test on CPAN for a taste.

Summary

Error handling, like multithreading, is associated with object-oriented programming. This is largely a matter of tradition, but it lets object interfaces establish a contract with the code using the object. On one hand, it warns that certain exceptions may need to be dealt with by the code using the object. On the other, it promises that certain other exceptions will be handled internally. Some languages do elaborate checking to make sure every error that may be thrown is handled somewhere. This is tedious, and programmers more often than not write sweeping rules to catch all errors and do nothing just to avoid having to make and comply with these declarations.

Forcing programmers to write CATCH { when X { } } in every subroutine and method is clearly overkill, but you should give extra consideration to methods other programmers have to use. Methods should at least clearly communicate how failure is signaled, be it an undef return value with a message stuffed in $@ or a raised exception. Methods should handle errors that they can usefully cope with rather than letting unexpected errors kill the program. Errors should be dealt with as close to the true source of the error as possible.

Failure should be silently ignored only in throwaway scripts and in places where the failure truly is of no consequence. Consider it a feature of Perl that every failed system call doesn't automatically terminate the program for want of cut-and-pasted exception-handling code.

CHAPTER 16

■ ■ ■

Type Safety

Intellectuals solve problems: geniuses prevent them.

—Albert Einstein

The phrase *object-oriented programming* brings two things to mind: calling methods in objects and declaring types. Perl lets you do the first without requiring you to do the second, and people are perfectly happy with this arrangement—so happy that this arrangement isn't expected to change, ever, in Perl.

Type safety is a form of stricture, and support for more forms of stricture is part of the general pattern of changes in Perl 6. By voluntarily specifying types, the language can check for a whole class of errors.

Automated testing is preferred to manual testing, but eliminating errors at their source beats automated testing. It's a form of false hubris to believe that the programs you or your team write won't fall prey to datatype errors. Small programs typically won't fall prey, but scaling up to larger programs requires preventive action, just as medium-sized programs benefit from strict and warnings even though they only get in the way for one-liners.

As programs grow larger, it becomes exponentially more difficult for the programmer to think through every possible interaction. This is *state explosion*, where each new variable or argument causes the possible states of a program at any moment to increase many fold. A program's state is the combination of the values of the variables, where file handles are pointed, and where in the program the processor currently is. A scenario where the program state is valid but atypical of the common case is a *corner case*. The program isn't in an inconsistent state, but it soon will be, as the program logic can't deal with the state it's in.

Corner cases aren't in themselves errors, but, by definition, programmers forgot to deal with them. Corner cases have crashed rockets launching satellites, taken nuclear reactors offline, and caused an extended outage of the entire U.S. phone system. A programmer discovering the cause of a mysterious behavior in a program will sometimes exclaim, "Oh, I didn't realize that could happen"—he just found a corner case.

Large programs tend to have corner-case errors arising from a lack of precision of exactly what kind of data is accepted and returned. This starts to happen as interfaces grow for internal usage rather than merely calling a series of methods in external objects, such as objects from CPAN. Often one programmer will use interfaces in another part of the program created by another programmer and will use them in a way they should handle but their author didn't consider.

Technically, any algorithm may fail to deal with a corner case, but subroutines are about the right size to establish a clear interface, spelling out concrete expectations. Type safety is a tool that sounds out, with the computer's help, exactly what possibilities exist and which you're taking into account. Should you fail to consider a possibility, you'll be notified. Type safety still applies inside a subroutine definition, of course.

These type checking calculations use set logic. The computer examines the set of types a complex type represents (that is, the type itself and all the types of classes from which it inherits). This is compared against the set of things expected. This is done for each argument in a method call and for the return value in a method return. Should the set provided expand beyond the set expected, the programmer has failed to take a situation into consideration. These tests require creation of types (objects) to represent each clearly defined set of state that cannot be internally inconsistent (possibly because the object constructor and mutators enforce consistency).

Unlike some topics covered in this book, type safety *isn't* an everyday programming technique. It's *tedious* to declare types because you have to communicate facts to the compiler, and that means lots of typing *at the keyboard*. Every tool has its place, though, and if you can recognize the signs of *not* having everything under control, you'll know when you're ready for this one. Waging a rough guess, I'd say type safety is more useful than troublesome at around 10,000 lines of code or 5 programmers, whichever comes first.

typesafety, the Perl 5 implementation, is limited. Type errors aren't caught that should be, and things are allowed that shouldn't be. (It's likely to improve over time, given feedback.) Interoperation with other modules is still very poor in typesafety. See the list of caveats in the later "Caveats" section.

Like tainting, type safety tracks how values move through the program and identifies things that aren't, well, safe. Unlike tainting, this is done when the program is compiled, not as it runs, and potentially unsafe constructs are found before the code even runs. The passing, return, and assignment of typed data are analyzed. Each of these operations must be consistent with the declarations of the types: what class they were defined as being or holding a reference to, what they're being stored as, what they're being passed as, and what kind of type is expected.

Perl 5 may or may not know whether a function (non-object-oriented subroutine) is defined anywhere in the program, so it never complains about the lack of a definition during compilation. Only when the program is run and no function definition is found does Perl emit the diagnostic Undefined subroutine &main::foo called. When a function is prototyped using Perl 5's type-only prototypes, discussed in Chapter 11, Perl is able to tell whether the arguments passed are of the correct number and type. Without the typesafety module, Perl 5 is unable to check the prototypes of methods in method calls as it does with functions. The typesafety module adds diagnostics in all these cases: completely undeclared functions, blatantly missing object methods, and object method prototypes that disagree with the types actually being passed in.

Changes for Perl 6

Type safety is part of the core language. You get it when you get Perl 6. No module needs to be downloaded. I hope it follows some of the ideas of typesafety, but that part of the specification just hasn't been written or discussed yet. Larry Wall has committed to *programming in the small* applications of Perl, where small, disposable programs are written to get a job done with minimum fuss. Typeless operation will still be the default. On the other hand, there are more chances for optimizations when strong types are used with type safety built into the language.

About the typesafety Module

In the interest of full disclosure, I wrote the typesafety module. In case you're interested in the implementation of the module, I've heavily commented the code. It uses the B back end, specifically B and B::Generate, to do its job.

A question people tend to ask me is, "Why?" (they're usually shaking their head as they ask this). Type safety is painful to use and requires drastic changes to how you're used to working, but I'd rather use type safety in Perl than another language. (I'm not a Perl snob; I just happen to know and enjoy writing Perl.) I'd rather sacrifice Perl's weak typing and retain the other features and benefits of Perl than have to throw Perl away and use another language just because Perl *lacks* the ability accept typing information. I've seen many meetings where a language had to be selected for a purpose and Perl was immediately ruled out without further discussion because the project was large and developer coordination demanded the ability to specify and check types. This is somewhat tragic when most of the people at the table know and like Perl. My goal is to extend the reach of Perl, not to diminish the fun of programming in it. An earlier account of my reasoning for creating typesafety was to irritate Python people, but the real reason is closer to doing it for the hack value.

The Case Against Type Safety

Ask ten Java programmers off the street if they'd program in a language without strong typing. They'll say no. Ask ten Perl programmers off the street if they'd program in a language with type safety. They'll say no.

Perl programmers tend to work alone or in small teams. There's no need to make members of the programming team behave responsibly, they say. Type safety makes code bureaucratic. When working in a medium-sized team, programmers trust everyone on the team at least enough to communicate effectively. No matter what kind of stricture you create, people will always create bad code, and trying to point the blame for problems in a project won't make the problems go away. We all need to break the rules some times, and Perl is a language that lets you break the rules and doesn't burden you with too many restrictive rules in the first place. Type checking goes against the spirit of Perl. That's the case against it, anyway.

Type checking checks for only a certain class of logic errors; it does nothing to detect off-by-one errors, overflow errors, other math errors, bottomless recursion, race conditions, priority inversion, and a whole host of other kinds of errors. Type safety ultimately only helps programmers remember what scenarios are being handled by routines and communicate requirements and compliance. Type checking is no silver bullet.

The Case for Type Safety

What is it about this technology that brings such joy to the developer's heart? It provides a safety net, that's what. Instead of perennially wondering whether you've accidentally broken some code while working on an unrelated piece, you can make certain at any time. If you want to make a radical change to some interface, you can be sure that you've fixed all the dependencies....

—Peter Scott, on the subject of automated testing in Perl Medic, (Addison-Wesley, 2004)

Type safety is one of those things where if you aren't forced at an early age to use it, you never get in the habit. And you wouldn't want to go through life with weak types, now would you?

Strong typing is a formalization of the boundaries between programmers. Done correctly, it prevents other programmers working on the same project from misusing your objects and methods. When one programmer is working on a project, the question of blame is obvious: the lone programmer is responsible for all problems. Given a team of 12 people and a project plagued with bugs, project managers and the programmers not responsible for the problems begin to seek a way of making programmers responsible for their programming dysfunction. If you use a module and call its constructor, passing some data that seems like it should work but it blows up, or it blows up a little down the road, whose bug is it? Is it a bug of the person making the call or the person who wrote the constructor? It becomes a matter of interpretation of the documentation, how well the module is error checking its input, and how well you feel it ought to be validating its input. The constructor may not be dealing with cases that it should be, but whether this is an intentional omission or a bug is up for debate. The constructor hasn't committed to handling that case or not. By requiring that typed objects be passed into the constructor, the module shares the work of validating with those objects. Many CPAN modules require an IO::Handle object as one of their arguments, for example. But even a lone programmer forgets how to use his own methods or just has mental lapses. One must plan to account for mistakes.

The following are some advantages to using type safety:

Inconsistencies are found at compile time, rather than much later at run time.

Specification of the types returned and accepted by routines are separate from the implementation of the routine. If a routine advertises that it takes an IO::Socket::INET object but blows up when one is provided, it isn't fulfilling its contract. The author of the routine is clearly at fault for failing to provide the interface he specified. Conversely, if someone tries to pass an IO::Handle object, the program won't even compile, as the routine explicitly isn't able to handle that case—it handles only a more specific subclass. When an object of the wrong type is passed, the programmer doing the passing is clearly at fault.

Error checking logic is reused. Data must be validated at least while the program is being debugged, and by requiring a specific type of object, you're reusing that object's own error-checking logic. If an IO::Handle object is passed in, you know that it may not be open, but you don't have to check that a filename refers to a file that isn't readable, doesn't exist, or has a path longer than the system-defined maximum. Those things just can't happen.

Type information specified may be used to automatically convert data structures to and from what another language expects, saving the tedium of having to write wrapper classes in Perl.

Perl 6 hopes to play nicely with numerous other languages through language bindings, linking, and common runtime systems such as Parrot. To be able to exchange data between programs where the data is more complex than just integers, strings, and arrays of both, Perl needs to be able to map its more complex types to the complex types of other languages, and that means objects. If you've ever written code using the excellent Inline::C or the remarkable Inline::Java, you know that moving data structures and objects between the two languages isn't automatic and requires Perl glue. For Perl 6 to cooperate with other languages, via Inline, via Web Services, or by tricks of linking or virtual machines, Perl must be able to specify complex types for its own variables.

Interoperating with CORBA, ADO, Web Services, and any other object technology that allows reuse of components or communication between parts hinges on types. These technologies map types between systems and languages, making programs work together over networks. XS uses typemap, a translation of types between C and Perl, as glue. Making one system talk to another means mapping types between them. When writing XS, you have typemap to help, but if you create your own types (structs) in C, you have to extend typemap. CORBA and XML likewise need to know how to fit types from one language into another language.

Within a program, type checking is useful for detecting inconsistencies in the program arising from incompletely executed changes. The following are the tasks in which type checking aids:

- When the order or number of arguments to a subroutine changes, type checking tells where calls to that subroutine need to be adjusted to reflect the changes.

- When a routine is changed to return a new value to signal an exceptional condition that didn't exist before or wasn't handled correctly before, all calls to that routine must be updated to cope with the new return value, and type checking tells you where those calls are.

- If you've removed or renamed a method, you want to know that no code still depends on it, and type checking will confirm this for you.

- When a new method needs to be added to an object, type safety will warn the programmer if an equivalent method needs to be added to other object types as well. This situation arises when two object types are used interchangeably at some point in the program.

The examples in this chapter demonstrate how typesafety handles these situations.

Whereas objects avoid many cases where the programmer must change code all over his program to keep it consistent when something is changed in another place, type safety prevents cases where a programmer even has to look through his program to find things that may need to change.

Dynamic Typing

Perl is a dynamic language. The types of variables don't need to be pre-established (that is, the types don't need to be declared), and they may change on the fly. At any given moment, any variable may hold any kind of value.

```
# Untyped variables in Perl may take on different types as the program
# executes, Perl 5

my $x = 0;
$x = "Hi there\n";
$x = CGI->new;
$x = [CGI->new, 0, "Hi there\n"];
$x = { object => CGI->new, number => 0, string => "Hi there\n" };
```

$x is first a number, then a string, then an object, then an array reference, and finally a hash reference.

Since any function may return any value, and any variable may hold any kind of data, you can't safely write a sequence of code to operate on a return value or datum without first doing elaborate and numerous checks on the data. Or, perhaps you safely can, but you have no assurance that it will stay safe in the future—someone else could come along, return an unexpected value, and gum up the works.

Compiled languages seldom offer this flexibility, and when they do, they do so at great cost to their execution time and memory usage. Common wisdom says that if you're making an interpretive language, you may as well make it a dynamic language. For example, Python is a dynamic language, in stark contrast to its object-oriented tendencies.

Compile-Time vs. Run-Time Type Checking

As I said, not knowing for sure what kind of value you have at any moment, you must write elaborate checks. These checks are performed as the program runs; hence, they're called *run-time* checks. A well-written module will be helpful to people writing code to use it and will check that it has been provided with the correct argument types. These types of checks also tend to be written as the program is debugged, and then the author is loathe to remove the checks after the bug is fixed lest the problem return undetected. Listing 16-1 has some such tests.

Listing 16-1. *Manual Type Checking in an Example "Sink"*

```perl
# A helpful method makes sure it has the correct types, Perl 5

package Sink;

sub new { bless {}, $_[0] };

sub bathe {

  my $self = shift;
  my $pet = shift;
  my $soap = shift;

  $pet->isa('Washable') or
      die "first argument to bathe() must be Washable";

  $soap->isa('Shampoo') or
      die "second argument to bathe() must be Shampoo";

  repeat:
      $pet->apply(Water->new);
      $pet->apply($soap);
      $pet->lather;
      $pet->rinse;
      goto repeat if $pet->is_dirty;

}
```

Each object passed in is tested to see if it fits that type. The isa method requires that the object either be blessed into specified package directly or, alternatively, must inherit from it. If one class inherits from another, it's a good bet that the first class has all the features of the second.

Performing type safety checks at compile time has these advantages over run-time checking:

- You don't have to perform coverage testing to execute each line to make sure it's valid, which saves time on testing.

- As each type check is done only once initially as the program starts, the program executes much quicker.

- Compile-time type checks are implicit, so they clutter the program much less than explicit checking.

- Compile-time type checking is systematic whereas explicit run-time checks only spot-check.

The net result is improved code quality, reliability, and reduced verbosity compared to a typical degree of assertion testing.

Type-Checking Examples

Given a get_pet method, you may try to bathe the input (as in the Sink package defined in Listing 16-1). If it's always a dog during testing, everything is fine, but sooner or later, you're going to get a cat. In the "Compile Time vs. Run-Time Type Checking" section, I gave an example of an object-oriented sink that did explicit type checking using assertions, just like a good CPAN module would do. Listing 16-2 shows a modified version of Listing 16-1 that performs these checks implicitly.

Listing 16-2. *Implicit Type Checking with an Example "Sink"*

```
# A helpful method makes sure it has the correct types, Perl 5

package Sink;

use typesafety;

sub new { bless {}, $_[0] };

sub bathe (Washable; Washable, Shampoo) {

  my $self = shift;
  my $pet = shift;
  my $soap = shift;
```

```
repeat:
    $pet->apply(Water->new);
    $pet->apply($soap);
    $pet->lather;
    $pet->rinse;
    goto repeat if $pet->is_dirty;
}

$pet;

}


typesafety::check;
```

Compared to Listing 16-1, the lines starting with $pet->isa and $soap->isa are gone, and I've thrown in a strange-looking prototype.

Listing 16-3 shows the same example again, this time in Perl 6.

Listing 16-3. *Sink Class Example Updated for Perl 6*

```
class Sink;

method bathe returns Washable (Washable $pet, Shampoo $soap) {
 loop {
     $pet.apply(Water->new);
     $pet.apply($soap);
     $pet.lather;
     $pet.rinse;
     last unless $pet.is_dirty;
 }
   $pet;
}
```

Any argument given to this method must have type information associated with it, and it must be the correct type or some subclass of the correct type.

The first thing in the prototype in Listing 16-2, Washable, corresponds to returns Washable in the prototype in Listing 16-3. Both return the object given to them, so their return value is the same as their first argument. These aren't the normal prototype pills you saw in Chapter 11 that allow only scalars, arrays, hashes, and generic references as datatypes.

For the purposes of these examples, the classes that have an inheritance tree look like Figure 16-1.

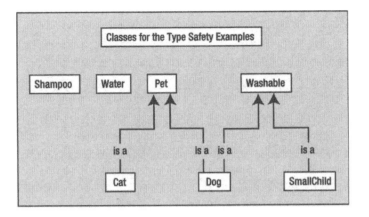

Figure 16-1. *Inheritance tree of example classes in this chapter*

Here are some definitions needed by later examples in this chapter. You'll need to type or paste these into module files to follow along with later examples. These probably won't help you understand the examples, so don't let them distract you. Washable's rinse, is_dirty, apply, and lather methods aren't interesting themselves other than they exist in the Washable class. Listing 16-4 defines the Pet, Washable, Dog, and Shampoo classes.

Listing 16-4. Pet, Washable, Dog, *and* Shampoo

```
# Pet, Washable, Dog, Shampoo, and Water classes, Perl 5

package Water;

sub new { bless {}, $_[0]; }

package Shampoo;

sub new { bless {}, $_[0]; }

package Pet;

sub new { bless {}, $_[0]; }

package Washable;

use autobox;
use autobox::Core;

sub new      { bless { 'fur' => [] }, $_[0]; }
sub rinse    { my $self = shift; $self->{fur}->undef }
sub is_dirty { my $self = shift; $self->{fur}->size }
```

```perl
sub apply    {
 my $self = shift;
 my $stuff = shift;
 $self->{fur}->push($stuff);
}

sub lather    {
  my $self = shift;
  $self->{fur} = $self->{fur}->grep(sub { ! $_[0]->isa('Dirt') });
}

package Dog;

use base 'Pet';
use base 'Washable';

sub new { Washable::->new }

sub chase_tail {
  my $dog = shift;
  # tail chasing stuff here
}

package Cat;

use base 'Pet';

package SmallChild;

use base 'Washable';
```

The earlier examples and future examples depend on these definitions. Dog doesn't have a new method (constructor) of its own. It inherits it from one of its base classes. If you don't like the inherited definition, you could write one of your own. The same goes for Cat and SmallChild.

Assignment and Type Checking

A variable with a specified type can only contain items of that type or some subclass of that type. Attempts to store other things in it fail.

```perl
# Testing our definitions for Pet, Washable, Dog, and so on - Perl 5

package main;

my Dog $dog = Dog->new;

# These tests will always be true by definition
```

```
die unless $dog->isa('Pet');
die unless $dog->isa('Washable');
```

This doesn't die. use base worked. Dogs are Washable, and they're also Pets. A Dog is of course usable as a Dog, so the assignment isn't flagged as being unsafe.

The die unless lines are redundant. Because my Dog $dog creates a variable, $dog, that can only be a Dog, these checks aren't ever needed. It's impossible for $dog to contain something other than undef or a Dog object. All Dogs are Washable because Dog subclasses are (inherit from) Washable. This relationship was established when the code for Dog said use base 'Washable'.

Unless prototyped otherwise, constructors are assumed to return an object of the same type as the package the constructor was called in. This works correctly with inherited constructors.

■**Unsafe code vs. incorrect code** When something is *safe*, it's provably safe. Not only does it not contain an error, but software can prove that it doesn't. That's what *type safety* refers to—provable correctness. There are expressions that don't contain errors but can't be proved to be safe, or at least typesafety isn't smart enough to prove that they're safe. These things are flagged as unsafe and a fatal error thrown. It can be annoying to have code you know to be correct flagged as unsafe, but remember that to verify your thought process, Perl must be able to follow your thought process.

■**Impossibility and types** typesafety can be tricked. One way is to pass a typed variable as an argument and then modify the parameter list entry directly. This is sure to confuse things badly. You could also use the PadWalker module to reference a variable in a way that isn't subject to type checking. typesafety can't be aware of everything that might be done, but it could be aware of more things. Some languages, such as Ocaml, have no holes in their type checking, but most languages aren't *entirely* type safe. See the notes in Chapter 3 about impossibility.

Assigning a Dog to something that wants a Dog works, of course, but the flip side is that things that can't be proven to be a Dog aren't allowed in assignments to variables typed to hold only Dogs.

```
# Assigning non-Dog things to $dog and failing, Perl 5
my Dog $dog = Pet->new;
typesafety::check;
```

This fails with the following diagnostic message:

```
unsafe assignment : type mismatch: expected:  scalar variable named, $dog,
type Dog, containing the literal value "Pet", defined in package main, file
dog.pl, line 92 ; got:  constructor, new, type Pet, containing the literal
value "Pet", defined in package Pet, file dog.pl, line 92  in package main,
file dog.pl, line 92
```

That's a lot of information. The general pattern of the diagnostic messages is constant. It tells what type was expected, what type it got, and where in the program each type was established. The Pet type was established by the constructor new for the Pet package. Roughly paraphrased, this error message you tells that a Dog was expected, but instead you got only a Pet. This information isn't all relevant in every case. The information about the literal value contained is unlikely to be accurate. typesafety guesses at this information to follow the logic in constructors as things are blessed.

A Dog is a specific kind of a Pet, and a Pet is something more generic than a Dog. That is, a Pet isn't necessarily a Dog. This relationship is one way just as inheritance normally is one way.

■Circular inheritance trees It's possible to declare circular inheritance trees in Perl 5. Obviously, a tree isn't circular, so this isn't really an inheritance tree. This is an artifact of perl not checking for cycles until it tries to follow inheritance looking for a method it can't find, in which case it will throw a fatal error similar to Recursive inheritance detected while looking for method 'baz' in package 'Bar'. You should probably refrain from creating such abominations. The two classes inheriting from each other could logically be considered the same class with the advantage of not confusing poor perl.

It could be argued that not all dogs are pets, but I'm ignoring that for the purposes of this example. Since a Dog is a specific kind of a Pet, you can count on it to do things that Pet may not be able to, such as chase its tail. Iguanas have tails, but they don't chase them. Cats chase other cats' tails, but they don't chase their own. Tail chasing is uniquely Dog.

```
# Subclasses and other derived types work as their base type, Perl 5
my Pet $pet = Dog->new;
typesafety::check;
```

This works fine. A Dog is usable as a Pet, so typesafety considers this safe. You can always store something more specific than is required but not the other way around. A Pet isn't safe anywhere that a Dog is.

```
# Try and fail to hold a generic Pet object in a variable that requires a
# Dog or some subclass of Dog, Perl 5

my Dog $dog = Pet->new;
typesafety::check;
```

This isn't good enough. The code may later try to call the chase_tail method on $dog, and if it holds a Pet, you don't know for sure that this method will be defined. Since it contains only a Pet, $dog might actually contain a Chimpanzee. typesafety rejects this.

Existence of Methods

Type checking requires that methods actually exist for a given type.

```
# Try to call a method that doesn't exist for a class, Perl 5

my Pet $pet = Pet->new;
$pet->chase_tail;
typesafety::check;
```

The method being called must exist in the object referenced. If a reference is known to hold some kind of Pet object, and you try to call a method on that object, that method must actually exist in the Pet class or a class from which it inherits. Anything less would be a mistake and an error. Since I've declared $pet as a reference to type Pet and only type Dog has a chase_tail method, typesafety knows for a fact that this would fail if it were to be executed.

typesafety doesn't try to figure out the actual subclass of a Pet that $pet holds at any given time but rather goes on the information you give it. Here, it only knows that $pet is either a Pet or some subclass.

```perl
# chase_tail() doesn't exist in Pet and typesafety only knows that $pet is
# a Pet, Perl 5

my Pet $pet = Dog->new;
$pet->chase_tail;
typesafety::check;
```

This is something that *would* work if typesafety weren't employed. For the purposes of type safety, $pet is considered to be a Pet, not necessarily a Dog, even though it happens to hold a Dog in this example. As the program goes on, a Bird might be assigned in. A Dog may be assigned to $pet, but the method chase_tail can't be safely be called in $pet. typesafety goes with what's *provably* safe, ignoring what's *actually* safe.

Method Return Type

new is assumed to return an object of the type in which the package new is called. That's why the following works even when new doesn't have an explicit prototype:

```perl
my Dog $dog = Dog->new;
```

Nonconstructors can have return types, too. Looking at the definition of bathe, that's the first thing, before the semicolon, in its prototype.

```perl
# Somewhere in package Sink is a bathe method - Perl 5

sub bathe (Washable; Washable, Shampoo) {
  ...
}
```

Chapter 11 introduces prototypes, but the prototypes it introduces don't contain type information, only context clues and parameter names. The prototype is the parentheses with the list of types in it in this example. That's (Washable; Washable, Shampoo). Context-only prototypes look something like ($\%\@;$). The semicolon has a different meaning. Using typesafety, it separates the single return type (which might be undef) from the list of argument types.

Number of Arguments

So far I've shown that type matters in assignment and for the value on which methods are being called. Assignments can only be made to equally specific or less-specific types, never to more specific types. Methods can be called only on types that are known to have that method. Beyond that, you must pass in the correct number and types of arguments to method calls.

```
# Attempt to bathe a dog, Perl 5

package main;

my Dog  $dog  = Dog->new;
my Sink $sink = Sink->new;

$sink->bathe($dog);

typesafety::check;
```

This outputs insufficient number of parameters - only got 2, expecting 3. The diagnostic message includes the line number and package name. For me, it was dog.pl, line 90.

This diagnostic wouldn't be emitted if the bathe method wasn't prototyped, even if the items sent to it had types specified. Since bathe was prototyped, perl knows the number and types of arguments. The actual parameter list looks like this:

```
# Somewhere in package Sink is a bathe method - Perl 5

sub bathe (Washable; Washable, Shampoo) {
  ...
}
```

This method takes a Washable object and some Shampoo to wash it with, and it returns a Washable object, which you can only assume is clean. These examples manually process arguments using the Perl 5 style rather than using named parameters.

If undef appears in the prototype, typesafety stops paying attention at that point. Both the type and number of arguments after that point don't matter. This is useful for optional parameters and variable-sized parameter lists.

Casting types You can employ type safety to distinguish between objects that are known to be clean (in the sense of the pet-washing examples), and the bathe method could return objects of a special Clean subclass to mark them as such. To do this, declare bathe with the prototype (Clean; Washable, Shampoo). $pet must then be converted from an instance of Washable to an instance of Clean, and the way to do this is to write the constructor in the Clean package to accept a Washable object from which to initialize itself. The Washable class constructor might then use bless to change the type of the object, or it might copy the instance data over manually. Reblessing objects is equivalent to *type casting* in other languages. object dog = (Dog) cat in another language is comparable in purpose to the Perl statements: my $dog = $cat; bless $dog, 'Dog';. Systems with absolute type safety don't allow type casts, as type casts essentially bypass the type system by making assertions that the type system can't verify.

Types of Arguments

Each argument is inspected for compatibility. The prototype of the method is compared with the known types of the arguments.

```
# Attempt to bathe a pet, Perl 5

package main;

my Pet $pet        = Pet->new;
my Sink $sink      = Sink->new;
my Shampoo $soap   = Shampoo->new;

$sink->bathe($pet, $soap);
```

Not all Pets are washable. bathe specifically wants a Washable. This fails with the diagnostic message:

```
argument number 1 type mismatch: must be type 'Washable', instead we got a(n)
Pet  in package main, file dog.pl, line 97
```

A Dog is Washable. A Cat isn't. A Pet may be a Cat for all you know. That would be bad. Changing my Pet $pet = Pet->new to my Dog $pet = Dog->new fixes this.

■**Reading typed arguments** Not all idioms of reading arguments are understood by the typesafety module. See the notes on processing arguments in the "Caveats" section later in this chapter.

Thanks to objects, you don't have to modify all the code when part of the program changes. Thanks to type checking, you're told exactly where you *do* have to make changes when another part of the program changes. Not only do you not have to change large amounts of code, but you don't have to search for the places you do have to change. In very large applications, it's generally worth the pain of using explicit types for this convenience.

Transitive Nature of Typing Rules

If a method requires a specific type as an argument, that type could come from a variable of that type, or it could come from another method call.

```
# Anything that returns typed information may be used as something of that
# type, Perl 5

Sink->new->bathe(Dog->new, Shampoo->new);
```

This is a version of the previous "attempt to bathe a pet" example, but I'm using the return values of the constructors of the various types directly without first assigning them to typed variables. This works fine and is fully type checked.

Mixing Strict Types, Loose Types, Arrays, and Hashes

Strict types can always be used in places where typeless data is expected. Loose types can never be used in places where strictly typed data is expected.

Strictly typed data may be passed to methods where no particular type is required and assigned to variables lacking a declared type. Data that has no type information associated with it can't be assigned to variables that are typed or passed to methods that require typed arguments.

Arrays and hashes don't currently accept type information but instead deduce it from their usage in conjunction with types assigned to them and types required of them.

Arrays are considered collections of similarly typed data and aren't useful as records containing collections of different kinds of things. Type information for an array is deduced from the least common denominator of types stored in its subscripts. That is, the most general of the types ever assigned to it is its effective type. Should a Dog be assigned at one point, and then later a Cat, it'll assume the type of Pet, which is the base class for both Dog and Cat.

Hashes are useful as records. %hash{'foo'} can be used as a typed variable of inferred type, and %hash{'bar'} is considered another other typed variable. If a variable key is used, the entire hash typesafety enforces consistent types for the entire hash.

Typed Arrays

Arrays become typed by virtue of being assigned only typed values.

```
# Arrays are typed when used only with typed variables

use Perl6::Variables;

my @array;

@array[0] = Washable->new;
@array[1] = Dog->new;

Sink->new(@array[int rand @array], Shampoo->new);
```

Since Washable is the most general of all the things assigned to @array, values taken from @array are considered to be of type Washable. If a Sink had also been signed in, no common type would exist, and values from @array would be useless as Sinks and as Washables. Since arrays automatically downgrade to the common type among all the types stored in them, none of the elements could be used as a Dog even though one of them was a dog. The built-in functions push, pop, shift, and unshift work as expected, returning something usable as the common type of the array.

Generics Other languages have *generic types*, also known as *generics* or *templates*. A generic is a class that works on a specific type, but that specific type hasn't yet been specified. Usually containers of some sort that are meant to be reusable rather than restricted to one type or no type will use this feature. For example, given a Bucket, you may want a Bucket that holds only Nails and another Bucket that holds only CoffeeGrounds. Rather than creating two different classes, you can use one class with a configurable strong type. typesafety's implementation of array typing bypasses the need for this complexity, at least in this simple scenario, and was inspired by Ocaml's type system.

Typed Hashes

Hashes have inferred types like arrays do, but type information is inferred separately for each key when constant values are used as subscripts. This facilitates writing classes in Perl 5, as classes are usually built on top of hashes and each hash key considered to be a different instance variable. See Listing 16-5.

Listing 16-5. *Using Type Inference with Hashes to Hold Instance Data*

```
# A class that packages together a Sink and Shampoo and offers a wash()
# method. $self->{sink} and $self->{shampoo} are individually and
# automatically typed.
# Perl 5

package Washer;

sub new {
  my $type = shift;
  bless {
      sink    => Sink->new,
      shampoo => Shampoo->new,
  }, $type;
}

sub wash (Washable; Washable) {
  my $self = shift;
  my $washable = shift;
  $self->{sink}->bathe($washable, $self->{shampoo});
  $washable;
}
```

$self is a hash reference, blessed into the Washer package. It holds references to two other types: a Sink and a Shampoo contained in $self->{sink} and $self->{shampoo}, respectively. These can be used where strong types are required. Of course, methods could be written to set and return these fields, like so:

```
# Accessors for our typed hash entries in $self, Perl 5

sub get_sink (Sink; undef) { my $self = shift; $self->{sink}; }
sub set_sink (Sink; Sink)  { my $self = shift; $self->{sink} = shift; }

sub get_shampoo (Shampoo; undef) { my $self = shift; $self->{shampoo}; }
sub set_shampoo (Shampoo; Shampoo) {
  my $self = shift; $self->{shampoo} = shift;
}
```

Should any code attempt to store a value in this hash using a subscript computed by a function or contained in a variable (or otherwise coming from some expression), then the separation will collapse, and the type of the entire hash will be considered to be that of the common type between everything stored in it. Hashes used with variable or computed keys are subject to the same rules as arrays.

Abstract Factory

An Abstract Factory is a design pattern documented in *Design Patterns: Elements of Reusable Object-Oriented Software* (Addison-Wesley, 1997) by Erich Gamma, Richard Helm, Ralph Johnson, and John Vlissides. An Abstract Factory delivers objects of some type according to some specification, but the exact class of the object returned is actually some subclass of the expected type. If the caller requires a Washable, it could return a Dog, a Chimp, an Elephant, or a SmallChild. You only care that whatever is returned be Washable.

```
# Abstract factory example - Perl 5

package WashableFactory;

sub give_me_something_to_wash (Washable; undef) {
  my $self = shift;
  my $desired_size = shift;
  return SmallChild->new if $desired_size < 40;
  return Dog->new        if $desired_size < 60;
  return Chimp->new      if $desired_size < 100;
  return Elephant->new;
}
```

This can be invoked with a call of WashableFactory->give_me_something_to_wash(75) to get a nice, new Washable. This concept centralizes the decision-making process of which of several actual implementations to use. This code may otherwise be scattered around the program, or one object may be trying to do too many things, and there is a desire to split it up into separate objects. Object-oriented programming cares about what an object can do, not where it came from, and this decouples the name of the class from the calls to objects created. In other words, the name of the type of the class isn't hard-coded all over the program, so if multiple implementations are introduced, the program needs to be changed at only one point—at the Abstract Factory.

All the configurations named in *Design Patterns: Elements of Reusable Object-Oriented Software* are designed to work within a typed language's type system.

Null Pointer Problem

The most popular strongly typed, object-oriented languages benefit greatly from the provable correctness type safety introduces. At least, they do to the degree that that type safety can prove the correctness of the program. When it comes to *null pointers*, it all falls down. A variable that's meant to hold a reference to a Dog might actually contain undef. Each language has its own equivalent, such as 0, null, nil, and so on. In each of these languages, including Perl, attempting to invoke a method on the null pointer is a fatal error.

```
$ perl -e 'undef->foo;'
Can't call method "foo" on an undefined value at -e line 1
```

Programs spontaneously closing are the hallmark of this class of bug. Perl will happily fail to open a file and keep on trucking, so why should a method call failure be any more serious? Larry has suggested Perl 6 will silently fail in this case, and the method call on undef will generate an unthrown error that may be thrown with syntax such as undef.foo err die;. Perl 5 can emulate this behavior.

```
# Trapping method calls on uninitialized object references - Perl 5

package Foo;

use typesafety;

sub new { bless { }, $_[0] }
sub bing { print "bing!\n"; }

# main

package main;

use typesafety;

use Class::BlackHole;
use autobox UNDEF => 'Class::BlackHole';

undef->bing; # fails - silently

my Foo $foo = Foo->new;
$foo->bing;  # no problem

my Foo $bar;
$bar->bing; # fails - also silently
```

autobox, presented in Chapter 14, associates methods with primitive types. One of the neat things it does is let you create an UNDEF package to serve as the class implementation for the undef value. This example tells it to use the Class::BlackHole package for method calls on the undefined value. Class::BlackHole uses AUTOLOAD to collect method calls to unknown methods and do nothing with them. And of course, typesafety never bats an eye at all this, oblivious to the concept that $bar might not actually contain the Foo it was typed as. To completely emulate

Perl 6's behavior, `Class::BlackHole` could be replaced with a custom `AUTOLOAD` method that creates `Error` objects and stuffs them into `$@` and then returns `undef`. `undef->foo err die;` would then work as it does in Perl 6 and may be trapped with an `eval { }` block.

Caveats

`typesafety` and `Perl6::Parameters` fight over the parameter list. Both can't be used at the same time.

You must use the `proto` function to prototype methods that use types with `::` in their names, as Perl 5 doesn't tolerate these characters in prototypes.

```
proto 'bathe', returns => 'Roles::Washable',

    takes => 'Roles::Washable', 'Soap::Shampoo';
```

`typesafety` attempts to follow the logic in Perl code that reads typed parameters in method definitions. However, it may fail. When `unshift`, `pop`, and the array subscript syntax are used on parameters, `typesafety` does the right thing. If values are pushed or unshifted onto the parameter list, `@_`, or if the parameter list is assigned to another variable before processing, `typesafety` will lose track of the types. `splice`, `grep`, `map`, and everything else, when applied to `@_`, will confuse `typesafety`. The same caveats apply to constructors, except that `typesafety` attempts to follow the type of the class as it's assigned to variables. This is done to support the `sub new { my $type = shift; bless { }, $type; }` idiom. `ref` may be used on $type, too.

REFERENCES AND THANKS

The Web page at `http://perldesignpatterns.com/?TypeSafety` links to resources on object-oriented design and type theory. It's also a place to ask questions about the `typesafety` module, report bugs, and suggest features.

Mark Jason Dominus's excellent Perl Mongers presentation called "Strong Typing and Perl" (or "Strong Typing Doesn't Have Suck") explains the concepts I've adopted for `typesafety`. This is no coincidence, as Dominus's article turned me onto the ideas, for which I'm grateful. The article is at `http://perl.plover.com/yak/typing/`.

Arthur Bergman's module, `types`, was a reference while I wrote versions of `typesafety` after version 0.2. `types` provides strong typing exclusively on simple types: integers, floating-point values, and strings. `typesafety` owes a lot to `types`. I'd like to thank Arthur for his collaboration and encouragement while I worked on later versions of `typesafety`. Of course, Arthur isn't responsible in any way for my bugs or omissions.

Summary

Most Perl programmers will never have the occasion to write code that benefits from strong typing, but times are changing. Applications are getting larger and so are software development projects. A host of technologies support these large development efforts: versioning systems, bug-tracking systems, automated testing, and collaborative groupware systems such as those offered by http://savannah.gnu.org, http://sourceforge.net, and http://freshmeat.net. All these have been well documented by other Perl (and non-Perl-specific) books. Automated testing took a foothold among Perl developers, and Perl programmers are enthusiastic CVS (and other versioning system) users.

Strong typing is just another tool for developers writing large applications. It helps both single and multiple developers keep things straight. It helps you model problems not just in software but your own mind. It makes the code self-documenting for junior members of the programming team who are otherwise inclined to misunderstand internal program interfaces.

And even if you're never involved in a large software project, it's just plain nice to be able to say, "Yeah, Perl can do that"; it's also fun to have a language that seems to know more about your application than you do and cleverly points out your mistakes.

CHAPTER 17

■■■

Multithreading

A thread is a *thread of execution*. This is simply the path the processor takes through the program as the program runs. When a subroutine is called, the thread winds through the body of that subroutine and then returns. The thread of execution winds around loops and dodges between conditionals. A processor winding its way through a program can solve any computational task, but certain problems don't map well to this model. A *multithreaded* program has several threads, each taking their own path of execution in a program. Programs that frequently stop to interrogate the state of things and then depending on this state conditionally do one task or another are prime candidates for multithreading.

At any point in a program that two tasks need to be done but the order depends on availability of resources, a threaded program simply attempts to do both tasks at the same time. It doesn't explicitly compute which of the two should be attempted. The program doesn't need to constantly invoke or return to a handler. Program logic doesn't need to be broken up into small pieces, each guaranteed never to attempt to use resources that might not yet be available. Each thread checks that resources are available immediately before they're used. Should some resource be unavailable, that thread of execution will pause until it becomes available. In this way, checks about resource availability become implicit rather than explicit.

Changes for Perl 6

Threads are enabled by default. Threads, coroutines, and continuations all work together correctly. No longer must you choose between threads and coroutines. Objects may be passed between threads by way of queues and shared variables. Objects don't become unblessed as they do in Perl 5, but this loose end may eventually be tied up in Perl 5.

In modern Perl 5, when the implementation of threads offered by the threads module is used, each thread logically has its own copy of each variable unless the variable is explicitly shared with :shared. This resembles what the fork call does except that variables may be shared upon request. Perl 6 may or may not share all variables by default, but it likely will. This follows other languages' implementations of threads and requires less CPU and memory.

Little is known about the exact semantics or syntax of threads in Perl 6. This chapter concentrates on the concepts and Perl 5 implementation.

Threads

For handling concurrent tasks, threads are the mainstay of the Win32 and VMS worlds and are widely deployed on modern Unix-like systems.

The basic skills for using threads are spawning new threads, sharing variables, locking access to variables, and using locks to coordinate access to other resources. You must also master coping with the effectively simultaneous execution of threads.

Configuring for Threads

perl doesn't enable threads by default when built from source. Test thread availability with the following one-liner:

```
# Test for availability of threads in Perl 5 at the shell
$ perl -e 'use threads;'
```

If threads are available, no output is generated. If threads aren't available, you'll get a message starting with the following:

```
This Perl hasn't been configured and built properly for the threads
module to work.  (The 'useithreads' configuration option hasn't been used.)
```

The message goes on to explain how all the XS modules (those modules partially implemented in C or linked against a C library) will need to be rebuilt should you build and install a new Perl that enables threads. This applies to Unix-like systems. Any libraries linked to, such as glib, will themselves need to be built with thread support enabled, or at least built in a "thread-safe" mode. It may not even be possible to rebuild some XS modules. Libraries for the most popular databases are thread safe. Many of the modules introduced in this book are XS modules but don't depend on any external C libraries that would need to be rebuilt.

If you aren't confident rebuilding C language libraries, rebuilding with threads may be out of the question. You may want to skim the rest of this chapter and then skip to Chapter 21, as the Coro module doesn't have this requirement that XS modules be rebuilt.

To rebuild perl with thread support, follow the instructions in Chapter 1, but provide the -Duseithreads argument to ./Configure. You may want to use the -Dprefix=/path option to place the threaded Perl in a place other than where the primary perl is.

Spawning Threads

threads::shared is the current recommended threading implementation for Perl 5, and it offers two ways to create a new thread of execution.

```
# Perl 5 - thread creation syntax
use threads;
threads->create(sub { ... }, @arguments); # creates a thread
async { ... };                            # also creates a thread
```

Both of these execute the code that should be placed where the ... is. This places a relatively short sequence of code in the middle of other code and runs the short sequence whenever its resources are available. Execution continues in the code immediately after the statement that creates the thread, and execution continues, in a new thread, in the code block provided to async { } or threads->create. Coro also provides an async { } block. See Chapter 21.

```
# Perl 5 - thread creation syntax
use threads;
threads->create(\&function_name, @arguments);
async { function_name(@arguments);
```

Both of these call a subroutine, giving that subroutine its own thread to run in. If there's no contention over resources, both threads run at logically the same time. That is, they don't run in any particular order, and the computer may flop back and forth between runnable threads.

Resources Threads Need

Earlier I said that two threads should be created when two things need to be done in indeterminate order, where the order depends on availability of resources. Three general kinds of resources may or may not be available.

- Threads communicate with each other through program variables and queues; queues are a special case of variables. These variables are resources.

- Threads communicate with the outside world through I/O handles. Input data is a resource.

- Threads depend on availability of the CPU. Given only one CPU, it must be shared between threads. CPUs are treated as resources.

When a needed resource isn't available, the thread gives up control of the CPU and waits until the resource is available.

Resources That Threads Have

Each thread knows its own current position in the program. It has locks on variables. It has variables that only it can see. These may be private copies of variables created because the original wasn't marked :shared, or they may be variables created in the thread, perhaps with my. When a thread is sleeping waiting for a task, it knows what it's waiting for—I/O, a timer to expire, or a lock on a variable. When a thread has finished executing, it has a result value that join may read. Each thread is represented by a thread object, available as threads->self from within the thread.

Sharing the CPU

The thread that's currently running obviously doesn't lack the CPU resource, but the threads that aren't running do lack the CPU. Some protocol for deciding how to share the CPU is in order. Programs have only indirect control over this resource. Calling sleep causes a process to give up control of the CPU. When the sleep has finished, the thread will again run. In the meantime, the CPU might as well be given to another thread that wants it, so it is. Calling threads->yield also gives up control of the CPU but then takes the CPU back as soon as it's available.

```
# Perl 5 - threads run whenever they can

use threads;
```

```perl
my $thread1 = threads->create(\&count_and_yield_1);
my $thread2 = threads->create(\&count_and_yield_2);
sub count_and_yield_1 {
    for my $counter (1 .. 4) {
        print "thread1: $counter\n";
        threads->yield;
    }
}

sub count_and_yield_2 {
    for my $counter (1 .. 4) {
        print "thread2: $counter\n";
        threads->yield;
    }
}

$thread1->join;
$thread2->join;
```

The output from this is as follows:

```
thread1: 1
thread2: 1
thread1: 2
thread2: 2
thread1: 3
thread2: 3
thread1: 4
thread2: 4
```

This example creates two additional threads beyond the main thread of execution you always get. The main thread has an important job to do—it waits for the threads that it created to finish executing. That's the purpose of $thread1->join and $thread2->join. This is similar to the wait call, used with processes. These prevent the program from exiting while threads are still running.

As you can see, the outputs of the two threads are intermingled. The bodies of both subroutines called effectively run at the same time. Without the threads->yield call, it would probably, though not certainly, do something like this:

```
thread1: 1
thread1: 2
thread1: 3
thread1: 4
thread2: 1
thread2: 2
thread2: 3
thread2: 4
```

Some threading implementations don't automatically move the CPU between different threads, and the output will most certainly look like that. To help the thread system along, explicitly yield at strategic points. I talk about this in the "Cooperative Threading Systems vs. Preemptive Threading Systems" section later in this chapter.

There's no reason two entirely different blocks of code need to exist to create multiple threads. The same block of code can be run in any number of threads, and each is separate from the others.

```
# Perl 5 - one code block may be run by multiple threads

use threads;

my $thread1 = threads->create(\&count_and_yield, 'thread1');
my $thread2 = threads->create(\&count_and_yield, 'thread2');
sub count_and_yield {
    my $message = shift;
    for my $counter (1 .. 4) {
        print "$message: $counter\n";
        threads->yield;
    }
}

$thread1->join;
$thread2->join;
```

These two new threads are both copies of the count_and_yield function, but each copy is passed a slightly different argument. The second through last arguments to threads->create become arguments to the code block from which the thread is created. count_and_yield prints out this argument inside a loop along with the loop iterator.

It might seem like running the same code twice at the same time would cause problems, but this is very easy for the computer to do. Using the same shared variables (those marked with :shared) from different threads is what causes problems.

Threads aren't confined to the code block passed to threads->create. Threads may call subroutines and methods and pretty much do what they please. Each thread is its own little program.

Variables As Resources

Let's imagine two roommates who can't stand being in the same room as each other. Both of them sleep a lot (see Listing 17-1).

Listing 17-1. *Locking on Variables As Resources*

```
# Perl 5 - contention over resources by two threads

use threads;
use threads::shared;
```

```perl
my $kitchen    :shared;
my $bathroom   :shared;
my $livingroom :shared;

my $hatfield = threads->create(sub {
    do {
        print "Hatfield wants the kitchen\n";
        lock $kitchen;
        print "Hatfield has the kitchen\n";
        sleep 10;
    };
    do {
        print "Hatfield wants the bathroom\n";
        lock $bathroom;
        print "Hatfield has the bathroom\n";
        sleep 10;
    };
    do {
        print "Hatfield wants the livingroom\n";
        lock $livingroom;
        print "Hatfield has the livingroom\n";
        sleep 10;
    };
});

my $mccoy = threads->create(sub {
    do {
        print "McCoy wants the kitchen\n";
        lock $kitchen;
        print "McCoy has the kitchen\n";
        sleep 10;
    };
    do {
        print "McCoy wants the bathroom\n";
        lock $bathroom;
        print "McCoy has the bathroom\n";
        sleep 10;
    };
    do {
        print "McCoy wants the livingroom\n";
        lock $livingroom;
        print "McCoy has the livingroom\n";
        sleep 10;
    };
});

$hatfield->join;
$mccoy->join;
```

This eventually prints what's shown in Listing 17-2. (I added the (pause) lines; they aren't printed.)

Listing 17-2. *Variable Locking Example Output*

```
Hatfield wants the kitchen
Hatfield has the kitchen
McCoy wants the kitchen
(pause)
Hatfield wants the bathroom
Hatfield has the bathroom
McCoy has the kitchen
(pause)
Hatfield wants the livingroom
Hatfield has the livingroom
McCoy wants the bathroom
McCoy has the bathroom
(pause)
McCoy wants the livingroom
McCoy has the livingroom
(pause)
```

The (pause) lines represent the ten-second sleeps. This program won't finish in less than 40 seconds.

In this example, two roommates are trying to use the same rooms in the same order, and the first roommate, Hatfield, keeps getting there first, making the second roommate, McCoy, wait. The computer has made sure each gets to where they're going as soon as they can.

I said that sleep allows other threads to run. That was half true. It lets other threads run as long as nothing else is preventing them. lock is used to gain exclusive access to a variable (which may reference a data structure). The lock stays in effect until the end of the block it was created in, so this example has the locks placed inside do { } blocks. A lock doesn't prevent other threads from accessing the locked variable; it only prevents another thread from locking the variables. This follows the semantics of flock.

These locks are called *mutex* locks—a contraction of *mutually exclusive*. One lock excludes other threads from locking the same variable. It may be locked by one thread exclusively.

Listing 17-3 shows an extreme case that's not a good application of threads, but it does serve to make mutex locks work really hard. The previous example assumes each roommate honestly needs to use these resources in this certain order. If they didn't, six threads could be created— one for each of the three rooms times two for each roommate. The two roommates would spend less time waiting for each other and make better use of the rooms of the apartment.

Listing 17-3. *Locking on Finer-Grained Resources*

```
# Perl 5 - contention over resources part two - less contention

use threads;
use threads::shared;
```

```perl
my $kitchen    :shared;
my $bathroom   :shared;
my $livingroom :shared;

my $hatfield= threads->create(sub {
    my $thread3 = async {
        print "Hatfield wants the kitchen\n";
        lock $kitchen;
        print "Hatfield has the kitchen\n";
        sleep 10;
    };
    my $thread4 = async {
        print "Hatfield wants the bathroom\n";
        lock $bathroom;
        sleep 10;
        print "Hatfield has the bathroom\n";
    };
    my $thread5 = async {
        print "Hatfield wants the livingroom\n";
        lock $livingroom;
        print "Hatfield has the livingroom\n";
        sleep 10;
    };
    $thread3->join;
    $thread4->join;
    $thread5->join;
});

my $mccoy = threads->create(sub {
    my $thread6 = async {
        print "McCoy wants the kitchen\n";
        lock $kitchen;
        print "McCoy has the kitchen\n";
        sleep 10;
    };
    my $thread7 = async {
        print "McCoy wants the bathroom\n";
        lock $bathroom;
        print "McCoy has the bathroom\n";
        sleep 10;
    };
    my $thread8 = async {
        print "McCoy wants the livingroom\n";
        lock $livingroom;
        print "McCoy has the livingroom\n";
        sleep 10;
    };
```

```
    $thread6->join;
    $thread7->join;
    $thread8->join;
});

$hatfield->join;
$mccoy->join;
```

This makes better use of the resources but requires that the rooms not need be visited in any certain order, because they won't be. There's no reason to spawn two threads to create the three threads for each roommate. All six room-grabbing threads could have been done in the main program. Listing 17-4 shows the output.

Listing 17-4. *Locking on Finer-Grained Resources Example Output*

```
Hatfield wants the kitchen
Hatfield has the kitchen
Hatfield wants the bathroom
Hatfield wants the livingroom
Hatfield has the livingroom
McCoy wants the kitchen
McCoy wants the bathroom
McCoy wants the livingroom
(pause)
Hatfield4 has the bathroom
McCoy has the kitchen
McCoy has the bathroom
McCoy has the livingroom
(pause)
```

Again, the (pause) lines aren't actually in the output. This example has far fewer pauses than the previous example. Both roommates are able to sleep at the same time, so the program executes in just about 20 seconds. Dropping the restriction that rooms be visited in a prescribed order made it finish twice as quickly. The sleeps finish in a fixed amount of time.

Listing 17-4 shows why things should sometimes run at the same time, but you might not have noticed that it also shows why things sometimes shouldn't run at the same time. The ghastly roommates are visiting multiple rooms at the same time!

```
Hatfield has the kitchen
Hatfield has the livingroom
```

To avoid this, you could create variables representing the roommates and lock them when a roommate goes into a room.

Input As a Resource

Typically, threads will be created to tap different resources, such as I/O handles, but a few resources, such as data structures, will be shared between threads. The threads will rarely, and for very brief periods of time, wait for each other. Instead, they'll both spend large amounts of time waiting for input on their respective file handles.

I'm generalizing a bit here. A thread doing I/O may also be suspended when sending data over a network socket or to the disk when it has filled up the send buffer and it can't send more data until some data has cleared the buffer. See Listing 17-5.

Listing 17-5. *Multithread Between Input and Output*

```perl
# Perl 5 - display a file while reading user input

use threads;
use threads::shared;

my $delay :shared = 1;
open my $fh, '<', __FILE__ or die $!;
my $thread1 = threads->create(sub {
    while() {
        print $_;
        sleep $delay;
    }
});

my $thread2 = threads->create(sub {
    while(<STDIN>) {
        chomp;
        $delay = $1 if /(\d+)/;
    }
});

$thread1->join;
$thread2->join;
```

This program opens its own code for reading if you save it into a file and then run it. Or you may replace __FILE__ with shift(@_) to read the first command-line argument as a file to read. Every second, it displays a line of the file. At any time, you may enter a number, and it will use this as the amount of time to wait between showing lines. The file scrolls at a variable speed. No locks are used—I'm cheating by not locking it, but I know I can get away with that in this case because only the instantaneous value of the variable is needed. If the value changes immediately after being read, no harm is done. The variable isn't read and then used to make a decision or perform a calculation. If it were, then this example would require locks.

Listing 17-6 shows another example. Network servers that must accept and service multiple incoming connections can use their primary thread to listen for new connections and then create a new thread for each accepted connection.

Listing 17-6. *Multithread Between Multiple Connections*

```perl
# Servicing multiple network connections - Perl 5:
use threads;

use IO::Socket::INET;
```

```perl
my $server = IO::Socket::INET->new(
    Listen => 10,
    LocalAddr => '0.0.0.0',
    LocalPort => 5000,
) or die $!;

while(1) {
    my $conn = $server->accept;
    threads->new(\&service_connection, $conn);
}

my $printing :shared;
use ops ':default', 'entereval';

sub service_connection {
    my $conn = shift;
    $conn->autoflush(1);
    while(my $line = <$conn>) {
        do {
            lock $printing;
            *STDOUT = $conn;
            eval $line;
            $conn->print($@, "\n> ");
        };
        threads->yield;
    }
}
```

This creates a little Perl server that accepts telnet connections on port 5000 and lets users issue Perl commands.

```
$ telnet localhost 5000
Trying 127.0.0.1...
Connected to Knoppix.
Escape character is '^]'.
print "hi\n";
hi
```

Commands typed at the server are evaled, and the results are printed back at the user. Unsafe operations are avoided with the ops module (which is a lower-level interface to the magic that the Safe module uses). All code compiled after it is restricted from performing any operation not explicitly allowed. More than one person may use the server at a time. Should one user take a long time to enter a command, other users may still connect and run their own commands.

When to Use Threads

Threads aren't useful where they would both just wait for each other constantly, such as where they're fighting over only the CPU and no other resource.

Threads are most useful where different resources are being used, such as different I/O handles, and the threads won't fight over resources. Threads are also useful when one thread is processing I/O, such as a controlling a user interface, and the other thread is making use of the CPU or some network connection.

If the program needs to do a large amount of I/O, and disk latency, not throughput, is the bottleneck, then threads might be able to keep the CPU busy with the result of one I/O operation while other I/O operations are still pending.

Threads are useful when the order things may be done in is somewhat flexible. There's little point to using threads when tasks need to be done in a fixed order. Dealing with input from various sockets and file handles where data may arrive at any time necessarily means that logic will run without any fixed order.

Threads don't make programs faster except in a few rare circumstances. They use additional CPUs in a multiple CPU system or a cluster. Threads frequently make programs go slower. They introduce computational overhead, and they increase the total memory requirements of the program, adding to swapping.

Threads don't lend themselves well to casual use because of complexity and overhead. Use coroutines for that.

Tricks and Techniques

The examples so far showed the basics. The following sections provide details to accomplish more involved tasks.

Returning Results from Threads

Threads may return results. This value is made available as the result of calling join on that thread's objects.

```
# Perl 5 - result values from threads:
use threads;
my $thread = threads->create(sub {
    rand for 1 .. 1000;
    rand;
});
# Do something else with the CPU here...
print "Random number: ", $thread->join, "\n";
```

This creates, and throws away, a lot of random numbers, which is useful for foiling sequence prediction attacks. After throwing a bunch away, it returns one to be used. Since it could take a while to generate a lot of random numbers and throw them away, this is done in a child thread while the main program presumably attends to something else.

Joining All Threads

It's nice to be able to launch threads, let them do the work, and not worry about tracking them all. Especially when threads are creating other threads, or when threads are created in a loop, it becomes a chore to store references to the thread objects. Thankfully, the thread package has a method that tracks all the threads in existence. Just join all of them, like this:

```perl
# Perl 5 - joining all threads

use threads;

threads->create(sub {
    sleep 2;
    print "thinking...\n";
    sleep 2;
    print "done...\n";
});

threads->create(sub {
    sleep 2;
    print "working...\n";
    sleep 2;
    print "done...\n";
});

(threads->list)[0]->join while threads->list;
```

This last line iterates through all the threads, joining each one in turn.

Queues

One thread producing information may feed its results to another thread through a locked, shared scalar. This works, but it's too much like a bucket brigade. Between any two threads, there is at most one value that has been produced and is ready to be processed. A queue is more like a conveyer belt. Each thread is free to move as fast as it can, assuming there are values to process and the queue isn't full (see Listing 17-7).

Listing 17-7. *Creating Your Own Thread Queue*

```perl
# Perl 5 - simple queue built on top of an array

use threads;
use threads::shared;
my @queue :shared;
```

```perl
my $producer = threads->create(sub {
    while(1) {
        do {
            lock @queue;
            push @queue, int rand 100;
            cond_signal(@queue);
        };
        threads->yield;
    }
});

my $consumer = threads->create(sub {
    while(1) {
        do {
            lock @queue;
            if(! @queue) {
                cond_wait(@queue);
            }
            print shift @queue, "\n";
        };
        threads->yield;
    }
});

$producer->join;
$consumer->join;
```

One thread produces random numbers as fast as it can, and the other prints as fast as it can. Should the thread doing the printing run out of values to print, it'll cond_wait. cond_wait gives up the lock on the variable fed to it, waits for another thread to perform a cond_signal on that variable, and then attempts to get the lock back. Even though many values may be present in the @queue at any given moment, @queue is always locked. It'd be a mistake to test if @queue is empty and then wait for a cond_signal; between the moment the program inspects @queue and it starts listening for a cond_signal, the cond_signal may have come and gone. This is a race condition (see the "Race Conditions" section).

Now that you know how to build a queue, you also know that it isn't as much fun as it sounds. When I tell you to use Thread::Queue when you need a queue, you'll know you're saving having to write this much code. Thread::Queue does all the locking and signaling for you (see Listing 17-8).

Listing 17-8. *Using the Standard Queue*

```perl
# Perl 5 - using the standard queue object

use threads;
use Thread::Queue;
```

```perl
my $queue = Thread::Queue->new;
my $producer = threads->create(sub {
    while(1) {
        $queue->enqueue(int rand 100);
        threads->yield;
    }
});

my $consumer = threads->create(sub {
    while(1) {
        print $queue->dequeue, "\n";
        threads->yield;
    }
});

$producer->join;
$consumer->join;
```

This does the same as previous example, but it does it with much less code. See the documentation in perldoc Thread::Queue for more background on Thread::Queue.

Semaphamores

Semaphores communicate status information between threads. In their simplest form, they communicate a single bit of data, but they do so in an inherently thread-safe way. Semaphores are used to build locks, though a higher-level version of semaphores is provided to programmers to build more complex shared structures with. A lock or a queue suits most purposes better, but see the documentation for Thread::Semaphore if you'd like to know more.

Thread Gotchas

Threads are a can of worms, so to speak. By using them, you're open to a whole new set of potential problems that just don't exist in the single-threaded world. Threads aren't worth using unless you're able to effectively recognize and avoid these problems.

The CPU will switch between running threads at any moment without notice on a *preemptive* threading system. A preemptive thread system will interrupt a running thread when its time slot is up. Always program as if there were thread->yield calls between each argument of every operation of every expression. Obviously, the CPU doesn't switch threads that often, but before any operation or operand, it could. Threads don't wait for the end of the statement. Botching this gives you a *race condition* or a *deadlock* scenario. These terms are properly defined in the coming sections, but first I'll explain the circumstances under which threaded programs fail.

On a *nonpreemptive* thread system, the CPU is never taken away from a running thread unless the thread explicitly yields or implicitly yields by attempting I/O on a blocked handle or accessing a queue. To avoid deadlock, the thread should use queues and semaphores to wait for resources from other threads.

The problems created by threads are notoriously difficult to find. Threaded programs may run fine throughout testing but then fail intermittently and mysteriously in production. These failures may only manifest themselves infrequently. The cause of these sorts of problems isn't obvious when looking at isolated parts of the program—they stem from how parts of the program interact.

Another problem arises when a thread must wait for something but uses all the CPU while waiting. This is a *busy spin*.

Deadlock

The examples so far have always locked one resource at a time. This will get you only so far. If you need two resources at the same time, you must lock both at the same time. Trying to lock one, copy it, lock the other, and do something with both is a *race condition*, a problem that I'll discuss in the next section. It's possible, and easy, to lock two variables at the same time, but it must be done with caution or the program may deadlock and stop responding (see Listing 17-9).

Listing 17-9. *Example Deadlock*

```perl
# Perl 5 - example deadlock - this program contains an ERROR

use threads;
use threads::shared;

my $foo :shared = 5;
my $bar :shared = 10;

my $thread1 = threads->create(sub {
    lock $foo;
    threads->yield;
    lock $bar;
    print $foo + $bar, "\n";
});

my $thread2 = threads->create(sub {
    lock $bar;
    threads->yield;
    lock $foo;
    print $foo * $bar, "\n";
});

$thread1->join;
$thread2->join;
```

The threads->yield calls wouldn't normally be written, but the CPU may switch which thread it's executing at any moment, so this turns a latent bug into an unavoidable one.

This is what happens: $thread1 starts to run, and it gets as far as locking $foo before the CPU is suddenly yanked to run $thread2. $thread2 starts off by locking $bar. Its next step is to lock $foo, but $foo is already locked, so it waits until the lock is released. The lock is never released.

$thread1 is given the CPU again because $thread2 is waiting for a lock, and $thread1 immediately attempts to lock $bar. $bar is already locked by $thread2, so $thread1 gives up control of the CPU until it becomes available. At this moment, there are *no* runnable threads. Both threads wait indefinitely for the other to give up their locks. Neither will go first.

Perhaps you noticed that $thread1 tried to lock first $foo and then $bar and that $thread2 tried to lock first $bar and then $foo. That is, $thread2 is locking the two variables in reverse order. That's the root of the problem. Had they been locked in the same order, $thread2 never would have gotten the first lock, and $thread1 would have then been allowed to finish.

Processes (created with fork) may experience deadlock as well. This can happen for instance when both processes are trying to flock multiple files.

The moral of the story is this: Always lock all resources in the same order.

Another form of deadlock called *priority inversion* may appear when you start to play with thread priorities, but that's beyond the scope of this book; see perldoc perlthread for an explanation.

Race Conditions

Race conditions usually take the form of a test performed on a shared variable and then some operation done on it. Even something as simple as $a = $b + $b may be a race condition. $b should be locked here and so should $a if it's :shared. Race conditions may be insidiously complex or deviously simple.

I've already mentioned that when performing a cond_wait on a shared variable, it must first be locked. If it wasn't locked, the cond_signal might have come and gone already. This is a race condition that could easily turn into a deadlock. It's likely that no replacement cond_signal would ever be performed, leaving the poor thread to wait forever for a signal that's already gone by, much like a guy late for an appointment might wait, not knowing whether his companion had come and gone already.

Race conditions are often security holes. When a sort of authorization or security test is performed and then a privileged action is taken when it passes, a malicious user may have changed something between the moment the test was performed and the action taken. Not until recently were many Unix-like systems able to safely execute a script with the setuid bit (so the script would run with the privileges of another user). The kernel would first check the permissions on the file, decide that it was both executable and setuid, and then open the file, read the shebang line, and execute that program with those permissions. The problem is that between the time the permissions were read and the file is opened, the file may have been replaced with another program that's not setuid but is then executed with setuid permissions.

Busy Spins

None of the thread examples in this chapter will use as much CPU as is available except when actually and actively computing values. In each of these cases where one of these threads needed some kind of resource, it did something that caused it to go to sleep and give up the CPU until the resource was available. Attempting to read from a file handle or socket puts a thread to sleep until the data is available. The thread doesn't need to check over and over again, wasting CPU. Attempting to lock a shared variable likewise automatically wakes the thread when the lock is available.

An improperly written program will use as much CPU as it can get, even when doing nothing but waiting for a resource. This is called *busy spinning*. The loop that checks for the availability of a resource is called a *busy spin*. To avoid this, use locks or semaphores to signal between threads that a resource is available. This works when one thread knows when something is available but others otherwise wouldn't.

Sometimes the resources are external to the entire program, and there's no operating system–independent way to detect when it becomes available. *Polling* is the only solution in this case. Check for it repeatedly, as in a busy spin, but insert a sleep statement with some reasonable number. This will use a small amount of CPU rather than a huge amount.

Cooperative Threading Systems vs. Preemptive Threading Systems

Strange bugs appear when some threaded programs are moved between systems with different flavors of threads.

On some thread systems, one thread will dominate the CPU, preventing other threads from running. This happens on *cooperative* threading systems. Cooperative threading systems never steal the CPU from a thread. Threads cooperate by explicitly giving up the CPU using threads->yield.

Running a program written for cooperative threads on a preemptively threaded system will expose race conditions masked by the cooperative thread system.

Not every Perl program must be portable, of course, but those that do will need to be aware of these problems. Cooperative threading systems are relatively rare. Microsoft Windows, Apple Mac OS X, and modern Linux and FreeBSD systems have preemptive threads. To satisfy the greatest number of users, be more concerned with avoiding deadlocks and race conditions than dealing with a thread system that requires you to explicitly yield during long-running computations.

Perl Thread Limitations

Two unusual problems limit Perl 5 threads, and a third problem common of many thread implementations needs mention. You can work around all these limitations, but it's useful to understand them as being disadvantages to using threads for concurrency on Perl 5.

Sharing References

Any reference that's shared between threads must be marked :shared. This avoids accidentally trouncing data. It also makes it difficult to share complex data structures. When a reference is shared, only the thing it immediately contains is also considered to be shared.

```
# Perl 6 - sharing data structures
my $x :shared;
$x = [1, 2, 3];        # okay - shared
$x = [\@foo, \@bar];   # not okay - @foo and @bar are not shared
```

To make @foo and @bar visible outside the current thread, even by reference, declare them using :shared. Alternatively, feed them to the share function, provided by threads::shared.

```
# Perl 6 - sharing data structures
my $x :shared;
share(@foo);
share(@bar);
$x = [\@foo, \@bar];  # okay - @foo and @bar are shared
share($x->[0]);       # not okay - silently fails
```

You may not build a data structure and then mark the entire data structure as being shared after the fact. You must construct it to be shared from the beginning, even if you have to copy the whole thing, feeding each node to share.

perldoc perlthrtut has a longer explanation of this problem.

Coroutines don't have this limitation. Any data structure assigned into a variable that's in scope in multiple coroutines is available in its entirety between those coroutines. This automatic sharing of data by references makes sharing data structures much easier.

Objects

An object created in one thread may not be shared back into other threads. If the object is built out of a blessed hash reference, other threads will see it as a hash reference. It simply comes unblessed. If it refers to other objects, those references fail, per the last caveat. Coroutines don't have these limitations.

Memory Leaks

Threads may lose track of memory. This manifests itself in long-running applications that slowly gobble up more and more memory. This isn't a usual problem, and it isn't specific to threads or Perl, but the nature of threads causes it to be tickled slightly more often than nonthreaded code. Perl 6's garbage collection should resolve this problem. As noted in Chapter 8, it's possible for a Perl 5 programmer to cause data structures to hold onto memory even after they're destroyed.

I haven't said anything about a few basic, useful arrangements of threads. perldoc perlthrtut explains them and includes examples. perldoc threads and perldoc threads::shared are the standard Perl thread references.

Threads are one solution to one kind of problem; related problems are solved by event systems, such as the POE family of modules (from CPAN) and the Event module. The traditional Unix multiprogramming approach is based on processes, which are created with the fork system call. Perl also forks a new process for you with the system built-in and with the '-|' and '|-' file modes to the open built-in.

Summary

Threads are useful for understanding other multiprogramming and concurrency systems. They're useful for solving certain problems that otherwise would be unbearable, such as making CPU-intensive programs responsive. Threads are the only real option when long-running computational tasks need to be done at the same time as other interactive tasks, and both need to closely share data. The complexity of thread systems and their low-level nature make them powerful enough for this, but this comes at a cost in program complexity and the associated potential for bugs. I've tried to steer you to other options or at least make you aware of the relative virtues of the various options. You should of course use the system that best suits the task at hand, but remember that threaded programming is a valuable and rare skill.

PART 4

■■■

Computer Science

■ ■ ■

## CHAPTER 18

Any and All

Nested loops usually do one of two things. They apply an operation to each element of a data structure, or they perform set operations between two partially overlapping sets of data. Intersections and differences between sets are computed far more often today than operations such as logical *and* and *exclusive-or* on bitmasks. Actually, logical operations on bits are set operations; they're just set operations on very small sets, where each element in the set contains one bit. Programmers won't stop doing set operations, but they've stopped using bits to do them. It's only natural that a high-level language would co-opt the bitwise logic operators to do logic operations on sets of strings, numbers, references, objects, and other sets.

New in Perl 6

any(), all(), and one() perform operations on sets. & and | are the operator versions of the any() and all() functions. These functions and operators are core and thus are fast. They complement hyper operators, outlined in Chapter 6. Except for core availability, these features exist in Perl 5.

Quantum Mechanics

Software tends to work fine until it's demonstrated for clients or high-level management, whereupon the act of being observed causes it to fail. Your car consistently misbehaves until you take it to the mechanic, whereupon it works just fine. It seems as if important observers possess a kind of power to influence the thing being observed. The Copenhagen Interpretation of quantum physics says that your paranoia is justified, if only on a subatomic level. The observer really does influence the outcome of events. Observing a subatomic particle forces it to commit to one of its possible states. Quantum computing aims to make machines that process *qubits*, quantum bits. A qubit may be logically 0, 1, or both 0 and 1 at the same time. This allows permutations to be computed completely in parallel (see Table 18-1).

Table 18-1. *Rules for and Under Conventional Logic Rules*

Input 1	Operation	Input 2	Result
0	*and*	0	0
1	*and*	0	0
1	*and*	1	1

This is an abbreviated, standard logic table for the logical *and* operation between two bits. When standard logic operations are applied to bits that are both 0 and 1 at the same time, the results may be both 0 and 1 at the same time (see Table 18-2).

Table 18-2. *Combinational Logic Rules for the and Operation*

Input 1	Operation	Input 2	Result
0&0	*and*	0	0
1&1	*and*	1	1
1&0	*and*	0	0&1
1&0	*and*	1	0&1

& signifies superposition here, because it does in Perl 6. 0&1 is a superposition of 0 and 1. && and and both represent normal, old-fashioned boolean logic.

Computing boolean operations in parallel is useful for two tasks. It considers several scenarios and tells you if *any* of those are true, and it considers several scenarios and tells you if *all* of them are true.

The case with the *or* operation isn't as interesting, as a 1 anywhere causes the result to be 1. Permutations collapse rather than proliferate. *Exclusive-or*, or *xor*, is interesting, though, but you'll need to built that out of *and*, *or*, and *not*.

Any and All Functions and Operators

Perl 6 defines the function any and the function all. Perl 6 defines | to mean any, and it defines & to be the same thing as all.

Quantum::Superpositions gives Perl 5 any and all, but & and | continue to be plain, old-fashioned bitwise operators in Perl 5. Chapter 6 contains details of operator arrangements in each version of the language.

To use superpositions of states with normal logic, you must decide whether 0&1 should be considered logically true or whether it must be 1&1. That is, must all the permutations be true, or does only one need to be true?

```
# any() in a comparison is something like grep - Perl 5
use Quantum::Superpositions;
# These two lines are equivalent:
die if any(1, 2, 5) == 3;
die if grep { $_ == 3 } (1, 2, 5);
```

These don't die. Boolean tests performed on superpositions created with any are considered true if the test is true for any of the eigenstates. The word *eigenstates* comes from particle physics; it describes the collection of states that have been superimposed on the same particle. By the way, any and all work on stuff other than just bits. They take numbers, strings, array references, hash references, any other kind of reference, objects, and, of course, other sets. Quantum::Superpositions combines any number of items, not just two. After all, Perl is a high-level language.

```
# all() in a comparison - Perl 5
use Quantum::Superpositions;
# These two lines are equivalent:
die unless all(1, 2, 5) < 10;
foreach (1, 2, 5) { die unless $_ < 10 };
```

There aren't really two kinds of superpositions—merely two ways of deciding how boolean truth should be determined.

This would be of little use if superpositions couldn't be compared to superpositions. Luckily, they can.

Set Operations

Just as code often performs operations on sets of data, a lot of code is spent doing set membership tests. Membership tests between sets of data are a natural extension of Perl's support for aggregates of values, such as lists and arrays.

Three basic set operations exist: union, intersection, and difference. *Union* is the combination of two sets. The sets are literally added together. *Intersection* looks for overlap between two sets. *Difference* looks for the items in one set that aren't in the other.

The following examples are written for Perl 5. The Perl 6 examples would be similar, but some of the equivalents aren't yet known. The syntax isn't that interesting anyway—only the concepts are.

Intersection

The intersection of two sets is the portion that overlaps.

```
# Find some intersection between sets - Perl 5
use Quantum::Superpositions;
die unless any(1, 2, 5) == any(1, 2, 3, 4, 5);
```

This example looks for some intersection between two sets and finds it, so it doesn't die. 1, 2, and 5 all satisfy the requirement of "some intersection". To do this without Quantum::Superpositions, you'd need nested loops or a hash for lookup. This tells you only if any intersection exists. It doesn't tell you what that intersection might be. You need the eigenstates function to find the actual intersecting items.

```
# Compute intersection between sets - Perl 5
use Quantum::Superpositions;
print join ', ', eigenstates(any(1, 2, 3) == any(3, 5, 7));
print "\n";
```

This prints 3. eigenstates collapses the superposition down to all its states. In the case of disjunctive superpositions, created with any, this includes everything that was fed into it. In the case of conjunctive superpositions, created with all, this includes the commonality between everything fed into it. As a boolean, a superposition is true if it contains anything and false if it's empty.

I said you could build sets of sets. It turns out that this is very useful.

```
# Compute intersection between sets - Perl 5
use Quantum::Superpositions;
my $set1 = any(5, 10, 20);
my $set2 = any(10, 20, 30);
print join ', ', eigenstates(all($set1, $set2));
print "\n";
```

This prints 10, 20. all can be fed any number of superpositions, making it trivially easy to look for the intersection between three, four, or hundreds of sets. This example was based directly on an example in the excellent Quantum::Superpositions documentation. The eigenstates() expression could also have been written eigenstates(any(1, 2, 3) == any(3, 5, 7)). See the later "Permutations" section.

Union

Unions are also easy. They combine all the elements from both sets.

```
# Find union of two sets - Perl 5
use Quantum::Superpositions;
my $set1 = any(1, 2, 3, 4);
my $set2 = any(4, 5, 6, 7);
print join ', ', eigenstates(any($set1, $set2));
print "\n";
```

This prints 6, 4, 1, 3, 7, 2, 5 on my machine.

This is identical to the example in the earlier "Intersection" section, but the all was swapped for a third any. @union = (@set1, @set2) serves the same purpose if you don't mind duplicate values.

Difference

Difference asks what's in one set that's not in the other. Given two sets, there are two difference operations—items in the first set that aren't in the second set and items in the second set that aren't in the first set.

```
# Find difference between two sets - Perl 5
use Quantum::Superpositions;
my $set1 = any(1, 2, 3, 4);
my $set2 = all(4, 5, 6, 7);
print join ', ', eigenstates($set1 != $set2);
print "\n";
```

This asks for anything in $set1 that's not in $set2. It prints 1, 3, 2.

Perl Cookbook, Second Edition (O'Reilly, 2003), contains a recipe for finding the difference between two sets. My old, battered, first-edition copy says approximately the following:

```perl
# Difference between two sets - adapted from the Perl Cookbook - Perl 5
my @set1 = (1, 2, 3, 4);
my @set2 = (4, 5, 6, 7);
my %seen = ();
my @aonly = ();
foreach my $item (@set2) { $seen{$item} = 1 }
foreach my $item (@set1) {
    unless ($seen{$item}) {
        # it's not in %seen, so add to @aonly
        push(@set1only, $item);
    }
}
print join ', ', @set1only;
print "\n";
```

This prints 1, 2, 3. %seen tracks whether something has been seen in @set2. It's just a temporary value to save having to iterate through each value of @set2 once for each element of @set1. @set1only is the output. *Perl Cookbook* has a more idiomatic version that initializes %seen using a hash slice assignment, but Quantum::Superpositions still saves you two temporary variables and most of the code.

I said that you could build *exclusive-or* from other operations. *Exclusive-or* asks for elements that exist only on one side but may be on either side. It's like a plain old *or* operation except it doesn't like it when the value exists on both sides. It must be one or the other. That's why it's exclusive.

```perl
# Exclusive-or built out of two difference operations and a union
# Perl 5
use Quantum::Superpositions;
my @set1 = (1, 2, 3, 4);
my @set2 = (4, 5, 6, 7);
print join ', ',
    eigenstates(any(any(@set1) != all(@set2), any(@set2) != all(@set1)));
print "\n";
```

This prints everything but the 4. It performs two difference operations, reversing the sets for the second one, and then merges the results with a union operation. You could also build this out of unions, intersections, and logical *not* operations, per DeMorgan's theorem. DeMorgan's theorem is beyond the scope of this book; any introductory symbolic logic text teaches the transformations, but I personally recommend the humorously written *Introduction to Logic: Propositional Logic,* Third Edition (Prentice Hall, 1999), by Howard Pospesel.

Permutations

The examples for intersection and difference started down the permutations path.

In the expression any(1, 2, 3) == any(3, 5, 7) from the intersection example, the result set is the set of things for which == is true when each combination of things from each list is considered. These permutations were generated and evaluated (see Table 18-3).

Table 18-3. *Possibilities Considered by Tests Between Junctions*

Left-Hand Set	Right-Hand Set
1	3
1	5
1	7
2	3
2	5
2	7
3	3
3	5
3	7

This sort of evaluation of permutations is known as a *Cartesian product*. When the 3 from any(1, 2, 3) is compared with the 3 from any(3, 5, 7), a match is found. If there were more matches, they'd be found, too.

The example for computing set differences is a little trickier.

```
# Nothing can equal everything in an all() set - Perl 5
use Quantum::Superpositions;
die "1 == " if 1 == all(1, 2, 3);  # false
die "1 != " if 1 != all(1, 2, 3);  # false
die "4 == " if 4 == all(1, 2, 3);  # false
die "4 != " if 4 != all(1, 2, 3);  # true
```

This dies with 4 != at - line 6. Nothing can be logically equal to everything in a set, when the set contains different things. In 1 == all(1, 2, 3), 1 == 1 is true, 1 == 2 isn't true, 1 == 3 isn't true, and all specifies that all permutations must be true for the whole expression to be true. 4, on the other hand, isn't equal to 1, and it isn't equal to 2 or 3. 4 != all(1, 2, 3) is true.

An all superposition can equal something else if it contains only one thing or it's flattened to one thing from several copies of the same thing.

```
# An all() set with one thing in it can equal other things - Perl 5
use Quantum::Superpositions;
die "1 == " if 1 == all(1, 1, 1);  # true
```

The differences example takes advantage of these properties of all superpositions.

```
# Difference of two sets - Perl 5
any(1, 2, 3, 4) != all(4, 5, 6, 7);
```

This computes a new superposition composed of the elements for which ! = is true between the permutations of elements.

```
# Long version of difference of two sets above - Perl 5
1 != all(4, 5, 6, 7);  # true
2 != all(4, 5, 6, 7);  # true
3 != all(4, 5, 6, 7);  # true
4 != all(4, 5, 6, 7);  # false
```

Operations between two superpositions result in a new superposition that uses the any() rules for booleanification if the set on the left is an any() set. If the set on the left is an all() set, then the set produced is itself an all() set.

< and > are especially useful. The following finds a set of numbers from one set that are less than all the other numbers in a second set:

```
# Elements of one set that are less than all elements in a second set
# Perl 5
use Quantum::Superpositions;
print join ', ', eigenstates(any(1, 2, 3, 4) < all(4, 5, 6, 7));
print "\n";
```

This prints 1, 3, 2. It could also have been written as follows:

```
# Elements of one set that are less than all elements in a second set
# alternative implementation using List::Util - Perl 5
use List::Util 'min';
my $min = min(4, 5, 6, 7);
print join ', ', grep { $_ < $min } (1, 2, 3, 4);
print "\n";
```

And conversely, permutations between sets can find elements larger than the largest in a second set.

```
# Elements of one set that are greater than all elements in a second set
# Perl 5
use Quantum::Superpositions;
print join ', ', eigenstates(any(4, 5, 6, 7) > all(1, 2, 3, 4));
print "\n";
```

This prints 6, 7, 5.

This could have been written as follows:

```
# Elements of one set greater than all elements in a second set
# alternative implementation using PDL - Perl 5
use PDL;
my $max = pdl([1, 2, 3, 4])->max;
my $set1 = pdl([4, 5, 6, 7]);
print $set1->where($set1 > $max), "\n";
```

This prints [5 6 7]. Print the intermediate values to understand how this does what it does. $set1 > $max creates a mask Perl Data Language (PDL) array, composed of 0s and 1s. For each position in $set1 that contains a value greater than $max, the same position in the mask contains a 1. where() takes this mask and selects the values back out of $set1 for each position in the mask that contains a 1. All in all, three sets are created. This is a roundabout way of doing it, but it's very fast and very general. Complex machinery can be built from these primitives. This PDL example doesn't automatically permutate sets, but you can attain this sort of behavior. Matrix operations are an obvious example.

```
# Permutations example using PDL - Perl 5
use PDL;
my $row = pdl([1, 2, 3, 4]);
print "Row:\n", $row, "\n\n";
my $col = pdl([4, 5, 6, 7])->dummy(0, 1);
print "Column:", $col, "\n";
print "Result:", $row * $col, "\n";
```

This gives the following output:

```
Row:
[1 2 3 4]

Column:
[
 [4]
 [5]
 [6]
 [7]
]

Result:
[
 [ 4  8 12 16]
 [ 5 10 15 20]
 [ 6 12 18 24]
 [ 7 14 21 28]
]
```

This PDL example performs a few useful tasks that superpositions don't. Duplicate values are retained, and the result is a multidimensional array. The x and y coordinates of any result are the x coordinate from the row of input data and the y coordinate from the column of input data. Result values may be easily correlated with the values from which they were generated. For large data sets, it's much faster than Quantum::Superpositions.

dummy(0, 1) needs an explanation. It inserts a dummy (empty) dimension. The first argument, 0, is the position to insert the dimension, and the second argument, 1, is the size of the dimension. Used this way, it inserts a dummy dimension that's one unit wide, which just happens to turn a row of values into a column of values. See Chapter 7 for more examples.

Nonboolean Operators and Functions on Superpositions

Logic operations are useful for set intersection tests and such, but the permutating logic works with any operator.

```
# Operators operate on every state of a superposition - Perl 5
use Quantum::Superpositions;
die unless any(1, 3, 7) * 3 == 9;
```

Three times three is nine, and any only requires that one of the values satisfies boolean tests, such as ==, so this doesn't die.

Multiplication, or any other binary operation between two sets, gives a set as a result.

```
# Operations permutate every state of two superpositions - Perl 5
use Quantum::Superpositions;
print join ', ', eigenstates(any(1, 3, 7) * any(2, 4, 6));
print "\n";
```

I get the following output:

```
6, 28, 12, 2, 14, 42, 4, 18
```

The result is computed from these permutations (see Table 18-4).

Table 18-4. *Operations on Set Permutations*

Left Set	Right Set	Result
12	2	24
1	4	4
1	6	6
3	2	6
3	4	12
3	6	18
7	2	14
7	4	28
7	6	42

Superpositions don't contain duplicates. Printing the result of permutations won't show any single number twice. The result of an operation that permutates can be tested with == or other boolean tests, or it may be used as input to another operator.

perldoc Quantum::Superpositions has an excellent example of comparing a set against a number using the modulo operator, %, to test for primes. The heart of it reads $n % all(2 .. sqrt($n)+1) != 0. This computes a set of all whole numbers between 2 and the square root of the number and then tries to divide that number by every number in that set. This builds a set of remainders, as the modulo operator, %, is used. This set is an all set, as it was created from performing an operation on an all set. If no 0 exists in the modulo result set, then none of the numbers in the original set was able to originally divide the original number. If it can't be divided evenly by a whole number, it's a prime. See perldoc Quantum::Superpositions for the actual example. The definitions for minima and maxima are alone worth the price of admission.

Superpositions As Function Arguments

Functions, including built-in functions, don't automatically work on superpositions, but you can tell Quantum::Superpositions to wrap logic around functions to make them work. Specifically, the result value of the function isn't a superposition of all possible results unless the function is wrapped or special care is taken. See the documentation for Quantum::Superpositions for examples.

Summary

Superpositions compute all possibilities in parallel, but present-day computers execute these possibilities in serial, that is, unless you happen to have an infinite number of processors and a really good threading implementation. Because of this, Quantum::Superposition isn't recommended for processing large data sets. Use PDL for that. PDL also defines any and all functions that don't permutate but do apply the two definitions of truth established in this chapter.

any is true if the test is true for any member of the set, but all requires the test to be true for every member of the set. perldoc PDL::Impatient gives the example of $b = $a->log10 unless any ($a <= 0); as a way of testing if a floating-point exception would be triggered before performing an operation. Perl 6 moves Quantum::Superposition-style behavior into the core, making it fast, and it will work with lightweight, true multidimensional arrays such as PDL gives you. The two have significant overlap, but Perl 6 merges these concepts.

Hyper operators are another story. They complement set operations. Perl 6 uses hyper operators to apply some operation to each element of a set, regardless of whether the values are being modified directly or a list of results is being generated. For Perl 5, Quantum::Superpositions does this. It isn't beyond the scope of the idea of superpositions, but it is beyond the scope of the basic idea of any and all, and Perl 6's set operations boil down to those two functions and their corresponding operators. Language::Functional defines any and all functions that perform this test on lists, too. Quantum::Superposition is unique in automatically permutating between sets and in operating on sets composed of other sets. The sets of sets are considered not only in parallel but also recursively. Complex conditionals may be hidden away in a scalar packed full of alternatives.

## CHAPTER 19

Lexical Closures

*L*exical *variables*, created with my, are in scope until the end of the current block. Lexical variables are "lexical" because a quick glance at the code shows where they're available—there's no need to trace the flow of the program to figure out where a variable might be changed.

It naturally follows that they're in scope and usable in blocks inside the current block, since those blocks appear before the end of the current block. Chapter 10 introduced this concept, but that was a simplification of what really happens. Variables continue to be useful in a block of code after that code has stopped running—as long as any references to them exist. In other words, the rules could be read as, "my variables are in scope until the end of the block—no matter what". The magic happens when code creates references to lexical variables merely by using them, and references to code keep those references alive.

Closures are immensely useful for creating structures out of logic, where the arrangement of the logic isn't exactly known when the program was written. Code like this isn't just written for artificial intelligence applications; it's useful for solving hard problems in general.

Coroutines, covered in Chapter 21, share variables between threads of execution according to the rules of lexical scope. Coroutines can be explained only in terms of lexical scoping rules. The idea is simple but not obvious; the implications of this simple idea are interesting, though. If you haven't already, you'll eventually have an "a-ha" moment when it starts to jell for you.

Changes for Perl 6

Subroutines may be defined with a lexical scope using my $foo = sub { }, as discussed in Chapter 11. This works in both Perl 5 and Perl 6 and is the only way to get a closure in Perl 5. Perl 6 also takes a closure when a reference is created to a lexically scoped, named subroutine. The code reference maintains references to the lexical variables it uses.

```
# Perl 6 - named subroutines may be closures
sub create_counter {
    my $counter;
    my sub counter_logic {
        $counter++;
    }
    return &counter_logic;
}
my $foo_counter = create_counter();
print $foo_counter.(), "\n" for 1 .. 10;
```

Regular functions, like counter_logic() in the previous example, may bind to lexical variables in Perl 6.

Perl 5 code would do tricks with glob assignments and local to avoid having to refer to closures as scalars, like $counter_logic->(). The anonymous subroutine syntax could have been used instead, but in some cases it reads better with the subroutine call syntax. When a subroutine is called repeatedly, counter_logic() reads better than $counter_logic.(), $counter_logic->(), or even the Perl 6 implied dot version, $counter_logic().

Any code block may now potentially be a closure—not just anonymous subroutines created with the sub { } syntax. There isn't a lot of distinction between code blocks and anonymous subroutines; a do { } block is conceptually just a closure that runs immediately, and it's a closure that no reference is kept to, except that it doesn't exist according to caller and except that return ignores it.

Code blocks in reference context (where a code reference is expected) turn into closures, much as arrays in reference context turn into references to themselves. Assignment (to an untyped variable) and other operations default to reference context.

Lexical Scope

If you agree that statements such as do { $bar = 30; foo(); print $bar; } should print 30, then you agree that subroutines generally shouldn't modify variables in other parts of the program. $bar shouldn't be in scope in this hypothetical other part of the program that corresponds to the hypothetical foo() routine. If this hypothetical other routine wants a variable named $bar, it should create its own. This simple rule breaks down when a subroutine is defined in the middle of a block of code.

```
# Anonymous subroutines and variable scoping - pseudo-Perl
$bar = sub {
    $foo = 20;
};
$foo = 10;
$bar->();
print $foo, "\n";
```

Depending on how variables are implemented in the language, this could print either 10 or 20. If it prints 10, then subroutines don't have their own private data when they're nested inside other code. If it prints 20, then nested subroutines can't work on variables in the surrounding code. Neither of these scenarios is always desirable, so you have a choice. Use my to create a new, private variable. The previous example will print 20. If I had written the $foo = 20 line as my $foo = 20 instead, it would print 10. That would have worked with local, too, but local isn't adequate in the following example:

```perl
# Anonymous subroutines and variable scoping - pseudo-Perl
$foo = 10;
sub print_foo {
    print $foo, "\n";
}
$bar = sub {
    local $foo = 20;
    print_foo();
};
$bar->();
```

This prints 20 even though the local $foo = 20 statement is clearly in another block. The value has leaked out. Globalism has snuck back in. Change the local to my, and this then starts printing 10. Only then is $foo and the $foo = 20 assignment truly private to the sub { } block.

Code references created with sub { } have references to the my variables they reference from surrounding scopes.

```perl
# Anonymous subroutines and lexical scoping - Perl 5 and Perl 6
my $counter = do {
    my $counter_value = 0;
    sub {
        ++ $counter_value;
    };
};
print $counter->(), "\n" for 1 .. 10;
```

Here, $counter is a reference to a small subroutine that consists in its entirety of ++ $counter_value. The code reference created by sub { } falls off the end of the do { } block. $counter_value is scoped to this do { } block. The code reference created by the sub { } is assigned to $counter and has a reference to $counter_value. Not only can anonymous subroutines see lexical variables that are in their parents' scope, but they also provide references to keep them alive. As long as a reference to this code reference exists, it'll hang onto its reference to $counter_value, and the $counter_value variable won't be forgotten. An anonymous subroutine that references variables in any enclosing block is called a *closure*. It's said to *close over* those variables. One sub { } may take several closures.

```perl
# Each closure has its own data - Perl 5 and Perl 6
# use Perl6::Variables; # uncomment for Perl 5
my @counters;
for ( 1 .. 10 ) {
    my $counter_value = 0;
    push @counters, sub {
        ++ $counter_value;
    };
};
print @counters[rand @counters]->(), "\n" for 1 .. 10;
```

@counters contains ten different closures created from the same sub { }. Each closure has attached to a different instance of $counter_value, so ten different $counter_value variables are alive at the same time. The print statement with the for clause on it picks out a random closure from the list, invokes it, and prints the result. Had there only been one $counter_value variable, this would count from 0 to 9 as did the previous example. You should get several 1s, a few 2s, and perhaps a 3 or two.

Reference-Counted or Garbage-Collected Variables

Technically speaking, my variables are allocated on the heap rather than the stack; they aren't necessarily freed when the current function returns or block ends. Most languages free storage associated with temporary variables when the current block ends or the current subroutine returns, as the variables must be cleared off the stack to return.

As variables may or may not be reclaimed when a block exits, another way is needed to decide when a variable is no longer being used. Perl 5 does this one way; Perl 6 running on Parrot does it another way.

Perl 5 counts how many things can see a variable as the program runs. Every time a reference is created, the reference count goes up. When a reference is lost, the reference count goes down. In the parlance of Chapter 5, references to containers are counted, and references may be names in symbol tables or references stored in other variables. When a variable name goes out of scope, a reference is lost. When a reference stored in a variable is overwritten or that variable goes out of scope, a reference is lost. When there are no references to the container (storage) associated with a variable, Perl reclaims the storage for future use.

Perl 6 on Parrot does something similar, but it doesn't keep a running count. Instead, Parrot goes through and looks for references to variable containers after the fact. Every now and again, Parrot will look through data structures, the program stack, and so on, to see which variables have references and can be seen. Parrot won't free a data structure the moment no references exist to it, but instead this condition will be detected some time in the future. This is called *mark-sweep garbage collection.*

Closures and Scope

Perl programmers often ask how to avoid using file-scoped variables in callbacks. File::Find is a popular, useful module and one of the first encountered that uses a callback. To locate the perl installations on a large multiuser machine, you could write something like that shown in Listing 19-1.

Listing 19-1. *An Anonymous Subroutine Sharing Lexically Scoped Data*

```
# Find Perl installations that scripts depend on
# Demonstrates call-backs - Perl 5

use File::Find;
use Perl6::Variables;

my %perls;
```

```perl
find(sub {
    return unless m/\.pl$/;
    open my $pl, '<', $_ or return;
    (my $shebang) = <$pl> =~ m/^#!(\S+)/ or return;
    %perls{$shebang}++;
}, '/');

for my $perl (
    sort { $b->[1] <=> $a->[1] }
    map [ $_, %perls{$_} ],
    keys %perls
) {
    print $perl->[1], ' ', $perl->[0], "\n";
}
```

On my laptop, I get the output shown in Listing 19-2.

Listing 19-2. *Sample Output from Callback Example*

```
/usr/bin/perl 434
perl 55
/usr/local/bin/perl 43
/usr/bin/env 18
/ford/thishost/unix/div/ap/bin/perl 12
/usr/local/bin/perl5.9.1 8
./perl 7
/bin/perl 4
../xperl 3
../miniperl 2
./miniperl 2
/usr/athena/bin/perl 2
/usr/lib/perl 2
/ford/thishost/unix/div/ap/bin/perl5.00404 1
/ford/thishost/unix/div/ap/bin/xperl 1
/usr/bin/perl-thread 1
/usr/home/bin/perl 1
/usr/home/vrpa/usr/local/bin/perl5.8.0 1
/usr/local/bin/perl5.8.0 1
/usr/pkg/bin/perl 1
env 1
perl.exe 1
```

/usr/bin/perl dominates handily. I'm not sure that I want to know what some of the others are.

The callback is the first argument to find(). It specifies what File::Find::find() should do with each file it finds. Information is communicated out of the callback routine by stuffing values into %perls. Some sort of channel such as this is needed, as values returned with return go to the find() routine, not the code that called find(). This works fine as a small stand-alone script, and it works well as part of a larger script as well. Enclose everything but the use statements in a block, and this still works correctly; %perls is private to that block.

Chapter 20 contains a *continuation* version of this example. This demonstrates another way to move values out of a block without exiting the block.

Evals vs. Closures

Chapter 3 suggested using closures instead of eval "" for security reasons; when eval "" is used with user-supplied data, malicious Perl may be interjected into the program. In most places that eval "" is used, only a few variables are filled in. Rather than generating a string to eval later, create a code reference to dereference later using ->() or .(). Rather than substituting in values, stuff them into lexical variables and close over them.

```
# Storing logic to execute later using eval - Perl 5
# Don't do this if it's possible to avoid it
my $answer = 10;
my $code = qq{ print "The answer is $answer.\n"; };
# Later in the program...
eval $code;
```

If $answer contained a ', the string would end prematurely. If $answer was read from data external to the program, it may contain something malicious, such as '; unlink $0; print '. No matter what quoting character is chosen, you can't trust input to not contain it. What if input is a copy of the program itself? The quoting character would certainly appear. References lose their magic when interpolated into a string, so data structures, objects, file handles, code references, or compiled regular expressions can't directly be provided to code stored in an eval "". Closures safely store arbitrary binary data, making them more secure and, in this certain way, more powerful. They also save memory in cases where eval "" is used repeatedly with more than a small amount of code. Closures reuse a single compiled copy of the code, even if the sub { } is used in a loop to generate multiple closures. Closures are faster for the same reason.

```
# Storing logic to execute later using a closure - Perl 5:
my $answer = 10;
my $code = sub { print "The answer is $answer.\n"; };
# Later in the program...
$code->();
```

The eval "" example copies the data in $answer into the string that's later evaled. The closure example takes a reference to $answer. If the value in $answer changes before the closure is executed, the change affects the closure. You're probably wondering how you could possibly build anything useful just closing over variables. Remember that you can close over other code references and that you can curry code references to customize them.

```
# Build more complex logic incrementally from simpler logic by closing on
# closures and currying - Perl 5

use autobox;
use autobox::Core;
```

```
my $add = sub { $_[0] + $_[1] };
my $gt  = sub { $_[0] > $_[1] };
my $add_two  = $add->curry(2);
my $add_five = $add->curry(5);
my $two_gt_five = sub { $gt->($add_two->(7), $add_five->(1)) };

print "2 + 7 is greater than 5 + 1\n" if $two_gt_five->();
```

You can use small pieces of logic to build complex machinery by closing over other closures. A calculator application could be built with a small parser that creates a tree of operations and data and then executes it. (This hypothetical application could also build a tree and then feed it to a specialized interpreter, but that isn't analogous to eval "". I assume you specifically want to use Perl's interpreter.) That tree looks something like Figure 19-1.

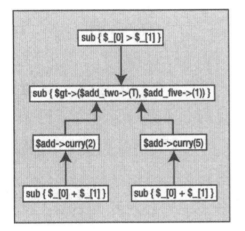

Figure 19-1. Structure created from the example system of code references

It isn't always practical to build all the small parts needed using closures, so eval "" is still useful in certain cases.

Summary

Closures customize and configure subroutines. Think of closures as lightweight objects of a sort, and think of lexical variables as instance data of a sort. Closures, when run, read arguments, just like a normal subroutine, but the feature of automatically referencing lexical variables minimizes the need for this. Rather than being instantiated with a call to new(), the closure latches onto the current set of variables in scope. This greatly simplifies construction. Because closures are just subroutines, as far as their user is concerned, the interface is simple, well understood, and well supported.

Closures may be blessed into objects. Closures may be stored in arrays and hashes. A closure may reference other closures and form a greater logic, created at run time. A closure may serve as a callback, being passed in as an argument to a subroutine to further specify what needs to be done. They may be used to specify policy and may be passed to a routine that specifies a mechanism to cleanly separate policy from mechanism.

Use closures to build small pieces of easily constructed, reusable logic. When simplifying program logic into subroutines, look for routines that were hard to factor out because they take too many arguments. These are the prime candidates for "closurehood".

CHAPTER 20

■■■

Continuations

One of the particular problems that often comes up is this: if you have a piece of code producing data, and another piece of code consuming it, which should be the caller and which should be the callee?

—Simon Tatham

Coroutines make peers of subroutines, letting multiple subroutine calls exist at the same time. Coroutines are still a little bit too low level for what programmers usually need, but they're very powerful, and they're the subject of the next chapter. A programmer still needs to wire the coroutines together, and *continuations* offer one way to accomplish that. But rather than having to think about the problem in terms of joining threads together through a queue, continuations use the plain old functional call idiom. In a coroutine, results are passed back from the called coroutine via yield rather than return. yield temporarily returns control to the caller without exiting the current subroutine. A continuation can yield a series of values from a loop, for instance, returning the value from the next loop iteration each time that continuation is called. It can call other routines, each of which can have if() statements, while() statements, and calls to other routines, and *those* can yield values.

The yield keyword temporarily suspends the function call to the current continuation and returns control to the caller. Continuations are created with the :Cont attribute to subdefinitions and with the csub { } keyword that generates anonymous continuations. The Coro module implements these features for Perl 5.

Continuations do something that's difficult but highly sought after in threading systems—they explicitly pass control back and forth between two places in the program, bypassing the uncertainty and complexity of the scheduler and resource locks.

Chapter 19 talked about doing away with the stack for allocating variables, instead allocating and freeing memory as needed. Closures let you have two or more copies of a variable alive at once. Coroutines let you have two or more copies of a subroutine alive at once.

The next chapter, Chapter 21, talks about using coroutines in places where you'd use threads. Continuations build on the idea of coroutines, but the concept is simple despite its power. Since continuations don't require you to think about things in terms of tasks or threads, I'm using them as an introduction to coroutines.

New for Perl 6

Continuations are in core and are faster, as they're designed into the language. Continuations don't sport a lot of extra or optional features, so there really isn't anything to change and add. Most of the modules in this book aren't well supported or recommended for production work; Coro is unusual in that it's stable, it's well supported, and it's considered by many to be exceptionally good style.

Producers and Consumers

A *producer* generates data, and a *consumer* gobbles it up. Sometimes a producer calls the consumer to feed it data; in other cases, a consumer calls a producer to request more data. Consider the Gnutella network protocol. Each Gnutella protocol packet starts with a 23-byte header that includes the command number and, depending on the command, the size of the trailer. The trailer contains any command-specific data and concludes the packet. The packets are sent as a stream of data, composed of TCP packets. A simple routine to decode packets could look like Listing 20-1.

Listing 20-1. *Reference* read_packet() *Implementation*

```
# Noncontinuation version - read Gnutella packet streams - Perl 5

sub read_packet {
    my $connection = shift;
    while(1) {
        read $connection, my $header, 23;
        my ($msgid, $cmd, $ttl, $hops, $length) = unpack 'a16CCCV', $header;
        read $connection, my $trailer, $length;
        process_packet($msgid, $cmd, $ttl, $hops, $length, $trailer);
    }
}
```

I didn't need to create a bunch of scalars to hold the parts of the header. I could have accomplished the same thing with an array, but I wanted to show you what's actually in the header. The trailers are far more complex to decode for most commands. Elsewhere in the program is the code shown in Listing 20-2 to decode an incoming stream of packets.

Listing 20-2. *Reference* process_packet() *Implementation*

```
# Noncontinuation version - dispatch (partially) decoded packets - Perl 5

use Perl6::Variables;
sub process_packet {
    while(1) {
        my @packet = read_packet();
        my $cmd = @packet[1];
        Packet::Ping->process(@packet)    if $cmd == 0x00;
        Packet::Pong->process(@packet)    if $cmd == 0x01;
        Packet::Bye->process(@packet)     if $cmd == 0x02;
```

```
        Packet::Keywords->process(@packet) if $cmd == 0x20;
        Packet::Push->process(@packet)     if $cmd == 0x40;
        Packet::Query->process(@packet)    if $cmd == 0x80;
        Packet::QueryHit->process(@packet) if $cmd == 0x81;
    }
}
```

This code suffers a fatal flaw—each subroutine calls the other. To make this work in a traditional, top-down programming world, one routine must be the caller and the other the callee. The callee does one small task and then returns. But which routine should be the callee and which the caller?

If process_packet was the caller and read_packet the callee, programmers could create alternate implementations of process_packet. Those alternate implementations would be able to reuse the logic read_packet, since read_packet may be called as a sort of helper routine. This would be useful for creating custom subclasses of the packets, specialized or extended for some purpose, such as to add support for protocol extensions (of which there are many). More if statements could be added to recognize new commands.

If read_packet called process_packet, programmers could create alternate implementations of read_packet. Alternate implementations of read_packet would be useful for reusing the packet-processing code in different thread systems and event models, and each implementation could reuse the logic in process_packet. read_packet could be replaced with glue to turn this Gnutella implementation into a POE component. (See http://poe.perl.org for information on POE, the Perl Object Environment.) Or, the programmer could use the Event module or the select system call to figure out which handle is ready to be read from, read from that handle, and then pass the data to process_packet.

In the traditional, top-down programming world, things don't work this way. One subroutine must be closer to main and "higher up", and the other must be below it, merely a subservient "helper" routine.

Continuations Introduction

Each time a continuation yields, it stops and returns a value. Next time it's called, it continues immediately after the yield rather than at the start.

```
# Yielding returns a value and then resumes after the yield next call
# Perl 5

use Coro::Cont;
sub producer :Cont {
    yield 1;
    yield 2;
    yield 3;
}

print producer(), "\n";
print producer(), "\n";
print producer(), "\n";
```

:Cont makes producer into a continuation. producer returns 1 on the first call. On the second call, it returns 2, and on the third, it returns 3. Should it be called a fourth time, it could come back with 1 again, as it starts execution at the top after it falls off the bottom. producer provides values, but the block never actually exits until execution hits the end of the block or a real return is executed. This means that lexical variables and loops stay just how they were left.

```perl
# Yield from within a loop in a continuation - Perl 5

use Coro::Cont;
sub producer :Cont {
    for my $i ( 1 .. 3 ) {
        yield $i;
    }
}

print producer(), "\n";
print producer(), "\n";
print producer(), "\n";
```

This prints 1, 2, and then 3, just like the previous example. Continuations receive their argument list in @_, just as normal subroutines do.

```perl
# Yield from within a loop in a continuation with arguments - Perl 5

use Coro::Cont;
sub producer :Cont {
    my @numbers = @_;
    yield;
    for my $i (@numbers) {
        yield $i;
    }
}

producer(5 .. 10);
print producer(), "\n";
print producer(), "\n";
print producer(), "\n";
```

Each call to producer may pass arguments, and these appear in @_ as parameters. Because of this, information may be passed to continuations as well as passed out of it using yield.

```perl
# yield from within a loop in a continuation with initial and
# incremental arguments - Perl 5

use Coro::Cont;
use Perl6::Variables;

sub producer :Cont {
    my @numbers = @_;
    yield;
```

```
    for (my $i = 0; $i < @numbers; $i++) {
        yield @numbers[$i];
        $i += shift if @_;
    }
}

producer(5 .. 25);       # create a sequence
print producer(1), "\n";  # skip one number
print producer(3), "\n";  # skip 3 numbers
print producer(10), "\n"; # skip 10 numbers
```

A modified version of the Gnutella examples in Listing 20-1 and Listing 20-2 could make either or both of the two complementary subroutines into a continuation. This gets around the producer-consumer distinction and allows both routines to use lexical variables, loops, if statements, and function calls in the normal fashion. Our requirements go beyond that, though. People extending the program should be able to replace either subroutine with another version. To this end, let's make *both* routines into continuations and then wire them together. Listing 20-3 reworks Listing 20-1 to use coroutines.

Listing 20-3. *Coroutine Implementation of* read_packet()

```
# Continuation version - read Gnutella packet streams - Perl 5

sub read_packet :Cont {
    my $connection = shift;
    while(1) {
        read $connection, my $header, 23;
        my ($msgid, $cmd, $ttl, $hops, $length) =
        unpack 'a16CCCV', $header;
        read $connection, my $trailer, $length;
        yield $msgid, $cmd, $ttl, $hops, $length, $trailer;
    }
}
```

The function call to process_packet was replaced with a yield statement. Even though read_packet executes a while(1) { }, it's absolutely no problem to call it repeatedly, and upcoming examples do just that. Each call picks up where the last yield left things. In this case, it does the next while(1) { } loop. process_packet has been extended with a built-in ping counter as a simple illustration of creating and using lexical variables inside continuations. Listing 20-4 rewrites Listing 20-2 to use coroutines.

Listing 20-4. *Coroutine Implementation of* process_packet()

```
# Continuations version - process Gnutella packet - Perl 5

sub process_packet :Cont {
    my $ping_counter;
    while(1) {
        my @packet = @_;
        my $cmd = @packet[1];
```

```
        if($cmd == 0x00) {
            'Packet::Ping'->process(@packet);
            $ping_counter++;
        }
        Packet::Pong->process(@packet)      if $cmd == 0x01;
        # ...
        Packet::Query->process(@packet)     if $cmd == 0x80;
        Packet::QueryHit->process(@packet) if $cmd == 0x81;
        yield;
    }
}
```

$ping_counter keeps its value, even as the routine repeatedly yields and is called again. You'll get a new $ping_counter should the routine ever actually return and then be called again. If this had been written as a continuation generator, each generated continuation would get its own private $ping_counter. When a function is called again after a yield, it resumes with any parameters from the most recent call stuffed in @_. Each while(1) { } loop iteration, @packet gets new data.

With the top-down approach to programming, only one of the routines could be written in a reusable way. With continuations, both could be written with no knowledge of how they might be called, allowing either or both to be modularly reused or replaced.

Here's the glue to bind these two functions:

```
# Connect process_packet() and read_packet() continuations - Perl 5

while(1) {
    my @packet = read_packet($connection);
    process_packet(@packet);
}
```

This assumes that process_packet() is modified to perform a while(1) { } loop and yield after each iteration.

read_packet(), as a continuation, can read packets in a loop. process_packet(), as a continuation, can keep values around needed to process packets. Neither of them suffers any disadvantage for yielding rather than playing the role of the caller.

Continuations and Callbacks

Chapter 19 contained an example of communicating information out of a callback, using File::Find::find() as an example. It used a variable that's in scope in the callback as well as the surrounding block. (In other words, the callback closed over the variable.) Listing 20-5 shows the example, repeated.

Listing 20-5. *Reference Perl Finding Implementation*

```
# Find Perl installations that scripts depend on
# Demonstrates call-backs - Perl 5
```

```
use File::Find;
use Perl6::Variables;

my %perls;
find(sub {
    return unless m/\.pl$/;
    open my $pl, '<', $_ or return;
    (my $shebang) = <$pl> =~ m/^#!(\S+)/ or return;
    %perls{$shebang}++;
}, '/');
for my $perl (sort keys %perls) {
    print $perl, ' ', %perls{$perl}, "\n";
}
```

The callback routine can communicate results using a continuation without needing a variable to buffer results. Rather than accumulating all the results in variable, such as %perls in this example, the data may be fed out of the routine as it's computed. For potentially large result sets, this allows processing of the results to begin immediately rather than waiting until they've all been found. It also prevents filling memory with intermediate results. Listing 20-6 is a rewrite of Listing 20-5 that has been modified to use coroutines.

Listing 20-6. *Coroutine Version of Perl Finding Routine*

```
# Find Perl installations that scripts depend on
# Demonstrates continuations - Perl 5

use Coro;
use Coro::Cont;
use File::Find;
use Perl6::Variables;

sub get_next_perl :Cont {
    find(sub {
        return unless m/\.pl$/;
        open my $pl, '<', $_ or return;
        (my $shebang) = <$pl> =~ m/^#!(\S+)/ or return;
        yield $shebang;
    }, '/');
    return undef;
}

while(my $_ = get_next_perl()) {
    last unless defined $_;
    print $_, "\n";
}
```

The get_next_perl subroutine is new as of this example, and it encloses the call to File::Find::find. Rather than doing %perls{$shebang}++, it simply does yield $shebang to tunnel the value out of the callback, straight through File::Find::find, out of get_next_perl, and right back to the while loop calling get_next_perl. The :Cont property applies to everything above it on the call stack, not only the present routine, so the anonymous subroutine passed to find can use yield even though the :Cont property is allied to the get_next_perl subroutine.

Continuation Generators

A continuation created with :Cont has one set of variables. Multiple parts of the program may simultaneously access this continuation, but any change to the state of the continuation applies to the whole program. This is the desired behavior in some cases, but to truly offer reusable logic, you need a continuation generator.

A continuation generator creates copies of continuations, each with their own set of variables, just as a closure creates copies of subroutines, each with their own set of variables. Listing 20-7 rewrites Listing 20-6 to use a continuation generator.

Listing 20-7. *Finding Perl Installations with Continuation Generators*

```
# Find Perl installations that scripts depend on
# Demonstrates continuation generators - Perl 5

use Coro;
use Coro::Cont;
use File::Find;
use Perl6::Variables;
sub get_shebang_generator {
    my $pattern = shift;
    csub {
        find(sub {
            return unless $_ =~ $pattern;
            open my $pl, '<', $_ or return;
            (my $shebang) = <$pl> =~ m/^#!(\S+)/ or return;
            yield $shebang;
        }, '/');
        return undef;
    };
}

my $get_next_perl = get_shebang_generator(qr/\.pl$/);
while(my $_ = $get_next_perl->()) {
    last unless defined $_;
    print $_, "\n";
}
```

get_shebang_generator takes the pattern that filenames must match as an argument. It returns a code reference that's both a closure and a continuation. Because the continuation is a code reference, you can create several of those and run them at the same time. You and other programmers on the project can reuse them in several parts of the program without fear of contention. A routine may create a continuation using the generator, pull a few values from it, and then call another routine without fear that the other routine will upset the state of the continuation. Each generated continuation is entirely private.

RESOURCES

The included documentation, `perldoc Coro::Cont`, has a neat example. Marc A. Lehmann wrote Coro and Coro::Cont. Some of the examples included with Coro in the eg/ directory do nifty things with using continuations such as blocks to sort and map to create criteria blocks with persistent lexical state.

This chapter quoted and initially followed the structure of http://www.chiark.greenend.org.uk/~sgtatham/coroutines.html by Simon Tatham. This article has an interesting work-around to C not saving or restoring the current point of execution between repeated calls. This work-around also serves to illustrate the problem that coroutines and continuations solve.

Chapter 11 poked at the idea of *lazy lists*, where only as much data as is needed is generated, and then only as needed. Want was used to decide how much data should be returned. This idea combines well with the idea of continuations, where more data can later be requested and the algorithm picks up generating data where it left off.

Closures, when used as callbacks, accomplish two of the things that coroutines do for you. They allow logic to be plugged together like building bricks, and they provide data storage that's persistent between calls. They require extra infrastructure, don't allow the callee to declare its own variables, and don't offer the same options for tunneling data into and out of routines, but they're important concept for structuring programs. Chapter 19 documents this technique.

Similar to closures, object references may be passed into routines to create pluggable logic. One method may also call methods on `$self`, allowing inheritance to override implementations.

Summary

Procedural programming takes the idea of stepwise scripting and adds a notion of calling a subroutine (also known as a *procedure*). Large subroutines are broken down into smaller subroutines by busting off parts of the large subroutine, turning them into auxiliary subroutines, and then inserting a call to the new auxiliary subroutine. The main subroutine calls the smaller ones, and the smaller ones are sort of utilities or helpers. The subroutines form a sort of treelike structure (a directed graph, actually) that's known as *top-down programming*. A subroutine may always use a subroutine that's below it on the tree, but things go sour when a subroutine tries to call a subroutine that's next to or above it. Some large, complex programs, such as Unix kernels, will draw lines, creating a "top half" and a "bottom half"; they mandate that no subroutine below the line ever be allowed to call a subroutine above the line. There may be several of these divisions. This was originally done to segregate interrupt-handling code, but the idea has spread. (It's become a pastime of technology writers to discuss how things are like or unlike top-down programming.)

Continuations give you all the parts needed to make subroutines into things that can truly be used modularly rather than merely "structured"; objects give a similar sort of modularity, but they're heavier on the syntax and overpowered in some ways. They lack the ability to suspend execution in the middle of a loop, conditional, or even other method, `yield`, and then resume at the exact same point. Even though an object has its instance data to keep variable values between calls, it isn't practical to glue two methods together. The methods would have to dispatch depending on internal state, which may entail complex heuristics. An object's instance data isn't stored on a stack, so a method that calls itself (or calls another method that calls the first method again) will overwrite the state data. This is another common source of bugs in object-oriented programming.

Rather than calling another routine by name (and rather than invoking a callback), continuations let you simply `yield` values. This minimizes the rigidity of a strict top-down ordering stricture and lets you write minimal pieces of logic to connect them without fuss or hassle.

CHAPTER 21

■ ■ ■

Coroutines

Anyway, a continuation is essentially a closure that, in addition to closing over the lexical environment, also closes over the control chain.

—Dan Sugalski

Coroutines let programs operate more like humans do. Program flow control already has concepts of queues and stacks from real life, but a concept of multiple, separate workspaces is missing. Humans don't often do two things at exactly the same moment, but we have many tasks in progress that we start and stop at will. We step away from a partially finished task, leaving all the papers, screws, or whatever parts just laying out on the workbench or desk, and we walk over to another counter and work on something else for a while. It'd be painful to have to pack everything up in neat little boxes when you're smack dab in the middle of working on a project. Coroutines and threads both offer execution contexts, which are "workspaces" in this analogy. Coroutines don't attempt to multiplex the CPU between tasks, making them a lightweight, simpler alternative to threads that's suitable for structuring logic in a program besides just dealing with multiple network connections or pipes. Coroutines let a programmer say, "Do this, oh, and do this, too"; coroutines let programmers specify what's to be done without dealing with the minutia of sequencing the exact order of events.

As with continuations, you can set up workflow paths between independently executing routines. As with threads, it's impossible to know beforehand what order various connections will provide data (and guessing wrong means deadlock). Each coroutine will run whenever its resources are available, for as long as its resources are available.

This chapter demonstrates the syntax for creating coroutines, getting result values from them, passing control between them, passing values between them, camping out waiting for other events, and waiting for all coroutines to finish.

This chapter takes extra time to cover the Coro::Socket and Coro::Event modules.

As coroutines don't try to simulate multiple CPUs, they don't intercept attempts to perform I/O and yield the CPU to other threads. The coroutine notion of *events* closely follows that of event-driven systems such as POE, but rather than a callback function being called when an event transpires, execution in the current coroutine is allowed to continue. A small amount of programmer awareness is required for several coroutines to sustain several I/O connections without blocking each other.

Not Covered

This chapter neglects the concept of locking. Coroutines should still coordinate access to resources and should use Coro::Semaphore to do so. One coroutine will block another from running when they both want the same resource, which is both dangerous and useful. Most of what Chapter 17 says about locking applies, except you should consider coroutines to be cooperative threads, and operations such as sleep won't relinquish the CPU (but read on).

async { }, introduced in this chapter, creates a new execution context that runs independently of the context in which it was created. This is useful, but communication is a bit too minimal for many cases. Chapter 20 introduced the sub foo :Cont syntax, which is useful for creating a new execution context with tighter communication between the created and creating context. The caller blocks when expecting a value from the called routine, and the called routine blocks after yielding until it's called again. When called again, it resumes immediately after the yield. This is comparable to setting up a Thread::Queue object for communication, calling threads->create(\&foo), and reading values from the queue. But I don't cover this here—it deservingly has a whole chapter dedicated to it.

New in Perl 6

The object library included with the system will be aware of coroutines. Special versions of included I/O objects, such as IO::Handle, won't be needed. All special variables will likely be context specific in Perl 6 whereas only a few are in Perl 5 Coro.

$/ is global across all contexts; to be confident of its value, each coroutine must explicitly set it before performing a readline. $/ dictates the end-of-line for readline. (An old idiom performs a local $/ = undef to slurp in a whole file.) Perl 6 moves away from variables with global effect in favor of traits on specific file handles, and Coro::Handle::readline() accepts an additional argument to do the job of $/.

In Perl 5, threads and coroutines aren't currently completely integrated, as Coro isn't thread safe—only one thread may safely use Coro. There's plenty of reason to want to use both; for example, you should be able to use coroutines in a module without concern that the person using your module may create a thread. Each thread may want to casually create several coroutines, using coroutines to structure the program and threads to give long-running tasks access to the CPU.

The specifics haven't been written yet, so I'm presenting the Perl 5 interface. The interface will change, but the concepts directly translate. Most of the modules in this book aren't well supported or recommended for production work—Coro is unusual in that it's stable, it's well supported, and it's considered by many to be very good style.

Coro Install Notes

Before installing Coro, install the latest version of Event. Event isn't a hard dependency, but Coro comes with extra magic and glue in the form of Coro::Event that you get when Event is already installed, and this chapter uses this. loop and unloop are keywords provided by Event. Event is especially handy for writing clients and servers with Coro but of little consequence to the classical use of coroutines—using coroutines to structure program logic. Coro doesn't require a POSIX (or other) thread implementation on the machine, but it's an XS module, so access to a C compiler and make utility is required.

Coroutine Context Creation and Reaping

Both threads and coroutines create an *execution context*—that is, the collection of variables private to a thread, the place in the program current being executed by that thread, and values for important variables such $_.

Threads privatize all the important variables; Coro does @_, $_, $@, and $^W, which are respectively the current parameter list, the default variable, the failure text or object from the last eval, and the current warnings mask.

Context Creation

The interface is similar to that of the threads module (I did say coroutines were lower level than continuations).

```
# Coroutine creation conversions versus threads - Perl 5

use Coro;                           use threads;
async { stuff(); };                 async { stuff(); };
my $c = async { stuff(@args); };    my $t = threads->create(sub { }, @args);
```

$c is an instance of a coroutine object, and $t is an instance of a thread object. Like threads, a context ends when the async { } block ends, when the subroutine returns, or when execution falls off the end. Note that async { } isn't a Perl built-in, and Perl 5 requires that blocks not attached to built-ins end with a semicolon. (Perl 6 makes the rules consistent—see Chapter 10.)

It's certainly possible to wrap a subroutine call in an async { } block, but for small swathes of inline logic, placing the code directly in the async { } blocks saves having to pass and read the arguments. The variables may be used directly; the async { } block closes over any lexical variables, as discussed in Chapter 19.

```
# Lexical binding to variables by a coroutine async { } block - Perl 5
my @arguments = qw/one two three/;
async {
    # do something with @arguments here
};
```

Lexically scoped variables are shared to a coroutine if they were in scope of the async { } block. Lexically scoped variables are private to a coroutine when created after the execution context was created (inside the block). Coroutines may spawn other coroutines—these rules apply recursively. The async { } block also shares any package variables.

threads also works correctly with lexical variables, allowing them to be shared when in scope and marked is shared.

Coroutine Objects and Coroutine Return Values

When using threads, an async { } block will return a thread object. When using Coro, an async { } block returns a coroutine object. To get the result value of the block, perform a join method call on this object.

```
# Coroutine reaping versus thread - Perl 5
use Coro;                              use threads;
my $five = async { 2 + 3 }->join;   my $five = async { 2 + 3 }->join;
```

This isn't the same join that joins strings together; it's a method of the threads or Coro class. join suspends the current context until the context being joined completely finishes and a value is returned or drops off the end. join comes back with this value, tunneling it from the context that ended to the one waiting.

Switching Contexts

cede pauses a coroutine, giving others a chance to run. yield does the same for cooperative threading systems, should you happen to have one of those beasts, though preemptive thread systems don't need this. Coroutines need at least one cede somewhere, as async { } blocks and :Coro subroutines always queue a task to run later; without a cede, execution will fall off the end of the program before any spawned coroutines have a chance to run.

More typically, context will switch when attempting I/O on Coro::Handle or Coro::Socket. To do this, use the Coro::Socket class and perform operations inside an async { } block or :Coro subroutine.

```
# Some file operations that work correctly with Coro - Perl 5

use Coro;
use Coro::Socket;
use Socket;

my $socket = Coro::Socket->new(
    PeerAddr => 'localhost',
    PeerPort => 79,
) or die $!;

my $line = readline $socket; # or: my $line = <$socket>;
$socket->read(my $ten_bytes, 10) or die $!;
$socket->print("OK\n") or warn $!;

my $listen = Coro::Socket->new(
    LocalPort => 79,
    Listen    => SOMAXCONN,
) or die $!;

$listen->listen();
while(my $client = $listen->accept()) {
    # ...
}
```

These are sample usages of accept, print, listen, readline, read, and Coro::Socket->new(). This isn't a coherent program—just several syntax examples. Each of these operations switches to another context if another context is available to run and the I/O operation can't be immediately completed.

Waiting for All Contexts to Run

Threaded applications avoid using the main thread. The main thread prevents the program from exiting before all threads have finished running by tracking the threads and joining them. Applications using coroutines may track and join threads by the objects returned from threads->create() and async { }, or they may ask the threads module for a list of threads and join each one. Applications using coroutines should take advantage of Coro::Event.

```
# Coroutines - collecting all coroutines before exit - Perl 5
use Coro;
use Coro::Event;
async { print "hi $_\n" } for 1 .. 10;
Event::loop;
```

Without the Event::loop or something functionally equivalent, this would exit before any of the coroutines created by async { } could run. You could use lock variables instead, as used in Chapter 17, but this is cumbersome. Performing a cede in a while loop or something equivalent would attempt to use all the CPU in a busy spin. Event::loop is smart—it knows whether anything is running and whether anything is ready to run, and it puts the CPU to sleep (or rather hands it off to entirely other programs than the perl program you wrote) when nothing can immediately be done.

Waiting for Events

Waiting for an event implies switching contexts, assuming one is available to switch to. Should none be available, the program gives up the CPU to other programs.

Code in a suspended context waits for a certain event, such as the following:

- Getting enough data on a network connection

- Data available to be read from a file handle

- Time passing

- Data arriving in a queue from another coroutine

- A semaphore (shared with another coroutine) going down

Coro::Socket works almost like IO::Socket::INET, but the current context suspends and waits until data is available should an accept, a connect (usually done via new), a read, or a readline is attempted. I'll show Coro::Socket examples in the "Coroutine Example" section.

Coro::Handle replaces IO::Handle; it switches context when I/O is attempted on a handle that isn't ready for it.

Coro::Event glues Coro and Event together. It lets you intermingle code written for an event-oriented, callback framework with event-oriented coroutines. Event provides primitives for waiting for the availability of data on a pipe or the like, as well as elapsed time.

Coro comes with modules to handle intercoroutine communication. These are Coro::Channel, Coro::Signal, Coro::Semaphore, and Coro::RWLoc. These let one coroutine pass data to another coroutine that's able to wait until data arrives or to unblock another coroutine until some programmatic resource is available.

Waiting on Timers

Use Coro::Event to wait on timers. Create a Coro::Event object outside an async { } block (or outside the main Use Coro::Event loop in an async { } block), and then call next on that object to wait for that event.

```
# Passing time with Coro and Coro::Event - Perl 5

use Coro;
use Coro::Event;

async {
    my $timer = Coro::Event->timer(interval => 10);
    while(1) {
        $timer->next();
        print "ding\n";
    }
};

Event::loop;
```

Do this instead of calling sleep or similar functions directly. When $event->next is called, the current context will be suspended until the specified amount of time has elapsed. Rather than interval => 10, you could just as easily say at => time() + 10. Both take a number of seconds; interval takes a number of seconds to wait, and at takes an absolute epoch time, such as time returns. See perldoc -f time. Your system probably supports fractional numbers of seconds; this depends on the Time::HiRes module to work.

Waiting on File Accesses

You could use Coro::Event in place of Coro::Socket and Coro::Handle if you were so inclined.

```
# Perl 5 - construct an Event object to wait on for input
my $event = Coro::Event->io(fd => fileno $file_handle, poll => 'r');
```

The poll argument may be any combination of r, w, and e to trigger events when data is available to read, when buffer space is available to write data to, or when a pending event exists. The io method also accepts a timeout parameter—see perldoc Event for details. Rather than using Coro::Event->io and fileno on file handles to wait until data is available, convert it to an instance of Coro::Handle with the Coro::Handle::unblock method.

```
# Converting an existing file handle into a Coro::Handle object
use Coro;
use Coro::Handle;
open my $fh, '<', '/tmp/sock.0' or die $!;
$fh = Coro::Handle->unblock($fh);
$fh->read(my $buffer, 1024);
```

$fh will now correctly cede to other contexts should it be read from while no data is available. The I/O operation methods readline, read, print, printf, sysread, syswrite, and close work like the IO::Handle methods of the same name but switch contexts and wait for the operation to be completed in cases where the operation can't be immediately completed.

The readable and writable methods suspend pending data to be read or buffer space available for writing to. These are implied by other I/O operations but may be handy for other operations.

timeout specifies the maximum amount of time the coroutine will spend waiting for an I/O operation to complete before it continues executing regardless. autoflush and fileno work as in IO::Handle. Methods not directly available from Coro::Handle but available from IO::Handle may be accessed by fetching the underlying IO::Handle from the Coro::Handle object.

```
$coro_handle_object->fh->truncate(0);
```

High-performance applications will want to unblock everything, but there is no harm in not doing so on regular file operations if your concern is merely servicing user requests on different pipes or sockets in whatever they come in.

Waiting on Other Coroutines

Listing 21-1 shows how to move data between coroutines. It creates two execution contexts, both of which have $queue in scope. The first waits for availability of input from standard input, reads from standard input, pushes the read data onto the queue, and then bails if in fact undef was read, indicating the end of input. (Control+D at the keyboard will end input.)

Listing 21-1. *Creating a Channel Between Coroutines*

```perl
# Pass data between coroutines using a Coro::Channel as a queue - Perl 5

use Coro;
use Coro::Channel;
use Coro::Event;

my $queue = Coro::Channel->new(10);

async {
    my $event = Coro::Event->io(fd => fileno STDIN, poll => 'r');
    while(1) {
        $event->next();
        my $input = <STDIN>;
        $queue->put($input);
        last unless defined $input;
    }
};

async {
   while(1) {
      my $output = $queue->get;
      last unless defined $output;
      print "got: $output\n";
   }
};

Event::loop;
```

If no coroutine is eligible for the CPU as both are waiting, the program uses no CPU. This happens when the first async { } block is waiting for keyboard input as it executes $event->next, and the second async { } block executes $queue->get to wait for data from the first. Written without using Coro::Channel or at least an array variable and Coro::Semaphore, this example would consume all available CPU while waiting for input. Note that my $input = <STDIN> will eventually read an undef, and I want to pass this through the queue to tell the other coroutine to exit as well, so I'm not using the preferred idiom of while(my $input = <STDIN>).

For simple cases where one block needs to pipe data to another, continuations are preferred over coroutines—see Chapter 20.

This example was adapted from the eg/prodcons3 example included with the Coro distribution.

Remarks on Coroutines and Threads

Coroutines default to sharing variables whereas threads requires the is shared trait (*property* in Perl 5 parlance).

Threads and coroutines have striking parallels, but you're discouraged from thinking of them as the same thing. (Some people will even be offended that I've performed a comparison as if they were.) The differences are briefly outlined in Chapter 17; threads should be used to keep a program responsive even as long-running computations are being made. For other applications, threads are overkill in features and overhead (though Perl 6 threads are designed to be fast and light). Enforcing threads's level of privacy requires CPU cycles and memory; it isn't practical to spawn thousands of threads, but a thousand coroutines is entirely doable. Coroutines were intended as a tool for structuring difficult to structure programs.

threads automatically change context when I/O is attempted on a file handle that isn't ready or an attempt is made to sleep(), making use of specialized objects for I/O unnecessary. Threads work at the system call level; coroutines don't, in their basic form, try to keep an execution context from stalling the CPU for other execution contexts.

It's harder to deadlock the program with a coroutine than a thread. Locks almost never need to be employed with coroutines, but in threads, locking is omnipresent. Context changes only when explicitly required. This makes it less likely for the program to be in an inconsistent state; the programmer is always aware of where in the program context may change.

Coroutine Example

Listing 21-2 shows a simple finger protocol server that dishes out the goods on any user on your system. Unix-like systems come with a finger command client to access this service, such as with finger scott@perl6now.com.

Listing 21-2. *Finger Daemon Implemented As a Coroutine*

```
# Simple finger daemon to demonstrate coroutines and I/O - Perl 5

use Coro;
use Coro::Socket;
use Socket;
use IO::Handle;
use Error ':try';
```

```perl
my $listen = Coro::Socket->new(
    LocalPort => 79,
    Listen    => SOMAXCONN,
) or die $!;

$listen->listen();

async {
    while(my $client = $listen->accept()) {
        async {
            try {
                my $username = <$client>;
                ($username) = grep m/[^-]/, split /\s/, $username or
                    throw Error::Simple("No username");
                ($username) = $username =~ m/([a-z0-9_]+)/ or
                    throw Error::Simple("Bad username '$username'");
                my ($name, undef, $uid, $gid, $quota, $comment, $gcos,
                    $dir, $shell) = getpwnam($username) or
                    throw Error::Simple("User '$usernamne' not found");
                $client->print(
                    "Login: $name\t\t\tName: $gcos\n",
                    "Directory: $dir\t\t\tShell: $shell\n",
                );
                if(-e "/var/mail/$name") {
                    $client->print("Mail last read ",
                        scalar localtime(-m "/var/mail/$name"), "\n");
                }
                if(open my $plan, '<', "/$dir/.plan") {
                    $plan->read(my $plantext, -s $plan);
                    $client->print("Plan:\n$plantext\n");
                }
            } catch Error::Simple with {
                $client->print($_[0]->{'-text'}, "\n");
            }
        };
    }
};

Event::loop;
```

Initially, there's one context (other than the Event::loop itself), and that's the outer async { } block, stopped at the $listen->accept() line to get an incoming connection. After a connection is received, this while loops and starts waiting for another connection but spawns a context in the process by executing the inner async { } block. This new context reads a username (with a trailing newline) from the newly accepted connection. Note that the finger client could wait a long time to send the username (the network may be slow, or they may be trying to pull something), so it's important that it service other connections and accept new connections while it waits. Coro switches to any other ready to run contexts when the `<$client>` line is executed, and it doesn't come back to this context until the request can be completed (a line is available to read). After that, it's mostly output generation, which itself is mostly showing off getpwnam (see `perldoc -f getpwnam`).

Forking, Threading, and Event Loops

Event systems, fork, threads, and coroutines all have special purposes at which they excel. Use fork before invoking exec to call another program. open does this when output is being piped to or from another program.

```
# Some forms of open() imply fork() - Perl 5
open my $mailprogram, '-|', '/usr/sbin/sendmail' or die $!;
```

Using fork indirectly or directly is the only sane way to execute other programs on Unix-like systems. (Windows users will use the Win32:: modules to create a process.) This is something that coroutines can't do.

User interfaces and network protocol handlers usually have an event loop meant to take control once things have been set up. Your code runs only when invoked by this event loop. Problems arise when two different modules need to be used at the same time, where both modules have an event loop that wants to take control of the CPU. If you're trying to use two modules, each of which has their own event loop, coroutines don't directly work—you have to break the event loop down.

For example, let's say you're using Net::IRC with Tk. Net::IRC wants you to call Net::IRC::start to hand over control of the program. Tk wants you to call Tk::MainLoop to give up the CPU. You have a dilemma—which event loop do you call? If you're using coroutines too, you'd want to call Event::loop too. Threads solve this by creating additional "virtual CPUs" with each CPU executing an event handler. Coroutines only help you juggle your single CPU. One approach is to extract the relevant file handles from each. For Net::IRC, the file handle can be extracted as `$irc_object->{_read}->handles()`, where $irc_object was created from Net::IRC->new(...). This would then be read inside an async { } block, using a Coro::Event instance to suspend pending, available data. When data is available, the Net::IRC::do_one_loop() method would be used like `$irc_object()->do_one_loop()`. Likewise for Tk, the socket would have to be extract and waited for I/O on, and then a single sweep for events would be done in Tk's event system. These are the steps required for making a module with an event loop of its own to work with Coro instead. Of course, if a module uses the Event generic framework, Coro works with it naturally.

Coroutines in Algorithms

Because of constraints of most languages, depth-first recursion logic must be implemented iteratively. Rather than recursing back into itself, it loops, and when it finds more possibilities to consider, they're pushed onto the end of the queue being looped over. The data pushed onto the queue must include a snapshot of the current state of the algorithm, and the programmer is charged with manually capturing and saving this state.

Coroutines, by contrast, consider possibilities in depth-first recursion *in parallel*. Chapter 8 has an example of breadth-first recursion nonoptimally solving simple mazes. This depth-first

version reliably and optimally solves complex mazes. At each turn, this example spawns
a coroutine to explore each possible route in parallel, stopping as soon as it finds the destination.
See Listing 21-3.

Listing 21-3. *Parallel Evaluation with Coroutines for Breadth-First Recursion*

```perl
# Highway navigation example modified to search breadth-first
# and in parallel - Perl 5

use autobox;
use autobox::Core;
use Perl6::Variables;
use Sub::Lexical;
use Coro;

my %ref_to_name;
my $i101n = [];  %ref_to_name{$i101n} = 'Interstate 101 North';
my $i101s = [];  %ref_to_name{$i101s} = 'Interstate 101 South';
my $i10   = [];  %ref_to_name{$i10}   = 'Interstate 10';
my $i202  = [];  %ref_to_name{$i202}  = 'Interstate 202';
my $us60  = [];  %ref_to_name{$us60}  = 'U.S. Route 60';
my $sr51  = [];  %ref_to_name{$sr51}  = 'State Route 51';
$i101n->push( $sr51, $i202, $i101s );
$i101s->push( $sr51, $i202, $i10, $i101n, $us60 );
$i202->push( $sr51, $i101s, $i101n );
$us60->push( $sr51, $i101s );
$sr51->push( $i101s, $i101n, $i10, $us60 );
$i10->push( $sr51, $i101s, $i202 );

my $location = $i10;
my $destination = $us60;

# This is the old depth-first recusive solution from Chapter 8:
# while($location ne $destination) {
#     $location = $location->[int rand $location->elems];
#     print "Take the ", %ref_to_name{$location}, " exit.\n";
# }
# print "And you're there!\n";

sub solve_maze {
    my $location = shift;
    my $destination = shift;
    my %already_did = ($location => 1);
    my @solved;
    my sub solve_maze_inner {
        my $location = shift;
        for my $exit ($location->flatten) {
            if($exit eq $destination) {
```

```
                @solved = (@_, $exit) unless @solved;
                return;
            }
            next if exists %route{$exit};
            %route{$exit} = 1;
            solve_maze_inner($exit, @_, $exit) and return;
        }
        return;
    };
    async { solve_maze_inner($location); };
    cede while not @solved;
    return @solved;
}

my @res = solve_maze($location, $destination);
for my $i (@res) {
    print "Take the ", %ref_to_name{$i}, " exit.\n";
}
print "And you're there!\n";
```

Unlike the depth-first version of this example in Chapter 8, this example returns the same route every time. Also unlike the other example, this one always returns the shortest route.

REFERENCES AND THANKS

Dick Grune is credited with coining the term *coroutine* and introducing the concept in his 1977 paper "A View of Coroutines" that's published in *ACM SIGPLAN Notices*, v.12 n.7, p.75–81. Donald Knuth's famous *Art of Computer Programming* (Addison-Wesley, 1998) discusses coroutines as well. Dan Sugalski's quote comes from his Squawks of the Parrot blog at http://www.sidhe.org/~dan/blog/archives/000156.html.

A few examples are included with Coro in the eg/ directory of the distribution; among them is a little Web server, a program to do parallel DNS lookups on blocks of IPs, and an asynchronous finger client.

Summary

Coro works well with other modules written to use the communal event loop in Event. It also works well with modules written without any event at all. Modules that subclass IO::Handle or IO::Socket::INET are perfect, as fileno works on them, and this may be fed to Coro::Event->io(). Modules that reference a file handle and allow you to query it work with Coro::Event in a similar way. One coroutine may wait on each connection created with a protocol module or on a connection representing a user interface.

Coro may be used to build a "pipeline" where one coroutine produces data, another performs an operation on it and then passes it on, and the last one displays or stores the information. Stages may be inserted in the pipeline, and infinite lists may be processed; only an infinite amount of time is required, not an infinite amount of memory, and results come out continuously rather than in one large batch.

Coroutines are useful for when multiple things are going on, and each should have its own lexical environment—regardless of whether there are network connections.

Perl 5 vs. Perl 6 Operators

The tables in this appendix summarize operators in Perl 5 and their Perl 6 equivalents. Table A-1 describes numeric operators.

Table A-1. *Numeric Operators*

Perl 5	Perl 6	Description
< > <= >= == != <=>	(Same)	Numeric comparison operators
0+	+	Explicitly forces numeric context (when used where a term is expected)
+	+	Adds numbers (when used where an operator is expected)
-	-	Negates numerically (when used where a term is expected)
-	-	Subtracts (when used where an operator is expected)
++	++	Increments
--	--	Decrements
*	*	Multiplies
/	/	Divides
%	%	Modulus
**	**	Power

Table A-2 describes string operators.

Table A-2. *String Operators*

Perl 5	Perl 6	Description
lt gt le ge eq ne cmp	(Same)	String comparison operators don't change
.	~	Concatenates
x	x	Repeats scalar
q	q	String constructor without interpolation
qq	qq	String constructor with interpolation
qx	(Unknown)	Shell execution
=~	~~	Match, substitution, or translation binding (binds to //, m, s, rx, or an expression)
!~	!~	Negated match, substitution, or translation (binds to //, m, s, rx, or an expression)
//	//	Regex: Perl 5: m; Perl 6: m or rx, depending on context (when term is expected)
m	m	Matches against regular expression or rule
s	s	Substitutes against regular expression or rule
tr	tr (?)	Transliteration
qr	rx	Regex/rule constructor

■**Unknown and uncertain operators** The *shell execution* operator for Perl 6 is listed as *(Unknown)* because no official word has been given about it, and I'm also unable to find an unofficial plan. Transliteration with the tr operator, marked with *(?)* in Table A-2 will probably exist in Perl 6, but the topic hasn't been addressed in earnest yet; preliminary discussion suggests the final version will get enhanced and unified semantics.

■**Built-in functions perform most string operations** Few string operators exist beyond binding to regular expressions, as string operations are primarily performed by built-in functions (or, under autobox, methods of the string API), as documented in perldoc perlfunc.

Table A-3 describes list operators.

Table A-3. *List Operators*

Perl 5	Perl 6	Description
,	,	List constructor
=>	=>	Perl 5: stringifying comma, Perl 6: pair constructor
(None)	*	Slurps when on left of assignment, flattens when on right
(None)	|	Interleaves elements of two lists into one list (same as zip())
qw< >	<< >>	Quotes list of words
x	xx	Repeats list

Table A-4 summarizes the low-precedence boolean operators, which run as *late* as possible, after other high precedence terms have been evaluated. Table A-5 shows the high-precedence boolean operators.

Table A-4. *Low-Precedence Boolean Operators*

Perl 5	Perl 6	Description
? :	?? ::	Conditional
(None)	true	Forces boolean context
not	not	Logical *not*
and	and	Logical *and*
or	or	Logical *or*
xor	xor	Logical *xor*
err	err	Logical *defined-or* (Perl 5.9.2 or later only)

Table A-5. *High-Precedence Boolean Operators*

Perl 5	Perl 6	Description
(None)	?	Forces boolean context
!	!	Logical *not*
&&	&&	Logical *and*
||	||	Logical *or*
(None)	^^	Logical *xor*
//	//	When operator is expected; logical *defined-or* (Perl 5.9.2 or later only)

▰**Booleans evaluate to strings, numbers, and other datatypes** Boolean operators provide boolean context to their first term for the purpose of testing its truth, but they don't actually convert the value to a boolean. The result is the unconverted term that satisfies the condition of the logical test. If a boolean test is performed on two numbers, for example, the result will always be a number.

Bitwise operations always return numbers or strings (depending on their arguments in Perl 5 or the operator used in Perl 6). The number or string contains a series of bits. They provide string or numeric context. Table A-6 summarizes the bitwise operators.

Table A-6. *Bitwise Operators*

Perl 5	Perl 6	Description
~	^	Bitwise *not*
&	+& ~&	Bitwise *and* (+ for num, ~ for string)
		+| ~|	Bitwise *or* (ditto)
^	+^ ~^	Bitwise *xor* (ditto)
<<	+< ~<	Shift bitwise (ditto)
>>	+> ~>	Shift bitwise (ditto)

Table A-7 describes reference operators.

Table A-7. *Reference Operators*

Perl 5	Perl 6	Description
(None)	=:=	Reference equality test
->	.	Dereference/method call
\	\	Creates reference to existing variable or value

Table A-8 describes junction operators.

Table A-8. *Junction Operators*

Perl 5	Perl 6	Description
(None)			any() junction
(None)	&	all() junction
(None)	^	one() junction

■None junctions Perl 6 also defines a none() function to build junctions of values that must all be false. I don't know of an operator version of the none() function, however.

Table A-9 describes miscellaneous operators, and Table A-10 describes permutations of other operators.

Table A-9. *Miscellaneous Operators*

Perl 5	Perl 6	Description
=	=	Assignment
(None)	:=	Runs time alias
(None)	::=	Compiles time alias
..	..	Range, flip flop (may be string, numeric, or boolean depending on arguments)
...	(Unknown)	Flip flop—sed emulation

Table A-10. *Permutations of Other Operators*

Perl 5	Perl 6	Description
op=	op=	Mutating assignment
(None)	>>op	Left vector op
(None)	op<<	Right vector op
(None)	>>op<<	Double vector op

■Few Perl 6 operators mutate This table lists ways other operators may be modified to alter their behavior. Relatively few operators in Perl 5 can be made to mutate (+= is a mutating operator), but any Perl 6 operator can be made to mutate if it makes sense to do so.

Index